Federal Courts

WILLIAM A. FLETCHER

*Circuit Judge, United States Court of Appeals for the Ninth Circuit
and Richard Jennings Professor Emeritus
University of California Berkeley School of Law*

JAMES E. PFANDER

*Owen L. Coon Professor
Northwestern University Pritzker School of Law*

Sixth Edition

Gilbert Law Summaries is a trademark registered in the U.S. Patent and Trademark Office

© West, a Thomson business, 2008
© 2014 LEG, Inc. d/b/a West Academic
© 2019 LEG, Inc. d/b/a West Academic
444 Cedar Street, Suite 700
St. Paul, MN 55101
1-877-888-1330
West, West Academic Publishing, and West Academic are trademarks of West Publishing Corporation, used under license.

Printed in the United States of America

ISBN: 978-1-64242-702-8

Summary of Contents

Gilbert Exam Strategies

Federal Courts is the study of the jurisdictional structure of the federal court system. This Summary is designed to supplement any Federal Courts or Federal Jurisdiction course, but you may also find it useful to supplement a first year Civil Procedure course or an upper-level course in Constitutional Litigation, as it covers many jurisdictional issues taught in those courses.

Questions on a Federal Courts exam can cover a wide range of issues. Specific topics, and the approach to answering exam questions on those topics, are discussed in the chapter approach sections located at the beginning of the chapters. Some general guidelines, useful in answering all Federal Courts exam questions, are given below.

1. **General Policies vs. Detailed Rules**

    Federal Courts questions often combine broad governmental structure and policy issues, on the one hand, and intricate technical and procedural issues on the other. Therefore, you must be prepared to address Federal Courts issues on both levels.

2. **Two Basic Issues**

    Questions concerning federal jurisdiction often involve, at least to some degree, two basic issues:

    a. **Separation of powers**

        Keep in mind that the federal courts are one of three coequal branches of the national government. The jurisdiction of the federal courts helps determine the relative powers of the judicial, executive, and legislative branches.

    b. **Federalism**

        Don't overlook the importance of the state courts. Federal courts have overlapping jurisdiction with the state courts, and hence, share power with them. The jurisdiction of the federal courts thus helps determine relative powers of the federal and state governments.

3. **History of Federal Judicial System**

    Note that the study of Federal Courts is unusually dependent on an understanding of the history of the federal judicial system. More than in other areas of the law, you must understand the historical forces that have shaped the federal court system and be able to analyze a number of the old "landmark" cases to write a complete and well-reasoned exam answer.

Federal Courts

Sixth Edition

Chapter One

Historical Sketch of the Federal Court System

CONTENTS	PAGE

Key Exam Issues

Compared to other law school courses, Federal Courts focuses to an unusual degree on historical materials. Therefore, before moving on to the study of specific doctrines, you need a general understanding of the historical background of the federal court system. This chapter briefly sketches the creation and growth of the federal judicial system. Although you will study more historical detail on particular points later in this Summary, this overview provides a structure that will enable you to understand those details in a meaningful way.

A. Article III—Foundation for the Federal Judiciary

1. Created Supreme Court and Authorized Creation of Inferior Federal Courts

The United States Constitution provides for federal courts in Article III, sometimes referred to as the "judicial article." Article III created, of its own force, the Supreme Court; but it merely *authorized* the creation of inferior federal courts, leaving to Congress the decision whether actually to create them or rely on state courts instead. Often referred to as the Madisonian compromise, Article III's provision for Congress to create federal courts or to rely on state courts instead informs a variety of structural issues of concurrent state and federal jurisdiction.

B. Judiciary Act of 1789

1. Introduction

The first Congress was convened in the year after the adoption of the Constitution. This Congress enacted the Judiciary Act of 1789. In the Act, Congress *exercised the authority* conferred by Article III and established a system of courts for the new federal government. Much of the structure of the modern federal court system can be traced back to this Act.

2. Circuit and District Courts Under the Act

The Act created circuit and district courts, although these courts were quite different from their modern equivalents. The circuit courts were staffed by Supreme Court Justices who "rode circuit" in their assigned circuits, and by district judges who resided in the circuit. The district courts were staffed by district judges.

a. Circuit and District Court Jurisdiction

The circuit courts had an original jurisdiction, and an appellate jurisdiction over the district courts. The district courts had only an original jurisdiction.

(1) Diversity Jurisdiction

Probably the most important original jurisdiction under the Act was diversity jurisdiction in the circuit courts. [Judiciary Act of 1789 ("Judiciary Act") § 11] This jurisdiction was exercised concurrently with the state courts, as it is today. The modern jurisdictional provision conferring diversity jurisdiction on federal trial courts is 28 U.S.C. section 1332.

(2) Removal Jurisdiction over Diversity Cases

The circuit courts were also empowered to hear diversity cases removed from the state courts. [Judiciary Act § 12] Such removal was permitted when the defendant was an out-of-state citizen, as it is today. The modern jurisdictional provision conferring removal jurisdiction in diversity cases is 28 U.S.C. section 1441(a).

(3) Admiralty Jurisdiction

Another important original jurisdiction was admiralty jurisdiction in the district courts. [Judiciary Act § 9] As is true today, this jurisdiction was exclusive in the federal courts. The modern jurisdictional provision conferring admiralty jurisdiction on the federal trial courts is 28 U.S.C. section 1333.

(4) Federal Criminal Jurisdiction

District courts were given jurisdiction over relatively minor federal criminal offenses; circuit courts heard the more serious crimes.

(5) No General Original Federal Question Jurisdiction

There was *no* general original federal question jurisdiction in either the circuit or district courts. (The circuit courts were briefly given general original federal question jurisdiction in 1801, but it was taken away the following year.) The failure to confer general original federal question jurisdiction may seem surprising, but the failure to grant such jurisdiction was of much less significance in 1789 than it would be today because there were relatively few federal rights at that time (and hence relatively few federal question cases) and because specific grants of subject matter jurisdiction were frequently granted to enable individuals to enforce those rights in court.

3. Supreme Court Jurisdiction

a. Original Jurisdiction

The Supreme Court was given original jurisdiction over certain cases, including suits between states, and suits between states and citizens of other states. [Judiciary Act § 13] This jurisdiction is substantially similar to the original jurisdiction of the Supreme Court today, although the ratification of the Eleventh Amendment curtailed jurisdiction over certain suits against the states. Today, the Supreme Court's original jurisdiction is specified in 28 U.S.C. section 1251.

b. Appellate Jurisdiction

(1) Appellate Jurisdiction over State Courts

The Supreme Court was given appellate jurisdiction over decisions of the state courts when a right was claimed under federal law and the decision of the state court was unfavorable to the federal right claimed. [Judiciary Act § 25] Although relatively few cases came to the Supreme Court on this basis, this grant of jurisdiction was of great importance because it established the power of the Supreme Court to act as the supreme expositor of federal law. The modern jurisdictional provision conferring appellate jurisdiction over state court decisions is 28 U.S.C. section 1257.

(2) Appellate Jurisdiction over Federal Courts

The Supreme Court was also given appellate jurisdiction over decisions of the circuit courts. [Judiciary Act § 22] In the early years, by far the greatest number of such appeals were in diversity cases. The Supreme Court's modern appellate jurisdiction over the inferior federal courts is conferred by 28 U.S.C. sections 1253 and 1254.

(3) The All Writs Act and Supervision

Apart from these grants of jurisdiction, the Judiciary Act also conferred "power" on the Court to issue writs of mandamus to courts of the United States and to federal officers, as well as writs of prohibition to district courts, sitting in admiralty, and writs of habeas corpus on behalf of anyone held in federal custody. The provision for issuance of these supervisory writs gave the Court broad power, in its discretion, to oversee the work of lower federal courts.

4. "Rules of Decision Act"

The Judiciary Act also provided that federal courts should follow the laws of the states in cases "where they apply." [Judiciary Act § 34] This provision has proved enormously important. It was the basis for the Court's decisions in **Swift v. Tyson**, 41 U.S. 1 (1842), and in **Erie Railroad v. Tompkins**, 304 U.S. 64 (1938). In its present form, this provision is known as the Rules of Decision Act. [28 U.S.C. § 1652]

5. Importance of Judiciary Act of 1789

In sum, the Judiciary Act of 1789 did several important things:

a. Created a Federal Court System

Article III of the Constitution had left to Congress the decision whether to establish a system of federal courts to handle the judicial business of the new nation, or whether to leave that business to the state courts. In the Judiciary Act, Congress took the earliest opportunity to create a genuine federal court system.

b. Granted Narrower Jurisdiction than That Authorized by Article III

The inferior federal courts established by the Act were given some, but not all, of the jurisdiction authorized by Article III. Although the jurisdiction conferred on the federal courts has been increased since then, Congress has followed the example of the 1789 Act in never conferring the full scope of the constitutionally authorized jurisdiction.

c. Established Categories of Suits Within Federal Courts' Jurisdiction

The Act empowered the federal court system to hear several important categories of suits that present-day federal courts continue to hear, including those that involve:

(1) Domestic Commerce and Possible Prejudice Against Out-of-State Citizens

The circuit courts were empowered to hear diversity suits within their original and removal jurisdiction.

(2) Foreign Commerce and International Relations

The district courts were empowered to hear admiralty cases within their original jurisdiction. The circuit courts were also empowered to hear disputes between citizens and aliens.

(3) Assertion of Federal Rights

The Supreme Court was empowered to hear federal question cases within its appellate jurisdiction over decisions of the state courts.

(4) Special Jurisdictional Grants

Federal courts were also given special responsibilities, such as oversight of federal revenue collection in the nation's ports and the power to confer naturalized citizenship on petitioning aliens who met the statute's requirements.

JUDICIARY ACT OF 1789—A SUMMARY

THE JUDICIARY ACT OF 1789:

☑ Created the federal court system;

☑ Established inferior federal courts that were given *some* jurisdiction authorized by Article III;

☑ Gave *circuit* courts the authority to hear diversity cases within their original and removal jurisdiction;

☑ Gave *district* courts the authority to hear admiralty cases within their original jurisdiction;

☑ Gave *district* courts the authority to hear disputes between citizens and aliens; and

☑ Gave the *Supreme Court* the authority to hear federal question cases within its appellate jurisdiction over decisions of state courts and to oversee all decisions by lower federal courts.

C. Emergence of the Modern Federal Judicial System

1. Civil War Amendments and Civil Rights Act of 1871

The structure of the federal court system remained relatively stable from its creation until the Civil War. The Civil War produced profound changes.

a. Civil War Amendments

The passage of the Thirteenth, Fourteenth, and Fifteenth Amendments after the Civil War created significant federal rights that had not previously existed. Congress was given explicit power to implement these amendments "by appropriate legislation." Congress moved promptly to employ its new powers.

b. Civil Rights Act of 1871

Three years after the adoption of the Fourteenth Amendment, Congress passed the Civil Rights Act of 1871. Section 1 of that Act prohibited anyone acting "under color of state law" from depriving any person of rights under the Constitution. The Act conferred jurisdiction on the inferior federal courts to hear cases brought under the Act. The lineal descendant of the substantive provisions of the Act is 42 U.S.C. section 1983, the statute upon which much of our modern civil rights law depends. The lineal descendant of the jurisdictional provision of the Act is our present-day 28 U.S.C. section 1343(3).

2. General Original Federal Question Jurisdiction

Four years after the passage of the Civil Rights Act of 1871, Congress conferred general original federal question jurisdiction on the federal circuit courts. [Act of March 3, 1875] The statute conferred jurisdiction over cases "arising under" federal law. This jurisdiction was at first construed to be as broad as the constitutional grant of "arising under" jurisdiction in Article III [**Pacific Railroad Removal Cases**, 115 U.S. 1 (1885)], but by the end of the century, the "arising under" language of the statutorily conferred federal question jurisdiction had been reduced by judicial construction to its modern dimensions. The modern jurisdictional provision for original federal question cases is 28 U.S.C. section 1331.

3. Creation of Circuit Courts of Appeals Under Evarts Act

In 1891, in the Evarts Act, Congress created what have become our modern circuit courts of appeals. The Evarts Act accomplished two primary things:

a. Creation of Circuit Courts of Appeals

The Act allocated to the district courts original diversity and federal question jurisdiction, and created new circuit courts of appeals with appellate jurisdiction over those suits.

b. Relief for Supreme Court Justices from Circuit Court Duties

The Act also provided for the appointment of new circuit court judges to staff the newly created courts of appeals, relieving the Supreme Court Justices of the burden of sitting as circuit court judges.

4. Growth of the Supreme Court's Certiorari Jurisdiction

Until 1891, all cases within the appellate jurisdiction of the Supreme Court were appealable as of right. In an effort to reduce the burden on the Supreme Court and the considerable backlog of cases, the Evarts Act made some of the Supreme Court's appellate jurisdiction discretionary. For cases coming within this discretionary jurisdiction, the Supreme Court could take or refuse to take a case by granting or denying a writ of certiorari.

a. Note

The Supreme Court's certiorari jurisdiction was expanded by later statutes. Under the Judges' Bill of 1925, the great bulk of the Supreme Court's appellate jurisdiction became discretionary. Finally, in 1988, the Supreme Court's appellate jurisdiction became almost completely discretionary. The modern statutory provisions governing the Supreme Court's certiorari jurisdiction are 28 U.S.C. sections 1254 and 1257.

D. Specialized Courts

1. Introduction

The federal courts described so far have relatively unspecialized jurisdiction. But Congress can also establish courts with specialized jurisdiction.

2. Article I Courts

Congress has a limited power to create federal courts under the authority granted in Article I of the Constitution. Congress has employed its power to create a number of Article I "legislative" courts of relatively narrow and specialized jurisdiction. A few of these courts were later reconstituted as Article III courts.

a. Military Courts

The Constitution authorizes Congress to provide for a military and promulgate rules for the discipline of its members. Exercising this power, Congress has authorized courts martial to hear claims that service members violated the code of military conduct. These military courts were staffed by officers of the armed services who lacked the life tenure and salary guarantees of the Article III judiciary. While federal courts did not directly review the sentences of courts martial, they could intervene if the court martial exceeded its jurisdiction. Today, a non-Article III US Court of Appeals for the Armed Forces hears military matters, subject to further review in the Supreme Court.

b. Territorial Courts

Congress has provided Article I federal courts to serve the territories of the United States. Since the long-term status of territories is often uncertain, and since Article I judges do not have the life tenure of Article III judges, Congress has preserved flexibility in deciding whether to abolish territorial courts as conditions change. The constitutionality of establishing territorial courts as Article I courts was sustained in 1828. [**American Insurance Co. v. Canter**, 26 U.S. (1 Pet.) 511 (1828)]

c. District of Columbia Courts

Local Article I courts for the District of Columbia were first created when the "federal district" was created. [Act of 1801] These courts have continued to exist, in one form or another, ever since. At the present time, local District of Columbia courts are constituted as Article I courts under the Court Reorganization Act of 1970. The constitutionality of the Act was sustained in 1973. [**Palmore v. United States**, 411 U.S. 389 (1973)]

d. Court of Federal Claims

The Court of Federal Claims has been an Article I court since its reorganization in 1982 and renaming (from "claims court") in 1992. [Act of April 2, 1982; Act of 1992] The Court of Federal Claims has trial jurisdiction over non-tort monetary claims against the United States government. Appeals are to the U.S. Court of Appeals for the Federal Circuit, an Article III court.

(1) Note

The original claims court, then called the Court of Claims, was created as an Article I court in 1855 to take over from Congress the task of deciding monetary claims against the government. It remained an Article I court for almost a century. In 1953, Congress declared by statute that the Court of Claims was an Article III court, and the Supreme Court confirmed this status in 1962. [**Glidden v. Zdanok**, 370 U.S. 530 (1962)] The Court of Claims remained an Article III court until its reorganization in 1982.

e. Court of Customs and Patent Appeals

The Court of Customs and Patent Appeals was created in 1909 as an Article I court to handle certain customs and patent matters. In 1958, Congress declared by statute that the Court of Customs and Patent Appeals was an Article III court. The Supreme Court confirmed this status in 1962. [**Glidden v. Zdanok**, *supra*]

(1) Note

The Court of Customs and Patent Appeals was *abolished* in 1982, and its jurisdiction taken over by the U.S. Court of Appeals for the Federal Circuit. [Act of April 2, 1982]

f. Tax Court

The present United States Tax Court was created as an Article I court in 1969. Previously, its adjudicative function had been performed by an administrative tribunal within the executive branch.

3. Adjunct Courts

Congress has created some non-Article III tribunals to act as "adjuncts" to Article III courts. They are sometimes referred to as Article I courts and sometimes as "adjunct" courts.

a. Bankruptcy Courts

Until 1978, bankruptcy disputes were decided by district judges with the assistance of a bankruptcy "referee." In 1978, a new Bankruptcy Act greatly expanded the powers of the bankruptcy courts, conferring new jurisdiction on what are now called bankruptcy "judges." In 1982, the Supreme Court held that at least part of the newly conferred jurisdiction could not constitutionally be exercised by a non-Article III federal tribunal. [**Northern Pipeline Construction Co. v. Marathon Pipe Line Co.**, 458 U.S. 50 (1982)] Congress passed a new statute in 1984, conferring on the bankruptcy courts a narrower scope of jurisdiction, solely concerning core bankruptcy matters. As for other matters, bankruptcy judges serve as adjuncts to the district courts.

The Court reaffirmed **Northern Pipeline** in 2011, holding that the bankruptcy court could not entertain an action for tortious interference with an expected inheritance. [**Stern v. Marshall**, 564 U.S. 462 (2011)] The decision was primarily noteworthy for reviving **Northern Pipeline**'s categorical approach to the power of bankruptcy courts. The Court found that the bankruptcy court was not an adjunct, because it had power to issue a judgment; that the consent of the litigants to appear before the bankruptcy court was not voluntary; that the claim in question was properly characterized as a private rights claim and would not fit within the public rights exception to Article III. If the parties consent, however, the bankruptcy court can exercise jurisdiction over so-called **Stern** claims. [**Wellness Int'l Network Ltd. v. Sharif,** 135 S.Ct. 1932 (2015)]

b. Federal Magistrates

Since 1968, federal magistrates have handled a variety of tasks for federal district judges. In fact, under a 1979 statute expanding their powers, federal magistrates may even conduct criminal misdemeanor and some civil jury trials. Before 1968, magistrates were known as commissioners. Magistrates often hear preliminary issues in criminal proceedings, acting as adjuncts to the district courts, and can hear a range of civil matters if the parties consent. These magistrate powers were approved in 1980. [**Raddatz v. United States**, 447 U.S. 667 (1980)]

(1) Note

Agencies, established by federal law, often perform initial adjudication of disputes subject to judicial review in an Article III court.

E. Summary of Historical Development

1. Power of Congress

Congress is explicitly given power by the Constitution to "constitute tribunals inferior to the Supreme Court." Although Congress has exercised that power from the beginning, it has never granted to the inferior federal courts the full extent of the constitutionally authorized jurisdiction under Article III.

2. Growth of Federal Power and Growth of Federal Courts

As federal power has expanded, the jurisdiction of the federal courts has expanded more or less commensurately. This phenomenon was particularly apparent after the Civil War, when federal substantive power and the jurisdiction of the inferior federal courts were both substantially expanded.

3. Federal Jurisdiction Responds to Allocations of Substantive Power in Federal Structure

Although the historical developments summarized in this chapter show the growth of federal power, a broader point may be inferred—*i.e.*, that federal jurisdiction can be expanded or contracted to correspond to prevailing allocations of power between the federal and state governments. The ability of the federal jurisdictional structure to change in response to shifts in the federal-state balance accounts for a number of doctrinal shifts in the past century.

4. Power of Congress to Create Specialized Article I Tribunals

Congress has from the beginning exercised its Article I power to create "legislative" and "adjunct" courts for particular purposes. This power has been employed with increasing frequency in recent years, but, as seen in *Northern Pipeline Construction Co. v. Marathon Pipe Line Co.* and *Stern v. Marshall* (*supra*, p. 8), this power is not without limit.

Chapter Two

"Case or Controversy" and Justiciability

Key Exam Issues

This chapter is concerned with the "case or controversy" requirement and the justiciability doctrines of *advisory opinions, feigned cases, ripeness, mootness, standing,* and *political questions.* These doctrines are important because they limit the number of cases the federal courts can hear and because they shape the way the cases are presented to the courts. The doctrines overlap with one another to a considerable extent, and they are seldom capable of application with absolute precision. Thus, if you see an exam question in this area, you will probably need to consider the applicability of several of these doctrines.

As you learn these doctrines, keep in mind the underlying structural and political purposes they serve. For example, the "case or controversy" and justiciability doctrines have sometimes been interpreted to duck politically awkward cases and other times to take cases in which the Supreme Court is particularly interested. Therefore, in answering questions dealing with these doctrines, be alert not only to the doctrinal details in the particular question but also to the larger structural and political issues that may be involved.

A. Introduction

1. Judicial Review Exercised by Courts of Limited Competence

Federal courts created under Article III of the Constitution are bodies of limited competence. They have the enormously important power of judicial review, which enables them to declare unconstitutional the acts of the other two branches of the federal government and of the states. But that power is limited in a variety of ways.

2. Limitations on Courts' Power

a. "Case or Controversy" Limitations

One of the most important limitations is that federal courts may only decide questions presented to them in justiciable "cases or controversies." The "case or controversy" limitation is a constitutional limitation.

b. Justiciability Limitation

Federal courts are also limited to deciding "justiciable" disputes. The source of the justiciability limitation is not altogether clear. It is sometimes seen as part of the constitutional "case or controversy" limitation. But a determination of justiciability often involves careful consideration of nonconstitutional "prudential" factors, which sometimes result in a federal court's refusing to decide a dispute that satisfies the constitutional "case or controversy" requirement. The Supreme Court may be restricting this prudential avoidance power.

B. Judicial Review

1. Introduction

The power of judicial review and the related limitations imposed by case or controversy and justiciability doctrines may be traced to the beginning of the federal court system.

2. *Marbury v. Madison*—Foundation of Judicial Review

In **Marbury v. Madison**, 5 U.S. (1 Cranch) 137 (1803), the Supreme Court held that it had the power to declare an act of Congress unconstitutional.

a. Facts

The case arose when Marbury brought suit in the original jurisdiction of the Supreme Court for the delivery of a commission appointing him Justice of the Peace of the District of Columbia. Outgoing President John Adams had signed the commission just before leaving office. The incoming administration of President Jefferson objected to the appointment of such "Midnight Judges," and Secretary of State James Madison refused to deliver the commission.

b. Opinion

Chief Justice Marshall, writing for the Court, found that Marbury had been validly appointed and that he was entitled to his commission. However, Marbury was not entitled to the mandamus remedy he sought. The Judiciary Act of 1789 purported to confer upon the Supreme Court the power to issue writs of mandamus to federal officers in the original jurisdiction of the Court. But Marshall held that Article III of the Constitution barred the Court from hearing such a mandamus proceeding in the exercise of the Court's *original jurisdiction.* Thus, the attempt by Congress to authorize the writ in a suit brought in the Court's original jurisdiction was unconstitutional.

c. Comment

Marshall's opinion was in some respects cautious. Narrowly read, it said only that the Court could not be compelled to perform an act that was in its opinion unconstitutional. The rhetoric of the opinion, however, was more expansive. Probably the most famous, and today the most widely quoted, sentence reads: "It is emphatically the province and duty of the judicial department to say what the law is."

3. Legitimacy of Judicial Review

Although there was some controversy at the time of **Marbury v. Madison** over the legitimacy of judicial review, modern historical scholarship has concluded that judicial review was not a creation out of whole cloth by the Marshall Court. In its present form, the power of judicial review goes well beyond the mere refusal of the judiciary to enforce what it regards as an unconstitutional statute.

4. Modern Scope of Judicial Review

In the modern era, the Supreme Court has used the power of judicial review to:

(i) *Declare unconstitutional acts of Congress and state statutes;*

(ii) *Substitute its constitutional judgment* for that of the President and order the President to perform acts that the President claims are constitutionally privileged [**United States v. Nixon**, 418 U.S. 683 (1974)—ordering President Nixon to produce tape recordings]; and

(iii) *Order state officers* to perform acts that the Court has concluded are required by the Constitution [see, e.g., **Cooper v. Aaron**, 358 U.S. 1 (1958)].

In modern cases, the Court frequently quotes the famous sentence from **Marbury v. Madison** (*supra*, p. 13), and has referred to itself as the "ultimate interpreter of the Constitution." [**Baker v. Carr**, 369 U.S. 189 (1962); **Powell v. McCormack**, 395 U.S. 486 (1969)] These claims of judicial supremacy have long attracted critical reactions, most recently in response to the

Court's invalidation of the federal Defense of Marriage Act. [**United States v. Windsor**, 570 U.S. 931 (2013) (Scalia, J., dissenting) (describing the Court's majority as operating under an "exalted conception of the role of this institution in America")]

MODERN SCOPE OF JUDICIAL REVIEW—A SUMMARY	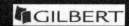

THE SUPREME COURT USES THE POWER OF JUDICIAL REVIEW TO:

- ☑ Declare *acts of Congress unconstitutional;*
- ☑ Declare *state statutes unconstitutional;*
- ☑ *Substitute its constitutional judgment* for that of the President and *order the President* to perform acts that the President claims are constitutionally privileged; and
- ☑ *Order state officers* to perform acts that the Court has concluded are required by **the** Constitution.

5. Responsibility of Other Branches to Determine Constitutionality

The Court's description of itself as the "ultimate interpreter of the Constitution" does not mean that the other branches of government must always secure the view of the Court on matters of constitutional interpretation. Nor does the power of judicial review, even broadly construed, mean that nonjudicial officers of the government are excused from exercising their own judgment as to what the Constitution requires. A governmental officer frequently must exercise her best independent judgment as to what the Constitution requires because there may be no applicable federal court order and no settled precedent clearly governing the situation. And governmental officers are always required to obey the Constitution whether or not under court order to do so.

6. Relation of Judicial Review to "Case or Controversy" and Justiciability Doctrines

The power of judicial review is of great significance. It gives the Supreme Court the power to interpret the Constitution and to require the other branches of the federal government, and the state governments, to follow that interpretation.

a. Insulation of Article III Judges from Political Pressures

The Justices, as Article III judges, are appointed for life subject only to the power of impeachment. They are thus protected to a great extent from the political pressures that influence the other branches of government.

b. Limits and Controls on Judicial Power

Because of the great significance of judicial review and because of the great political insulation our system provides to Article III judges, it is critically important that the power of judicial review be limited and controlled. The primary methods of limitation and control are to: limit the *number of questions* that come before the Justices; control the *timing* of such questions' presentation; and control the *form and manner* in which the questions are presented. Those methods are facilitated by the related doctrines of "case or controversy" and justiciability.

C. "Case or Controversy" and Justiciability

1. In General

a. Origin of Phrase "Case or Controversy"

Article III of the Constitution describes the categories of cases that are within the constitutionally authorized jurisdiction of Article III federal courts. To each head of jurisdiction set out in Article III is appended either the word "cases" or "controversies." For example, Article III refers to "all *cases* in Law and Equity, arising under this Constitution . . .," to "all *cases* of admiralty and maritime Jurisdiction," and to "*controversies* . . . between citizens of different states" (emphasis added). From this textual pattern has grown the habit of saying that Article III federal courts are authorized to hear only cases and controversies.

b. Meaning of "Case or Controversy"

The "case or controversy" requirement has come to mean that a question must be presented to the court as part of a *judicially cognizable dispute.*

c. Justiciability as a Subconstitutional Doctrine

It is also sometimes said that a dispute must be "justiciable." Although the meaning of the term is not stable, justiciability usually refers to subconstitutional factors, based on "prudence," that dictate whether a dispute should be decided. The Court reaffirmed the importance of the prudential branch of the doctrine in characterizing the adverse-parties requirement as prudential. [**United States v. Windsor**, 570 U.S. 931 (2013)]

d. Complicated, Overlapping Doctrines

What constitutes a "case or controversy" or a "justiciable" dispute cannot be quickly described. The following sections describe various overlapping doctrines that are used to decide whether a dispute should be heard by an Article III federal court. These doctrines include:

(1) *Advisory opinions;*

(2) *Feigned cases;*

(3) *Ripeness;*

(4) *Mootness;*

(5) *Standing;* and

(6) *Political questions.*

2. Advisory Opinions

The "case or controversy" limitation prevents Article III federal courts from issuing advisory opinions. This prohibition contains the following sub-elements:

(i) A federal court will *not answer inquiries from a coordinate branch of the federal government about the legality of contemplated conduct.* In other words, it will not give legal advice.

(ii) There must be *adverse parties* seeking the resolution of a *concrete and bona fide dispute.*

(iii) A federal court will not decide a case if its decision is *made subject to review by one of the coordinate branches.*

(iv) In other words, a federal court can adjudicate only when its decision *will finally resolve the parties'* dispute subject only to the possibility of further review within the federal court system.

a. Note—Other Doctrinal Headings Sometimes Used

These sub-elements of the advisory opinion prohibition appear under other doctrinal headings as well—*e.g.*, feigned cases, ripeness, mootness, and standing.

b. Prohibition Against Advisory Opinions Not Applicable to Article I Courts or State Courts

(1) Article I Federal Courts

Article I courts or tribunals, sometimes called "legislative courts," are established outside the authority of Article III of the Constitution. (*See* discussion, *infra*, pp. 76 *et seq.*) Article I courts are not prohibited from providing advisory opinions. For example, until 1953 the Court of Claims was an Article I court and exercised a "congressional reference jurisdiction" under which it advised Congress about various pending bills. In 1982, Congress restored the reference jurisdiction when it returned the Court of Federal Claims to Article I status. (Note that the Article III judges of the predecessor court were not displaced; they succeeded to positions in the new Article III US Court of Appeals for the Federal Circuit.)

(2) State Courts

State courts are not created under Article III of the federal Constitution. They are created under the authority of state constitutions and are not bound by the federal "case or controversy" limitation. A few states permit their state courts to issue advisory opinions. For example, the Massachusetts Supreme Judicial Court is authorized to give advisory opinions "upon important questions of law, and upon solemn occasions" to the legislature and to the governor.

EXAM TIP　　　　　　　　　　　　　　　　　　　　　　　**▮GILBERT**

If a fact pattern presents you with a state court providing an opinion to a state executive, remember that the Article III prohibition against issuing advisory opinions *does not apply to state courts or Article I courts*. (Of course, a state is free to impose such a limit by state statute or in the **state** constitution.)

---

c. No Legal Advice to Coordinate Branches

Article III federal courts from the beginning refused to give legal advice to coordinate branches of federal government.

(1) Refusal to Answer Hypothetical Questions

An Article III court will not answer hypothetical questions but will decide only questions in an actual case before it.

 Example: In 1793, Secretary of State Thomas Jefferson sent a letter to the Supreme Court requesting answers to a number of legal questions arising out of the United States' status as a neutral country in relation to the warring countries of Great Britain and France. Chief Justice John Jay and the Associate Justices replied that since the "three departments of the government [are] in certain respects checks upon each other," and since the Supreme Court is "a court in the last resort," it would be improper for the Justices to answer these questions "extrajudicially." [Correspondence of the Justices]

(a) Justifications for the Refusal

The conclusion of the Justices may perhaps have been compelled by the language of Article III conferring only the "judicial power" on the federal courts. But it was also compelled by a variety of structural reasons:

1) No Premature Decisions

Since the Court might eventually be called upon to decide actual cases in which these legal questions arose, it would be unwise for the Court to commit itself to answers that it might regret upon more mature reflection.

2) Hypothetical, Abstract Questions

The questions posed are hypothetical and relatively abstract. Judicial decisions are more likely to be sound if rendered in a particularized, relatively detailed factual setting.

3) No Adverse Parties

There are no interested parties arguing both sides of the questions. This means that the Court is not as likely to be fully informed about the ramifications and actual consequences of their answers as they would be if the questions were posed in an actual litigated dispute.

4) Legal Advice Available Within Particular Branch

The President and other government officials have the resources to secure expert legal advice from within their own branch of government.

(2) No Attempts to Obtain Advice by a Set-up Case

Congress cannot obtain legal advice by artificially setting up a case. The strength of this prohibition against set-up cases is unclear, however, as may be seen by the Court's decision in the famous *Muskrat* case and by the later undercutting of *Muskrat.*

(a) *Muskrat v. United States*

Congress had allotted tribal lands and cash to certain Indians. Congress later enlarged the group of people entitled to share in that property, and passed a statute authorizing several specifically named individuals to sue for a declaratory judgment that the Fifth Amendment was not violated by enlarging the group of allottees. The statute provided for attorneys' fees to the named private litigants if the courts decided that the group could not constitutionally be enlarged. The Supreme Court refused to decide the case, holding that the statute authorizing the individuals to seek a declaratory judgment was an attempt to obtain an advisory opinion. The Court's judgment would amount "to no more than an expression of opinion upon the validity of the acts in question." [**Muskrat v. United States**, 219 U.S. 346 (1911)]

1) Elusive Rationale

The precise rationale of the Court's holding in *Muskrat* has always been difficult to determine. The totality of the circumstances resulted in the Court's conclusion that the question was not presented in a "case or controversy." It was probably significant that the parties were specifically named by the statute, and it may have been significant that attorneys' fees were provided. Of perhaps the greatest significance was the fact that a declaratory judgment was sought. Declaratory judgments were *not clearly permitted* in Article III federal courts for another 25 years. [*See* **Aetna Life Insurance Co. v. Haworth**, 300 U.S. 227 (1937), *and see infra*, p. 23]

(b) Possible Abandonment of *Muskrat*

Although *Muskrat* has become a standard citation for the proposition that Article III courts will not issue advisory opinions, two more recent cases make clear that the citation is more to a general principle for which the case supposedly stands than to the case itself.

1) *South Carolina v. Katzenbach*

The Voting Rights Act of 1965 authorizes a state to seek a declaratory judgment that a *proposed change* in state voting practices does not violate the Act. Despite a dissent by Justice Black arguing that permitting a state to seek advance authorization violated the principle of *Muskrat,* the Supreme Court sustained the Act. [**South Carolina v. Katzenbach**, 383 U.S. 301 (1966)]

2) *Northern Cheyenne Tribes v. Hollowbreast*

Congress had allotted tribal land to individual members of the tribe, with the provision that legal title would not pass to the allottees until 1976. In 1968, Congress passed a superseding statute purporting to revest the land in the tribe. In the 1968 statute, Congress specifically authorized the tribe to sue for a declaratory judgment that the revesting of the property in the tribe did not violate the Fifth Amendment rights of the individual allottees. Only after that judicial determination would the revesting actually take effect. Despite the marked similarity to *Muskrat*, the Court decided the Fifth Amendment question on the merits without even alluding to a possible "case or controversy" difficulty. [**Northern Cheyenne Tribes v. Hollowbreast**, 425 U.S. 649 (1976)]

d. No Executive or Legislative Revision

Article III federal courts, from the beginning, have also refused to issue judgments subject to revision by the coordinate branches of the federal government.

(1) Based on Separation of Powers

If a federal court judgment may be reversed or set aside by either the executive or legislative branch, such an action would violate the principle of separation of powers. It would interfere with the independence of the judicial branch by depriving its judgments of finality.

Example: After the Revolutionary War, Congress established a statutory compensation system for American servicemen who had been injured during the War. Federal circuit courts were directed to find whether servicemen were disabled and to transmit their finding to the Secretary of War. However, if the Secretary suspected "imposition or mistake," he had the power to withhold the claimant's pension. Supreme Court Justices, sitting on three circuit courts, refused to hear servicemen's claims because the statute raised problems of both executive and legislative revision. The Secretary was specifically authorized by statute to ignore the court's opinion if he thought there had been "imposition or mistake." Furthermore, even if a claimant were approved by the Secretary, Congress could refuse to pay the claimant's pension. Thus, the courts could not properly proceed because under the Constitution "neither the Secretary of War, nor any other Executive officers, nor even the Legislature, are authorized to sit as a court of errors." [**Hayburn's Case**, 2 U.S. (2 Dall.) 409 (1792)]

Example: A federal statute provided that a money judgment issued against the United States by the Court of Claims would be paid only after "an appropriation therefor shall be estimated by the Secretary of the Treasury." The Supreme Court held that an Article III court could not decide an appeal from such a judgment because of the lack of finality: "All that the Court is authorized to do is to certify its opinion to the Secretary of the Treasury, and if he inserts it in his estimates, and Congress sanctions it by appropriation, it is then to be paid but not otherwise." [**Gordon v. United States**, 117 U.S. 697 (1864)]

Example: The Supreme Court held, contrary to the holdings of most lower federal courts, that there was a short statute of limitations in federal securities fraud cases. [**Lampf, Pleva, Lipkind, Prupis & Petigrow v. Gilbertson**, 501 U.S. 350 (1991)] Because of the decision in *Lampf*, lower federal courts dismissed a number of pending securities cases. Congress then passed corrective legislation re-establishing the longer statute of limitations and reinstating the suits that had been dismissed by the lower courts after *Lampf*. The Supreme Court held that Congress was powerless to reinstate suits where dismissal had resulted in final judgments. If the congressional legislation had been given effect, it would have revised final judgments by Article III courts: "When retroactive legislation requires its own application in a case already finally adjudicated, it does no more and no less than 'reverse a determination once made, in a particular case." [**Plaut v. Spendthrift Farms, Inc.**, 514 U.S. 211 (1995)]

Compare: In a case where an appeal of the dismissal is pending—*i.e.*, in a case where there is no final judgment—Congress has the power to change the law and to require application of the new law. "When a new law makes clear that it is retroactive, an appellate court must apply that law in reviewing judgments still on appeal that were rendered before the law was enacted." [**Plaut v. Spendthrift Farms, Inc.**, *supra*]

Compare: Many procedural systems provide limited grounds on which a party may petition to reopen an otherwise final judgment. [*See, e.g.*, Fed. R. Civ. P. 60(b)] (In general, a post-judgment change in the applicable law does not warrant post-judgment relief.)

(2) Outer Limits of Prohibition Against Executive and Legislative Revision

The mere possibility of executive or legislative revision is *not* enough to prevent an Article III court from hearing a case. The problem in **Hayburn's Case** and in **Gordon v. United States** was that revision by the other branches was *explicitly* *written* into the statute. Had the Supreme Court been willing to proceed, this explicit statutory authorization would have operated as a legitimization of the executive and legislative revision.

Example: In 1806, the Supreme Court upheld an award of damages against a US naval officer who had wrongly seized a Danish vessel on the high seas. The officer, one Maley, did not appear as a defendant; instead, the government arranged to have his interests defended by the US attorney, apparently with a view toward facilitating the judicial determination of the claim as a prelude to its payment by act of Congress. The Court did not view either the officer's absence or the government's control of the litigation as creating the sort of feigned case that lay beyond judicial power. Nor did it view Congress's control over the appropriation of funds as fatal to its power to hear the case against Maley. [**Maley v. Shattuck**, 7 U.S. 458 (1806)]

Example: In 1962, the Supreme Court held that Congress had validly reconstituted the Court of Claims as an Article III court. [**Glidden v. Zdanok**, *supra*, p. 7] The Court noted that there was no power in the judicial branch to compel payment of the Court of Claims' money judgments against the United States, but that the United States regularly paid Court of Claims judgments against it. Thus, while the other branches had the raw power to ignore Court of Claims judgments, the power was neither authorized in the statute granting jurisdiction to the Court of Claims nor frequently exercised. It was enough, for purposes of the Article III requirement of finality, that the Court of Claims could rely on the "good faith of the United States." [**Glidden v. Zdanok**, *supra*]

Example: The practical finality on which the Court based its decision as to the Court of Claims [**Glidden v. Zdanok**, *supra*] also supports a federal judicial role in reviewing benefit determinations by federal agencies such as the Social Security Administration, in that Congress pays benefits to successful claimants as a matter of course.

(3) Prohibition Against Revision Does Not Apply to Judicial Revision

The prohibition against an Article III court's issuing judgments that will be revised by the executive or legislative branches derives from the principle of separation of powers. To allow the coordinate branches to revise a judgment of the judicial branch would erode the independence of the judiciary. But the principle of separation of powers does *not* prohibit the *judicial revision* of prior judicial decisions. [**Tutun v. United States**, 270 U.S. 568 (1926)—naturalization decisions may be set aside in later de novo judicial proceedings]

3. Feigned Cases

Article III federal courts cannot hear feigned cases, in which the parties merely pretend to be adversaries. A true "case or controversy" requires that the parties have, and seek to promote, their adverse interests in the litigation.

Example: In a case from 1850, the Supreme Court both approved of the use of feigned cases to clarify the law in the case of a legitimate dispute and warned against the use of feigned cases when doing so might prejudice the rights of third parties. Explaining that the feigned case was proper but there must be an actual controversy and adverse interests, the Court foreclosed the use of feigned cases when doing so was meant to procure an advantageous precedent for use against parties not before the court. [**Lord v. Veazie**, 49 U.S. (8 How.) 251 (1850)]

Example: On the day a new state statute regulating railroad fares went into effect, plaintiff tried to buy a ticket at the new statutory rate. The railroad refused, and plaintiff sued for damages. The parties conceded that the case was a "friendly suit" in which there was no true antagonism between them. (The plaintiff did not really wish to buy a ticket at the statutory rate. Rather, he sought to facilitate the railroad's challenge of the fares.) The Supreme Court refused to hear the suit. A federal court can decide a case brought only "in pursuance of an honest and actual antagonistic assertion of rights by one individual against another." [**Chicago & Grand Trunk Railway v. Wellman**, 143 U.S. 339 (1892)]

Example: A tenant in property covered by federal wartime rent controls sued to challenge his rent as too high. But, in fact, the landlord had instigated the litigation, paid plaintiff's lawyer, and controlled the course of the litigation. Even though the United States intervened to defend the rent controls, the Supreme Court required that the suit be dismissed. The presence of the United States as an intervening defendant could not cure the fundamental lack of "case or controversy" caused by the fact that there was no "genuine adversary issue between the parties." [**United States v. Johnson**, 319 U.S. 302 (1943)]

Example: Plaintiff brought suit against her employer, the state of Arizona, asking that she be permitted to speak Spanish on the job. After the district court granted injunctive relief, she resigned from her position, thus rendering her claim moot. Encouraged by the federal court of appeals, the state attorney general consented to an award of nominal damages in order to give plaintiff the appearance of a stake in defending against an appeal. In holding the case moot on appeal, the Supreme Court wrote, "In advancing cooperation between [plaintiff] and the Attorney General regarding—nominal damages, the Ninth Circuit did not home in on the federal courts' lack of authority to act in friendly or feigned proceedings." [**Arizonans for Official English v. Arizona**, 520 U.S. 43 (1997)]

Compare: Plaintiff brought suit to challenge the government's imposition of a federal estate tax that, as required by the Defense of Marriage Act (DOMA), refused to give her credit for being the surviving spouse of her deceased same-sex partner, even though the two had been married under otherwise applicable law. The government continued to demand payment of the tax, even as it agreed with the plaintiff that DOMA was unconstitutional as applied to her. Meanwhile, members of Congress, in an association known as BLAG, the Bipartisan Legal Advisory Group, intervened to defend DOMA. The Court concluded, over a sharp dissent, that the parties were sufficiently adverse to satisfy the requirements of Article III. The majority opinion treated the plaintiff as having standing to challenge the denial of a spousal tax credit and viewed the adverse parties requirement as a matter of prudence. For the majority, then, the appearance of BLAG and the sharply opposed views it presented were sufficient to ensure the concrete adverseness needed to sharpen the issues for judicial resolution. [**United States v. Windsor**, 570 U.S. 744 (2013)]

a. Test Cases and Institutional Reform Suits Not Necessarily Feigned Suits

(1) Test Cases

As long as the interests of the parties are genuinely adverse, the fact that the case may have been framed as test litigation does not prevent an Article III court from hearing it. Thus, if a black woman wishes to litigate the constitutionality of segregated public buses, it is enough for her to ride on such a public bus. It would not matter if she had never before ridden the bus, and that she had done so on this occasion solely to bring the constitutional challenge.

(2) Institutional Reform Suits

Reform suits brought against large institutions pose special problems of adverseness. The defendant is typically the head of a state institution (*e.g.*, the director of prisons). Often, the defendant will have sought increased funds from the legislature to improve the institution's conditions. Suit may be brought against that defendant asking for the sort of improvements for which the defendant himself has been seeking funds from the legislature. Does that mean that there is no adversary relationship between the parties? There has been surprisingly little discussion of this issue in the decided cases. The practical result has been that the suits are permitted, perhaps on the theory that the defendant is representing not only his own interest but that of the state as a whole. The fact that the defendant has been unable to obtain increased funding makes it clear that the state as a whole is acting adversely to the plaintiff.

b. Special Rules for Some Uncontested Matters

In a variety of situations, federal courts have agreed to hear uncontested proceedings. These include the entry of default judgments, consent judgments, and class action settlement judgments, the adjudication of applications for certificates of appealability in federal habeas proceedings and petitions for the grant of immunity as agreed to by the witness and the government, and the issuance of search warrants of various kinds. The party seeking a judicial decree does not, in these circumstances, feign a dispute but asserts a claim of right under the terms of a federal statute or rule that authorizes an ex parte proceeding. The Court has consistently upheld the power of federal courts to hear such matters. [See Pfander & Birk, 124 Yale L.J. 1346 (2015)]

4. Ripeness, Mootness, and Standing

Ripeness, mootness, and standing are related concepts. They all share the core requirement that is most explicitly articulated in standing: A litigant must be able to show, at the time of the suit, that she has a stake in the outcome. However, different elements are emphasized in the three doctrines:

a. Overview of the Doctrines

(1) Ripeness

Ripeness is the requirement that a dispute has progressed to the point that the parties are in clear disagreement over their legal rights and duties.

(2) Mootness

A case is moot when circumstances have changed to such an extent that the party can no longer obtain judicial relief that will be of any use.

(3) Standing

To have standing a plaintiff must show that she has suffered a legally cognizable injury; that the injury was caused by or attributable to the defendant's conduct; and that the relief she seeks will remedy the injury of which she complains.

b. Ripeness

Ripeness requires that a dispute have progressed beyond the point where a legal question is merely hypothetical. It is designed to ensure that an *actual, immediate, and concrete controversy* is presented to the court.

(1) Constitutional and Subconstitutional Doctrine

Ripeness is in part a requirement of the "case or controversy" limitation of Article III; if a question is too hypothetical or abstract at the time it is posed, it is beyond the constitutional competence of an Article III court. In some cases, although the constitutional minimum of Article III may be satisfied, the dispute may nevertheless be found not ripe for adjudication because of subconstitutional "prudential" reasons. But the line between constitutional and prudential ripeness is often blurred and vague and the continued application of prudential ripeness may be contested.

(2) Ripeness and Declaratory Judgments

For a number of years it was thought that the "case or controversy" limitation of Article III might prevent federal courts from granting declaratory judgments. The concern was that parties seeking a declaratory judgment would present questions in a premature, unripe form, and that such questions would not present the sort of actual, concrete dispute required by Article III.

(a) Historical Background

Although an early case seeking a declaratory judgment seemed to imply that Article III courts might not be able to grant declaratory judgments at all [**Willing v. Chicago Arbitration Association**, 227 U.S. 274 (1928)], the Supreme Court affirmed a declaratory judgment a few years later [**Nashville, Chattanooga & St. Louis Railway v. Wallace**, 28 8 U.S. 249 (1933)], thus indicating that at least some declaratory judgments were permissible. Encouraged by this decision, Congress in 1934 enacted the Declaratory Judgment Act. The Act declares that a federal court may issue a declaratory judgment in "a case of actual controversy." [28 U.S.C. § 2201] The Act did not purport to authorize federal courts to take cases not permitted by the "case or controversy" limitation of Article III, and the Court in upholding the Act emphasized that the Act authorized declaratory judgments only in justiciable controversies. [**Aetna Life Insurance Co. v. Haworth**, *supra*, p. 17—court may not render a judgment in a "dispute of hypothetical or abstract character"]

(b) Importance of Ripeness in Declaratory Judgment Cases

In damage suits, it is not necessary to articulate separately any ripeness requirement. In such cases, the dispute has already crystallized. In injunction suits, the ripeness doctrine is duplicative, for the traditional equitable requirement of immediacy of threatened injury serves to ensure that the dispute is sufficiently far advanced to satisfy the "case or controversy" doctrine. By contrast, in declaratory judgment suits, there is no factual pattern (as in damage suits) or doctrinal substitute (as in injunction suits) that ensures the concreteness of the dispute. Thus, in most suits for declaratory judgment, the ripeness requirement is separately articulated and considered.

(3) Formulation of Doctrine

The most widely employed doctrinal formulation for ripeness is that a court must "evaluate both the *fitness of the issues* for judicial decision and the *hardship to the parties* of withholding court consideration." [**Abbott Laboratories v. Gardner**, 387 U.S. 136 (1966)]

 Example: fitness of issues: Plaintiff sought a declaratory judgment that a state statute prohibiting distribution of anonymous handbills was unconstitutional. Plaintiff had once been convicted under the statute but made no showing that he would again engage in the sort of handbilling forbidden by the statute. The Court held that no case or controversy was presented. [**Golden v. Zwickler**, 394 U.S. 103 (1969)]

e.g. **Example: hardship:** The National Park Service ("NPS") issued rules that declared a federal government contract enforcement regime did not apply to contracts with NPS concessionaires. A concessionaire challenged the NPS rules. The Court found that the challenge to the agency's declaration of inapplicability was unripe. The NPS rules did not have the force of law, but only expressed the NPS view on the subject; ultimately the decision would rest with another agency, subject to judicial review. The issue was one of law (and thus arguably fit for resolution), but the Court viewed the concessionaire as facing little hardship. If and when a breach of contract dispute arose, review would be available. [**National Park Hospitality Association v. Department of Interior**, 538 U.S. 803 (2003)]

(a) Relation Between Ripeness and a Judge's View of the Merits

Professor Scharpf has suggested that Justices often find that a case is ripe or unripe depending on their view of the merits. [Scharpf, *Judicial Review and Political Questions*, 75 Yale L.J. 517 (1966)]

e.g. **Example:** Several federal civil service employees sought a declaratory judgment that the Hatch Act could not constitutionally prevent them from engaging in political activity. With one exception, the employees all described activities **in** which they *would engage* if the Act did not prohibit them. The majority of the Court refused to resolve a question involving a mere "hypothetical threat" to First Amendment rights; they had to know more precisely what the plaintiffs were actually going to do before judging the constitutionality of the Hatch Act's prohibition of that conduct. But Justices Black and Douglas both thought the case was ripe. Since Justice Black thought the Act was broadly unconstitutional, he did not need precise information about the particular conduct at issue. For him, the conduct was *all* protected. Justice Douglas attached particular importance to the First Amendment rights at issue, and thought it was more important to protect those rights than to insist punctiliously on a fully developed record of actual behavior. [**United Public Workers v. Mitchell**, 330 U.S. 75 (1947)] Notably, after dismissing some claims as unripe, the Court went on to reach the merits by addressing the obviously ripe claims of one employee.

(b) Ripeness as a Prudential Doctrine with Political Overtones

In some cases, the Court may find a case unripe because it views a decision as politically inexpedient or because it does not favor the type of relief sought.

e.g. **Example: politically inexpedient decision:** Plaintiffs were a married couple seeking a declaratory judgment that Connecticut statutes prohibiting the use of contraceptives and the dispensing of advice about their use were unconstitutional. Only one prosecution (a test case) had been brought under the statutes in more than 75 years. A plurality of the Court found that in the absence of a serious threat of actual enforcement of these statutes, the case was not justiciable. [**Poe v. Ullman**, 367 U.S. 497 (1961)] The Court was unwilling to enter the politically charged controversy about the availability of contraception in Connecticut.

Example: relief not favored by Court: Plaintiffs, 19 citizens of Cairo, Illinois, alleged a pattern of civil rights violations in the administration of the criminal justice system. Some, but not all, of the plaintiffs had been subjected to the alleged illegal practices. Plaintiffs sought a structural injunction that would have required government officials to bring their practices into conformity with the Constitution. The Court held that plaintiffs had not alleged a case or controversy: "We can only speculate whether respondents will be arrested, either again or for the first time, for violating a municipal ordinance or a state statute . . . ." Furthermore, the Court indicated that the requested injunction would be "nothing less than an ongoing federal audit of state criminal proceedings" and would be "intrusive and unworkable." [**O'Shea v. Littleton**, 414 U.S. 488 (1974)] *Comment: O'Shea* may be seen as a standing case rather than a ripeness case. Plaintiffs' injuries, caused by illegal practices in the past, were not redressable by injunctive relief aimed at future practices. [*See also* **City of Los Angeles v. Lyons**, 461 U.S. 95 (1983)— plaintiff in civil rights case had been subjected to chokehold by police after routine traffic stop; Court denied standing to seek injunctive relief to block use of chokeholds in the future because plaintiff could not show he was likely to be subjected to them again; however, plaintiff had standing to sue for damages]

(c) Doubts as to the Prudential Ripeness Doctrine

The Supreme Court questioned the legitimacy of some judge-made doctrines of prudential avoidance. [**Lexmark Int'l, Inc. v. Static Control Components, Inc.,** 572 U.S. 118 (2014)] The Court did not, however, have occasion to discuss the prudential ripeness doctrine.

c. Mootness

Like ripeness, mootness is concerned with timing. But whereas ripeness prevents a court from deciding a suit that is brought too early, mootness prevents a court from deciding a case *too late,* when the passage of time has made judicial relief irrelevant. For example, if the parties have settled their dispute, the case is moot. Or if the remedy sought by the plaintiff is no longer necessary, the case is moot.

EXAM TIP   **GILBERT**

It might help you remember ripeness and mootness by thinking of a case as being like a tomato plant. Just as you don't want to eat a tomato until it is ripe, the case can't be heard until it is ripe—*i.e.,* until it has reached the stage where there is an *actual, immediate, and concrete controversy*, and not something merely hypothetical or abstract or "green." On the other hand, when the frost comes and kills the tomato plant, it is too late for fruit. Likewise, when circumstances have changed so much that *judicial relief isn't really of any use*, a case is moot.

---

(1) Constitutional and Subconstitutional Doctrine?

(a) Constitutional Doctrine

Mootness is, in important part, a doctrine deriving from the Article III "case or controversy" limitation. If a case is moot, it is no longer of any direct concern to the litigants. Thus, the court's decision would not affect the parties but would merely resolve what has become a hypothetical question. For this reason, the mootness doctrine is sometimes described as preventing advisory opinions.

(b) Subconstitutional Doctrine

Mootness is also a subconstitutional or "prudential" doctrine. A case that is not moot in the Article III sense may nevertheless be dismissed for reasons of prudence or sound judicial administration. For example, in **Kremens v. Bartley**, 431 U.S. 119 (1977), the Supreme Court dismissed the case as moot because the statute that had been challenged in the suit had been changed. The Court based its dismissal on "policy" considerations against passing unnecessarily on constitutional questions rather than on "purely constitutional considerations."

(c) Doubts About Prudential Mootness

As with prudential ripeness, the Supreme Court's decision in **Lexmark v. Static Control** may cast doubt on federal judicial power to issue prudential mootness dismissals.

(2) Variety of Contexts

Mootness determinations are made in a variety of contexts.

Example: Plaintiffs moved to Colorado less than six months before an election. They challenged a Colorado statute that required six months' residency before newcomers were allowed to vote. The case was not heard by the Supreme Court until after the election. The Court dismissed the case as moot because (i) the election was now over and plaintiffs would have fulfilled the six-month requirement by the date of the next election; and (ii) in any event the Colorado statute had been changed so that it now required only two months' prior residency. [**Hall v. Beals**, 396 U.S. 45(1969)]

Example: Plaintiff had been convicted under a state statute prohibiting distribution of anonymous handbills. He then sought a declaratory judgment that the statute was unconstitutional. Since he had made no showing that he was now violating the statute or intended to do so, and since he had already been convicted and was not now in a position to challenge that conviction, the case was moot. [**Golden v. Zwickler**, *supra,* p. 24]

Example: Plaintiff, a white male, sued for admission to law school on the ground that an affirmative action admissions program had denied him equal protection of the law. The state trial court ordered him admitted, and the university appealed. By the time the Supreme Court issued its opinion in the case, plaintiff was in his final semester. The university conceded that it would not expel plaintiff even if it prevailed in the Supreme Court. The Court found the case moot. [**DeFunis v. Odegaard**, 416 U.S. 312 (1974)]

(3) Voluntary Cessation of Activity

The fact that a defendant has voluntarily discontinued its challenged activity does not necessarily render a case moot. *Rationales:* (i) If a defendant could thus render a case moot, the public interest in adjudicating the legality of the conduct would be frustrated; and (ii) a defendant, having obtained a strategic dismissal based on mootness, could begin the conduct again.

Example: The United States sought an injunction under the Clayton Act against individual defendants sitting simultaneously on boards of directors of competing companies. After the suit was filed, the defendants resigned the challenged directorships. The Court held that this did not render the case moot because "[t]he defendant is free to return to his old ways." [**United States v. W. T. Grant**, 345 U.S. 629 (1953)]

cf. **Compare:** Voluntary cessation may, however, render a case moot under some circumstances. For example, a defendant county had discontinued the employment practices that were challenged in the suit. Because the effects of the past actions had been eradicated, and because there was " 'no reasonable expectation . . .' that the alleged violation will recur," the Court found the case moot. [**County of Los Angeles v. Davis**, 440 U.S. 625 (1979)]

cf. **Compare:** One party can moot an existing litigation by delivering a broad and unconditional covenant not to sue its opponent. Nike Inc. sued Already Inc., alleging a violation of its Air Force 1 trademark. Already counterclaimed, alleging that the trademark was invalid. Eventually, Nike issued a broad covenant not to sue, applicable to existing Already products and any colorable imitations. The Court found that covenant sufficed to moot the case, notwithstanding Nike's voluntary cessation. Noting the burden on parties who seek a finding of mootness, the Court emphasized that the covenant must be phrased in terms broad enough to make it "absolutely clear [that] the allegedly wrongful behavior could not reasonably be expected to recur." [**Already LLC v. Nike, Inc.**, 568 U.S. 85 (2013)]

(a) Type of Relief Sought

Generally, a defendant's voluntary cessation of activity *before* suit is filed will block an action for injunctive or declaratory relief, but not an action for damages. [**Steel Co. v. Citizens for a Better Environment**, 523 U.S. 83 (1998)]

(4) "Capable of Repetition, Yet Evading Review"

The Supreme Court has developed an exception to the normal application of mootness principles where the question presented in the case can systematically evade review because it remains a concrete controversy for only a short time. [*See* Southern Pacific Terminal Co. v. Interstate Commerce Commission, 219 U.S. 498 (1911)—"capable of repetition, yet evading review"]

e.g. **Example:** Plaintiffs challenged Illinois election statutes, but the Supreme Court did not hear the case until after the election. The Court held the case not moot because the burden on prospective candidates as a result of the statutes controlled future elections; therefore, the issue presented was "capable of repetition, yet evading review." [**Moore v. Ogilvie**, 394 U.S. 814 (1969); *but see **Hall v. Beals** supra*, p. 26]

e.g. **Example:** Plaintiff challenged a Texas statute criminally prohibiting abortions. Plaintiff was pregnant at the time she filed suit, but was no longer pregnant when the Supreme Court decided the case. The Court noted that the "normal human gestation period is so short that . . . pregnancy litigation will seldom survive much beyond the trial stage, and appellate review will be effectively denied." The Court held the suit not moot because it was "capable of repetition, yet evading review." [**Roe v. Wade**, 410 U.S. 113 (1973)]

cf. **Compare:** The Court found that the dispute in **DeFunis v. Odegaard**, *supra*, p. 26, was not within the "capable of repetition" exception. The Court reasoned that, although the law school maintained its admissions policy, the plaintiff himself would not apply to law school again.

Recall that in real life, it generally takes a long time—often years—for a plaintiff to get her day in court. Thus, if you see an exam question where there is a *relatively short period of time for a meaningful remedy* (*e.g.,* facts involving a pregnancy or an upcoming election), be sure to consider whether this issue is *capable of repetition yet evading review.* But be careful to look for issues that are tied to events that typically occur in a person's life *only once* (*e.g.,* graduating from a law school)—such issues are unlikely to be "capable of repetition").

(5) Mootness in Class Actions

Mootness determinations pose special problems in class action suits because the legal rights of an entire class of litigants rather than of a single individual are at stake.

(a) Named Representative Need Not Have a Live Controversy

The claim of a single member of a class—even the named representative—may become moot without rendering the class action moot, because other members of the class may still have a live controversy.

Example: The named plaintiff moved to Iowa and sought a divorce. Iowa law required a one-year residency before a divorce could be obtained. Plaintiff challenged the Iowa one-year requirement in a class action brought on behalf of all newly arrived Iowa residents desiring divorces. She obtained class certification before the case became moot as to her, but by the time the case was argued in the Supreme Court, the named plaintiff had lived in Iowa more than a year and had even obtained a divorce in another state. The Court nevertheless held that case was not moot *as to the members of the class.* [**Sosna v. Iowa**, 419 U.S. 393 (1975)]

(b) Class Action as a Substitute for "Capable of Repetition, Yet Evading Review" Device

It is apparent from the Court's holding in *Sosna v. Iowa, supra,* that litigants whose claims are particularly time-sensitive need not rely exclusively on the "capable of repetition, yet evading review" rationale to avoid mootness. Where the criteria of Federal Rule of Civil Procedure 23 (class action) can be satisfied, the certification of a class will save the case from mootness.

(c) Class Certification Required

A class must be certified before the class action device can save a case from mootness.

Example: Plaintiffs sought to bring a class action challenging certain school regulations that they claimed interfered with the publication of their student newspaper. Class certification was denied. The plaintiffs continued to press this suit on the merits as individuals, but graduated before the Supreme Court heard the case. The Court held that in the absence of a class certification the plaintiffs' suit was moot. [**Board of School Commissioners v. Jacobs**, 420 U.S. 128 (1975)]

Compare: In a collective action proceeding under the federal Fair Labor Standards Act, the plaintiff sought to pursue an individual claim and a claim on behalf of others similarly situated. The employer made an offer of judgment to the individual, one that included back pay, attorney's fees and costs. The plaintiff conceded, perhaps incorrectly, that this mooted her claim. The Court ruled that once the individual claim was moot, the lower court correctly dismissed the collective allegations; without a live claim, the plaintiff could no longer purport to pursue relief on behalf of others. [**Genesis Healthcare Corp. v. Symczyk**, 569 U.S. 66 (2013)]

1) Appeal of Denial of Class Certification

If class certification has been denied, the named plaintiff may appeal the denial even after the suit has become moot as to him.

e.g. **Example:** Plaintiff sought parole from federal prison but was denied because he failed to satisfy the criteria of federal "Parole Release Guidelines." He brought a class action challenging the Guidelines, but class certification was denied. Plaintiff was released from prison before any appeal could be heard. The Supreme Court held that the narrow issue of class certification was not moot on appeal even though plaintiff had been released from prison. [**United States Parole Commission v. Geraghty**, 445 U.S. 388 (1980)]

e.g. **Example:** Plaintiffs sought to bring a class action, claiming that they had been charged usurious interest rates on their credit cards. Class action certification was denied. Defendant tendered to the named plaintiffs the full amount of damages claimed by them, and the district court entered judgment against plaintiffs over their protest. Plaintiffs appealed the denial of class certification. The Court held that the class certification issue was not moot because plaintiffs had not voluntarily accepted the settlement offer. Moreover, plaintiffs had a continuing personal stake in the class certification, because the costs of the litigation could be spread over a larger group if the suit were permitted as a class action. [**Deposit Guaranty National Bank v. Roper**, 445 U.S. 326 (1980)]

(6) Mootness in Criminal Cases

A criminal appeal is not moot merely because the sentence has already been served. As long as there may be *"collateral legal consequences"* stemming from the conviction (*e.g.,* inability to vote or impeachability as a witness), the criminal defendant continues to have sufficient personal stake in the validity of the conviction to prevent mootness. [**Sibron v. New York**, 392 U.S. 40 (1968)]

(7) Mootness as a Prudential Doctrine with Political Overtones

In some cases, it appears that the Court finds a case moot or not moot depending on whether it wishes to decide the case on the merits. For example, in **DeFunis v. Odegaard**, *supra,* p. 26, the Court appears not to have been ready to decide the complex and politically sensitive issue of affirmative action in university admissions. The Supreme Court cut back on the use of prudential standing doctrine in **Lexmark Int'l, Inc. v. Static Control Components, Inc.**, 572 U.S. 118 (2014), but it has not yet decided what impact that decision will have on prudential elements of the mootness doctrine.

(8) Manufacturing Mootness

Defendants, and plaintiffs, may have the power to manufacture mootness by making a unilateral offer of full relief to their opponents. Obviously, a mutually agreed upon settlement will moot a case (and may preclude any further litigation except to enforce the settlement agreement). But parties may also have a power of somewhat uncertain scope to moot cases by unilateral action. [**Genesis Healthcare Corp. v. Symczyk**, 569 U.S. 66 (2013) (assuming that a settlement offer that fully satisfies plaintiff's claim for relief would moot the case, even if the plaintiff refuses the offer)] Consider **Already, LLC v. Nike, Inc.**, 568 U.S. 85 (2013). Nike sued for trademark infringement; Already counterclaimed to invalidate the trademark. Eventually, Nike discontinued its litigation and issued a "covenant not to sue" in which it "unconditionally and irrevocably" agreed to refrain from making any claim or demand against Already in respect of its trademark. The Court found that this broad covenant covered any conceivable claim Nike might make and held that it mooted the case.

(9) Pick-off Settlement Offers and Class Action Mootness

Defendants seeking to avoid class action litigation following the decision in **Genesis Healthcare Corp. v. Symczyk**, supra, may attempt to "pick-off" the claims of the named plaintiffs by settling with them and thereby depriving the plaintiffs of standing to pursue claims on behalf of a class. What happens if the plaintiffs refuse to accept the defendant's offer of full relief? In **Campbell-Ewald v. Gomez**, 136 S.Ct. 663 (2016), the Court held that the defendant's unconditional offer to pay the full amount of the plaintiff's demand was not alone enough to moot the plaintiff's claim. Notably, the plaintiff declined to accept the offer, preferring to continue the litigation on behalf of the class. Left unresolved was whether the defendant's pick-off strategy would work if the defendant, instead of making an unconditional offer of payment, actually tendered the full amount of the claim and secured the entry of a judgment in the plaintiff's favor.

d. Standing

The three-part test of standing doctrine requires that a plaintiff allege "*personal injury* [that is] *fairly traceable* to the defendant's allegedly unlawful conduct and likely to be *redressed* by the requested relief." [**Allen v. Wright**, 468 U.S. 737 (1984)]

(1) Constitutional and Subconstitutional Doctrine

(a) Article III "Case or Controversy" Requirement

The requirement that a litigant have standing derives in important part from the "case or controversy" limitation of Article III. To satisfy Article III, the plaintiff must show that she *personally* has suffered some *actual or threatened injury*. [**Lujan v. Defenders of Wildlife**, 504 U.S. 555 (1992)] The plaintiff must also show that injury bears a *causal relationship* to the challenged conduct of the defendant; the Court has spoken of this as the *causation or fair traceability requirement*. [**Lujan v. Defenders of Wildlife**, *supra*; **Allen v. Wright**, *supra*] Finally, the plaintiff must show that the proposed relief will *redress or remedy the injury* in question. [**Simon v. Eastern Kentucky Welfare Rights Organization**, 426 U.S. 26 (1976)]

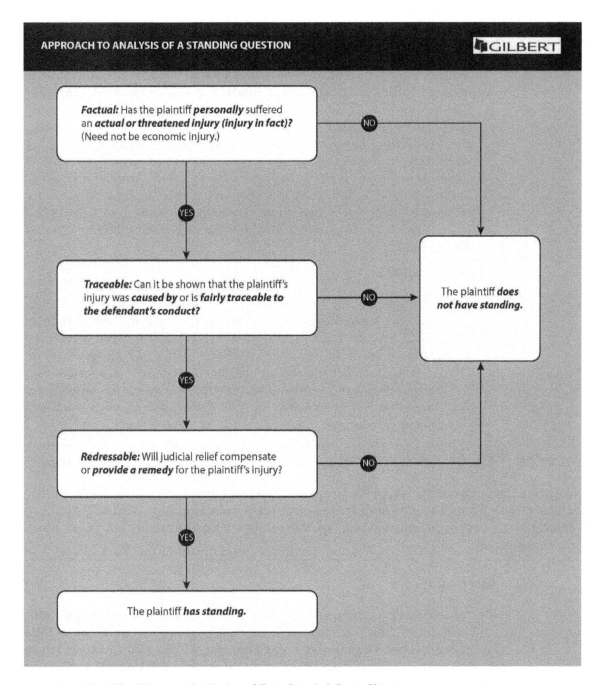

(b) The Uncertain Role of Prudential Standing

For many years, standing was said to have both a constitutional and prudential component. The Court on occasion would refuse to hear a case because of "prudential rules of standing that, apart from Article III's minimum requirements, serve to limit the role of the courts in resolving public disputes." [**Warth v. Seldin**, 422 U.S. 490 (1975)]

e.g. **Example:** In **Elk Grove Unified School District v. Newdow**, 542 U.S. 1 (2004), the Court denied prudential standing to a father who had challenged his daughter's exposure to a school policy that required recitation of the Pledge of Allegiance, with its reference to one nation "under God." Although the father may have suffered an injury in fact to his own interests as a parent, his claim may have conflicted with the interests of the girl's mother (who as the custodial parent had refused to authorize the suit) and those of the daughter herself. The Court's disposition enabled it to avoid any resolution of the merits of the father's religion clause challenge to the pledge.

More recently, the Court has significantly narrowed the doctrine of prudential standing. In **Lexmark Int'l, Inc. v. Static Control Components, Inc.**, 572 U.S. 118 (2014), the Court transformed the zone-of-interest test from an inquiry into prudential standing to an assessment of the meaning of the relevant statute. Instead of inviting judges to ask whether, as a matter of judicial discretion, they would agree to hear the matter, the Court called for an inquiry into whether **Congress** had made the plaintiff a proper party to enforce the rights in question. The move from a doctrine that focuses on judicial prudence to one that emphasizes legislative design means that parties may claim to fall within a statute's zone of interests only if Congress has placed them there by allowing them to sue.

1) Comment

Lexmark v. Static Control calls into question the legitimacy of such prudential justiciability doctrines as those barring the adjudication of generalized grievances, requiring a concrete dispute between adversaries, and requiring dismissal of moot claims. While the **Lexmark** Court indicated that the prohibition on the exercise of jurisdiction over generalized grievances was to be regarded as a matter of constitutional doctrine, it did not resolve the future treatment of other prudential justiciability doctrines.

EXAM TIP   **GILBERT**

When confronting a question that implicates a doctrine that arose from the exercise of judicial prudence and discretion, such as doctrines of justiciability and abstention (the subject of chapter 9), consider asking whether **Lexmark** calls for some reconsideration of the foundation of those doctrines.

---

(2) Nature of Injury

The "personal stake" requirement of standing includes a requirement that plaintiff show some injury. This is often referred to as "injury in fact." [**Association of Data Processing Service Organizations v. Camp**, *supra*] The Court has referred to standing as requiring an "actual or imminent injury" [**McConnell v. Federal Election Commission**, 540 U.S. 93 (2003)], one that is "distinct and palpable." [**Warth v. Seldin**, *supra*]

(a) Injury May Be Small

There is no requirement that plaintiff's injury be of any particular size. Small injuries are frequently sufficient for standing.

> **e.g.** **Example:** A federal taxpayer may have standing to challenge an expenditure as a violation of the Establishment Clause even though only a few cents of her total tax payment go to the challenged expenditure. [**Flast v. Cohen**, *supra*]

(b) Injury Need Not Be Economic

Injury is not confined to economic, or monetary, injury.

e.g. **Examples:** Injury may be to an aesthetic interest, such as environmental beauty. [**Sierra Club v. Morton**, 405 U.S. 727 (1972)] Or it may be to an interest in living in a racially integrated environment. [**Trafficante v. Metropolitan Life Insurance Co.**, 409 U.S. 205 (1972)] Or it may be to a student's interest in obtaining an education in a racially integrated school. [**Allen v. Wright**, supra p. 30]

(c) Injury Cannot Be Merely General

An injury is insufficient to confer standing if it is shared generally by the population and does not affect the plaintiff in particular.

e.g. **Example:** An allegation of injury that simply asserts that the government has violated the law is insufficient. [**Schlesinger v. Reservists Committee to Stop the War**, 418 U.S. 208 (1974)]

e.g. **Example:** An allegation of racial stigma arising out of governmental action asserted to be racially discriminatory is insufficient unless plaintiff alleges that he has personally suffered from the discriminatory treatment. [**Allen v. Wright**, *supra,* p. 30]

cf. **Compare:** In **Federal Election Commission v. Akins**, 524 U.S. 11 (1998), the Court distinguished concrete injuries that are widely shared and will nonetheless support standing (such as those resulting from a mass tort) from generalized grievances (abstract claims of injury to a common interest in compliance with law). (*See infra,* p. 34.)

(d) Injury Cannot Be Merely Speculative

A bare allegation that plaintiff fears that injury will occur is insufficient. More than mere speculation is required.

e.g. **Example:** Plaintiff was subjected to a chokehold by the Los Angeles police after a routine traffic arrest. Although plaintiff had standing to sue for damages for the chokehold that he had experienced, he did not have standing to seek injunctive relief against the police practice of using the chokehold. He was no more likely to be subjected to the chokehold in the future than was any person in Los Angeles. [**City of Los Angeles v. Lyons**, *supra,* p. 25]

cf. **Compare:** An individual landlord and a landlords' association challenged a rent control ordinance under which special rent concessions were required for "hardship tenants." Plaintiffs failed to allege in their complaint that they had hardship tenants, but stated at oral argument in the Supreme Court that association members had such tenants. Under such circumstances, there is "sufficient threat of actual injury to satisfy Article III's requirement." [**Pennell v. City of San Jose**, 485 U.S. 1 (1988)]

cf. **Compare:** Plaintiffs contended that an Interstate Commerce Commission ("I.C.C.") order increasing railroad freight rates would increase the cost of recycled products and would thus reduce the incentive to recycle. Plaintiffs contended that this would have adverse effects on the environment in the area in which the plaintiffs lived; thus, plaintiffs sought an order requiring the I.C.C. to prepare an Environmental Impact Statement ("EIS") before implementing the order. The Court ***granted*** standing. [**United States v. SCRAP**, 412 U.S. 669 (1973)] Although at first glance the relationship between the challenged rate order and the alleged environmental injury appears to be fatally speculative, the willingness of the Court to grant standing can be explained by looking at the relief sought. Plaintiffs sought to require the preparation of an EIS, which is statutorily required when a proposed action *may have* an adverse environmental impact. Thus, the statutory requirement for an EIS was triggered by the existence of a speculative relationship, and the function of the EIS was to require that the relationship be investigated and the results of the investigation reported.

cf. **Compare:** In **McConnell v. Federal Election Commission**, *supra,* p. 32, the Court denied standing to a United States Senator who wished to challenge certain rules that would limit his ability to purchase time on television stations in a future campaign. Because the Senator would not face reelection for five years, the injury was not sufficiently "actual and imminent" to confer standing.

cf. **Compare:** In 2013, the Court found that Amnesty International and a group of other plaintiffs lacked standing to challenge a federal law authorizing surveillance of certain non-US persons located overseas. The federal surveillance statute, as amended in 2008, authorized the Attorney General and the director of National Intelligence to request authority to conduct such surveillance, subject to the approval of the Foreign Intelligence Surveillance Court (FISC). The plaintiffs (lawyers, human rights activists, members of the news media) contended that they had ongoing contacts with non-US persons who were likely targets of such surveillance, thus creating a substantial risk that their own conversations would be intercepted. In a 5–4 decision, the Court ruled that the claim was too speculative to warrant standing. Plaintiffs could not show that their foreign contacts had been targeted or that the FISC would approve a request for their surveillance. Although the plaintiffs claimed that they had incurred substantial costs to protect the confidentiality of their communications with foreign contacts, the Court viewed these expenditures as the voluntary choice of the plaintiffs, a choice that could not manufacture standing in the absence of a "certainly impending injury." [**Clapper v. Amnesty International, USA**, 568 U.S. 398 (2013)]

(3) Causal Link to Defendant's Wrongdoing

Assuming the existence of a concrete injury, the standing doctrine requires a showing that the injury was *caused* by or is *fairly traceable* to the defendant's alleged wrongdoing.

e.g. **Example:** In **Allen v. Wright**, *supra,* p. 30, the Court found that the plaintiffs adequately alleged an injury to their interest in securing public education in racially integrated schools. But the injury to this interest was not viewed as "fairly traceable" to the government's conduct in providing tax deductions to racially discriminatory private schools. The causal link between the government's provision of tax benefits to *private* schools and the degree of integration achieved in *public* schools was seen as too weak to sustain standing.

(4) Ability of Court to Remedy Injury

Standing also requires a showing that the judicial relief requested would *remedy or redress* the alleged injury. [**Allen v. Wright**, *supra*] This redressability requirement focuses on the degree to which the proposed remedy would eliminate or redress the harm plaintiff allegedly suffered. Suits for damages to compensate for the invasion of a legally protected interest present an easy case for redressability; the award of damages would in theory make the plaintiff whole. Suits for injunctive and declaratory relief, particularly those that seek to compel the government to take action against some third party, can present a closer question.

Example: Plaintiffs challenged a new Internal Revenue Service ruling that reduced the obligation of a hospital to provide care to poor people while still retaining the tax status of a charitable organization. The Court denied standing because there was no showing that a different I.R.S. ruling would make the hospital provide more care to the poor. [**Simon v. Eastern Kentucky Welfare Rights Organization**, *supra,* p. 30]

Example: Plaintiff, the mother of an illegitimate child, had requested the district attorney to enforce a Texas criminal statute requiring fathers to pay child support, but the district attorney refused on the ground that the statute applied only to fathers of legitimate children. The Supreme Court refused to hear a suit seeking an order requiring Texas officials to prosecute fathers of illegitimate children. The Court found that only a "speculative" connection existed between the desired result (the payment of child support) and the remedy sought (criminal prosecution of delinquent fathers). [**Linda R.S. v. Richard D.**, 410 U.S. 614 (1973)] (*But note:* The rationale in this case is unconvincing. Both common sense and sociological studies support the plaintiff's contention that the threat of criminal prosecution will have a significant effect on the behavior of delinquent fathers. A different and possibly more convincing rationale was briefly suggested by the Court: Private citizens ordinarily are given little power to influence prosecutors' discretionary decisions about whom to prosecute.)

Example: A variety of low-income plaintiffs challenged allegedly exclusionary zoning ordinances. The Court denied standing on the ground that there was no showing that an invalidation of the challenged zoning ordinances would have resulted in the construction of housing that plaintiffs could have afforded. [**Warth v. Seldin**, *supra,* p. 31]

Compare: Low-income plaintiffs challenged, on exclusionary zoning grounds, the refusal to rezone a specific parcel of land to permit a particular proposed housing project. The Court found standing because there was a substantial probability that if the zoning were changed the project would be built and plaintiffs thereby benefited. [**Village of Arlington Heights v. Metropolitan Housing Development Corp.**, 429 U.S. 252 (1977)]

Compare: After finding that voters had suffered an injury to their right to certain campaign finance information under federal law, the Court treated the injury as redressable, despite the existence of prosecutorial discretion. Although the federal agency retained discretion whether to pursue claims to compel disclosure of the information by a third party, judicial review of the legal standard governing the disclosure issue could influence the exercise of that discretion and redress the injury to voters' informational interest. [**Federal Election Commission v. Akins**, *supra,* p. 33]

Compare: Plaintiffs lived near two nuclear power plants that were under construction. They wished to halt construction because of environmental and aesthetic concerns. They challenged the constitutionality of the Price-Anderson Act, which imposed a statutory limitation on the total liability of a nuclear plant in the event of an accident. They alleged that without the financial protection of the Act, the plants would not be completed. The Court permitted standing, agreeing that the plants probably would not be completed if the Act were invalidated; thus, the remedy sought by plaintiffs would prevent or redress the injury. [**Duke Power Co. v. Carolina Environmental Study Group**, 438 U.S. 59 (1978)]

(5) Distinguish Between Standing and the Right to Sue

The Court has frequently said that whether a plaintiff has standing to sue is not the same question as whether the plaintiff has stated a cause of action. **Lexmark**, *supra* p. 32 suggests a two-part inquiry that first focuses on whether the plaintiff can satisfy the Article III elements of standing and only then inquires whether the relevant statute permits the plaintiff to enforce the rights in question.

EXAM TIP   **GILBERT**

On your exam, don't confuse the concept of standing with the concept of stating a cause of action. For such a question, be sure to *start* by determining whether the plaintiff has standing (*see* chart, *supra*) and then address whether the plaintiff has stated a cause of action.

---

(6) Refusal to Permit "Supplemental" Standing

Article III requires a claim-by-claim analysis of the plaintiff's standing. Additionally, the concept of "supplemental standing" is inapplicable—each claim must be judged, for standing purposes, on its own.

e.g. **Example:** In **DaimlerChrysler v. Cuno**, 547 U.S. 332 (2006), the plaintiffs paid taxes both to municipal government and to state government, and sought to challenge a corporate tax rebate on the ground that it reduced tax revenues to both levels of government. (For more on taxpayer standing, *see infra,* pp. 38–41.) The Court agreed that the plaintiffs had standing as municipal taxpayers but concluded that they lacked standing as state taxpayers. The Court also refused to permit plaintiffs to rely on their standing as municipal taxpayers to provide the Article III foundation for their claim as state taxpayers. The Court distinguished **Mine Workers v. Gibbs**, 383 U.S. 715 (1967), which allowed district courts to exercise supplemental jurisdiction over nonfederal claims when they bear an appropriate relationship to claims within federal jurisdiction. [**DaimlerChrysler Corp. v. Cuno**, *supra*]

(7) Power of Congress to Confer Standing

It is a fundamental doctrine that Congress cannot confer on Article III federal courts jurisdiction not authorized by Article III. Thus, if a plaintiff lacks standing in the Article III sense, Congress cannot by statute confer standing on that person. In other words, Congress cannot do away with the standing and timing requirements discussed earlier.

e.g. **Example:** *Lujan v. Defenders of Wildlife:* The federal Endangered Species Act ("ESA") provides that "any person may commence a civil suit on his own behalf . . . to enjoin . . . the United States [or any agency thereof]" who is alleged to be in violation of the Act. Plaintiff environmental organizations challenged a rule promulgated by the Secretary of the Interior that required federal agencies to consult with the Secretary to ensure that agency-funded projects in the United States or on the high seas do not threaten endangered species, but did not require consultation for such projects in foreign countries. Plaintiffs contended that exclusion of activities in foreign countries was inconsistent with the ESA. Two projects that would have been covered by a broader rule were in Egypt and Sri

Lanka. Members of one of the plaintiff groups had previously travelled to Egypt and Sri Lanka and had observed the habitat of endangered animals (but not the animals themselves). Although they hoped to observe the animals in the future, at the time of the suit, they had no concrete plans to do so. The Court held that the members, and hence the organizations, did not have sufficient injury to satisfy Article III. Without such injury, it made no difference that Congress had authorized "any person" to bring suit to enforce the ESA. [**Lujan v. Defenders of Wildlife**, *supra,* p. 30] (*But note:* If the plaintiffs could show that defendants' actions caused them an "injury in fact," the ESA's grant of standing to "any person" would have allowed their suit to proceed. [**Bennett v. Spear**, 520 U.S. 154 (1997)])

cf. **Compare:** The Federal Election Campaign Act requires organizations to register as political committees if they meet certain standards. Voters filed a complaint with the Federal Election Commission ("FEC"), arguing that the American Israel Public Affairs Committee should be treated as a political committee and required to disclose information such as membership, contribution sources, and expenditures. When the FEC rejected their claim, they petitioned the district court to review the FEC's action under a statute that allowed suit by a party aggrieved by an FEC order. The Court held that the agency action undercut the voters' access to information, causing them an injury in fact that sufficed to support their standing. The creation by Congress of a right to information, though it was a right widely shared by all voters, was enough to satisfy Article III standards. [**Federal Election Commission v. Akins**, *supra,* p. 33] *Comment: Akins* does not overrule *Lujan.* Rather, the Court, despite a strongly worded dissent by Justice Scalia (the author of *Lujan*), provided Congress the means to authorize citizen suits by recognizing that Congress can create a right, the invasion of which would support Article III standing.

(a) Limited Congressional Power to Confer Standing

In a number of cases prior to *Lujan,* the Court upheld congressional grants of standing where the plaintiff would have been found to lack standing absent the statute. These cases are analytically consistent with *Lujan* in that the plaintiffs had sufficient injury in fact to satisfy Article III.

e.g. **Example:** A white resident in an apartment complex sought an injunction under the Civil Rights Act of 1968 against the landlord's racial discrimination against prospective nonwhite tenants. The Court found the white resident to have standing. [**Trafficante v. Metropolitan Life insurance Co.**, *supra,* p. 33] Justices White, Blackmun, and Powell concurred, noting that they would have had "great difficulty" finding Article III standing in the absence of the Civil Rights Act.

e.g. **Example:** Plaintiff sought to bring a class action challenging the Parole Commission's guidelines. Class certification was denied, and plaintiff was later released from prison. Even though plaintiff no longer had any personal stake in the application of parole guidelines, the Court permitted him to appeal the denial of class certification. The Court found that in passing Federal Rule of Civil Procedure 23 (class actions), Congress conferred a statutory right on a person in plaintiff's position even though he no longer had a personal stake in the controversy. Such a person served as a "private attorney general." [**United States Parole Commission v. Geraghty**, *supra,* p. 29]

e.g. **Example:** The Federal Fair Housing Act of 1968 makes it unlawful to "represent to any person because of race . . . that any dwelling is not available for . . . rental when such dwelling is in fact available." A black "tester" asked about the availability of an apartment and was falsely told that it was not available. The tester had standing to sue under the Act even though he had no desire to live in the apartment. [**Havens Realty Corp. v. Coleman**, 455 U.S. 363 (1982)]

(b) Special Status of the State as a Litigant

A decision of uncertain breadth suggests that Congress may have power to confer standing on states as preferred litigants. A variety of litigants filed a petition with the Environmental Protection Agency ("EPA"), asking it to regulate greenhouse gas emissions that have been linked to global warming. The EPA declined. The Court held that the state of Massachusetts (alone of the many petitioners) had standing to seek judicial review of the EPA's decision, even though one might question whether the state's injuries would be redressed by any action the EPA might take in the United States to address a problem of global proportions. The Court ascribed some significance to the special sovereign status of Massachusetts, and to Congress's decision to give the states (among others) a procedural right to challenge inaction by the EPA. As a consequence, the Court found that a somewhat less substantial showing of immediacy of injury and redressability would suffice to confer standing. [**Massachusetts v. EPA**, 549 U.S. 497 (2007)] The decision by a narrow five-Justice majority drew a sharp dissent, and provides an uncertain foundation for future expansions of state standing.

(c) Spokeo and the "No-Injury" Consumer Claim

Sometimes, instead of a broad grant of standing, Congress creates a new right, such as the right of every individual under the federal Fair Credit Reporting Act (FCRA) to accuracy in credit reports published about them. The Court has held that allegations of a violation of the statute do not automatically confer standing; plaintiffs must show Article III injury that is both concrete and particularized. [**Spokeo v. Robins**, 136 S.Ct. 1540 (2016)]

Acknowledging that an inaccurate credit report poses a particularized harm, the **Spokeo** Court focused on whether that individual's injury was "concrete." The Court found that intangible injuries (such as that occasioned by the publication of an inaccurate report) could be concrete, but not simply because Congress created a right to sue. Instead, the concreteness inquiry focuses on whether the individual has suffered a real or de facto injury that Congress has made cognizable by granting a right to sue for its invasion.

e.g. **Example:** The Court explained that a false report that misstated an individual's zip code might not occasion any injury and would not be actionable. But false reports that affected an individual's job prospects or credit score could well meet the test for concreteness.

Comment: The Court's decision may affect the viability of some consumer class actions, brought against a company to recover damages on behalf of a class of individuals. Many federal statutes, including the FCRA and the Telephone Consumer Protection Act, include provisions that entitle claimants to a stated award of damages (say $500 or $1000) for statutory violations. The greater specificity needed to establish standing after **Spokeo** may complicate the certification of such class actions.

(8) Taxpayer Standing

For many years, it was established that federal taxpayers could not rely on their status as taxpayers to confer standing to challenge allegedly illegal federal expenditures. [**Frothingham v. Mellon**, 262 U.S. 447 (1923)—taxpayer's interest too "remote, fluctuating, and uncertain"] But *Frothingham* has been modified so that taxpayer standing is now permitted in some cases.

(a) State and Municipal Taxpayers

The Supreme Court heard on the merits an appeal from a state court suit in which local taxpayers sought to challenge under the Establishment Clause of the First Amendment expenditures for busing children to Catholic parochial schools. The Court noted that plaintiffs were taxpayers but did not discuss the standing issue. [**Everson v. Board of Education**, 330 U.S. 1 (1947)] However, for there to be standing, there must be an expenditure of tax money. [**Doremus v. Board of Education**, 342 U.S. 429 (1952)]

> **e.g.** **Example:** When a state taxpayer sought to challenge required reading of the Old Testament in the public schools, the Supreme Court denied standing. According to the Court, this was not a "good faith pocketbook" action since no specific expenditure was challenged. [**Doremus v. Board of Education**, *supra*]

(b) Federal Taxpayers

Federal taxpayer standing has been permitted in extremely limited circumstances to challenge congressionally approved *expenditures alleged to be in violation of the Establishment Clause.*

1) Test

The Court formulated a two-part test for taxpayer standing: (i) the expenditure must be *an exercise of the taxing and spending power* rather than merely an "incidental expenditure" connected with a regulatory program; and (ii) the expenditures must be *prohibited by some specific constitutional limitation* rather than merely beyond the powers delegated to the federal government. [**Flast v. Cohen**, 392 U.S. 83 (1968)—limiting but not overruling **Frothingham v. Mellon**]

> **e.g.** **Example:** A federal taxpayer challenged federal expenditures used to finance instruction in religious schools. Plaintiff satisfied the test because the expenditures were an exercise of the taxing and spending power which she challenged as being inconsistent with the Establishment Clause. [**Flast v. Cohen**, *supra*]

2) No Taxpayer Standing in Non-Establishment Clause Cases

Despite the apparent generality of the test formulated in **Flast v. Cohen**, *supra,* the Supreme Court has permitted taxpayer standing *only* to challenge expenditures made pursuant to statutes alleged to be *in violation of the Establishment Clause.*

> **e.g.** **Example:** A federal taxpayer sought to challenge secret expenditures by the Director of the Central Intelligence Agency as in violation of Article I, Section 9, Clause 7 of the Constitution requiring a "regular Statement and Account" of expenditures of public money. The

Court denied standing. [**United States v. Richardson**, 418 U.S. 166 (1974)]

e.g. **Example:** Federal taxpayers sought to challenge the practice of members of Congress holding positions as military reservists, allegedly in violation of Article I, Section 6, Clause 2, prohibiting members of Congress from simultaneously holding any other "Office under the United States." Plaintiff alleged that congressional spending decisions were improperly influenced by the conflicting obligations of Members of Congress. The Court denied standing. [**Schlesinger v. Reservists Committee to Stop the War**, *supra*, p. 33]

3) Limitation and Virtual Abandonment of *Flast v. Cohen*

The Court has subsequently *denied* standing to federal taxpayers who brought an Establishment Clause challenge to a grant by the United States of real property to a religious school. The Court limited *Flast* to expenditures of funds under Article I, Section 8. It held that *Flast* did not apply to the "Property Clause" of Article IV, Section 3, Clause 2 giving Congress the "Power to dispose of. . . Property belonging to the United States." [**Valley Forge Christian College v. Americans United for Separation of Church and State**, 454 U.S. 464 (1982)]

a) Criticism

There is little difference, either in terms of the finances of the United States or in terms of the Establishment Clause, between expenditures of cash and grants of real property. The distinction between expenditures under Article I, Section 8 (for which standing is permitted) and grants under Article IV, Section 3, Clause 2 (for which standing is denied) seems formalistic rather than functional.

b) Further Limitation of *Flast v. Cohen*

In **DaimlerChrysler Corp. v. Cuno**, *supra*, p. 36, the Court rejected a state taxpayer's standing to mount a Commerce Clause challenge to certain corporate tax rebates offered by a state government. State taxpayers resembled federal taxpayers in that their payments were mingled with those of millions of others and their own share became so minute and indeterminate as to fail to provide a concrete stake.

c) Virtual Overruling of *Flast v. Cohen?*

In its most recent treatment, the Court rejected the attempt of taxpayers to mount an Establishment Clause challenge to an executive branch program that allowed faith-based groups to compete for federal grant money. The Court distinguished **Flast v. Cohen** on the ground that it involved an explicit congressional appropriation of funds to religious groups. Here, by contrast, Congress did not expressly allocate the funds to religious groups, but simply made general appropriations that the executive branch was to spend in the exercise of its discretion. [**Hein v. Freedom From Religion Foundation, Inc.**, 551 U.S. 587 (2007)] Although the Court did not expressly overrule *Flast,* its denial of standing to challenge discretionary spending decisions by the executive certainly enables the political branches to structure spending in ways that will evade any taxpayer challenge.

Compare: In 2010, the Court continued to treat the **Flast v. Cohen** decision as confined to its specific facts. The state of Arizona offered tax credits to those who donated money to groups that, in turn, helped pay the cost of religious school education. Despite the fact that the state program clearly conferred a financial benefit on religious groups in the form of reduced taxes, the Court rejected taxpayer standing. [**Arizona Christian School Tuition Organization v. Winn**, 560 U.S. 924 (2010)]

EXAM TIP

On an exam, if you see taxpayers seeking to challenge a federal expenditure, your first thought should be that they probably don't have standing. But remember that there is a *limited exception* to this rule if the challenge is based on the *Establishment Clause*. Also be sure to see if there has been an expenditure of tax money under a specific congressional appropriation and not a grant of property, the conferral of an indirect financial benefit, or the creation of discretionary executive spending authority, which would not be sufficient for taxpayer standing.

---

d) Taxpayer Standing Compared to Citizen Standing

Standing to sue merely as a "citizen" has consistently been denied by the federal courts. [*See, e.g.,* **Schlesinger v. Reservists Committee to Stop the War**, *supra*, p. 40]

(9) Congressional and State Legislative Standing

(a) Standing Based on Legislative Duties

Members of Congress and state legislators sometimes challenge laws and practices on the basis that they interfere with their legislative duties. Their standing depends on a showing that the law or practice they wish to challenge impedes their legislative duties; it's not enough simply to argue that the law does or does not violate the Constitution.

Example: Members of Congress challenged the constitutionality of the federal Line Item Veto Act, which permits the President to veto particular spending and tax provisions. Plaintiffs were four Senators and two members of the House of Representatives suing individually. They relied on no statute granting standing to challenge the Act. The Supreme Court denied standing: "[A]ppellees have alleged no injury to themselves as individuals . . ., the institutional injury they allege is wholly abstract and widely dispersed . . ., and their attempt to litigate this dispute at this time and in this form is contrary to historical experience. We attach some importance to the fact that appellees have not been authorized to represent their respective Houses of Congress in this action, and indeed both Houses actively oppose their suit." [**Raines v. Byrd**, 521 U.S. 811 (1997)]

Compare: Individual state legislators were granted standing to challenge the ability of the state lieutenant governor to cast the deciding vote on whether to ratify a constitutional amendment. If the lieutenant governor had not cast his vote, the position favored by plaintiffs would have prevailed.

In bringing suit, the legislators sought to "maintain the effectiveness of their votes." [**Coleman v. Miller**, 307 U.S. 433 (1939)] The Supreme Court in the *Raines* case distinguished *Coleman* on the ground that the *Raines* plaintiffs "have not alleged that they voted for a specific bill, that there were sufficient votes to pass the bill, and that the bill was nonetheless deemed defeated. In the vote on the Line Item Veto Act, their votes were given full effect. They simply lost that vote."

cf. **Compare:** The Arizona Legislature had standing to challenge a popular referendum that transferred control of drawing the lines of electoral districts from the legislature to a bipartisan commission. [**Arizona State Legislature v. Arizona Indep. Redistricting Comm'n**, 135 S. Ct. 2652 (2015)]

(b) Standing for Legislators When the Executive Declines to Defend

On occasion, the executive branch of state or federal government will decline to defend the constitutionality of a law before the federal courts. When members of the legislative branch or others intervene in the litigation to defend the law, their actions may raise a question of standing to appeal.

e.g. **Example:** In **INS v. Chadha**, 462 U.S. 919 (1983), the government declined to defend a federal law authorizing one house of Congress to veto discretionary non-deportation of aliens who overstayed their visas. The Court concluded that both the House and Senate were proper parties to petition for review of a decision invalidating such one-house vetoes, at least where the government continued to threaten deportation.

cf. **Compare:** After the Obama administration declined to defend the constitutionality of the Defense of Marriage Act (DOMA) (which prohibited the federal government from recognizing same-sex marriage for purposes of federal benefits), the Bipartisan Legal Advisory Group (BLAG) of the House of Representatives stepped in to do so. The Court's majority concluded that the United States had a financial interest in the case sufficient to confer standing on it to appeal, notwithstanding its refusal to defend DOMA's constitutionality on the merits. The government's interest was said to arise from its financial stake in defending a claim for the refund of federal taxes paid by the plaintiff, the same-sex partner of a decedent who was lawfully married under state law and would have been entitled to a marital exemption from the federal inheritance tax but for DOMA. The majority viewed the government's financial interest, together with BLAG's adversity, as sufficient to satisfy Article III. In an interesting and potentially important development, the majority viewed the adverse-parties requirement as a prudential matter, rather than a hard-and-fast element of Article III standing. BLAG was said to provide any requisite adverseness. [**United States v. Windsor**, 570 U.S. 931 (2013)]

(c) Standing for Private Parties When the Executive Declines to Defend

In **Hollingsworth v. Perry**, 570 U.S. 692 (2013), the State of California refused to defend Proposition 8, the ballot initiative that prohibited same-sex marriage in that state, after it was invalidated on constitutional grounds in the district court. Prop 8 proponents intervened, and sought to defend the law in the Ninth Circuit. After certifying a question to the California Supreme Court, the Ninth

Circuit ruled that the intervenors had standing to appeal as representatives of the state of California.

The Court rejected the intervenors' standing to appeal, finding that theirs was little more than a generalized grievance held in common with all of the supporters of Prop 8. While the intervenors had limited official status as the "proponents" of the measure, they had no official role in enforcing the measure and were acting in their capacity as private individuals. The Court's approach thus emphasizes the importance of some formal or official authorization as the key to defending a law's constitutionality in the wake of an executive branch refusal to defend.

(10) Association Standing

An association has standing to represent the interests of its members when (i) the *individual members would have standing* to sue in their own right; (ii) the *interests* the association seeks to protect are *"germane" to its purpose;* and (iii) the nature of the claim and the relief sought are such that the *presence of the individual members is not required.* [Hunt v. Washington Apple Advertising Commission, 432 U.S. 333 (1977)]

Example: An association of motor carriers may represent the interests of its members in challenging an order of the Interstate Commerce Commission. [**National Motor Freight Association v. United States**, 372 U.S. 246 (1963)]

Example: The National Association for the Advancement of Colored People ("NAACP"), in appealing an order requiring it to produce its membership lists, may rely upon the constitutionally protected associational rights of its members. The NAACP contended that both it and its members would be injured if the State of Alabama could require the membership list to be disclosed. [**NAACP v. Alabama**, 357 U.S. 449 (1958)]

Example: An association of associations has standing to bring suit on behalf of its member associations as long as they, in turn, would have standing to bring suit on behalf of their individual members. [New York State Club Association v. New York City, 487 U.S. 1 (1988)]

Compare: An association can have standing only if its individual members have standing. Thus, the Sierra Club has no standing if it fails to allege that any of its members will be injured by a challenged development. [**Sierra Club v. Morton**, *supra*, p. 33]

Compare: An individual who has a concrete aesthetic or recreational interest in the preservation of specific habitat or eco-systems may bring suit to challenge actions that threaten her interest. Accordingly, an environmental group or association will be granted standing if its members have the requisite connection to the habitat in question. But if an association settles claims in respect of the habitat in which its members have shown a concrete interest and fails to offer evidence that members have similar connections to other affected areas, the association will be denied standing to challenge federal administration of the habitat in question. [**Summers v. Earth Island Institute**, 555 U.S. 488 (2009)]

AN ASSOCIATION HAS STANDING TO REPRESENT THE INTERESTS OF ITS MEMBERS WHEN:
☑ The **association members would have standing** to sue in their own right;
☑ The interests the association seeks to protect are **"germane" to its purpose**; and
☑ The nature of the claim and the relief sought are such that **the presence of the individual members is not required.**

(11) Third-Party Standing

The Court may permit parties who meet the Article III "case or controversy" test to assert the interests of absent third parties in arguing their case.

(a) Difficult for the Third Party to Assert Rights

Third-party standing is likely to be granted where the third party will find it difficult to assert her own rights.

e.g. **Example:** A white person sold his property to a black purchaser despite a racially restrictive covenant purporting to prohibit such a sale. A white beneficiary of the covenant sued the seller for damages. In urging the invalidity of the covenant, the white seller was permitted to assert the interests of the black purchaser because such a purchaser would seldom be a party to a suit on a covenant. Thus, the seller was "the only effective adversary." [**Barrows v. Jackson**, 346 U.S. 249 (1953)]

e.g. **Example:** The NAACP can assert the rights of its members not to have their names revealed when the members assert a right to remain anonymous. If the members come into court on their own behalf, they will be forced to reveal their names and will thus automatically lose the right to anonymity that they wish to protect. [**NAACP v. Alabama**, *supra*]

cf. **Compare:** A death row inmate had knowingly and intelligently waived his right to appeal his conviction and death sentence. The Supreme Court denied third-party standing to a fellow inmate to appeal on his behalf. [**Whitmore v. Arkansas**, 495 U.S. 149 (1990)]

(b) Close Relationship Between Party and Third Party

Third-party standing is likely to be granted when there is a close relationship between the party and the third party.

1) Seller-Purchaser

A seller of beer asserted the right of an 18-year-old male who wished to purchase beer in challenging a statute that permitted the sale of beer to women beginning at age 18, but did not permit sales to males until age 21. The seller had standing. [**Craig v. Boren,** 429 U.S. 179 (1976); *and see* **Barrows v. Jackson**, *supra*—white seller permitted to assert right of black purchaser]

2) Doctor-Patient

A doctor may sometimes assert the rights of patients.

a) Right of Patient Seeking Abortion

A doctor may assert the right of a patient to an abortion when some direct interest *of the doctor* is also at stake. [**Doe v. Bolton**, 410 U.S. 179 (1973)—criminal penalties against doctor for performing an abortion; **Singleton v. Wulff**, 428 U.S. 106 (1976)—fees for performing abortion directly limited by the challenged statute]

1/ Distinguish

A doctor does not have standing to defend the constitutionality of a statute limiting the right to an abortion. For example, in **Diamond v. Charles**, 476 U.S. 54 (1986), the state had defended the statute limiting abortion on the merits in the court below. The lower court held against the state, and the state did not appeal the decision. In this circumstance, a doctor who wished to defend the statute but had no criminal liability and no direct financial interest at stake did not have standing to appeal the lower court's decision.

b) Right of Patient to Contraception

In contrast to the doctors in the abortion cases, a doctor seeking a declaratory judgment of the right of his patients to receive professional medical advice about contraception was *denied* standing. [**Tileston v. Ullman**, 318 U.S. 44 (1943)]

1/ Distinguish—Doctor Prosecuted Under Criminal Statute

A doctor who faces a *criminal* prosecution does have standing.

e.g. **Example:** A doctor and a director of Planned Parenthood were criminally convicted under an aiding and abetting statute for providing information and advice to married couples concerning the use of contraceptives. The Court upheld the defendants' standing to raise the patients' right to the information and advice. **Tileston v. Ullman**, *supra,* was distinguished on the ground that these defendants were criminally convicted, whereas Dr. Tileston merely sought a declaratory judgment. [**Griswold v. Connecticut**, 381 U.S. 479 (1965)]

2/ Others Prosecuted Under Criminal Statute

A defendant was criminally convicted for giving away a contraceptive to an unmarried person in violation of a state statute forbidding distribution of contraceptives by anyone except doctors and pharmacists and to anyone except married couples. The defendant was neither a doctor nor a pharmacist. The Court upheld the defendant's standing to raise the right of an unmarried person desiring to obtain contraceptives. [**Eisenstadt v. Baird**, 405 U.S. 438 (1972)]

3/ Comment

The Court's denial of standing in **Tileston v. Ullman**, *supra,* and its later grants of standing in **Griswold v. Connecticut**, *supra,* and **Eisenstadt v. Baird**, *supra,* may be partly explained by the distinction between a civil plaintiff seeking a declaratory judgment and a criminal defendant challenging a conviction. But an important contributing explanation is almost certainly the Court's desire in *Tileston* to avoid the then-controversial issue of contraception, and its willingness, 20 and 30 years later, to address that same issue.

4/ Second Thoughts About Third-Party Standing?

The Court may cut back on third-party standing to challenge abortion restrictions. Physicians challenged a federal statute that restricted access to a particular abortion procedure known as "intact dilation and extraction." The Court upheld the statute against a variety of challenges, including one based upon the claim that it did not adequately provide for exceptions to protect the life of the mother. Noting that a health-of-the-mother exception appeared in the statute, the Court concluded that the adequacy of the exception was to be adjudicated in an as-applied setting (perhaps involving a mother in a life-threatening situation) rather than in a facial challenge brought by physicians. [**Gonzales v. Carhart**, 550 U.S. 124 (2007)]

3) Teacher-Student

A Catholic parochial school challenged a state statute requiring all students to attend public school. The school was permitted to assert the rights of its students to attend the school of their choice. [**Pierce v. Society of Sisters**, 268 U.S. 510 (1925)]

4) Next Friend Standing in Habeas Corpus

As discussed at greater length later (*see infra,* pp. 252 *et seq.*), federal courts may entertain petitions for habeas corpus on behalf of individuals who wish to challenge the legality of their confinement. When detention deprives an individual of access to the court or to counsel, habeas law permits the individual's "next friend," often a parent or other close family member, to initiate proceedings. [28 U.S.C. § 2242; **Whitmore v. Arkansas**, *supra,* p. 44]

5) The Uncertain Implications of *Lexmark* for Prudential Tests

Many older decisions frame the third-party standing inquiry in terms of prudence. Recall that the **Lexmark** Court cast doubt on the viability of prudential standing doctrines. [**Lexmark Int'l, Inc. v. Static Control Components, Inc.**, *supra* p. 32] Note that the **Lexmark** Court did not classify third-party standing as constitutionally grounded, thereby raising questions about its future application.

a) Preserving Continuity

So far, most lower courts view third-party standing doctrine as having survived in prudential form. [**Ray Charles Foundation v. Robinson**, 795 F.3d 1109 (9th Cir. 2015) (describing a lower court consensus)]

Still, **Lexmark** encourages courts to evaluate questions of third-party standing by reference to the language of any applicable act of Congress, conferring a right to sue.

(12) Defendant's Standing

When a defendant is subjected to the operation of a statute, he will ordinarily not be permitted to object to the statute on the ground that, although validly applied as to him, it might be unconstitutional as to someone else.

 Example: A Mississippi statute required railroads to settle accident claims against them within 60 days or to pay a penalty of $25 for failure to do so. In a suit brought under the statute, the defendant railroad argued that the statute was unconstitutional because it imposed the duty to settle whether the damage claim was reasonable or extravagant. The Court refused to entertain the defense because the damage claim in this suit was reasonable. Thus, the statute was clearly constitutional as to this defendant. [**Yazoo & Mississippi Valley Railroad v. Jackson Vinegar Co.**, 226 U.S. 217 (1912)]

Example: Election officials were sued for violating the Federal Civil Rights Act of 1957. The officials argued that the Act was unconstitutional because it could be interpreted to prohibit activity whether or not state action was present. The Court refused to entertain the defense because state action was clearly present in this case. [**United States v. Raines**, 362 U.S. 17 (1960)]

(a) Rationale

The rationale behind defendant's standing cases such as those above is that the Court should not entertain constitutional challenges before it is necessary to do so. If the statute can be validly applied to the behavior of the actual defendants, the Court will not speculate as to possible future applications of the statute and the constitutionality of those applications.

(b) Exception—Free Speech

Where a criminal statute prohibits protected speech, a defendant prosecuted under the statute may defend on the ground that the statute impermissibly prohibits speech, even though the defendant's actual speech could have been prohibited under a narrowly drawn statute. For such a defense to be entertained, the statute must be substantially overbroad; *i.e.,* it must sweep a substantial amount of protected speech within its prohibition before a defendant may urge an overbreadth defense. [**Broaderick v. Oklahoma**, 413 U.S. 601 (1973)]

(13) Article III Standing in State Court

Since state courts are not bound by the Article III "case or controversy" doctrine, they may hear suits brought by plaintiffs without Article III standing, including suits based on *federal law.* [**Doremus v. Board of Education**, *supra,* p. 39]

(a) Appellate Jurisdiction of Supreme Court

Despite the fact that a plaintiff without Article III standing cannot originally bring his action in federal court, if the state court issues an opinion interpreting federal law, the Supreme Court can hear an appeal *by a losing defendant.*

Example: Plaintiffs without Article III standing obtained a state court judgment that mineral leases of state-owned real property were illegal under federal law. The Supreme Court reviewed the state court's decision at the request of the defendant-petitioners (lessees of the property) on the ground that the judgment posed a "serious and immediate threat to the continuing validity of [their] leases." This threat was sufficient injury to support standing to seek review of the state court judgment in the Supreme Court. [**Asarco Inc. v. Kadish**, 490 U.S. 605 (1989)]

1) Criticism

It is difficult to see how a judgment against defendants cures the "case or controversy" difficulty, since plaintiffs are just as much without Article III standing whether they win or lose in state court. In **Asarco v. Kadish**, the Supreme Court affirmed the judgment of the state court against defendants, producing a very odd result—plaintiffs, who were concededly without Article III standing, obtained a judgment in their favor from the highest Article III court in the land!

2) Distinguish—Losing Plaintiff

If the plaintiff without Article III standing loses in state court based on a federal claim, the Supreme Court cannot hear an appeal *by the plaintiff.*

Example: A state taxpayer brought a state court challenge to required Bible reading in the public schools based on the First Amendment; the state court held against the taxpayer-plaintiff on the merits. The Supreme Court declined to review the judgment because the plaintiff-appellant was without Article III standing. [**Doremus v. Board of Education**, *supra,* p. 39]

e. Comparison of Ripeness, Mootness, and Standing

(1) Ripeness and Mootness

Both ripeness and mootness are concerned with timing. If a dispute is brought to court *too early,* it is unripe. If a dispute is brought to court *too late* or remains in court *too long,* it is moot. A suit is justiciable only if it is brought to court in the interval of time after it has become ripe and before it has become moot.

(2) Ripeness and Standing

To some extent, ripeness and standing are both concerned with timing. Both may ask the question whether a dispute has progressed sufficiently far that a court may properly adjudicate it. But standing is concerned with the *plaintiffs injury,* whereas ripeness is concerned with the *suitability of a dispute for judicial resolution.* Thus, it is possible that a plaintiff may have standing in the Article III sense of injury or threatened injury, but a court may nevertheless find the case unripe if, by waiting, the court may eventually have the dispute presented to it in a better form.

Example: Plaintiffs sought a declaratory judgment that the Hatch Act, which prohibited political activity by federal employees, was unconstitutional. Plaintiffs could show injury sufficient to demonstrate standing because they were refraining from engaging in political activity. Nevertheless, the Court found the case unripe, despite plaintiffs' standing, because the case would be presented in a much clearer form if the Court waited until plaintiffs actually engaged in the prohibited activity. The dispute would then be ripe because the behavior would be actual rather than hypothetical, and the range of applications of the challenged statute presented for adjudication would be restricted to the actual behavior. [**United Public Workers v. Mitchell**, *supra*, p. 24]

 Example: In **McConnell v. Federal Election Commission**, *supra*, p. 32, a United States Senator sought to challenge campaign restrictions that would not affect him until his reelection campaign five years later. Without discussing ripeness, the Court denied the plaintiff standing on the ground that the injury failed to satisfy the "actual and imminent" requirement.

EXAM TIP   GILBERT

On your exam, keep in mind that although "ripeness" and "standing" are both related in part to timing, you must *analyze the issues separately*. Remember that a plaintiff may have standing, yet the court may nonetheless determine that the case has not yet progressed far enough for a judicial determination (unripe).

---

(3) Mootness and Standing

To some extent, both mootness and standing are concerned with timing. A plaintiff may have standing to seek an injunction, but if events progress to the point where the injunction *no longer serves a useful purpose*, the plaintiff no longer has standing. Another way of saying that a plaintiff no longer has standing is to say that the case has become moot.

 Example: Plaintiffs sought an injunction that would permit them to vote in an upcoming election. They had not fulfilled the state's statutory length-of-residence requirement, and they claimed the statute was unconstitutional. Plaintiffs had standing because they wished to vote and were prevented from doing so by the challenged statute. If the election took place, and/or plaintiffs lived in the state long enough to satisfy the statute, they would no longer have standing. Another way of saying that they no longer had standing is to say the case had become moot. [**Hall v. Beals**, *supra*, p. 26]

(4) Mootness as Standing in a Timeframe?

In the past, the Court linked the doctrines, referring to "mootness" as standing set in a timeframe. In such a view, unless all the elements of standing persist throughout the litigation, the case will be dismissed as moot. Now, however, the Court *explicitly rejects the linkage.* Standing functions at the outset of the litigation to ensure concrete stakes and adverse presentations. After the issues have been joined and resources devoted to current litigation, exceptions to the mootness rule may enable the court to retain the case even if the parties' interests would no longer support standing. [**Friends of the Earth v. Laidlaw Environmental Services, Inc.**, 528 U.S. 167 (2000)]

EXAM TIP   GILBERT

For your exam, remember that a court may retain a case despite the fact that the plaintiff could not show standing if the case were brought anew.

 Compare: Recent cases emphasize that the requirements of standing apply to "all stages of litigation." [**Hollingsworth v. Perry**, 570 U.S. 693 (2013)] Such an approach means that standing "must be met by persons seeking appellate review, just as it must be met by persons appearing in courts of first instance." [**Id.** at 2656] The notion that Article III standing requirements apply with undiminished rigor throughout the litigation stands in some tension with the Court's rejection of the notion that mootness operates as "standing in a time frame."

5. Political Question

The political question doctrine is less a single doctrine than a single label applied to a variety of questions that federal courts will not adjudicate. This refusal to adjudicate is what distinguishes political question cases from cases presenting ripeness, mootness, or standing problems. A case with a ripeness problem may eventually be decided; a case with a mootness problem could have been decided at an earlier time; and a case with a standing problem could be decided if presented by a litigant with a more personal stake in the matter. But a case presenting a political question simply *cannot be judicially decided,* no matter how ripe or live the dispute and no matter how great the plaintiff's personal stake. In some cases, a court's denial of standing will resemble a refusal to adjudicate political questions. For example, in cases involving a generalized grievance, there may be no plaintiff with the requisite personal injury and the denial of standing may, as a practical matter, foreclose review altogether.

a. Modern Relaxation of Political Question Doctrine

Since the Warren Court, the political question doctrine has permitted the federal courts to decide an increasing range of questions. The doctrine nevertheless remains an extremely important limitation on the federal judicial power.

b. Modern Formulation of Doctrine

The Court has set out six criteria for determining whether a political question exists:

(i) Is there a *"textually demonstrable constitutional commitment of the issue to a coordinate political department"*;

(ii) Is there a *"lack of judicially discernible and manageable standards for resolving"* the dispute;

(iii) Is the case impossible to decide *"without an initial policy determination of a kind clearly for nonjudicial determination"*;

(iv) Is the case impossible to decide without *"expressing lack of the respect due coordinate branches of government"*;

(v) Is there an *"unusual need for unquestioning adherence to a political decision already made"*; or

(vi) Is there potential for *"embarrassment from multifarious pronouncements by various departments on one question."*

[**Baker v. Carr**, *supra,* p. 13—equal protection challenge to malapportioned state legislature not a political question]

c. Underlying Considerations

Several related considerations are contained in the criteria of **Baker v. Carr**, *supra.*

(1) Separation of Powers

Probably the most important consideration is separation of powers. The political question doctrine compels the courts to recognize the limits of judicial competence and to leave certain issues to be authoritatively resolved by the executive and legislative branches.

(2) Amenability to Judicial Resolution

A second important consideration is a legal process concern about the amenability of the dispute to judicial resolution. For example, are there "judicially manageable standards" for resolving the dispute?

(3) Prudence

A third consideration is prudential. For example, is there an "unusual need" (*e.g.,* in a foreign relations matter) to defer to a decision that has already been made by another branch?

d. Case-by-Case Application

The Court in **Baker v. Carr**, *supra,* was careful to note that the determination of whether a political question exists is a "delicate exercise in constitutional interpretation" that must be made on a case-by-case basis.

(1) Illustration of Cases in Which a Political Question Has Been Found

e.g. **Example:** Plaintiff sued for damages for an alleged trespass. Defendants contended that they were representatives of the lawful government of Rhode Island, that plaintiff was engaged in insurrection, and that they had entered plaintiff's property to arrest him. Plaintiff contended that he, rather than the defendants, was acting on behalf of the lawful government of the state. The Court refused to hear evidence on the merits of the dispute over which faction to recognize as the lawful government of Rhode Island. [**Luther v. Borden**, 48 U.S. (7 How.) 1 (1849)]

e.g. **Example:** Plaintiff sought to enjoin execution of the post-Civil War Reconstruction Acts on the ground that they replaced the governments of the southern states and violated the Guaranty Clause of the Constitution. The Court held that the suit presented a nonjudicial political question. [**Georgia v. Stanton**, 73 U.S. (6 Wall.) 500 (1867)] *Note:* Other cases attempting to enforce the Guaranty Clause have all been held to present political questions. [*See, e.g.,* **Mountain Timber Co. v. Washington**, 243 U.S. 219 (1917); **Pacific States Telephone & Telegraph Co. v. Oregon**, 223 U.S. 118 (1911)]

e.g. **Example:** The length of time during which a proposed constitutional amendment may remain open for ratification, and the effect of a state's prior rejection and later ratification of an amendment, are political questions to be determined by Congress rather than the Court. [**Coleman v. Miller**, *supra,* p. 41]

e.g. **Example:** Several members of Congress challenged the President's unilateral termination of a treaty with Taiwan. The case was dismissed. A four-Justice plurality of the Court sustained the dismissal on the ground that the case presented a political question. [**Goldwater v. Carter**, 444 U.S. 996 (1979)— Rehnquist, J., concurring in the judgment]

e.g. **Example:** A former federal judge was impeached by the House of Representatives after he was criminally convicted of accepting a bribe. The Senate appointed a committee to take evidence and hear testimony. The committee then reported to the full Senate. The judge challenged this procedure, arguing that Article I, Section 3, Clause 6 of the Constitution, which gives the Senate sole power to "try all Impeachments," requires the full Senate to hear all evidence and testimony. The Court held that the manner by which the Senate "tries" a case of impeachment presents a nonjusticiable political question. [**Nixon v. United States**, 506 U.S. 224 (1993)]

e.g. **Example:** States have an obligation to draw the lines for voting districts in ways that respect minority voting rights as set forth in federal statutes and the Constitution, and the Court has agreed to review the line-drawing process. But the majority party at the state level may also draw the lines to achieve partisan political gain. Although the Court acknowledged that a severe partisan gerrymander would violate the Constitution, it proclaimed itself as yet incapable of defining judicially manageable standards with which to say when a partisan gerrymander goes too far. [**Vieth v. Jubelirer**, 541 U.S. 267 (2004)] Partisan gerrymanders thus present political questions, although the Court has since suggested that the emergence of manageable standards in a future case might call for a different conclusion. [**League of United Latin American Citizens v. Perry**, 548 U.S. 399 (2006)]

(2) Illustration of Cases in Which a Political Question Has Not Been Found

e.g. **Example:** Plaintiffs sought to require the reapportionment of the Tennessee state legislature on equal protection grounds. In a groundbreaking opinion, the Court held that this did not present a political question. [**Baker v. Carr**, *supra—overruling* **Colegrove v. Green**, 328 U.S. 549 (1946)]

e.g. **Example:** Congressman Adam Clayton Powell was elected to the United States House of Representatives, but the House refused to seat him because of financial and other improprieties. Defendants contended that Article I, Section 5 (providing that "Each House shall be the Judge of the . . . Qualifications of its own Members") was a textually demonstrable commitment to the legislative branch. However, the Court held that the commitment of Article I, Section 5 extended only to qualifications expressly set out in the Constitution, such as age, citizenship, and residence. Because the Court viewed those qualifications as exclusive, it interpreted Article I as barring the House from excluding Powell on other grounds and refused to treat the matter as a political question. [**Powell v. McCormack**, 395 U.S. 486 (1968)]

e.g. **Example:** An Indian tribe sought damages for occupation of land allegedly owned by the tribe. The Court held that the power given to Congress by Article I, Section 8, Clause 3 to regulate "Commerce . . . with the Indian Tribes" was not such a textually demonstrable commitment to a coordinate branch as to make the issue of land ownership a political question. [**County of Oneida v. Oneida Indian Nation**, 470 U.S. 226 (1985)]

e.g. **Example:** After the 1990 census, some states got more congressional districts and some got fewer, based on population changes since the previous census. Montana, which lost one of its two districts, challenged the federal statute under which the reapportionment of districts was made. The Court noted that the reapportionment decision was made by Congress, thus presenting separation of powers questions not presented in **Baker v. Carr**, *supra.* It nevertheless held the case justiciable and upheld the statute on the merits. [**United States Department of Commerce v. Montana**, 503 U.S. 442 (1992)]

e.g. **Example:** Congress adopted legislation authorizing US citizens born in Jerusalem to have Israel noted on their US passports as their place of birth. Previous State Department policy had been to list Jerusalem, but not Jordan or Israel, as the birthplace. When an individual sued to procure the congressionally authorized reference to Israel, the US government sought dismissal on the ground that the issue presented a political question. The lower courts agreed and dismissed, viewing the passport issue as one that would require the courts to decide the political status of Jerusalem. Rejecting that characterization, the Court framed the issue more narrowly as whether the individual had a right to record his birthplace on his passport. As framed, the question struck the Court as presenting a relatively familiar matter of statutory and constitutional interpretation, amenable to judicial resolution. [**Zivotofsky v. Clinton**, 566 U.S. 189 (2012)]

6. "Passive Virtues" Debate

For over 50 years, there has been an academic debate about the legitimate role of the justiciability doctrines in controlling the appellate jurisdiction of the Supreme Court, and of the jurisdiction of the federal courts in general.

a. Professor Bickel's Position

Professor Bickel argued that the Supreme Court should use the doctrines of ripeness, mootness, standing, and political question to practice the "passive virtues." [A. Bickel, *The Least Dangerous Branch* (1962)] Bickel agreed with Justice Brandeis's famous statement about the Court, "The most important thing we do is not doing." Bickel advocated that the Supreme Court frequently stay its hand, and he proposed that justiciability doctrines be employed by the Court *to avoid or postpone decision* in cases that were politically inexpedient or procedurally awkward.

Bickel had in mind the Court's decision to delay its resolution of **Brown v. Board of Education** until 1954, after having twice set the case down for reargument. Commenting on the arrival of Earl Warren as the new Chief Justice and the Court's eventual issuance of a unanimous opinion in **Brown**, Justice Felix Frankfurter later characterized the events as the only solid evidence of God he had seen in his lifetime.

b. Professor Wechsler's Position

Professor Wechsler has advocated that the Supreme Court formulate and apply *"neutral principles"* in deciding cases. [H. Wechsler, *Principles, Politics and Fundamental Law* (1961)] For Wechsler, "neutral principles" are important both substantively and jurisdictionally. That is, the Court should employ "neutral principles" both in deciding cases on the merits and in deciding which cases to decide. Bickel agreed emphatically with Wechsler that neutral principles should govern the decision of cases on the merits. But Bickel argued that if the appellate jurisdiction of the Court could be controlled by justiciability doctrines to avoid decisions in awkward cases, the Court could more effectively formulate and apply neutral principles in those cases it decided on the merits.

c. Professor Gunther's Position

Professor Gunther agreed strongly with Wechsler. [Gunther, *The Subtle Vices of the "Passive Virtues"—A Comment on Principle and Expediency in Judicial Review*, 64 Colum. L. Rev. 1 (1964)] Gunther relied on Chief Justice Marshall's famous statement in **Cohens v. Virginia**, 19 U.S. (6 Wheat.) 264 (1821), that the Court has "no more right to decline the exercise of jurisdiction which is given than to usurp that which is not given." Commenting on Bickel's view that the principle is more important in deciding cases on the merits than in deciding which cases to decide, Gunther called Bickel's position "100% insistence on principle, 20% of the time."

d. Limited Role of the "Passive Virtues"

It is easy to lose sight of the fact that the debate among Bickel, Weschsler, and Gunther is of critical importance only when the appellate jurisdiction of the court is mandatory. Even when Bickel was writing, the great majority of the Supreme Court's jurisdiction was controlled by the discretionary writ of certiorari. The Court can avoid decision in such cases simply by denying certiorari. (The Court does not publish explanations for its decisions denying certiorari and no one seems to contend that its grants and denials would pass a neutral principles test.) For cases within its mandatory appellate jurisdiction, the use of the justiciability doctrines to avoid decision took on more importance. But the Court treated even this jurisdiction as, in substantial part, de facto discretionary. Thus, employment of the justiciability doctrines was often not necessary if the aim was simply to avoid review.

(1) Note

Since 1988, the Court's appellate jurisdiction has been, for practical purposes, entirely discretionary under the writ of certiorari, thus further diminishing the importance of the "passive virtues" debate.

(2) Other Uses of the "Passive Virtues"

The Bickelian view nevertheless still has importance, because justiciability doctrines may be employed in various ways to permit the Court to discuss issues without deciding them; to duck a case for which it has already granted certiorari [*see, e.g.*, **DeFunis v. Odegaard**, *supra*, p. 29]; to decide some but not all questions in a particular case; and in various ways to engage in "colloquies" with the other branches through the use of the Court's opinions.

e. Awkwardness of Practicing the "Passive Virtues" When Lower Court Jurisdiction Is Affected

Since the doctrines of ripeness, mootness, standing, and political question apply to all Article III courts, they apply equally to the Supreme Court and the lower federal courts. To the extent that a justiciability doctrine has been employed for the Bickelian purpose of permitting the Supreme Court to avoid appellate review of a politically awkward case, there is danger of distorting the jurisdictional structure of the lower federal courts. For example, the Supreme Court may hold a case moot because it does not want to deal with the politically sensitive issue presented in the case, rather than because the case is genuinely moot. [*See, e.g.*, **DeFunis v. Odegaard**, *supra*] If such a mootness determination is taken at face value, the lower federal courts will hold some cases moot that they should decide on the merits.

e.g. **Example:** One lower court has relied on **Elk Grove Unified School District v. Newdow**, *supra*, p. 31, in denying standing to noncustodial parents to pursue claims other than the pledge of allegiance challenge that the **Elk Grove** Court apparently sought to avoid. [**Crowley v. McKinney**, 400 F.3d 965 (7th Cir. 2005)]

Chapter Three

Congressional Power over Federal Court Jurisdiction

Key Exam Issues

Congress has a great deal of power to regulate the jurisdiction of the federal courts. The contours of that power are, however, somewhat ill-defined. To understand the nature and extent of the power, you need an understanding of the history of congressional regulation of federal court jurisdiction and a detailed knowledge of several key cases.

In this area, you should *not* try to reduce all of the cases to clear rules. Many doctrines and principles are ambiguous and matters of continuing controversy. To answer examination questions, keep in mind the *history and structure* of the federal court system, and apply the *theories of the key cases* to the facts of your question.

A. Article III and Congressional Power—Historical Overview

1. Article III and the "Madisonian Compromise"

The delegates to the Constitutional Convention agreed that there should be a federal Supreme Court. But they were unable to agree on whether there should be inferior federal courts, and, if so, what their role should be. The delegates settled on what has come to be known as the "Madisonian Compromise." Essentially, the compromise consisted of giving Congress power to *create or not to create inferior federal courts*, as well as power to *regulate the jurisdiction of all the federal courts*, including the *appellate jurisdiction* of the Supreme Court.

a. Language of Article III

(1) Supreme Court

Article III, Section 1 of the Constitution provides: "The judicial Power of the United States, shall be vested in one Supreme Court . . . ." Article III, Section 2, Clause 1 describes the various categories of cases to which the "judicial power shall extend," including federal question, diversity, admiralty, and a number of other cases. It provides that the Court shall have *original jurisdiction* in cases affecting ambassadors and other public ministers and consuls and in cases in which a state is a party. In all other types of cases listed in Article III, Section 2, the Supreme Court shall have *appellate jurisdiction*, "both as to Law and Fact, with such Exceptions, and under such Regulations as the Congress shall make."

(2) Inferior Federal Courts

Article III, Section 1 provides: "The judicial Power of the United States, shall be vested . . . in such inferior courts as the Congress may from time to time ordain and establish." Article III, Section 2, Clause 1 then describes the various kinds of cases these inferior courts might be empowered to hear.

b. Conventional Reading of Article III

(1) Supreme Court

The conventional reading of Article III is that it created the Supreme Court of its own force. (That is, no further statutory authorization was necessary.) Furthermore,

Article III authorized the exercise of the Court's original jurisdiction of its own force. But it subjected the Supreme Court's *appellate jurisdiction* to the control of Congress by conferring the jurisdiction "with such Exceptions, and under such Regulations as the Congress shall make."

(2) Inferior Federal Courts

The conventional reading of Article III is that it authorized Congress to create inferior federal courts, but that it did not require Congress to do so. Congress thus had the option of creating no inferior federal courts and relying on the existing state courts to hear cases within the constitutionally authorized jurisdiction. By implication, Congress also had the option of creating inferior federal courts and conferring some, but not all, of the constitutionally authorized jurisdiction.

EXAM TIP   GILBERT

For your exam, it is helpful to remember that *Article III created the Supreme Court* by its own force, but that *further congressional statutory creation* was required for *inferior* federal courts.

---

c. Justice Story's Broad Reading of Article III

Justice Joseph Story appears to have had more than one interpretation of Article III. In his broadest interpretation, he read Article III as mandating the vesting in the federal courts of the entire judicial power described in Article III. In **Martin v. Hunter's Lessee**, 14 U.S. (1 Wheat.) 304 (1816), Story pointed out that the language of Article III provided that "the judicial Power of the United States *shall* be vested" (emphasis added) in the Supreme Court and in such inferior courts as Congress sees fit to establish. For Story, this meant that vesting of the jurisdiction was mandatory, and it extended to *all* the cases described in Article III, Section 2, Clause 1: "[I]t is a duty to vest the whole judicial power."

(1) Limit of Story's Position

Story said only that the judicial power had to be vested in *some* federal court. It has sometimes been suggested that Story argued for the vesting of the full extent of the constitutionally authorized jurisdiction in the inferior federal courts. But the language of Story's opinion is not so broad; even in his broadest interpretation, it was sufficient for the jurisdiction to be exercised as Supreme Court appellate review of state court decisions.

(2) Rejection of Story's Position

Congress has never conferred, and the federal courts have never exercised, the full extent of the jurisdiction authorized by Article III. As a matter of constitutional history, Story's position is debatable. As a matter of practice, Story's position has been uniformly and continuously rejected. Today it is widely assumed that Congress has significant and legitimate power to grant or withhold from the federal courts the jurisdiction described in Article III.

d. Professor Amar's Reading

Professor Amar has argued for a narrow version of Justice Story's position. According to Amar, Article III requires that the full extent of the judicial power be vested somewhere in the federal courts for three categories of cases: federal question cases, cases affecting ambassadors, and admiralty cases. Federal jurisdiction in these three categories is described in Article III as extending to "all" such cases. Article III does not require that the full extent of the constitutionally authorized jurisdiction be vested in other categories of cases (*e.g.,* diversity), since the jurisdiction for these cases is not described in Article III as extending to "all" such cases. [Amar, *A Neo-Federalist View of Article III: Separating the Two Tiers of Federal Jurisdiction,* 65 B.U. L. Rev. 205 (1985)] Professor Meltzer has concluded that the historical record does not clearly favor Professor Amar's reading. [Meltzer, *The History and Structure of Article III,* 138 U. Pa. L. Rev. 1569 (1990)]

Judge Fletcher has argued that, rather than mandating jurisdiction, the selective use of "all" in Article III may describe the scope of Congress's power to confer exclusive jurisdiction. On this view, Congress could extend the jurisdiction of the federal courts to, say, "all" ambassador and admiralty matters but not to "all" diversity matters. [Fletcher, *Congressional Power over the Jurisdiction of the Federal Courts: The Meaning of the Word "All" in Article III,* 59 Duke L.J. 929 (2010)]

2. Judiciary Act of 1789

During its first session, Congress passed the Judiciary Act of 1789, creating a system of federal courts. (*See supra,* pp. 2–5.)

a. Supreme Court

The Judiciary Act created positions for Supreme Court Justices and authorized the Supreme Court to exercise the original jurisdiction described in Article III. As stated above (*see supra,* p. 56), the consensus view is that Article III created the Court and established its original jurisdiction of its own force. Thus, this part of the Act was to some extent superfluous. The Act also conferred appellate jurisdiction on the Supreme Court over decisions of inferior federal courts and over certain decisions of the state supreme courts.

b. Inferior Federal Courts

The Judiciary Act created two levels of inferior federal courts, both district and circuit courts. The Act conferred diversity and admiralty jurisdiction on these courts and other jurisdiction not necessary to detail here. The Act did ***not*** confer general original federal question jurisdiction on these courts. (*See supra,* pp. 2–3.)

c. Significance of the Act

The Judiciary Act shows that at the earliest possible opportunity Congress created a federal court ***system.*** It was not content to have merely a federal Supreme Court supervising the state courts. The idea of having such a federal judicial system has prevailed ever since. The Act also shows that Congress did not agree with Justice Story's later reading of Article III, for it failed to confer the full extent of the jurisdiction authorized by Article III. Although the scope of the statutorily authorized jurisdiction has increased since the Act, it remains true today that the federal courts do not exercise the full jurisdiction authorized by Article III.

B. Congressional Power to Restrict Jurisdiction of the Federal Courts

1. In General

Congress has a certain amount of unquestioned power to restrict the jurisdiction of the federal courts. However, the boundary between the legitimate power to restrict jurisdiction and a questionable power to accomplish other aims, under the guise of jurisdictional restrictions, is not clearly delineated. The power to restrict jurisdiction, and the outer boundary of that power, will be considered in turn.

2. Clear Congressional Power to Restrict Jurisdiction

An essential premise of the Madisonian Compromise is that Congress has the power to grant, to withhold, and to regulate the original and appellate jurisdiction of the lower federal courts, and to do the same with the appellate jurisdiction of the Supreme Court. In most cases, the exercise of this power is beyond serious challenge. The examples that immediately follow pose no problems because Congress is merely regulating the flow of business in the court system. Congress is not abridging any substantive right and it has no invidious purpose.

a. Trial Court Diversity Jurisdiction

Congress conferred diversity jurisdiction on the federal trial courts by the Judiciary Act, but it did not confer the full constitutionally authorized diversity jurisdiction. The refusal to confer the full jurisdiction has persisted to this day. [28 U.S.C. § 1332—present statute]

e.g. **Example:** Plaintiff, a New York citizen, was an assignee of a bond and mortgage. He had received the assignment from a Michigan citizen. Plaintiff sued another Michigan citizen on the bond and mortgage. The Supreme Court held that there was no diversity jurisdiction under Section 11 of the Judiciary Act of 1789 because the statute looked to the citizenship of the assignor rather than the assignee. [**Sheldon v. Sill**, 49 U.S. (8 How.) 440 (1850)] *Note:* The "assignee clause" restriction was eliminated from the diversity statute in 1948, making it clear that the lack of jurisdiction in *Sheldon v. Sill* was due to the statutory restriction rather than any limitation in Article III.

e.g. **Example:** Plaintiff is a citizen of state A. She sues two defendants, one a citizen of state A and the other a citizen of state B. No statutory diversity exists because the statute requires "complete diversity"—*i.e.*, that no defendant be a citizen of the same state as any plaintiff. [**Strawbridge v. Curtiss**, 7 U.S. (3 Cranch) 267 (1806)] Complete diversity is not a requirement of Article III, but is a requirement set by Congress. [**State Farm Fire & Casualty Co. v. Tashire**, 386 U.S. 523 (1967)—applying the federal interpleader statute, which does not require complete diversity]

For your exam, it is important to remember that although only *minimal* diversity (*one* plaintiff must be of diverse citizenship from *one* defendant) is *constitutionally* required, Congress has not conferred full jurisdiction on the federal courts. Rather, *complete* diversity (*all* plaintiffs must be of diverse citizenship from *all* defendants) is *statutorily* required.

b. Trial Court Federal Question Jurisdiction

Congress did not confer general original federal question jurisdiction on the federal trial courts by the Judiciary Act. Rather, general original federal question jurisdiction was not durably conferred until 1875, and that statute is interpreted under the "well-pleaded complaint" rule—*i.e.,* for there to be federal question jurisdiction, the federal question must appear in a *well-pleaded complaint*, not in the defendant's answer or in the complaint as an anticipation of a defense. [28 U.S.C. § 1331—present statute]

Example: Plaintiffs sued to enforce a contract for free lifetime railroad passes, asserting in their complaint that the defendant railroad would defend on the ground that federal law forbade the issuance of the passes. The Court refused to hear the case, holding that plaintiffs could not confer federal question jurisdiction by *anticipating* a federal defense that might be made in the answer. [**Louisville & Nashville Railroad v. Mottley**, 211 U.S. 149 (1908)]

When answering an exam question, be sure to remember that in almost every case the plaintiff's *complaint is the only pleading that is considered* when determining whether federal question jurisdiction is present. If the federal question arises in the plaintiff's well-pleaded complaint, there is typically federal question jurisdiction. On the other hand, if the plaintiff pleads a claim under state law so that no federal question appears in the complaint, there generally is no federal question jurisdiction; a defendant may not remove the action to federal court alleging a federal defense. Thus, a plaintiff may refrain from asserting federal claims to keep the case in state court.

c. Supreme Court Appellate Jurisdiction

The Judiciary Act of 1789 did not confer appellate jurisdiction on the Supreme Court to hear all cases coming up from the state courts involving federal questions. Rather, the Act conferred jurisdiction only when a claim of right under federal law had been *denied* by the state court. (The present statute confers jurisdiction more broadly. [28 U.S.C. § 1257—*see infra*, pp. 85 *et seq.*])

3. Questionable Uses of Congressional Power to Restrict Jurisdiction

On some occasions, Congress has used its power to regulate the federal courts' jurisdiction in questionable ways. When cases raising such questions have come before the Supreme Court, the power of Congress has almost always been *sustained.* But the contours of Congress's power over the federal courts' jurisdiction are not altogether clear. The best way to understand the issues involved is to look closely at several important cases.

a. Supreme Court Appellate Jurisdiction

(1) *Ex Parte McCardle*

McCardle, a Southern newspaper editor held in custody after the Civil War by federal military authorities on charges arising out of publication of articles hostile to Reconstruction, sought release on habeas corpus from the federal trial court in Mississippi. McCardle took a direct appeal to the Supreme Court under a new statute granting the right to such an appeal. (The old statute, which had not been repealed, provided for a complicated and time-consuming appeal process in habeas cases.) A central issue in McCardle's appeal to the Supreme Court was the constitutionality of the Reconstruction Acts. Since a majority of the Supreme Court was hostile to Reconstruction, it seemed likely that the Court would strike down some or all of the Acts. After McCardle's case had been argued to the Court but before it was decided, Congress repealed the new appeal statute to prevent the Court from invalidating the Reconstruction Acts. The Court's unanimous opinion simply noted that Congress's power to "make exceptions to the appellate jurisdiction of this court is given by express words." It did not comment on the fact that the case was already before the Court when the jurisdiction was repealed, stating, "We are not at liberty to inquire into the motives of the legislature." Finally, the Court noted that the old, more cumbersome statute giving the detainee a right to petition the Supreme Court in habeas cases was still intact. [***Ex parte* McCardle**, 74 U.S. (7 Wall.) 506 (1869)]

(a) Historical Significance of *McArdle*

The opinion in *McCardle* seems relatively innocuous. According to one possible reading, Congress merely took away one route of appeal in habeas cases while leaving another route intact. But in fact, the case was much more than that. It was an occasion on which Congress deliberately used its power over the Court's appellate jurisdiction to achieve a political result in a particular case.

(b) Modern Significance of *McCardle*

Justices Douglas and Black in 1962 voiced the opinion that "[t]here is serious question whether the *McCardle* case could command a majority view today." [**Glidden v. Zdanok**, *supra*, p. 20—Douglas, J., dissenting] The Court, however, continues to cite *McCardle* as good law. If *McCardle* simply stands for the proposition that Congress has power to regulate the Court's appellate jurisdiction, the case is clearly good law. But whether *McCardle* also means that Congress can deprive the Court of jurisdiction over a case by repealing the jurisdictional statute after the case has been argued is open to some doubt. Finally, and perhaps most importantly, *McCardle* stands for the political proposition that an aroused Congress can use its power over jurisdiction to intimidate and control a politically weak Court. In this respect, *McCardle* states an important structural truth about the balance of power among the three branches of the federal government.

(2) *United States v. Klein*

During the Civil War and several times thereafter, the President offered pardons and restoration of property to those who had participated in the rebellion. By statute, Congress granted jurisdiction to the Court of Claims (and to the Supreme Court on appeal) to restore to pardoned persons the property seized from them by the government. By a later statute, Congress purported to take away jurisdiction from the Supreme Court whenever a litigant relied upon a pardon in a suit for restoration of property. The Court held that Congress could not take away jurisdiction in this fashion. The statute's "great and controlling purpose" was to deprive Presidential pardons of their proper effect, and it tried to prescribe a particular evidentiary effect as resulting from the pardon. The Court heard the case to protect the "constitutional power of the Executive" in granting pardons and characterized the purported jurisdictional withdrawal as merely "a means to an end." [**United States v. Klein**, 80 U.S. (13 Wall.) 128 (1872)]

(a) Narrow Reading of *Klein* Principle

The Court has adopted a narrow view of the *Klein* principle. In **Bank Markazi v. Peterson**, 136 S.Ct. 1310 (2016), the Court considered a statute that broadened the range of Iranian government assets that were subject to levy to satisfy the judgment in a specific case, a case that Congress identified by docket number. The majority upheld the statute, concluding that Congress had power to change the law by broadening asset availability and to make that rule applicable to a pending case that had yet to become final. The dissent argued, unsuccessfully, that Congress had effectively decreed the outcome of a pending piece of litigation in violation judicial branch independence. See also **Robertson v. Seattle Audobon Society**, 503 U.S. 429 (1992) (rejecting *Klein*-based challenge to law that changed the rules governing preservation of forest land and made it applicable to pending cases, thereby determining the result of the litigation).

1) Comment

In evaluating congressional power to change the law and apply it to a pending case, the Court has refused to insist that Congress adopt laws of general applicability. Both the Iranian asset law and the forest preservation law were adopted with specific cases in mind. Rather, the Court will focus on whether Congress had constitutional power to adopt the law in question. In Klein, the Court questioned congressional power, given its retrospective impact on property rights and its imposition on the president's pardon power.

(3) Comparison of *Klein* and *McCardle*

Klein suggests a potentially useful limitation on *McCardle*. When an impermissible substantive end is sought to be achieved by prescribing a particular evidentiary or substantive rule under the guise of a jurisdictional regulation, the attempt to withdraw jurisdiction *may be disregarded* as merely a "means to an end." However, this formulation is not susceptible of precise or definitive application.

(4) *Felker v. Turpin*

In **Felker v. Turpin**, 518 U.S. 651 (1996), the Supreme Court sustained a restriction on its appellate jurisdiction in habeas corpus cases. The Antiterrorism and Effective Death Penalty Act of 1996 provides that second and later habeas petitions to federal courts are allowed only under very limited circumstances, and that such petitions must be authorized by a federal court of appeals. The Act provides that a decision of the court of appeals in this "gatekeeping" capacity is not reviewable by the Supreme Court. The Court held that this restriction on its appellate jurisdiction was permissible under Article III because a prisoner has the right to file an original habeas petition directly in the Supreme Court under a separate statute. [28 U.S.C. § 2241] Justice Souter, concurring, contended that even though such a petition is original in the sense that it is filed directly in the Supreme Court, it is "nonetheless for constitutional purposes an exercise of this Court's appellate (rather than original) jurisdiction." Additional mechanisms for Supreme Court review of a court of appeals' decision include interlocutory review by certified question [28 U.S.C. § 1254(2)], and an order under the All Writs Act [28 U.S.C. § 1651].

(5) Possible Limit Based on Court's Supremacy

Academic commentators argue that the Court's supremacy may require that the Court retain oversight and control of inferior federal courts. At the time Article III was ratified, the Supreme Court enjoyed both as-of-right appellate jurisdiction and discretionary power to review the work of lower courts through such common law or supervisory writs as prohibition and mandamus. Congress's power to regulate the Court's appellate jurisdiction might apply only to the as-of-right jurisdiction conferred in Article III; on such a view, Congress may have an obligation to respect and preserve the Court's supervisory powers as an entailment of the Court's supremacy. The Court might draw on its supremacy in resisting far-reaching restrictions on its power to engage in discretionary review. [Pfander, *Jurisdiction-Stripping and the Supreme Court's Power to Supervise Inferior Tribunals*, 78 Tex. L. Rev. 1433 (2000)]

b. Federal Court Jurisdiction Generally

(1) Norris-LaGuardia Act

During the first decades of the 20th century, the Supreme Court several times struck down state legislation forbidding or limiting remedies to enforce a "yellow dog" contract (contract by which an employee agrees not to join a labor union). In 1932, Congress passed the Norris-LaGuardia Act [29 U.S.C. §§ 101–115], which provided in part that no federal court has jurisdiction to grant legal or equitable relief to enforce a "yellow dog" contract. [29 U.S.C. §§ 101, 103] The Act was purposely drafted in *jurisdictional terms* because the Court had struck down state legislation that had forbidden such contracts or had limited remedies to enforce them. [*See* **Truax v. Corrigan**, 257 U.S. 312 (1921)—striking down limitation of remedies; *and see* **Coppage v. Kansas**, 236 U.S. 1 (1915); **Adair v. United States**, 208 U.S. 161 (1908)—striking down legislation forbidding such contracts]

(a) Supreme Court Reaction

The Supreme Court has never addressed the "yellow dog" contract provisions of the Act. However, in 1938, the Court *sustained* another part of the Act [29 U.S.C. § 107], which imposed strict prerequisites for the granting of injunctions in other kinds of labor disputes. [**Lauf v. E.G. Shinner Co.**, 303 U.S. 323 (1938)] This section of the Act was also drafted as a limitation on the federal courts' jurisdiction, but the prerequisites imposed by the section were variations of the traditional requirements for the exercise of equity jurisdiction (*e.g.,* irreparable injury and no adequate remedy at law). In sustaining this section of the Act, the Court stated, "There can be no question of the power of Congress *thus* to define and limit the jurisdiction of the inferior courts of the United States." [**Lauf v. E.G. Shinner Co.**, *supra* (emphasis added)]

(b) Significance of Norris-LaGuardia Act and *Lauf v. E.G. Shinner Co.*

The theory behind the "yellow dog" provision of the Norris-LaGuardia Act was that Congress could prevent the federal courts from enforcing such contracts by withdrawing jurisdiction to grant any relief for their violation. The Court's opinion in *Lauf* can be read broadly to endorse the use of the jurisdictional limitation device to accomplish indirectly what Congress cannot accomplish directly.

1) Caveat

There are, however, two factors that argue for a narrow reading of *Lauf*: First, the Court actually upheld only that part of the Norris-LaGuardia Act that imposed traditional equitable limitations on the injunctive power, and the Court's language referred to the power of Congress "thus" to limit jurisdiction; it is not clear that the Court's statement was intended to refer to the "yellow dog" provisions of the Act which were not before the Court. Second, by 1938 (when the *Lauf* case was decided), the Supreme Court's view of the Constitution had substantially changed. By then, a majority of the Court probably would have sustained a statute openly outlawing "yellow dog" contracts. Thus, even if the Court's language can be read to refer to the "yellow dog" provisions, the Court probably did not see the Norris-LaGuardia Act as an attempt to achieve an unconstitutional purpose by way of a purported jurisdictional limitation.

(2) Portal to Portal Question

The Fair Labor Standards Act of 1938 provided that overtime rates had to be paid for work in excess of a 40-hour work week. In several decisions in the mid-1940s, the Supreme Court had defined the "work week" of miners to include time spent traveling underground to and from the mine face, as well as other time spent in other preliminary and incidental activities. These decisions created enormous (and unexpected) retroactive liabilities for many employers. To permit employers to avoid these liabilities, Congress passed the Portal to Portal Act of 1943, which defined the "work week" as *not* including these preliminary and incidental activities. The Act then prescribed retroactively that no federal court had jurisdiction to hear any suit for overtime pay arising out of a broader definition of "work week." The Second Circuit upheld the Portal to Portal Act but did not agree that Congress had unlimited power to accomplish forbidden ulterior purposes by the regulation of federal jurisdiction. According to the court, the power to regulate jurisdiction was "subject to compliance with at least the requirements of the Fifth Amendment." [**Battaglia v. General Motors Corp.**, 169 F.2d 254 (2d Cir. 1948)] Only after the court was satisfied that Congress had the substantive power, consistent with the Fifth Amendment, retroactively to eliminate the liability for accrued overtime pay did the court sustain the "jurisdictional" limitation.

(3) Comparison of Norris-LaGuardia Act and *Battaglia*

If the Second Circuit's approach in *Battaglia* were applied to the "yellow dog" provision in the Norris-LaGuardia Act, the use of the jurisdictional limitation device might not have saved the provision from constitutional scrutiny of the substantive question. That is, the *Battaglia* court sustained the jurisdictional restriction *only after it was satisfied* that the underlying consequence of the Portal to Portal Act was constitutional. If the Court had applied this approach to the Norris-LaGuardia Act, it would have examined the constitutionality of a limitation on the power to enforce "yellow dog" contracts, and if such a limitation was unconstitutional, the Court would have invalidated the jurisdictional limitation.

(4) Modern Example: Indian Trust Land

A long-running battle over an effort to take land in Michigan into trust for a native tribe there, perhaps for use as a casino, illustrates the importance of evaluating the constitutionality of congressional changes in the law that accompany jurisdictional restrictions. In **Patchak v. Zinke**, 138 S.Ct. 897 (2018), the Court upheld provisions that seemingly directed an outcome in an identified federal court litigation. After the plaintiff sued the federal government to block federal acquisition of the land, Congress enacted the Gun Lake Trust Land Reaffirmation Act, ratifying the trust designation of the land and withdrawing federal jurisdiction in cases relating to the land, specifically mentioning "an action pending in a Federal court as of the date of enactment of this Act." Over a dissent that argued this was directing the outcome of a specific case, the Court upheld the law and the dismissal of the action. Apparently central to the majority's fractured decision was the shared assumption that Congress had power, prospectively, to direct the redesignation of the land in question.

> **Note:** the plaintiff, a resident living near the land in question, did not claim title to the property in question (as did the claimant in *Klein*) but only sought to prevent its use for the designated tribal purpose.

c. Modern Proposals to Limit Federal Court Jurisdiction

Unpopular Supreme Court decisions have prompted numerous proposals to curtail Supreme Court appellate jurisdiction or federal court jurisdiction generally. For example, in the 1950s, Senator Jenner proposed a bill that would have eliminated Supreme Court appellate jurisdiction over cases involving employees' security programs, state laws regulating subversive activities, and state bar admissions; and in the 1970s, several proposals were made to eliminate Supreme Court appellate jurisdiction over abortion, school busing, and school prayer cases. Similarly, in the 1960s, proposals were made to prohibit *any* federal court from reviewing state court criminal convictions in which confessions by the accused were admitted into evidence, and from hearing reapportionment cases. In the 1970s, numerous proposals were also made to prohibit any federal court from hearing busing cases. Legislation proposed in 2004 and 2006, some of which was adopted by the House but not the Senate, would have withdrawn federal jurisdiction over constitutional challenges to limits on recognition of gay marriage, to prayer by public figures, and to the Pledge of Allegiance.

d. Constitutionality of Jurisdiction-Curtailing Proposals—Large Areas of Uncertainty

Very few cases involving questionable uses of the congressional power to restrict federal court jurisdiction have reached the Supreme Court. **United States v. Klein**, *supra*, p. 61, is the only case in which the Court has held that Congress was without power to restrict jurisdiction because the power was used merely as a "means to an end." The cases described above (p. 61) are suggestive, but the cases are so few (and the opinions so cryptic) that they are incapable of providing definite answers to many questions involving jurisdiction restrictions.

(1) Modern Academic Arguments

A number of suggestions has been advanced in modern academic literature:

(a) "The Essential Role of the Supreme Court in the Constitutional Plan"

Professor Hart suggested that Congress could not make exceptions to the Court's appellate jurisdiction that would destroy "the essential role of the Supreme Court in the constitutional plan." [66 Harv. L. Rev. 1362 (1953), excerpted and updated in *Hart & Wechsler's The Federal Courts and the Federal System* 295–97 (6th ed. 2009)—commonly referred to as "The Dialogue"] According to Professor Hart, the restriction on habeas corpus appeals to the Supreme Court in *Ex parte* **McCardle** was consistent with the Court's "essential role" because Congress left intact an alternate route of appeal to the Court in habeas cases. As Hart recognized, however, his test is "pretty indeterminate."

(b) "Discrete and Disfavored Constitutional Claims"

Professor Sager argued that Congress must provide federal jurisdiction, either original or appellate, over all federal *constitutional* claims. He has further suggested that Congress cannot use its power to restrict the jurisdiction of federal courts in general to "shav[e] off discrete and disfavored constitutional claims with deep prejudice to judicially protected rights." [95 Harv. L. Rev. 17 (1981)]

(c) Modern Conditions Make Lower Federal Courts Constitutionally Required

Professor Theodore Eisenberg has argued that the growth of federal law and federal court caseloads means that inferior federal courts are no longer the "luxury" they were for our "young nation." According to Eisenberg, because of the greatly increased importance of federal law, inferior federal courts are now a constitutional necessity. Thus, Eisenberg claims, the original "Madisonian Compromise" (*see supra*, p. 56) has been overtaken by events, and Congress now has the constitutional obligation to leave intact *some* inferior federal courts. As a corollary, Eisenberg contends that Congress cannot "restrict jurisdiction over busing, reapportionment, or any other narrowly defined class of cases." [83 Yale L.J. 498 (1974)]

(d) The Court's "Supremacy" and the Corollary Inferiority of Other Courts Entails a Power of Ongoing Supervision

Professor James Pfander has argued that Article I and Article III require that all courts and tribunals given power to hear federal cases must remain inferior to the Supreme Court. The correlative requirements of supremacy and inferiority impose limits on the power of Congress to place the work of lower courts beyond the Supreme Court's oversight and control. On this view, Congress has power to regulate both the original and appellate jurisdiction of the federal courts so long as it preserves the Supreme Court's discretionary power to ensure that lower court decisions comply with federal law and respect established limits on their power. [Pfander, One Supreme Court: Supremacy, Inferiority, and the Judicial Power of the United States (2009)]

SOME MODERN ARGUMENTS INCLUDE:

- ☑ The exceptions to jurisdiction cannot destroy *"the essential role of the Supreme Court in the constitutional plan."*

- ☑ There must be federal jurisdiction, either original or appellate, *over all federal constitutional claims.*

- ☑ Due to the expansion of federal law and federal rights, *some inferior federal courts are now a constitutional necessity.*

- ☑ Although Congress can regulate the jurisdiction of the Supreme and inferior federal courts, it **cannot place lower courts beyond the supervisory oversight and control of the nation's one Supreme Court.**

e. Consequences of Restricting Federal Court Jurisdiction—The Relevance of State Courts

State courts have an obligation equal to that of the federal courts to follow and enforce federal law. Moreover, since Congress has not been given a general power to restrict state court jurisdiction, Congress may not have the power to prevent adjudication by the state courts of suits involving federal rights. That is, state courts of general jurisdiction have the power, and probably even the duty, to hear federal claims without separate and explicit congressional authorization to do so, at least when no federal court has the power to hear those claims. The power of Congress to curtail or eliminate federal court jurisdiction must be seen in light of this state court power.

(1) Restriction of Supreme Court Appellate Jurisdiction

The aim of many modern proposals that seek to eliminate Supreme Court appellate jurisdiction in certain types of cases is to make the *state courts* and lower federal courts the final arbiters of *federal rights* in these cases. Even though these courts would be required to follow federal law, the elimination of Supreme Court appellate jurisdiction would have several important consequences:

(a) Flouting of Federal Law

A state court could disregard federal law once the Supreme Court lost its power to review state court decisions on appeal. Such a flouting of federal law would be constitutionally forbidden, but as a practical matter there would be little to stop a state court from engaging in such behavior.

(b) Little Further Development of Federal Law

Assuming, however, that state courts attempt conscientiously to follow applicable federal law, federal law might develop at a much slower pace, for there would be no court with a final authoritative voice on federal matters.

(c) Little Coordination of Federal Law

To the extent that federal law would develop in the state courts, there would be little ability to coordinate that development since there would no longer be any central authoritative tribunal.

IF THE SUPREME COURT WERE DEPRIVED OF APPELLATE JURISDICTION IN "FEDERAL RIGHTS" CASES, THE FOLLOWING CONSEQUENCES COULD ENSURE:

☑ Nothing would prevent a state court from *flouting federal law*;

☑ Federal law would be *developed at a slower pace*; and

☑ The development of federal law would *not be coordinated* by any one entity.

(2) Restriction of Federal Court Jurisdiction in General

If *no* federal court—Supreme Court or inferior federal court—is authorized to hear certain types of federal claims, the problems described above will be accentuated. If inferior federal courts are unable to hear federal claims, there will be no body of federal law being decided parallel to that being decided in the state courts. In that event, there would be several additional important consequences:

(a) No Federal Court Example

State courts would not be able to look to *any* federal court for assistance in discovering the governing federal standard or establishing the federal precedent.

(b) No Collateral Control by Federal Courts

Under present law, federal courts have collateral power to review state criminal convictions on habeas corpus and a limited collateral power to enjoin state criminal and civil proceedings. (*See infra*, pp. 253 *et seq.*, 233 *et seq.*) This collateral control over the state courts would be eliminated to the extent that federal courts had no jurisdiction to hear certain types of cases.

(3) Restriction of Inferior Federal Court Jurisdiction

If inferior federal courts were deprived of jurisdiction over federal claims, but the Supreme Court appellate jurisdiction remained, the Supreme Court would have statutory power to review state court decisions of these claims. Thus, in theory, federal court jurisdiction would remain. In practice, however, Supreme Court review would be largely unavailable because of the Court's already heavy caseload.

4. Functions of Congressional Power over Federal Court Jurisdiction

Congressional power to regulate federal court jurisdiction operates at two levels:

a. Efficient and Appropriate Allocation of Judicial Business

(1) Efficient Allocation

Most congressional regulation of federal court jurisdiction is designed simply to regulate the flow of judicial business. Factors such as caseloads, administrative convenience, and expertise are important and noncontroversial considerations. The jurisdictional regulations described in pp. 59–60, *supra*, are primarily influenced by such factors.

(2) Appropriate Allocation

Factors having to do with sympathies of a court system can also be legitimate considerations. For example, Congress has given jurisdiction over federal question cases to the federal courts in substantial part because of the perception that the federal courts should be the "*primary* and powerful reliances for vindicating every right given by the Constitution, the laws, and treaties of the United States." [**Steffel v. Thompson**, 415 U.S. 452 (1974) (emphasis in original)]

b. Political Control by Congress

Cases such as *Ex parte* **McCardle** stand on a different footing from the noncontroversial considerations mentioned above. *McCardle* shows that when Congress and the Court are in profound and passionate political disagreement, Congress may use its power over jurisdiction to achieve particular political ends.

(1) Power of Congress Ambiguous

To some extent, as seen in pp. 61–64, *supra*, Congress's power to effect political ends through jurisdictional control is fairly clear. However, to a significant extent, the power of Congress to achieve political ends through jurisdictional regulation is ambiguous. This ambiguity is useful in one very important respect: Partly because the power of Congress in this area is unclear, Congress and the Court have generally acted so as to avoid direct confrontation. Despite the many modern proposals for limitation on federal court jurisdiction over such things as busing and abortion cases, Congress has not passed any of these bills. Yet the threat of Congress's doing so serves as a reminder to the Court of this and other political checks on the Court's power to make law. The end result is what many regard as a salutary pressure on both Congress and the Court to compromise and cooperate.

5. Congressional Power to Curtail Review by Limiting Access to the Writ of Habeas Corpus

Since the Judiciary Act of 1789, the federal courts have been given the power to review the legality of detention by writ of habeas corpus. What's more, the Constitution declares that the privilege of the writ shall be not suspended except when in cases of rebellion or invasion the public safety may require it. A growing body of law suggests that the non-suspension clause imposes important limits on the power of Congress to curtail review of the legality of present custody.

a. Habeas Corpus and the War on Terror

(1) Review of Enemy Combatant Detention

Shortly after the United States invaded Afghanistan in November 2001 under the congressional authorization for the use of military force, the military established a secure detention facility at Guantanamo Bay, Cuba to house enemy combatants captured in the hostilities. Eventually, Guantanamo Bay was to house individuals captured around the world as part of the Bush Administration's global war on terror. Detainees eventually brought challenges to their detention in the federal courts, raising questions about the legality of detention. These questions ranged broadly, including challenges to the factual predicate for the government's enemy combatant finding, to the power of the government to house combatants without affording them the protections of international law, and to the power of the government to punish the detainees for engaging in unlawful modes of combat. The government consistently took the position that the federal courts had no power to review these matters.

(a) Rasul and the Military Commission Act of 2006

In 2004, the Court ruled that the general statutory grant of power to issues writs of habeas corpus empowered the federal district courts to hear applications for review of detention filed by aliens housed at Guantanamo Bay. [**Rasul v. Bush**, 542 U.S. 466 (2004)] Congress responded by narrowing the scope of such review in the Military Commission Act of 2006, eliminating review by way of habeas corpus and providing for extremely limited review by the US Court of Appeals for the D.C. Circuit of the legality of detention and any imposition of criminal sanctions.

(b) *Boumediene* and the Non-Suspension Clause

Detainees challenged this restriction on habeas review. The Court agreed that Congress had gone too far, finding for the first time that a restriction on federal habeas review violated the non-suspension clause. Critical to the Court's decision was its finding that the writ extended to the detention facility in Cuba (as held in **Rasul**), that the aliens enjoyed the constitutional privilege of habeas corpus to test their detention, and that Congress had restricted access to the Great Writ without affording an adequate substitute. In particular, the Court found that the factual issues surrounding the legality of detention were better developed through the plenary hearings available on habeas review at the district court level than through the limited appellate review available at the D.C. Circuit. [**Boumediene v. Bush**, 553 U.S. 723 (2008)]

EXAM TIP   ◤GILBERT

When assessing a constitutional challenge to restrictions on the power of the federal courts to review detention by way of habeas corpus, be sure to consider the adequacy of any forms of substitute judicial review Congress has made available.

---

b. Habeas Corpus and Immigration Reform

(1) The Roots of Habeas Review

Aliens detained at the border or placed in deportation or removal proceedings have long been permitted to seek review of the legality of their custody, and by implication the legality of the removal proceeding, through petitions for a writ of habeas corpus. Now, an elaborate administrative machinery precedes any order of removal and aliens have statutory entitlements to judicial review of adverse agency action. Habeas corpus provides an additional tool of judicial review, at least for aliens in custody.

(a) St. Cyr

During the 1990s, Congress adopted two important immigration law reform measures. Among other things, these reforms put in place a regime of presumptive deportation or removal for undocumented aliens and for lawful resident aliens who committed specified criminal offenses. One such lawful resident who pled guilty to a criminal offense, St. Cyr, invoked the attorney general's discretion to waive deportation. But the attorney general took the position that Congress had eliminated discretion by statute. What's more, the law proclaimed that "no court" shall have jurisdiction to review any such final order of removal. St. Cyr argued that this language effected an unlawful suspension of the privilege of the writ. Although the Court held that the provision in question foreclosed review by state courts and by the federal appellate court, it found that the language did not clearly curtail district court review. Any other interpretation would have presented grave questions concerning the constitutionality of the legislation under the habeas non-suspension clause. [**INS v. St. Cyr**, 533 U.S. 289 (2001)] While the Court stopped short of concluding that the non-suspension clause foreclosed the jurisdictional restriction, the combined force of **St. Cyr** and **Boumediene** suggest that the Constitution requires some habeas review of deportation issues, at least in the absence of substitutes.

1) The Availability of State Courts?

Shortly after the Civil War, the Court ruled that state courts may not entertain petitions for habeas review of federal official detention. [**Tarble's Case**, infra p. 219] As a result, in considering alternatives to federal judicial review by way of habeas corpus, the state courts do not provide a viable alternative forum.

C. Congressional Power to Allocate Jurisdiction Among the Federal Courts

1. Power to Allocate Jurisdiction Among Article III Courts

a. Power to Assign Whole Cases

Congress has unquestioned power to allocate jurisdiction over particular kinds of *cases* among Article III federal courts. For example, when the United States Court of Claims was an Article III court, Congress required that most monetary claims against the United States be brought in the Court of Claims rather than in the federal district court. Furthermore, Congress may divide up the original and appellate jurisdiction of the inferior federal courts in whatever way it deems best.

b. Power to Assign Exclusive Jurisdiction over Certain Questions

Although Congress has not done so often, it may also assign to certain federal courts exclusive jurisdiction to decide certain *questions*, forbidding other federal courts to inquire into or decide such questions.

Example: During World War II, Congress created an Article III Emergency Court with exclusive power to provide injunctive relief against the enforcement of regulations promulgated under the Federal Price Control Act. Plaintiff sought an injunction in federal district court, restraining the United States attorney from enforcing certain price regulations, on the ground that both the Price Control Act and the regulations were unconstitutional. The Supreme Court held that the Emergency Court had exclusive jurisdiction to grant injunctive relief to restrain enforcement of regulations under the Act or of the Act itself. [**Lockerty v. Phillips**, 319 U.S. 182 (1943)]

Example: A successor case to **Lockerty v. Phillips**, *supra*, established a more far-reaching and possibly dangerous principle. A criminal prosecution was brought in federal district court for violation of a price control regulation. The Price Control Act provided that the legality of a regulation could not be raised in the district court as a defense in a criminal prosecution. The Court sustained this restriction on the district court's jurisdiction on the ground that the defendant could have challenged the regulation by bringing an earlier and separate suit in the Emergency Court. Having "failed to avail himself of an adequate separate procedure," defendant may be barred from raising the issue as a defense in the district court criminal proceeding. [**Yakus v. United States**, 321 U.S. 414 (1944)]

2. Power to Allocate Jurisdiction Between Article I and Article III Courts

a. Basic Distinction Between Article I and Article III Courts

Article I of the Constitution confers upon Congress the power to create so-called *"legislative courts"* outside the framework of Article III. Such courts now include military courts (courts-martial), territorial courts, the Tax Court, the United States Court of Federal Claims, administrative courts, United States Magistrates' courts, District of Columbia local courts, and bankruptcy courts. Article III of the Constitution (the "judicial article") creates the Supreme Court and confers upon Congress the power to create inferior federal courts (*e.g.*, the courts of appeals and district courts). Courts created under Article III are sometimes referred to as *"constitutional courts."* Article III court judges are appointed for life ("during good Behavior"), and their salary may "not be diminished during their Continuance in Office."

b. Characteristics of an Article III Court

Establishing criteria for distinguishing between Article I and Article III courts has not been easy. The best test is probably the two-part test established by Justice Harlan in **Glidden v. Zdanok**, *supra,* p. 61 (*and see infra*, pp. 73–74):

(i) Is the subject matter jurisdiction over the dispute *authorized by Article III*; and

(ii) Are the *judges independent* and the *judgments final?*

To understand the present law fully, you should consider the now-abandoned cases that led up to *Glidden.*

CHARACTERISTICS OF AN ARTICLE III COURT	GILBERT
ACCORDING TO JUSTICE HARLAN'S TWO PART TEST FOR DISTINGUISHING BETWEEN AN ARTICLE I AND ARTICLE III COURT AN ARTICLE III COURT MUST HAVE THE FOLLOWING CHARACTERISTICS:	
☑ The *subject matter* over the dispute must be authorized by Article III; and ☑ The judges must be *independent* and the judgments must be *final*.	

(1) Early Cases

(a) *Ex Parte Bakelite Corp.*

At one time, the now disbanded Court of Customs Appeals decided some matters that did not constitute cases or controversies because the court's decisions lacked finality. The Supreme Court held that this lack of finality was permissible because the Court of Customs Appeals was a "legislative" court even though Congress had given life tenure to the judges of the court. According to the Supreme Court, what determined the character of the Court of Customs Appeals was the type of jurisdiction conferred upon it. Although many of the customs appeals decided by the court had sufficient finality to be cases or controversies, these did not "inherently or necessarily require [a] judicial determination." Rather, the decisions in such cases could be decided by executive officers. [*Ex parte* **Bakelite Corp.**, 279 U.S. 438 (1929)]

(b) *Williams v. United States*

When Congress reduced the salaries of the judges of the Court of Claims, it was objected that the Court of Claims was an Article III court, whose judges were protected by the Constitution from a diminution in salary. The Supreme Court held that the Court of Claims was a legislative court, because it entertained cases brought by private citizens against the United States. The Court held that such suits were not included under the bases for jurisdiction authorized by Article III, and therefore such a suit could only be brought in "legislative" courts. [**Williams v. United States**, 289 U.S. 553 (1933)]

(2) Assessment of *Bakelite* and *Williams*

Williams, and possibly *Bakelite*, were based on the idea that there are two types of cases: those that are "inherently judicial" and those that are not. Inherently judicial cases can be brought only in Article III courts. Other suits can be brought only in legislative courts.

(a) Criticism

The tidy division between inherently judicial business and other suits proved unrealistic and unworkable, and threw into disarray the theoretical structure of Article III court jurisdiction. The *Bakelite* rationale was unsound, because even though customs appeals could be decided by an executive branch officer, such disputes could also be cast as cases or controversies that could be decided by the normal judicial process. And the conclusion in *Williams* that suits against the United States were not authorized by Article III was contradicted by the terms of Article III, which granted jurisdiction over "controversies to which the United States shall be a Party." It was also contradicted in practice by many decades of the Supreme Court's hearing appeals from the Court of Claims of money judgments against the United States.

(3) Modern Approach—*Glidden v. Zdanok*

In 1953, Congress declared by statute that the Court of Claims was an Article III court, and it did the same for the Court of Customs and Patent Appeals in 1958. The validity of these statutes was challenged in the Supreme Court. In 1962, a seven-Justice Court held that the Court of Claims and Court of Customs and Patent Appeals *were* Article III courts. [**Glidden v. Zdanok**, *supra,* p. 72]

(a) Plurality Opinion

Justice Harlan, joined by two other Justices, concluded that *Bakelite* and *Williams* had been wrongly decided. He was willing to assume that the disputes presented to the Court of Claims and the Court of Customs and Patent Appeals were not "inherently" judicial business and thus could be assigned, if Congress so desired, to Article I tribunals. *Bakelite* and *Williams* said that if these cases were not inherently judicial business, they ***had*** to be assigned to Article I courts, but Harlan concluded that Congress could assign them to ***either*** Article I or Article III tribunals as it chose.

(b) Tests for Article III Status

To decide whether the Court of Claims and the Court of Customs and Patent Appeals were Article III courts, Harlan established two tests:

1) Article III Head of Jurisdiction

The dispute must come under a head of jurisdiction described in Article III. That is, the business of the court must be "the federal business . . . specified" in Article III.

2) Independence of Judges and Judgments

The judges must have tenure and salary protection as required by Article III, and the judgments must be final. That is, the "judges and judgments [must have] the independence . . . expressly or implicitly made requisite [in Article III]."

c. Article III Courts Have Limited Jurisdiction

Federal courts created under Article III cannot exercise any greater jurisdiction than that described in Article III. This basic principle of limited jurisdiction has two components.

(1) Case or Controversy Limitation

As described in the preceding chapter, Article III courts are not permitted to hear disputes unless they are presented as "cases or controversies" within the meaning of Article III.

(2) Described Bases of Jurisdiction

The bases for jurisdiction in Article III (diversity, federal question, admiralty, etc.) are extensive. They do not, however, include all categories of cases in which the federal government may have an interest. But if a case does not come under any of the Article III bases for jurisdiction, an Article III court ***cannot*** hear the case.

(a) The *Tidewater* Case

Congress passed a statute providing that citizens of the District of Columbia and the territories would be the equivalent of state citizens for purposes of diversity jurisdiction. But Article III confers diversity jurisdiction only over "controversies . . . between citizens of different ***states***" (emphasis added), making no mention of citizens of the District of Columbia or the territories. Plaintiff, a District of Columbia corporation, sued a Virginia corporation in federal district court, relying on diversity of citizenship. The Court upheld diversity jurisdiction, but there was ***no majority rationale*** for the decision.

[**National Mutual Insurance Co. v. Tidewater Transfer Co.**, 337 U.S. 582 (1949)]

1) Varied Rationales

Justice Jackson, joined by two other Justices, argued that Congress *had* the power under Article I to confer jurisdiction over cases of federal concern on Article III courts even if no jurisdictional head of Article III was applicable. (They relied on the examples of the then-existing "hybrid" courts of the District of Columbia and on bankruptcy cases involving state law questions, claiming that these cases were not covered by the heads of Article III jurisdiction.) Two other Justices argued that the diversity jurisdiction clause of Article III should be construed to include citizens of the District of Columbia and the territories, and thus the statute merely conferred jurisdiction already authorized by Article III. *But note*: Both of these views were *rejected* by different majorities of the Justices.

2) Summary of *Tidewater*

Although the result in *Tidewater* was to sustain the exercise of jurisdiction, the most important thing to remember is that six of the nine Justices rejected Justice Jackson's position. For these six Justices, it was fundamental doctrine that Congress *cannot* confer jurisdiction on Article III courts by statute when Article III does not authorize that jurisdiction.

3) Alternative Explanation

One might explain the result in *Tidewater* as an exercise of Congress's power to protect citizens of the United States living abroad, in the territories, or in the District of Columbia from possible discrimination by state courts in the enforcement of state law. Such an approach would treat US citizens as enjoying Fourteenth Amendment privileges and immunities in the even-handed enforcement of rights grounds in state law. On such a view, the grant of diversity jurisdiction upheld in *Tidewater* could be seen as an exercise of the Fourteenth Amendment enforcement power and cases within the grant as arising under federal law. [Pfander, *The Tidewater Problem: Article III and Constitutional Change,* 79 Notre Dame L. Rev. 1925 (2004)]

(b) Distinguish—Congressional Limitation of Jurisdiction

Tidewater thus stands for the proposition that Congress cannot *add* to the constitutionally authorized jurisdiction of Article III. But clearly Congress has the power to *subtract* from the jurisdiction authorized by Article III. Or, to put it more conventionally, Congress need not grant to the Article III courts the full extent of their constitutionally authorized jurisdiction.

(c) Distinguish—Supplemental Jurisdiction

While the majority position in *Tidewater* is that Article III federal courts cannot be granted jurisdiction not enumerated in Article III, this principle does not forbid supplemental jurisdiction. Under supplemental jurisdiction (formerly pendent and ancillary jurisdiction), an Article III federal court with proper jurisdiction over a case may decide *related* additional claims and may bring in *related* additional parties, even if there is no independent jurisdictional basis for those claims and parties. (*See infra*, pp. 146 *et seq.*)

e.g. **Example:** Plaintiff sues on a claim based on a federal question. Although there is no diversity of citizenship, plaintiff may nevertheless join an additional, related *state law* claim provided it arises out of "a common nucleus of operative fact." If the federal and state law claims are thus related, they are viewed as part of the same "case" for which Article III has authorized jurisdiction based on the existence of the federal claim. [**United Mine Workers v. Gibbs**, 383 U.S. 715 (1966)]

d. Congressional Power to Allocate Jurisdiction to Article I Courts

(1) Problem of Congressional Power Under *Glidden v. Zdanok*

Under the *Glidden* view articulated by Justice Harlan, Congress has considerable power to assign cases to Article I or Article III tribunals as it chooses. The problem is deciding how far Congress may go in assigning to Article I courts cases that it could have assigned to Article III courts. Justice Harlan's opinion explicitly left this issue open in *Glidden* (*see supra*, p. 74).

(2) "Madisonian Compromise" and the Analogy Between State Courts and Article I Courts

Under the "Madisonian Compromise" Congress had, and probably still has, the power to assign much or all of the lower federal court business to the state courts rather than to the federal courts. (*See* discussion *supra*, pp. 67–68.) One can argue that if Congress has the power to assign business to state courts, it should have the power to assign the same business to Article I federal courts. But the analogy between state courts and Article I federal courts is not entirely persuasive for two reasons:

(a) Implicit Assumption of Article III

Article III provides that the "judicial Power of the United States . . . shall be vested" in Article III courts. The implicit assumption of that language is that if federal courts are established, they will be Article III rather than Article I courts.

(b) Political Control over the Courts—A Separation of Powers Issue

An important aim of Article III was to protect Article III judges from the influence of the other branches of the federal government by providing constitutionally guaranteed life tenure and salary protection. Article I judges have neither constitutional life tenure nor salary protection, and thus are more vulnerable to attempts by the executive and legislative branches to influence their decisions. State judges are often subject to political pressures, but these pressures are not brought to bear by the other branches of the federal government. Thus, the Madisonian Compromise does not threaten the principle of separation of powers. But an ability to assign large amounts of judicial business to Article I courts would threaten that principle. [*See* **Northern Pipeline Construction Co. v. Marathon Pipe Line Co.**, *supra*, p. 9—Brennan, J.]

(3) Scope of Congressional Power to Assign Judicial Business to Article I Courts

The cases in which the Supreme Court has dealt with Congress's power to assign jurisdiction to Article I courts are not easy to synthesize, but there are a number of helpful judicial landmarks.

(a) Article I Courts That Have Been Approved

1) Territorial Courts

Territorial courts were the first Article I courts to be approved by the Supreme Court. [**American Insurance Co. v. Canter**, *supra,* p. 7]

2) District of Columbia Courts

Article I local courts of the District of Columbia are closely related to territorial courts. They have been explicitly approved. [**Palmore v. United States**, *supra,* p. 7]

3) Military Courts

The military may employ Article I military courts to try service-connected disciplinary cases. [**Dynes v. Hoover**, 61 U.S. (20 How.) 65 (1858)]

4) Other Article I Courts

The United States Tax Court and the United States Court of Federal Claims are presently Article I courts. At one time, the Court of Federal Claims and the Court of Customs and Patent Appeals were Article III courts (*see supra,* p. 7).

(b) Synthesis Suggested by *Northern Pipeline*

Under the Bankruptcy Act of 1978, Congress gave significantly increased jurisdiction over bankruptcy matters to Article I bankruptcy courts. Northern Pipeline filed for bankruptcy and subsequently filed a suit in bankruptcy court against Marathon Pipe Line, claiming on state grounds that Marathon owed it money under a contract. Marathon claimed that it was entitled to an Article III court determination of the contract dispute. Although there was no majority rationale, the Supreme Court held that the provisions of the Bankruptcy Act giving jurisdiction to the bankruptcy court over state law claims were *invalid.* [**Northern Pipeline Construction Co. v. Marathon Pipe Line Co.**, *supra,* p. 76]

1) Plurality Opinion

Justice Brennan, writing for a four-Justice plurality, stated that there are three kinds of permissible Article I courts:

(i) Territorial courts;

(ii) Military courts; and

(iii) Courts deciding "public rights" cases. Justice Brennan wrote that the distinction between "public rights" and "private rights" has never been "definitively explained" but that most public rights cases are suits brought by a private individual against the government. The argument in favor of Article I courts here is that since the government may constitutionally grant certain rights to private persons and may commit decisions about entitlements under those rights to nonjudicial executive administration, there can be no constitutional objection to Congress's using the "less drastic expedient of committing their determination to a legislative court or an administrative agency."

2) Criticism

Justice White, joined by two other Justices, criticized the plurality's three permitted categories of Article I courts as an "unrealistic attempt to cabin the domain of Article I courts."

(c) Result in *Northern Pipeline*

The bankruptcy court in *Northern Pipeline* was obviously not a territorial court or a court-martial. Nor was the suit a "public rights" case because it was a dispute between two private companies based on a state-law contract claim. The Court therefore struck down the assignment of the jurisdiction in question to an Article I bankruptcy court.

(d) Aftermath of *Northern Pipeline*

In 1984, Congress passed a new statute restricting the jurisdiction of the Bankruptcy Court to core bankruptcy matters. State law cases based on tort or contract (such as the claim involved in *Northern Pipeline*) are assigned to the district court with the bankruptcy judge acting as an adjunct.

(e) Definition of "Public Rights" Cases in Decisions After *Northern Pipeline*

The core of *Northern Pipeline's* definition of "public rights" cases was civil suits brought by private individuals against the government. Later decisions do not definitively resolve the breadth of the "public rights" exception.

1) Federal Scheme Entailing Adjudication Before Arbitration Panel

A federal statute requires a firm registering a pesticide to submit data to the Environmental Protection Agency ("EPA"). If the EPA uses the data to evaluate the registration of another firm's pesticide, the first firm is entitled to compensation from the second firm. The amount of compensation is determined in a suit between the two companies before an arbitration panel, subject to judicial review only for "fraud, misrepresentation, or misconduct." The Court noted that the suit was between private parties rather than between a private plaintiff and the government. Nevertheless, it sustained the scheme. According to the Court, the right to compensation bore "many of the characteristics of a 'public' right" because it was created as "an integral part of a program safeguarding the public health." [**Thomas v. Union Carbide Agricultural Products, Inc.**, 473 U.S. 568 (1985)] Notably, some first registrants under an earlier version of the law had sued the federal government, alleging that it had taken valuable property rights by allowing second registrants to rely on first registrants' (costly) submissions to the EPA. By creating a duty to compensate first registrants, Congress can be seen as acting in the shadow of such takings claims, which would clearly qualify as public rights matters.

2) State Law Counterclaim Before Administrative Tribunal

Plaintiff sought reparations from a commodity broker before the Federal Commodity Futures Trading Commission, an administrative tribunal. The broker counterclaimed for money owed under state law. The Court sustained the jurisdiction of the administrative tribunal over the counterclaim as a "de minimis" intrusion on Article III courts; the state law claim was "completely dependent upon" the federal reparations claims. [**Commodity Futures Trading Commission v. Schor**, 478 U.S. 833 (1986)] The Court suggested that it was shifting from the categorical approach of **Northern Pipeline** to something more closely resembling the balancing approach advocated by the **Northern Pipeline** dissenters.

3) Apparent Reaffirmation of *Northern Pipeline*

In 2011, the Court apparently returned to the categorical approach of **Northern Pipeline**, limiting the power of bankruptcy courts to hear Article III business. [**Stern v. Marshall**, 564 U.S. 462 (2011)] In **Stern**, as part of a long-running dispute between Vicki Marshall and E. Pierce Marshall over the estate of a wealthy oil man, a trustee in bankruptcy brought a common law claim on Vicki's behalf for tortious interference with an expected inheritance. Although similar to **Northern Pipeline**, the claim arose as a compulsory counterclaim to one that E. Pierce filed in Vicki's bankruptcy proceeding. (There was also probate litigation in the Texas state courts, giving rise to questions about the scope of the probate exception. *See infra* p. 142.)

The Court held that the counterclaim was within the scope of Article III and could not be assigned to an Article I bankruptcy court. As a common law claim between two private parties, the tort claim could not be considered a matter of public right. It was different from the arbitration claim in **Thomas**, which arose from a complex federal administrative scheme. And it was different from **Schor**, in that the tort claim was not dependent on a claim under federal law. While the Court did not need to go that far, the concurring opinion of Justice Scalia would have held that public rights claims must feature the government as a party.

4) Apparent Restatement of Public Rights

In **Oil States Energy Services, LLC v. Green's Energy Group, LLC**, 138 S.Ct. 1365 (2018), the Court based its approval of an expanded agency role in the resolution of disputed patent rights on the public rights doctrine. Congress gave the Patent and Trademark Office broader power to conduct so-called inter partes review of patents. Viewing the government's initial grant of patent rights as a matter of public right, the Court treated the expanded power of the PTO to hear a dispute over the patent as a reserved power to reconsider the initial grant.

(4) The Relevance of Consent

In **Commodity Futures Trading Commission v. Schor**, *supra,* p. 79, the Court recognized that Article III imposes structural limits on the scope of congressional power and creates an individual right to litigate certain claims before Article III courts. The Court further recognized that such an individual right was subject to waiver through a party's consent to litigation in an Article I court. In *Schor*, the party that later challenged the authority of the administrative tribunal had acceded to its jurisdiction over the counterclaim, and the Court found that this consent constituted a waiver of the individual's right to an Article III court.

Example: Litigants before the federal district courts may find that aspects of a case may be submitted to a federal magistrate, a non-Article III federal judge appointed by the district court. The dispositions of the magistrate are subject to de novo review by the district court, although in practice the review may not be exacting. Additionally, magistrates may try cases with the consent of the parties.

In **Wellness Int'l Network Ltd. v. Sharif**, 135 S.Ct. 1932 (2015), the Court upheld bankruptcy court's power, when the parties consent, to adjudicate *Stern* claims—claims typically governed by state law that have been brought to augment the bankruptcy estate. For the Court, consent resolved both the concerns with individual right of access to an Article III court and, as in *Schor*, seemed to call for a functional analysis of threat posed to judicial independence. Chief Justice Roberts, author of the more formalistic decision in *Stern*, dissented.

(5) Scope of Congressional Power to Assign Judicial Business to "Adjunct" Courts

Although they are sometimes referred to as Article I courts, there are other non-Article III tribunals that are often referred to as "adjunct" courts. They are in many respects indistinguishable from Article I courts, except that they are designed to serve as subsidiaries or "adjuncts" to Article III courts, rather than as independent tribunals.

(a) Illustrations of "Adjunct" Courts

The two most clear-cut examples of adjunct courts are:

1) Bankruptcy Courts

See supra, pp. 6–14.

2) United States Magistrates

Magistrates hear minor criminal matters and some civil matters. Their decisions are reviewed by Article III courts, usually the district court. The exercise of some power by United States magistrates was upheld in **United States v. Raddatz**, 447 U.S. 667 (1980). However, the constitutionality of the exercise of the full range of powers now statutorily granted to magistrates is still open to question. The Court's most recent decision upheld the magistrate's power to preside over jury selection in a felony trial, given that the parties consented. [*See* **Peretz v. United States**, 501 U.S. 923 (1991)]

3) Other Illustrations

Two other tribunals are sometimes referred to as "adjuncts": special masters, and administrative agencies when there is a right of appeal to an Article III court.

(b) Scope of Congressional Power

The analysis applied to determine the constitutionality of assigning a case to an "adjunct" rather than directly to an Article III court is largely the same as for assigning a case to an Article I court. The only significant difference is that provisions for **significant review** of the "adjunct's" decision by the Article III court may save what would otherwise be an unconstitutional assignment of jurisdiction. Although the outer limits on Congress's power to assign judicial business are not clear, two cases shed light on the matter.

1) *Crowell v. Benson*

Under the Longshoremen's and Harbor Workers' Compensation Act, injured employees could seek compensation from their employers in a proceeding before an administrative tribunal. An employer objected to an award of damages on the ground that he was entitled to an initial hearing before an Article III court. The Supreme Court sustained the award, noting that the agency's findings of fact as to matters clearly within the authority of the agency could be treated as final as long as they were sufficiently supported by evidence. Questions of fact going to the issue of **jurisdiction** of the agency, however, had to be reviewable de novo by the district court. [**Crowell v. Benson**, 285 U.S. 22 (1932)]

a) **Note—No "Public Right" Involved**

Crowell was an unusual case for an administrative determination in that the disputants were two private individuals, an employee and an employer. Had the case been a more typical administrative case in which the disputants were a private individual and the government, it would have been a "public rights" case in which it would have been clear that no Article III tribunal was required. (*See supra,* p. 77.)

b) **Present Significance of *Crowell***

Administrative determinations of fact touching on an agency's jurisdiction are generally given more finality today than they were in *Crowell,* and the part of *Crowell* requiring de novo review is almost certainly no longer good law. But the basic idea of *Crowell*—that there must be some meaningful review by an Article III court of a decision by an Article I or "adjunct" court—still retains vitality as a general principle.

2) *Northern Pipeline Construction Co. v. Marathon Pipe Line Co.*

In *Northern Pipeline,* the exercise of jurisdiction by an Article I bankruptcy court over a state law claim between private parties was struck down. (*See supra,* pp. 6–14.) Justice Brennan, in a plurality opinion, concluded that there was insufficient appellate review by the district court of the bankruptcy court to make its decision a permissible exercise of power by an "adjunct" court. [**Northern Pipeline Construction Co. v. Marathon Pipe Line Co.,** *supra,* p. 77]

3) *Stern v. Marshall*

In *Stern v. Marshall,* the Court followed *Northern Pipeline* in rejecting the argument that the bankruptcy court should be regarded as an adjunct to the (Article III) federal district court. Bankruptcy courts have broad subject matter jurisdiction and the power to issue judgments, making them courts rather than adjuncts. [**Stern v. Marshall,** *supra* p. 79]

Summary: On the exam, students should start by trying to connect the problem to a situation the Court has already addressed. In *Northern Pipeline*, for example, the Court treated territorial courts and military tribunals as established exceptions to Article III. For matters closer to the core of Article III, the public-private distinction bears some consideration: the Court has sometimes suggested that Congress has greater flexibility to withdraw access to Article III courts as to matters of public right. Finally, with regard to private law matters, students should consider whether the non-Article III decision-maker can be brought within the adjunct framework of *Crowell v. Benson*.

3. Congressional Power to Assign Jurisdiction to State Courts

Congress's power to regulate the jurisdiction of the federal courts includes the power to assign cases to the state courts rather than to the federal courts. This topic is discussed in Chapter VIII. (*See infra*, pp. 215 *et seq.*)

Chapter Four

Supreme Court Jurisdiction

Key Exam Issues

Federal Courts courses usually focus on the Supreme Court's **appellate jurisdiction over the state courts.** This jurisdiction is important in that it ensures that the state courts follow federal law faithfully. You should particularly be prepared for questions regarding:

1. The **independent and adequate state ground doctrine;**

2. The power of the Supreme Court to review **state court findings of fact;**

3. The necessity for a **final judgment;** and

4. The requirement that the judgment be by the **highest state court** in which a decision could be had.

In answering examination questions, keep in mind not only the technical requirements of these doctrines but also the institutional imperatives of the Supreme Court that may exert pressures on the doctrines in a particular case.

The Supreme Court's **original jurisdiction** is usually given fairly abbreviated treatment in a Federal Courts course. If your class has covered this topic, remember to distinguish between the Court's *exclusive* and *concurrent* original jurisdiction, and remember that the Court is generally *reluctant to take original jurisdiction cases.*

A. Appellate Jurisdiction of the Supreme Court

1. Appellate Jurisdiction over State Court Decisions

The Supreme Court has appellate jurisdiction over lower federal court decisions as well as over state court decisions. Federal Courts classes devote most of their attention to the Court's appellate jurisdiction over state court decisions because of the interesting federalism problems presented.

a. Foundation of the Power

(1) Constitutional Basis

Article III provides that except for cases within its original jurisdiction (*see infra,* pp. 104 *et seq.*), the Supreme Court "shall have appellate Jurisdiction, both as to Law and Fact, with such exceptions, and under such regulations as the Congress shall make." [U.S. Const. art. III, § 2, cl. 2]

(2) Judiciary Act of 1789

Section 25 of the Judiciary Act of 1789 provided for Supreme Court appellate review of state court decisions in which the state court decided **against a federal right** that had been asserted and in which the question presented immediately respected that federal right.

(3) Constitutionality of Supreme Court Review of State Court Decisions

In the early years of the 19th century, some states' rights advocates contended that the state courts were courts of distinct "sovereigns," and therefore could not be subjected to appellate review by the court of the federal "sovereign." They conceded that the state courts were obliged to follow federal law faithfully, but they objected to the Supreme Court's enforcement of that obligation. In the famous case of **Martin v. Hunter's Lessee**, *supra,* p. 57, the Supreme Court held that Congress had the power to authorize the Supreme Court to exercise appellate jurisdiction over questions of federal law decided in the state courts.

b. 1988 Statute

The present statute was passed in 1988. Under this statute, the Supreme Court's appellate jurisdiction over state court decisions is entirely discretionary, under the *writ of certiorari.* [28 U.S.C. § 1257]

(1) Prior Statute

Before 1988, the Supreme Court's appellate jurisdiction over state court decisions was divided between mandatory appeals and discretionary writs of certiorari. The Supreme Court was required (at least in theory) to hear cases within its mandatory appellate jurisdiction, but was allowed to pick and choose in its discretion among cases within its certiorari jurisdiction. (For a fuller discussion of the distinction between appeal and certiorari, *see infra,* pp. 100 *et seq.*)

c. Appellate Jurisdiction Limited to Federal Questions

(1) Historical Background

As mentioned, section 25 of the Judiciary Act of 1789 provided for Supreme Court review of state court judgments where the state court had decided against a claimed federal right (*see supra,* p. 84). Section 25 *restricted* that review to issues that "immediately respect[ed]" the federal question. In 1867, Congress amended section 25 by eliminating the restrictive sentence, so that the Supreme Court was no longer explicitly confined to what "immediately respect[ed]" the federal question. However, even without the explicit statutory restriction, the Court held that its review of state court decisions was still limited to the federal question or questions presented. [**Murdock v. City of Memphis**, 87 U.S. (20 Wall.) 590 (1875)]

(2) Importance of *Murdock v. City of Memphis*

The essential principle of **Murdock v. City of Memphis** is that the Supreme Court cannot decide questions of state law in cases coming up on appeal from the state courts. This principle follows from the fact that state courts are the authoritative expositors of their own law.

(a) Exception

The Court may decide questions of state law when the state court has manipulated state law to avoid the command of federal law. In its opinion in the *Murdock* case, the Court warned that it had "such powers as may be necessary to cause [its] judgment . . . to be respected."

(b) Distinguish—State Law Questions Coming up from Lower Federal Courts

Murdock does not prevent the Supreme Court from deciding questions of state law in cases coming up from the lower federal courts (*e.g.,* diversity cases, federal question cases with supplemental jurisdiction over state law claims, or federal question cases in which issues of state law are involved).

d. Independent and Adequate State Ground

An outgrowth of *Murdock* is the following important principle: The Supreme Court *will not decide a case* coming up from a state court if there is an independent and adequate state ground to support the decision. [**Fox Film Corp. v. Muller**, 296 U.S. 207 (1935)]

(1) Definition of "Independent and Adequate"

(a) "Independent"

An "independent" state ground exists when a decision is based on state law that is independent of whatever federal law might require. If state law is interpreted to make it consistent with the supposed command of federal law, or if state law incorporates federal law, the state law is not "independent."

Example: State law depending on federal law: The Utah Supreme Court sustained an exception from state income tax for a federal employee. The state court appeared to have done so with the understanding that federal law required the exception. If the decision of state law thus depended on an interpretation of federal law, the state law decision was not "independent." [**State Tax Commission v. Van Cott**, 306 U.S. 511 (1939)]

Example: State law incorporating federal law: A California statute exempted from state motor fuel tax any fuel sold for official use to a department of the United States. Since the state statute incorporated federal law for its definitions of a United States department and its official use, the state law decision was not "independent." [**Standard Oil of California v. Johnson**, 316 U.S. 481 (1942)]

(b) "Adequate"

To be "adequate," the decision of the state question must be fully dispositive, so that the decision of the federal question makes no difference to the outcome of the case.

(c) Parallel State and Federal Constitutional Provisions

Even if a state *constitutional* provision parallels a provision in the federal Constitution, a state court may rely on its own state constitutional provision as an ***independent and adequate ground*** for its decision.

Example: If a case is based on a clause in the state constitution prohibiting the taking of private property for public use without just compensation (parallel to the provision in the Fifth Amendment to the federal Constitution), there is an independent and adequate state ground for the decision, and the Supreme Court will not decide the case. [**Jankovich v. Indiana Toll Road Commission**, 379 U.S. 487 (1965)]

If you encounter an exam question that provides you with a state constitutional provision that closely mirrors a federal constitutional provision, don't automatically assume that the Supreme Court will grant certiorari because of that similarity—a state provision may be interpreted differently and thus *may provide an independent and adequate basis* for a state court's ruling.

(2) Rationales for the Rule

(a) No Advisory Opinions

A frequently invoked justification for the independent and adequate state ground doctrine derives from the prohibition against advisory opinions. The Supreme Court's decision of a federal question will have no effect on the outcome of a case if a state law ground is independent of federal law and fully dispositive. Thus, a decision on the federal issue could be seen as merely "advisory" because it would make no actual difference to the parties.

(b) Avoidance of Unnecessary Constitutional Adjudication

A further justification is that when a federal constitutional question is posed, the independent and adequate state ground doctrine will help the Court avoid making an unnecessary decision of a federal constitutional question.

(c) Docket Control

Note that the doctrine arose when the Court's appellate jurisdiction was mandatory. The doctrine thus served to limit access to a docket crowded with cases.

(3) Ambiguous Treatment of State Law Ground by State Court

It frequently happens that the state court opinion is written unclearly, so that one cannot be sure from the opinion whether the state ground is independent and adequate. The question arises whether, in such a case, the Supreme Court should decide the federal question despite the possibility of there being an independent and adequate state ground.

(a) Prior Practice

Until 1983, if it was unclear whether there was an independent and adequate state ground, the Court usually remanded the case to state court. Only after the state court made clear that no such state ground existed would the Supreme Court take the case. [**Minnesota v. National Tea Co.**, 309 U.S. 551 (1940)]

(b) Present Practice

The Supreme Court's present practice is to assume that there is *no* independent and adequate state ground unless the state court has clearly indicated that it is relying on such a ground. [**Michigan v. Long**, 463 U.S. 1032 (1983); **Ohio v. Robinette**, 519 U.S. 33 (1996)] Compared to the prior practice, the consequences are:

1) More Cases

The Supreme Court has a slightly larger pool of cases in which it can render decisions because of the presumption against there being an independent and adequate state ground.

2) Risk of Advisory Opinions

There is a risk of advisory opinions if the Supreme Court decides a case in which it is unclear whether there is an independent and adequate state ground. If on remand from the Supreme Court's decision the state court finds that there is, in fact, an independent and adequate state ground, the Supreme Court decision on the federal issue will not control the dispute's outcome.

3) Risk of Unnecessary Constitutional Decisions

There is risk of unnecessary constitutional decisions if the Supreme Court decides a case on the basis of the federal Constitution. If the state court after remand of the case finds that, in fact, there is an independent and adequate state ground, the constitutional decision will have been unnecessary.

4) More Political Exposure for State Courts

State courts wishing to achieve a particular result and to protect that result from Supreme Court reversal are obliged to make clear the state law basis for their decision. If the state court is thus forced to make visible the fact that state law and the state court are responsible for the result, the state political process may be more easily employed to change that result than if it was ambiguous whether state or federal law required the result.

(c) *Michigan v. Long Restated*

The Court reached a conclusion similar to that in **Michigan v. Long**, *supra* upholding its appellate jurisdiction to review a federal question in circumstances where the state court judgment failed to clarify the basis on which that court was acting to deny a federal challenge to the legality of jury selection in a capital case. [**Foster v. Chapman**, 136 S.Ct. 1737 (2016)]

In **Kansas v. Carr**, 136 S.Ct. 633 (2016), the Court reaffirmed the rule in **Michigan v. Long**, presuming despite some ambiguity that a state court opinion turned on federal law and was a proper object of appellate review. Justice Scalia's opinion for the Court highlighted a concern with state court's incentives to portray its potentially unpopular decisions as compelled by federal law.

(4) State Procedural Bar as Independent and Adequate State Ground

Failure to comply with valid state procedural requirements for raising an issue will prevent a litigant from presenting a federal issue to the Supreme Court on appeal. [**Michel v. Louisiana**, 350 U.S. 91 (1955)]

(a) Supreme Court Scrutiny of State Procedural Bar

The Supreme Court will scrutinize the asserted state procedural bar to ensure that it has been appropriately invoked. A state procedural bar will not prevent Supreme Court review in the following circumstances:

1) State Rule Unconstitutional

If a state procedural rule *violates constitutional due process,* either on its face or as applied, Supreme Court consideration of a federal issue *is not barred.* "As applied" decisions require close examination of the circumstances of a rule's application, and subtle factual differences between cases can produce different outcomes.

a) Unforeseeable State Court Rulings

If a later-imposed state court procedural rule is neither in effect nor foreseeable at the time it could have been obeyed, it violates due process to preclude a party from raising a federal issue for failure to obey the rule. [*Compare* **Brinkerhoff-Faris Trust & Savings Co. v. Hill**, 281 U.S. 673 (1930)—due process violation—*with* **Herndon v. Georgia**, 295 U.S. 441 (1935)—no due process violation]

b) Time Limits for Pretrial Motions

Application of strict time limits for making pretrial motions can, in certain circumstances, violate due process. [*Compare* **Reece v. Georgia**, 350 U.S. 85 (1955)—due process violation—*with* **Michel v. Louisiana**, *supra,* p. 88—no due process violation]

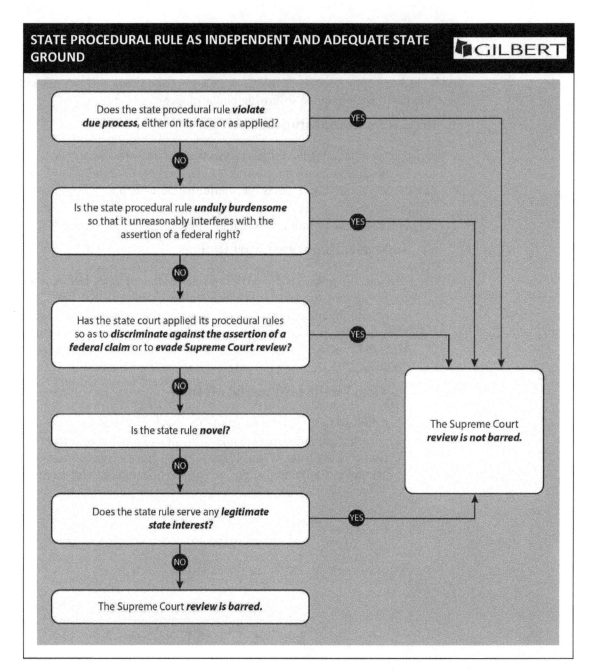

2) State Rule Constitutional

Even if a state procedural rule satisfies constitutional due process, the rule may be disregarded in certain circumstances.

a) Unduly Burdensome

If a state procedure is unduly burdensome, thus unreasonably interfering with the assertion of the federal right, an asserted state procedural bar will be disregarded. [**Davis v. Wechsler**, 263 U.S. 22 (1923)]

b) **Discrimination Against Federal Law or Evasion of Supreme Court Review**

If a state court applies its procedural rules so as to discriminate against the assertion of a federal claim [**Wolfe v. North Carolina**, 364 U.S. 177 (1960)], or to evade Supreme Court review [**Rogers v. Alabama**, 192 U.S. 226 (1904)], the Supreme Court may decide the federal issue despite the asserted state procedural bar.

c) **Novel State Procedural Rule**

If the state court uses a novel state procedural rule to bar the assertion of a federal claim, the Supreme Court may decide the federal issue. [**Ford v. Georgia**, 498 U.S. 411 (1991); **NAACP v. Alabama**, *supra*, p. 43]

d) **Discretionary State Procedural Rule**

While some older cases find no bar to review when a state court uses a "discretionary rather than jurisdictional" state procedural rule to bar the assertion of a federal claim [**Sullivan v. Little Hunting Park**, 396 U.S. 229 (1969)], more recent cases adopt a different view.

In **Beard v. Kindler**, 588 U.S. 443 (2009), a convicted felon sought to challenge his state court criminal conviction on federal grounds by applying for habeas review in federal court. (The adequate and independent state ground doctrine bars both direct review of federal issues in the Supreme Court and collateral review of such issues in federal habeas proceedings.) The state court had refused to reach the merits of the petitioner's federal claims, applying its fugitive felon rule as a procedural bar to the state judicial review of any issues he might have raised had he not escaped from prison. The Supreme Court held that further review of the state court decision was barred, even though the state court's rule applying the fugitive felon bar to review was discretionary rather than mandatory.

1. Note the argument for preserving review: when state courts exercise their discretion about whether to hear procedurally defaulted federal issues, they may base their decision on an assessment of the strength or weight of the federal ground (thereby suggesting that the state court's application of the procedural default was not truly independent of its evaluation of the federal ground).

2. The Court rejected that argument in **Beard**, reasoning that, like federal courts, state courts have a strong interest in exercising discretion about whether to grant particular litigants relief from procedural defaults.

e) **No Legitimate State Purpose**

In **Henry v. Mississippi**, 379 U.S. 443 (1965), the Supreme Court suggested, but found it unnecessary to decide, that a litigant's failure to comply with a state procedural rule should not "bar vindication of important federal rights" unless compliance with the state's procedural rule "serves a legitimate state interest."

1/ Current Status of *Henry v. Mississippi*

The Court has not often cited **Henry v. Mississippi** in recent years, casting doubt on the present status of its conclusion that the state procedural rule served no legitimate state interest. However, the Court has continued to examine the state interest in procedural rules and has occasionally excused a default after rejecting the legitimacy of the state interest.

e.g. **Example:** The defendant in a criminal proceeding argued through counsel that an issue was an element of the crime that the prosecution was obliged to prove. The state court found a default of the defendant's federal due process claim by virtue of counsel's failure to renew the objection later, at the time the jury was instructed. Renewal would not have served a legitimate state interest, given that the trial court was simply maintaining its earlier ruling. [**Osborne v. Ohio**, 495 U.S. 103 (1990)]

e.g. **Example:** The defendant planned to offer an alibi defense, but the alibi witnesses disappeared from the courtroom during a recess. Trial counsel requested a continuance, but the judge refused, citing docket concerns and personal issues. The state appellate court found a procedural default of a due process challenge to the denial of the continuance, due to counsel's failure to submit the motion in writing (something neither the prosecutor nor the trial court had mentioned). Citing *Osborne, supra,* the Court found no legitimate state interest to support application of the in-writing rule. [**Lee v. Kenma**, 534 U.S. 362 (2002)]

(b) Distinguish Between Direct and Collateral Review

The independent and adequate state procedural ground doctrine applies to direct (*i.e.,* appellate) review by the Supreme Court of state court decisions, including criminal convictions. The application of this doctrine to direct review cases has been described above. The doctrine also applies to collateral review, by habeas corpus, of state court criminal convictions. [**Beard v. Kindler; Lee v. Kenma**, *supra*] Additionally, a specialized set of rules governs the forgiveness of procedural defaults that would otherwise bar federal habeas corpus review of constitutional challenges to state court criminal convictions. Federal habeas review of state convictions is discussed in Chapter X (*see infra,* pp. 252 *et seq.*)

1) *Michigan v. Long* Applies to Both Direct and Collateral Review

For a state procedural bar to block federal habeas review of a state criminal conviction, the state court must make a "plain statement that its decision rests upon adequate and independent state grounds." [**Harris v. Reed**, 489 U.S. 255 (1989)]

2) State Procedural Grounds Must Meet Test of Adequacy on Collateral Review

The standards of adequacy, as developed in direct review cases, also govern the adequacy of state procedural defaults as a bar to federal habeas corpus review of state court criminal convictions. [**Lee v. Kenma**, *supra*]

e. Review of State Court Findings of Fact

(1) General Rule—No Review

Ordinarily, the Supreme Court will *not review* findings of fact by the state court.

(2) Exceptions

The Court *will* review state court fact findings in two situations:

(a) Question of Fact and Federal Law So Intermingled That Review of Findings of Fact Necessary

The Court will review state findings of fact where a conclusion of law as to a federal right and a finding of fact are "so intermingled as to make it necessary, in order to pass on the federal question, to analyze the facts." [**Fiske v. Kansas**, 274 U.S. 380 (1927)]

e.g. **Example:** Defendant was charged with violating Kansas's Criminal Syndicalism Act because he had sought to persuade people to join the Industrial Workers of the World ("I.W.W."). The sole evidence of the illegal purposes of the I.W.W. introduced at trial was the preamble to the I.W.W. constitution. The Supreme Court read the preamble and drew its own conclusions. [**Fiske v. Kansas**, *supra*] *(Comment:* The *Fiske* case was a particularly easy one in which to review the fact-finding of the state court. The sole relevant evidence was a single document. Thus, there was no need *to resolve contradictions in the evidence or to evaluate the truthfulness of witnesses*—tasks to which an appellate court is ill-suited.)

e.g. **Example:** Defendant was convicted on breach of the peace charges arising out of a civil rights demonstration. The Supreme Court conducted an independent review of the record, including a viewing of a news film of the demonstration, to evaluate defendant's claim that his conduct was constitutionally protected. [**Cox v. Louisiana**, 379 U.S. 536 (1965)]

e.g. **Example:** Defendant contended that he had been convicted by a jury from which blacks had been intentionally and systematically excluded. The Supreme Court conducted an independent review of the record to determine whether such exclusion of blacks had taken place. [**Norris v. Alabama**, 294 U.S. 587 (1935)]

(b) No Supporting Evidence in the Record

The Court will review state court findings of fact where a federal right has been denied as a result of a finding "shown by the record to be without evidence to support it." [**Fiske v. Kansas**, *supra*]

e.g. **Example:** Defendant was charged with violating a municipal anti-loitering ordinance. After examining the evidence, the Court held that there was "no evidence" that defendant had violated the ordinance. [**Thompson**

v. Louisville, 362 U.S. 199 (1960)] (*Note:* It was not literally true that there was "no" evidence that the defendant had violated the ordinance; there was merely insufficient evidence. The case may be best read as an attempt by the Supreme Court to warn the city of Louisville that conduct such as defendant's should not be criminally prosecuted without a much clearer indication that this was the intent of the ordinance.)

1) Fate of "No Evidence" Approach

The **Thompson v. Louisville** "no evidence" approach has been employed in a subsequent case in which the Court held that there was "no evidence" that the defendant had intentionally sold an obscene button to a minor. [**Vachon v. New Hampshire**, 414 U.S. 478 (1974)] But the "no evidence" standard of federal constitutional due process for criminal convictions has been replaced by a standard requiring evidence showing guilt "beyond a reasonable doubt." [**Jackson v. Virginia**, 443 U.S. 307 (1979)]

EXAM TIP   **GILBERT**

For your exam, remember that the Supreme Court will *not review* a state court's finding of fact unless: the *finding and federal law are so intermingled* as to make review necessary or (ii) there is *no evidence* (or, in a criminal case, insufficient evidence to support a finding of proof beyond a reasonable doubt).

---

(3) Importance of Constitutional Rights

In cases involving constitutional rights, the Supreme Court sometimes refers to its "duty. . . to make its own independent examination of the record when federal constitutional deprivations are alleged." [**Napue v. Illinois**, 360 U.S. 264 (1959)] The Court has been particularly apt to reexamine the record in cases involving First Amendment rights. [**Jacobellis v. Ohio**, 378 U.S. 184 (1964); **Cox v. Louisiana**, *supra*, p. 93]

f. Final Judgment Rule

The statute authorizing Supreme Court review of state court decisions explicitly restricts review to "final judgments or decrees" of the state court. [28 U.S.C. § 1257] Nonfinal judgments are not reviewable. What constitutes a final judgment is a somewhat complicated matter.

(1) Purposes of Final Judgment Rule

(a) Efficiency

In the great majority of cases, it is more efficient to provide appellate review only after the conclusion of the litigation, rather than to review questions in a piecemeal fashion throughout the litigation.

(b) Federalism

In addition, there are important, though crosscutting, federalism arguments. For example, it is often argued that the operation of the state courts should not be interfered with unnecessarily. The final judgment rule helps serve this goal by preventing premature and potentially unnecessary intervention by the Supreme Court.

1) But Note

State courts cannot always be trusted to treat sympathetically claims of federal right. This second argument cuts the other way, suggesting that in some cases the Supreme Court should intervene early in a state court case to protect the litigant asserting a federal right.

(2) Distinguish—Final Judgment Requirement for Appeals from Lower Federal Courts

Appellate review within the federal court system is for the most part also limited to review of final judgments. [*See, e.g.,* 28 U.S.C. § 1291—courts of appeals have jurisdiction of appeals from "final decisions" of the district court] But there are two important differences in the operation of the final judgment rule in Supreme Court review of state cases and lower federal court cases:

(a) No Statutory or Rule Exceptions for State Courts

There are both statutory and rule exceptions to the finality requirement for *federal* court judgments. For example, 28 U.S.C. section 1292 explicitly provides for interlocutory review in certain cases, and Federal Rule of Civil Procedure 54(b) permits what amounts to interlocutory appeal for some claims or parties. Also, once a case reaches a court of appeals, the Supreme Court has the power to hear many cases before rendition of judgment by the court of appeals. [28 U.S.C. §§ 1254(1)—certiorari; 1254(2)—certified question] But there are *no comparable exceptions* set out in the statute governing review *of state* court judgments. Thus, there is considerable pressure for judge-made exceptions to the finality rule of 28 U.S.C. section 1257.

(b) Federalism Concerns Influence Application of the Rule to State Courts

The occasionally contradictory goals of protecting the state courts from federal interference, and protecting litigants who assert claims of federal right in unsympathetic state forums, exert complicated pressures on the final judgment rule that do not exist for judgments coming up from the lower federal courts.

(3) Traditional Doctrine

The traditional doctrine of the final judgment rule requires that there be a decision that "terminates the litigation between the parties on the merits of the case" and in which nothing remains to be done but to require the lower court to perform the "ministerial act" of entering the judgment. [**Mower v. Fletcher**, 114 U.S. 127 (1885)]

e.g. **Example:** A judgment directing dismissal of a case is final, in that the only action left to be taken in the case is the entry of the order. [**North Carolina Railroad v. Story**, 268 U.S. 288 (1925)]

cf. **Compare:** A judgment *denying dismissal* is *not* final because further proceedings will be had. [**Southern Pacific Co. v. Giles**, 351 U.S. 493 (1956)] Likewise, *interlocutory injunction orders* are not final. [**Georgia Railway & Power Co. v. Town of Decatur**, 262 U.S. 432 (1923)] (In federal courts, by contrast, interlocutory injunction orders may be reviewed under 28 U.S.C. section 1292.)

(4) Exceptions

Even before the final judgment rule was significantly relaxed (*see infra,* 96–98), some exceptions arose:

(a) Collateral Order

A ruling on a collateral order may be deemed final even when the case or principal case is still not concluded.

Example: The state court temporarily enjoined labor union picketing despite objections that the National Labor Relations Board had exclusive jurisdiction over the dispute. The Supreme Court found the issue of state power to proceed in the face of a federal preemption claim to be collateral to and separable from the underlying merits of the dispute. [**Local No. 438 Construction & General Laborers' Union v. Curry**, 371 U.S. 542 (1963)]

Example: A ruling in a state proceeding may sometimes be challenged in a collateral state proceeding such as an extraordinary writ rather than in an ordinary appeal. A final judgment in such a state collateral proceeding may be reviewed by the Supreme Court even if the principal case is still not concluded. [**Bandini Petroleum Co. v. Superior Court**, 284 U.S. 8 (1931)]

(b) Orders Subject to Immediate Execution and Imposing Substantial Hardship

A ruling may require that specific property rights be immediately transferred based on a ruling of federal law even though further proceedings are also contemplated. At least where such a transfer imposes substantial hardship, and where the issue of federal law is confined to the resolution of the question of the property transfer, the judgment will be considered final. [**Radio Station WOW v. Johnson**, 326 U.S. 120 (1945)]

(5) Relaxation of Final Judgment Rule—*Cox Broadcasting*

In **Cox Broadcasting Corp. v. Cohn**, 420 U.S. 469 (1975), the Supreme Court significantly relaxed the final judgment rule. The Court set out four categories of cases in which Supreme Court review would be permitted despite the absence of a formal final judgment:

(a) Practical Finality

If the state appellate court remands for further proceedings, but it is clear that the *federal issue* already decided is *conclusive* in any such proceedings, the judgment will be considered final.

Example: A state supreme court sustained a state utility rate-setting statute against a federal constitutional challenge, and remanded to the state public utilities commission for further rate-setting proceedings. The Supreme Court reviewed the state court judgment because it was satisfied that the state court judgment was the "state's last word" on the constitutionality of the statute. [**Duquesne Light Co. v. Barasch**, 488 U.S. 299 (1989)]

Example: A demurrer on federal grounds to a criminal complaint was sustained by the state trial court but reversed in the appellate court and remanded for trial. In this particular case, it was apparent that the defendant had no other legal or factual defense to the prosecution, and to deny immediate review by the Supreme Court would constitute "inexcusable delay." [**Mills v. Alabama**, 384 U.S. 214 (1966)]

(b) Federal Issue Will Necessarily Survive

If the federal issue will survive and require decision regardless of the outcome of further state proceedings, the judgment will be considered final.

Example: In **Radio Station WOW v. Johnson**, *supra*, p. 96, the question of federal law involved in the transfer of property rights would be presented in an appeal regardless of the outcome of the further proceedings.

(c) Federal Issue Will Not Survive

If the federal issue will *not* survive further proceedings, the judgment will be considered final.

Example: A criminal defendant appealed his conviction on the ground that his confession had been improperly admitted. The state appellate court reversed the conviction and remanded for trial without the use of the confession. If the defendant were convicted in the new trial, the admissibility of the confession would have been moot. If he were acquitted, the state could not have appealed because a retrial would have constituted double jeopardy. Therefore, the state was permitted to appeal the denial of admission of the confession despite the further proceedings. [**California v. Stuart**, 384 U.S. 436 (1966)]

(d) Serious Erosion of Federal Policy

If "the state court decision might seriously erode federal policy," it may be reviewed even if there is no final judgment.

Example: A state appellate court upheld the application of a state civil racketeering statute to sales of allegedly obscene material against a First Amendment challenge, and remanded for trial. The Supreme Court reviewed the decision on the ground that if the state First Amendment holding was ultimately unreviewable (as it would be if the defendant prevailed on other grounds at trial), the federal policy of "adjudicating the proper scope of First Amendment protections" might be seriously eroded. [**Fort Wayne Books v. Indiana**, 489 U.S. 46 (1989)]

Example: A state appellate court held that a workers' compensation award could be increased above the base level because of violations of state safety regulations, and remanded for consideration of whether the safety regulations had in fact been violated. The company subject to the award was a federal nuclear contractor who argued that such safety-based increases were preempted by federal law. The Supreme Court reviewed the decision on the ground that if the state court preemption holding was ultimately unreviewable (as it would be if no safety violations were found after remand), the "unreviewed decision . . . might seriously erode federal policy in the area of nuclear production." [**Goodyear Atomic Corp. v. Miller**, 486 U.S. 174 (1988)]

Example: The Supreme Court reviewed a state court temporary injunction of labor union picketing because "postponing review would seriously erode the national labor policy requiring the subject matter . . . to be heard by the [NLRB], not by the state courts." [**Local No. 438 Construction & General Laborers' Union v. Curry**, *supra*, p. 96]

SUMMARY OF FINAL JUDGMENT RULE	**GILBERT**

RULE:

The Supreme Court can review only *final judgments* of the state court.

TRADITIONAL APPROACH:

To be final, the state court's decision must *terminate the litigation* between the parties on the merits such that *nothing remains to be done except for the ministerial act of entering the judgment*.

EXCEPTIONS TO THE FINALITY RULE

- A ruling on a *collateral order* may be deemed final.

- A ruling subject to *immediate execution and imposing a substantial hardship* on a party may be deemed final.

RELAXATION OF RULE HAS OCCURRED IN THE FOLLOWING CASES

- *Practical finality:* If the state appellate court remands the case to a lower state court, but it is nonetheless clear that the *federal issue has been determined conclusively*, the judgment is deemed final.

- *Survival of federal issue:* If the federal issue *will necessarily survive* and require decision regardless of further state proceedings, the judgment is deemed final.

- *No survival of federal issue:* If the federal issue *will not survive* further state proceedings, the judgment is deemed final.

- *Erosion of federal policy:* If the state court decision would *seriously erode federal policy*, it may be reviewed even if there is no final judgment.

---

(6) Assessment of *Cox Broadcasting*

The Court in **Cox Broadcasting Corp. v. Cohn**, *supra*, was trying to give itself considerable discretion in deciding whether to review state court decisions, and at the same time trying to provide meaningful guidelines for the exercise of this discretion. But the four exceptions to the final judgment rule are not easy to understand and apply. The Court's decision in Cox *Broadcasting Corp.* may eventually produce sufficient confusion that the Court will need to try again to create a systematic approach to the final judgment rule for state courts.

g. Highest State Court

The statute authorizes Supreme Court review of decisions by the "highest court of a state in which a decision could be had." [28 U.S.C. § 1257] This language has two consequences:

(1) Litigants Must Appeal Within State System

A litigant may seek review in the Supreme Court only after she has appealed her case as far as possible *within the state court system.* Even if review by the highest state appellate court is discretionary, she must also seek review in that court.

(2) Highest State Court Need Not Be State Supreme Court

In some cases, appellate review may not be available above a certain level in the state court system. In that event, review in the United States Supreme Court may be sought from any state court, as long as it is the highest state court from which a decision may be had in the particular case.

Example: The Supreme Court may review a criminal conviction in the Louisville Police Court when no further appeal is permitted within the state court system. [**Thompson v. Louisville**, *supra,* p. 94]

2. Appellate Jurisdiction over Lower Federal Court Decisions

a. Introduction

The Supreme Court actually reviews considerably more cases brought up from the lower federal courts than from the state courts. But Federal Courts classes usually pay relatively little attention to this part of the Supreme Court's appellate jurisdiction. For the sake of completeness, the outlines of the Supreme Court's appellate jurisdiction over the lower federal courts will be sketched below, but the discussion will be brief.

b. General Character of Jurisdiction

Essentially, the Supreme Court has the power to hear any case over which the lower federal courts have jurisdiction. Unlike in its review of state court decisions, where it is limited to questions of federal law, the Court may decide *any* question of law, whether state or federal, in cases coming up from the lower federal courts. As a matter of practice, however, the Court ordinarily limits itself to important questions of federal law.

c. Courts of Appeals

By far the greatest number of cases come from the courts of appeals. Under the present statute, enacted in 1988, there are two types of appellate jurisdiction. [28 U.S.C. § 1254]

(1) Certiorari

The Supreme Court may review any decision of a court of appeals by the discretionary writ of certiorari. [28 U.S.C. § 1254(1)]

(2) Certification

A court of appeals may certify to the Supreme Court "any question of law . . . as to which instructions are desired." Such certification seeks an ***answer to a particular question*** rather than a review of the entire case. The procedure is employed infrequently. [28 U.S.C. § 1254(2)]

(3) Prior Statute

Under the prior version of 28 U.S.C. section 1254, some appeals from the courts of appeals were within the Supreme Court's mandatory appellate jurisdiction and some were within the discretionary writ of certiorari.

d. District Courts

Almost all appeals from a district court are to a court of appeals. However, one rare kind of case—those before three-judge district courts—can be appealed directly to the Supreme Court. These constitute the last surviving remnant of the Supreme Court's mandatory appellate jurisdiction.

(1) Historical Background of Three-Judge Court Statute

Before 1976, suits seeking to enjoin the operation of state statutes alleged to be unconstitutional were heard by three-judge district courts. Appeal was directly to the Supreme Court. [28 U.S.C. § 2281—now repealed] This appellate jurisdiction proved burdensome, and the Supreme Court sought in a variety of ways to narrow the operation of the statute. The general statute was finally repealed in 1976.

(2) Present Three-Judge Court Statute

There are a few scattered statutes that still provide for three-judge district courts and direct appeal to the Supreme Court. [*See, e.g.,* 28 U.S.C. § 2284(a)—suits challenging apportionment; 42 U.S.C. § 1973aa–2, b, c—suits challenging voting practices]

3. Certiorari and Appeal

Virtually all of the Supreme Court's jurisdiction is now *discretionary*, meaning that the applicable statutes permit but do not require the Court to review the case. This discretionary jurisdiction is called "certiorari." As noted above, only appeals from three-judge district courts are *mandatory,* meaning that the Court is required to review the case. This mandatory jurisdiction is called "appeal." (The "mandatory" nature of appeal was to some degree subverted by the Court even before adoption of the 1988 statute eliminating most of the Court's mandatory jurisdiction. *See infra,* pp. 8–15.)

a. Historical Background

Prior to 1891, all of the Supreme Court's appellate jurisdiction in relation to state courts was mandatory. The Evarts Act, passed in 1891, for the first time created a category of cases that the Court reviewed by writ of certiorari. In certiorari cases, the Court could decline to review a case if it did not present a question of sufficient importance. The category of cases that the Court reviews on certiorari has substantially increased since the Evarts Act. Before 1988, cases seeking review by writ of certiorari constituted about 90% of the cases in which appellate review was sought. Since 1988, virtually all review is by writ of certiorari.

b. Certiorari

(1) State and Federal Courts

The Supreme Court reviews cases from both the state and federal court systems by certiorari.

(2) Grant of Certiorari—"Rule of Four"

A grant of certiorari requires an affirmative vote of four Justices under the so-called rule of four. Votes for or against certiorari are rarely made public or explained, although a Justice will occasionally write a short dissent from a denial of certiorari explaining why the Justice thinks the case is "cert-worthy."

(3) Factors Leading to a Grant of Certiorari

The grant or denial of a writ of certiorari is entirely discretionary, although certain factors that will increase the chances of a grant of certiorari may be identified. Such factors include:

(a) *Split of authority among the federal circuit courts of appeal* [Supreme Court Rule 10(a)];

(b) *Split of authority between a state court and another state court or a federal court of appeals on a federal question* [Supreme Court Rule 10(b)]; and

(c) *Important unsettled question of federal law* [Supreme Court Rule 10(c)].

GRANTING CERTIORARI

THE SUPREME COURT IS MORE LIKELY TO GRANT CERTIORARI WHEN THERE IS:

- ☑ A *split of authority* among the *federal circuit courts of appeal*;
- ☑ A *split of authority* between a state court and another state court or a federal court of appeals *on a federal question*; and
- ☑ An *important unsettled question of federal law*.

---

(4) No Precedential Value

The denial of a writ of certiorari carries with it no indication of the Supreme Court's view of the merits, and it has no precedential value.

c. Appeal

Since there is little mandatory jurisdiction left, the following is for historical perspective. When the Supreme Court took a case for review on appeal, it was said to *"note probable jurisdiction."*

(1) State and Federal Courts

The Supreme Court reviewed cases from both the state and federal systems by appeal.

(2) "Rule of Four"

As with granting certiorari, noting probable jurisdiction required an affirmative vote of four Justices.

(3) Refusals to Note Probable Jurisdiction—Summary Dispositions

The Court frequently refused to take a case on appeal even though it was theoretically within its mandatory jurisdiction. In such cases, the Court made a "summary disposition" of the appeal. Such summary dispositions were made without full briefing of the case on the merits and without oral argument.

(a) State Court Decisions

In the cases coming up from the state courts, the Supreme Court used one of two rationales to justify a summary disposition:

1) Dismissal for Want of Substantial Federal Question

Typically, the Court deemed the federal question at issue in the appeal not to be substantial and dismissed the case for want of a *substantial federal question.* [**Zucht v. King**, 260 U.S. 174 (1922)]

2) Dismissal for Want of Properly Presented Federal Question

Sometimes the federal question was substantial, but was presented in such a way that the Court could not easily or readily resolve it. In such cases, the Court sometimes (though rarely) dismissed it for want of a *properly presented* federal question. [**Rescue Army v. Municipal Court of Los Angeles**, 331 U.S. 549 (1947)]

a) Note

On at least one occasion, the Court used the rationale of want of a properly presented federal question to avoid deciding a politically sensitive case. [**Naim v. Naim**, 350 U.S. 891 (1955)—refusing to hear case in which Virginia Supreme Court had sustained the constitutionality of Virginia law forbidding interracial marriage] This use of the power to dismiss a politically sensitive case because of an assertedly improperly presented federal question has been the subject of intense academic debate.

(b) Lower Federal Court Decisions

When the Supreme Court desired to make a summary disposition of an appeal from a lower federal court, it employed a different vocabulary. Rather than "dismiss for want of a substantial federal question" as it did for state court cases, the Court summarily *affirmed.* Such "summary affirmances" were made without full briefing of the case on the merits and without oral argument.

(c) Precedential Value of Summary Dispositions

In disposing summarily of appeals, the Supreme Court obviously gave short shrift to those cases. For many years, it was an open secret that the Court treated much of its appeal jurisdiction as it treated its certiorari jurisdiction, taking only the cases of greatest significance and refusing to hear the remainder. The sheer number of cases for which review was sought meant that the Court disposed summarily of most of the cases appealed to it, even after **Hicks v. Miranda,** *infra.*

1) Decisions on the Merits

In **Hicks v. Miranda**, 422 U.S. 332 (1975), the Court held that summary dispositions of appealed cases, unlike decisions to grant or deny certiorari, were decisions on the merits.

2) Precedential Value in Lower Courts

The Court also held that lower courts were bound by the Supreme Court's summary dispositions in appealed cases, despite the lack of oral argument and briefing and the lack of an opinion by the Court. [**Hicks v. Miranda**, *supra*]

3) Precedential Value in Supreme Court

However, the Supreme Court itself does not accord to a summary disposition the same precedential value it accords to a plenary disposition with full opinion. [*See* **Edelman v. Jordan**, 415 U.S. 651 (1974)] In other words, the Court more readily disregards or overrules a summary disposition than a decision rendered after plenary review.

4) Effect on Justiciability Doctrines

In the great majority of cases, the Supreme Court avoided review in mandatory appeals by refusing to note probable jurisdiction, as just described. Sometimes, however, the Court used justiciability doctrines to avoid review in mandatory appeals. In such cases, the Court would find that the plaintiff lacked standing or that the case was unripe or moot. A sophisticated reading of the Court's justiciability decisions will take into account whether the case was within the Court's mandatory appellate jurisdiction. The Court sometimes stretched or distorted justiciability doctrines to avoid having to take a case within its mandatory jurisdiction. (*See* discussion *supra,* pp. 53–54, of Professor Bickel's famous "passive virtues.")

5) Grant, Vacate, and Remand

In an increasingly common disposition, the Court will *grant* certiorari, *vacate* the opinion below, and *remand* to that court for further proceedings. These grant, vacate, and remand (*"GVR"*) dispositions often direct lower court reconsideration of an issue in light of the Court's own resolution of a similar issue in another case. Note that the Court may also vote to "hold" a case (*i.e.,* delay acting on it) until another case that raises similar legal issues is resolved. If the resolution of the second case affects the law applied in the "held" case, the Court may then dispose of the held case by GVR.

e.g. **Example:** After the Court overturned an award of punitive damages, in **State Farm Mutual Insurance Co. v. Campbell**, 538 U.S. 408 (2003), it disposed by GVR of 10 cases in which petitions for review were being "held" by the Court. These GVRs required the lower court to reconsider their prior rulings in light of the decision in *Campbell.*

(d) Justification

"Holds" can be important in direct review of state court criminal convictions. Denial of certiorari in such cases terminates direct review and triggers the application of a more deferential standard of federal habeas corpus review. Holds and GVRs ensure application of the direct review standard to cases that the Court regards as similarly situated.

(e) Criticism

The use of holds and GVRs makes less sense on the civil side, at least where the final judgment rule has been relaxed and parties can pursue forms of interlocutory review. As to nonfinal judgments, state proceedings remain open to take account of any change in the law.

(f) Possible Extension

The Court used the GVR process in **Youngblood v. West Virginia**, 547 U.S. 867 (2006), apparently after concluding that the state supreme court had failed to address the defendant's constitutional challenge to the non-disclosure of exculpatory evidence. Dissenters criticized use of the GVR where no intervening decision or event had occurred.

B. Original Jurisdiction of the Supreme Court

1. Introduction

The Supreme Court has a seldom-invoked jurisdiction in which it acts as a court of original jurisdiction—*i.e.*, as a trial court. On the average, no more than two or three original jurisdiction cases per year are brought before the Court. The Court refers them to special masters who take evidence and submit proposed rulings to the Court. The Court is reluctant to take original jurisdiction cases and it frequently declines to hear a case within its jurisdiction if an alternative forum is available.

2. Constitutional Basis

Article III provides, "In all cases affecting Ambassadors, other public Ministers and Consuls, and those in which a state shall be a Party, the Supreme Court shall have original jurisdiction." [U.S. Const, art. HI, § 2, cl. 2] The most important part of the Court's original jurisdiction is suits between the states.

EXAM TIP   **GILBERT**

For your exam, remember that although the Supreme Court can act as a trial court—in cases within its *original jurisdiction*—this is very rare. The most important class of cases falling within the original jurisdiction of the Supreme Court is *suits between the states*.

---

3. Self-Executing

The Court's original jurisdiction is commonly assumed to be self-executing. That is, the jurisdiction is not dependent upon any statutory authorization for its existence and exercise. Nevertheless, Congress has prescribed the Court's original jurisdiction and has divided it between exclusive and concurrent jurisdiction. [28 U.S.C. § 1251; *see* below]

4. Exclusive and Concurrent Jurisdiction

The Court's original jurisdiction is divided into exclusive and concurrent jurisdiction. Where it is concurrent and a lower federal court has heard the case as an original matter, the case may later be heard by the Supreme Court as part of its appellate jurisdiction.

a. Historical Background—Treatment in *Marbury v. Madison*

Chief Justice Marshall wrote in **Marbury v. Madison** (*supra,* p. 13), that the division contained in Article III between the Supreme Court's original and appellate jurisdiction could not be altered by Congress. What was designated by Article III as appellate could not be made original, and what was original could not be made appellate. The first proposition—that the Court's appellate jurisdiction described in Article III could not be made original by statute—was the basis for the Court's holding in *Marbury* and remains true today. The second proposition—that the Court's original jurisdiction could not be made appellate—is no longer good law. As is discussed, *infra,* much of the original jurisdiction described in Article III is now concurrent with the lower federal and state courts. It is thus exercised as appellate jurisdiction by the Supreme Court when cases are brought in the original jurisdiction of the lower courts and review is later obtained in the Supreme Court.

b. Present Statutory Division

(1) Exclusive Original Jurisdiction

Under the present statute, the Supreme Court has exclusive original jurisdiction over controversies between two or more states. [28 U.S.C. § 1251 (a)]

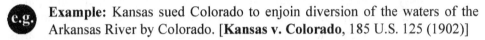 **Example:** Kansas sued Colorado to enjoin diversion of the waters of the Arkansas River by Colorado. [**Kansas v. Colorado**, 185 U.S. 125 (1902)]

Example: Kentucky sued Indiana to require Indiana to perform a contract between the two states to build a bridge across the Ohio River. [**Kentucky v. Indiana**, 281 U.S. 163 (1930)]

Example: New Jersey sued New York to quiet title to Ellis Island, located in New York Harbor. The Court ruled that New York retained title to the original land mass, but that the portion of the island that had been expanded by landfill belonged to New Jersey. [**New Jersey v. New York**, 523 U.S. 767 (1998)]

(2) Concurrent Original Jurisdiction

Under the present statute, the Supreme Court has concurrent original jurisdiction (with the state and lower federal courts) over three kinds of suits:

(a) Ambassadors, etc., Are Parties

"[A]ctions or proceedings to which ambassadors, other public ministers, consuls, or vice-consuls of foreign states are parties" are within the Court's concurrent original jurisdiction. [28 U.S.C. § 1251(b)(1)]

(b) United States and a State Are Parties

"Controversies between the United States and a State" are within the Court's concurrent original jurisdiction. [28 U.S.C. § 1251(b)(2)]

Example: The United States sued to establish title to land claimed by Texas. [**United States v. Texas**, 143 U.S. 621 (1982)]

(c) State Suing out-of-State Citizen or Alien

"[A]ctions or proceedings by a State against the citizens of another State or against aliens" are within the Court's concurrent original jurisdiction. [28 U.S.C. $1251(b)(3)]

Example: South Carolina sued the United States Attorney General, challenging the Voting Rights Act of 1965. The Attorney General was a citizen of another state. [**South Carolina v. Katzenbach**, *supra,* p. 18]

Example: Georgia sued 20 out-of-state railroad corporations alleging violation of the federal antitrust laws. [**Georgia v. Pennsylvania Railroad**, 324 U.S. 439 (1945)]

1) Distinguish—State as Defendant

When a state *is sued* by a citizen of another state or an alien, the Eleventh Amendment severely restricts the ability of any federal court (including the Supreme Court) to hear the case. (*See infra,* pp. 287 *et seq.*)

5. Discretionary Refusal to Exercise Jurisdiction

The Supreme Court often refuses to hear cases within its original jurisdiction. When it refuses to hear such cases, it employs the procedural mechanism of denying leave to file an action.

a. Concurrent Jurisdiction

Most of the cases the Court refuses to hear are within its concurrent original jurisdiction.

Example: The Supreme Court refused to hear a suit brought by Ohio against several out-of-state chemical companies to remedy mercury pollution in Lake Erie. The Court noted the complicated nature of the environmental issues involved, pointed out that the suit could be filed in other courts, and noted that the Supreme Court was much better adapted to sitting as an appellate rather than a trial court. [**Ohio v. Wyandotte Chemicals Corp.**, 401 U.S. 493 (1971)]

Example: Illinois sued four Wisconsin cities to abate pollution allegedly caused by them. The Supreme Court refused to take the case, noting that the merits of the case arose under federal law and that the federal district court had concurrent jurisdiction. [**Illinois v. City of Milwaukee**, 406 U.S. 91 (1972)]

Example: The United States sued California and Nevada for a declaration of rights to waters of a river flowing into and out of Lake Tahoe. The Supreme Court refused to take the case, noting that the federal district court had jurisdiction over the principal dispute. [**United States v. Nevada**, 412 U.S. 534 (1973)]

EXAM TIP　　　　　　　　　　　　　　　　　　　　　　　　**GILBERT**

It is important to note that even though a case may fall within the Supreme Court's original jurisdiction, and even though the case is one that the Supreme Court would be more inclined to hear (*e.g.,* a suit between the states), the Court *may decline jurisdiction,* and will be more inclined to do so if there is another court with subject matter jurisdiction.

---

b. Exclusive Jurisdiction

The Supreme Court has even refused to hear a case within its exclusive original jurisdiction. Arizona sought to enjoin New Mexico from taxing electricity generated in New Mexico but sold in Arizona. The Court noted that there was a pending state court suit in which private utilities challenged the New Mexico tax. Thus, although the actual case sought to be brought was within the exclusive original jurisdiction of the Court, the *issues* in the case were being litigated concurrently. [**Arizona v. New Mexico**, 425 U.S. 794 (1976)]

6. "Original" Writs of Mandamus and Habeas Corpus

Since 1789, the Supreme Court and its Justices have had the authority to entertain "original" petitions for mandamus and habeas corpus. These petitions begin with an initial filing at the Court, but they operate as appellate proceedings. The key to understanding their appellate quality is to recall that Article III forbids original mandamus in the Supreme Court to review the actions of **federal executive officials**. [**Marbury v. Madison,** *supra*] On the other hand, the Court has used mandamus and habeas petitions to "revise and correct" the work of **lower courts**. [*Ex parte* **Bollman**, 8 U.S. 75 (1807)] Though sometimes described as "original" writs when directed at lower courts, mandamus and habeas corpus operate in functional terms as an exercise of the Court's appellate jurisdiction.

Chapter Five

District Court Subject Matter Jurisdiction

Key Exam Issues

Subject matter jurisdiction is an important topic on Federal Courts exams. You must keep in mind: (i) a federal court *must have subject matter jurisdiction* to exercise judicial power, and (ii) this requirement *cannot be waived*. The two most important kinds of subject matter jurisdiction are:

1. **Federal Question Jurisdiction**

   The outer *constitutional* boundaries of federal question jurisdiction are somewhat unclear. To understand the nature of these boundaries, pay close attention to the *Osborn case, bankruptcy jurisdiction,* and the concept of *protective jurisdiction.* The *statutory* boundaries of federal question jurisdiction are narrower, but in some cases equally difficult to describe with precision. In analyzing this issue, pay close attention to the meaning of *"arising under"* federal law, the *well-pleaded complaint rule,* and the operation of the well-pleaded complaint rule in *declaratory judgment cases.*

2. **Diversity Jurisdiction**

   The constitutional and statutory boundaries of diversity jurisdiction are relatively clear. However, the doctrines involved can be quite complex. In studying this topic, pay close attention to what constitutes citizenship for both *natural and artificial persons,* and to the methods for determining whether the *jurisdictional amount* (over $75,000) has been satisfied.

An important tip for all examination questions involving issues of district court subject matter jurisdiction: Such questions often also involve issues of *supplemental jurisdiction, removal jurisdiction, venue,* and *forum non conveniens.* (These doctrines are covered in the next chapter.) Remember to think of *all* of these issues as part of the basic preliminary question of whether a district court may hear the suit.

A. Introduction to Subject Matter Jurisdiction of Federal District Courts

1. In General

The federal district courts are the basic trial courts of the federal court system. Their subject matter jurisdiction over civil cases rests on two *primary* bases: federal question and diversity. Their jurisdiction over civil cases also includes other bases such as admiralty.

EXAM TIP   **⬛GILBERT**

Be careful not to write something on your exam that you don't really mean! For example, many students, when discussing federal subject jurisdiction, will write something along the lines of: "A federal court is a court of limited subject matter jurisdiction. The two bases for federal subject matter jurisdiction are federal question jurisdiction and diversity of citizenship jurisdiction." Although such a statement, alone, probably would not affect the final grade, it does misrepresent federal subject matter jurisdiction: Federal question jurisdiction and diversity of citizenship aren't the **only** bases, they're the two **primary** bases.

---

a. Jurisdiction of Courts of Appeals

For purposes of this outline, it is unnecessary to consider separately the jurisdiction of the federal circuit courts of appeals. Except for appeals to the courts of appeals from decisions of federal administrative agencies, the jurisdiction of the courts of appeals is essentially commensurate with that of the district courts.

2. Courts of Limited Jurisdiction

The district courts are courts of limited jurisdiction. Jurisdiction must be explicitly conferred upon them for them to hear a case.

a. Contrast with State Trial Courts

State trial courts, by contrast, are typically courts of *general* jurisdiction. That is, state courts are typically authorized to hear any judicially cognizable dispute without the necessity for separate and explicit authorization of jurisdiction for each category of case.

3. Importance of Limitations on District Court Subject Matter Jurisdiction

The limited nature of the federal district courts' subject matter jurisdiction has been referred to as the "first principle" of federal jurisdiction.

a. Sua Sponte Inquiry

If the parties fail to raise a defect in subject matter jurisdiction, the federal courts have a *duty* to raise and decide the point sua sponte. [**Mansfield, Coldwater & Lake Michigan Railway v. Swan**, 111 U.S. 379 (1884)]

b. Defect Not Waivable

Parties cannot waive a defect in subject matter jurisdiction. This basic principle is incorporated into Federal Rule of Civil Procedure 12(h)(3).

c. Jurisdiction Not Conferred by Agreement

Parties cannot confer subject matter jurisdiction by agreement. [**Owen Equipment & Erection Co. v. Kroger**, 437 U.S. 365 (1978)]

d. Defect Can Be Raised for First Time on Appeal

A defect in subject matter jurisdiction can be raised in the court of appeals, even if it has not been raised in the district court. The Supreme Court has taken this principle so far as to hold that a party who has invoked the district court's subject matter jurisdiction and then lost on the merits may successfully move in the court of appeals to dismiss the case for want of subject matter jurisdiction. [**American Fire & Casualty Co. v. Finn**, 341 U.S. 6 (1951)—defendant removed to federal court, lost on the merits, and successfully appealed the judgment on the ground that the district court lacked subject matter jurisdiction]

e. Criticism of "First Principle" of Federal Jurisdiction

The ability of the parties, and the duty of the federal court, to raise a defect in subject matter jurisdiction at any stage in the proceedings has been heavily criticized by academic commentators. [*See, e.g.,* American Law Institute, *Study of the Division of Jurisdiction Between State and Federal Courts* 366 (1968)—"This fetish of federal jurisdiction is wholly inconsistent with sound judicial administration and can only serve to diminish respect for a system that tolerates it"] Despite such criticism, however, the strength of this "first principle" of federal jurisdiction remains unimpaired.

4. Rejection of "Hypothetical" Jurisdiction

As a consequence of Article III's limits, federal courts ordinarily must satisfy themselves at the outset of the litigation that they have subject matter jurisdiction, even where the parties fail to raise the issue. This view of subject matter jurisdiction as a structural limit forecloses the federal courts from assuming the existence of federal jurisdiction for purposes of resolving the case on the merits, even if the merits disposition would provide an easier and more obvious basis for resolving the case. [**Steel Co. v. Citizens for a Better Environment**, 523 U.S. 83 (1998)]

a. Breadth of Hypothetical Jurisdictional Bar Uncertain

It is unclear how far this prohibition against the use of hypothetical jurisdiction extends. District courts may reach other issues, such as the lack of personal jurisdiction, when those issues offer an easier and more obvious legal basis for disposing of the case than a difficult question of subject matter jurisdiction. [**Ruhrgas AG v. Marathon Oil Co.**, 526 U.S. 574 (1999)] Unlike the alternative basis for decision in *Steel Co., supra,* the personal jurisdiction issue in *Ruhrgas AG* did not go to the merits of the dispute and thus posed little threat that a court might bootstrap its way into a merits resolution of an action over which it lacked jurisdiction.

b. Other Issues That Pose Hypothetical Jurisdiction Problems

A variety of threshold issues might provide a more straightforward disposition that would enable the district court to avoid a difficult issue of subject matter jurisdiction and thus pose hypothetical jurisdiction problems. For example, district courts have discretion to dismiss for forum non conveniens, thereby refusing to exercise jurisdiction on the ground that the litigation should proceed in a more convenient forum. Also, defendants may argue that they enjoy state sovereign or official immunity from suit.

5. Scrutinizing Jurisdictional Characterizations

In part due to the significant consequences outlined above (p. 111), proposed jurisdictional characterizations now attract closer scrutiny. Rather than simply treating as jurisdictional every limit on the power of a federal court to hear a particular matter, the Court recognizes that some limits may operate less as jurisdictional limits than as rules to govern the processing of claims. Such claim-processing rules may be subject to waiver and equitable defenses that would be unavailable if a limit were characterized as jurisdictional.

a. Factors That Inform the Characterization Process

The Court has identified factors that aid in the characterization process. In general, claim processing rules, such as time limits, may be viewed as merely mandatory, rather than jurisdictional (meaning that the court will enforce the limit if it has been properly preserved for decision, but has no obligation to raise the limit on its own). If the time limit appears in a federal statute, however, the Court may be more likely to regard it as jurisdictional, especially if it qualifies a grant of jurisdiction to an Article III court.

 Example: Federal bankruptcy rules prescribe a time for filing complaints objecting to a debtor's discharge. The rule was not jurisdictional. [**Kontrick v. Ryan**, 540 U.S. 443 (2004)]

Example: Time limit for filing a motion for a new trial, specified in federal rules of civil procedure, was not jurisdictional. [**Eberhart v. United States**, 546 U.S. 12 (2005)]

Compare: Time limits for filing a notice of appeal, specified in 28 U.S.C. section 2107 **were jurisdictional.** [**Bowles v. Russell**, 551 U.S. 205 (2007)— emphasizing that the time limit in question appeared in a federal statute, rather than a rule of practice, and operated to restrict the authority of an Article III court]

Compare: Time limit for filing an administrative appeal by Medicare providers seeking to challenge amount of their reimbursement was **non-jurisdictional**, despite its having been set forth in a federal statute. [**Sebelius v. Auburn Regional Medical Center**, 568 U.S. 145 (2013)—concluding that the statutory 180 day time limit, which had been enlarged to three years by regulation, was neither jurisdictional nor subject to equitable tolling]

Compare: Federal statute prescribing time limit for filing an appeal with the Veterans Court, an Article I tribunal, did not operate as a jurisdictional requirement. [**Henderson v. Shinseki**, 562 U.S. 428 (2011)]

Compare: When the time limit was specified in a rule of court, rather than an act of Congress, the Supreme Court rejected its characterization as jurisdictional. [**Hamer v. Neighborhood Housing Services of Chicago**, 138 S.Ct. 13 (2017)]

Compare: Even statutory time limits may be subject to equitable tolling. The Federal Tort Claims Act specifies that individuals pursuing tort claims against the United States must file notice of claim with the relevant agency two years after the claim accrues and must file suit within six months after the agency acts. Over the government's objection, both time limits were held subject to equitable tolling. The Court gave voice to a rebuttable presumption in favor of viewing statutory time limits as subject to tolling and found that the presumption had not been overcome by a clear statement in the applicable statute. [**United States v. Kwai Fun Wong**, 135 S.Ct. 1625 (2015)]

EXAM TIP   GILBERT

Keep in mind the various factors that apparently inform the Court's approach. It will be more likely to treat as jurisdictional those limits that appear in a federal statute, that qualify the power of an Article III court, and that expressly speak in terms of the court's jurisdiction. A finding of non-jurisdictionality does not automatically trigger equitable tolling.

B. Federal Question Jurisdiction

1. In General

Federal question jurisdiction is *authorized* by Article III of the Constitution and is specifically *conferred* on the district courts by statute. With the exception of a statute passed in 1801 and repealed the next year, Congress did not confer general original federal question jurisdiction on the federal trial courts until 1875. The scope of the constitutionally authorized federal question jurisdiction is broader than that conferred by statute. The constitutional and statutory bases for the jurisdiction will be considered in turn.

2. Constitutional Basis

a. Article III

Article III of the Constitution provides that the "judicial power" shall extend to cases "arising under this constitution, the Laws of the United States, and Treaties made, or which shall be made under their Authority." [U.S. Const, art. III, § 2, cl. 1]

b. Scope of Constitutional Authorization

The constitutionally authorized federal question jurisdiction is quite broad. However, there are relatively few cases and areas of law in which the Supreme Court has explored the outer boundaries of the jurisdiction. These cases are considered below.

(1) *Osborn v. Bank of United States*

When Congress created the Bank of the United States by statute, in the same statute it authorized the Bank to sue and be sued in the federal courts. This jurisdictional authorization was not limited to cases involving some substantive federal right; the Bank could also sue in federal court on such things as ordinary contract claims under state law. The question in *Osborn* was whether such state law-based suits "arose under" federal law within the meaning of the constitutional grant in Article III. Chief Justice Marshall wrote that Congress could confer federal question jurisdiction over suits brought by the Bank because the Bank owed its existence to federal law. [**Osborn v. Bank of United States**, 22 U.S. (9 Wheat.) 738 (1824)]

(a) Broad Reading of Article III

Although in many cases the only disputed issues would depend on state law, Marshall reasoned that the Bank's capacity to act depended on federal law. Thus, the question of the Bank's capacity to act "forms an original ingredient in every cause. Whether [the question] be, in part, relied on or not, in the defense, it is still a part of the cause, and may be relied on." Thus, for Marshall, the *possibility* that a question of federal law might arise was sufficient to satisfy the "arising under" jurisdictional authorization of Article III.

1) Note

In *Osborn* itself, Marshall's discussion was dictum, for in that case the Bank had challenged a state taxation scheme on the ground that it interfered with the operation of the Bank in violation of **McCulloch v. Maryland**, 17 U.S. (4 Wheat.) 316 (1819). But in a companion case, the Bank sued on a purely state law claim for payment of certain notes. Thus, as to this companion case, Marshall's discussion was part of the holding. [**Bank of the United States v. Planters' Bank of Georgia**, 22 U.S. (9 Wheat.) 904 (1824)]

(b) Possible Rationale—Federal Instrumentality

One can argue that federal question jurisdiction was proper in *Osborn* because the Bank was a federal instrumentality that deserved the protection of a federal forum. The Bank was indeed an instrument of federal policy, and it was true that Congress authorized the Bank to sue in federal court because it was legitimately concerned about the extreme hostility of many states to the Bank. However, Marshall's opinion did not rely on the federal instrumentality rationale.

(c) Present Status

Justice Frankfurter criticized *Osborn,* contending that it adopted too expansive a view of the federal question jurisdiction authorized by Article III. [*See* **Textile Workers' Union v. Lincoln Mills**, 353 U.S. 448 (1957)—Frankfurter, J., dissenting] But the Supreme Court has recently reaffirmed *Osborn.* The federal statutory charter of the American National Red Cross authorizes it "to sue and be sued" in federal court. Relying on the charter, plaintiffs sued the Red Cross and other defendants in federal district court under state law, alleging that they had contracted AIDS from blood supplied by the Red Cross. Citing the "long-standing and settled rule" of *Osborn,* the Court held that federal incorporation was a sufficient basis for federal question jurisdiction. [**American National Red Cross v. S.G.**, 505 U.S. 247(1992)]

(2) *Pacific Railroad Removal Cases*

In 1875, Congress passed a statute giving the federal trial courts general original and removal jurisdiction over cases arising under federal law. The question arose soon thereafter whether railroads with a federal charter of incorporation were entitled to sue or be sued in federal court under the new statute. The Court held that federally chartered railroads were entitled to remove ordinary tort suits to federal court under the new federal question statute. [**Pacific Railroad Removal Cases**, *supra,* p. 6]

(a) Present Status

Congress later overturned the result in the *Pacific Railroad Removal Cases* by passing a statute that explicitly provided that a federal charter of incorporation was *not by itself a sufficient basis* for general federal question jurisdiction. The Supreme Court has also expressed doubt about the correctness of the original decision in the *Pacific Railroad Removal Cases.* [*See* **Gully v. First National Bank in Meridian**, 299 U.S. 109 (1936)—"Only recently we said after full consideration that the doctrine of the charter cases was to be treated as exceptional . . . ."]

(3) Bankruptcy Jurisdiction

Federal district courts for many years have had the power to decide bankruptcy cases in which no question of federal law is at issue. Such cases are typically brought by the trustee for the estate of the bankrupt against those who owe money to the bankrupt under state law.

(a) Constitutionality of Bankruptcy Jurisdiction

In **Northern Pipeline Construction Co. v. Marathon Pipe Line Co.**, *supra,* p. 81, the Supreme Court held that non-Article III federal judges could not adjudicate bankruptcy claims based on state law. Such cases had to be decided by Article III judges. The constitutionality of the exercise of this jurisdiction by the federal district courts was assumed without discussion.

(b) Elusive Rationale for Bankruptcy Jurisdiction

Although the constitutional power of the federal district court to hear such a case has never been in serious doubt, the rationale for bankruptcy jurisdiction has always been elusive.

1) Justice Frankfurter's View

In his dissent in **Textile Workers' Union v. Lincoln Mills**, *supra,* p. 115, Justice Frankfurter justified district court jurisdiction over state law-based bankruptcy claims by calling it "analytically outside the 'federal question' category, but sufficiently related to the main purpose of bankruptcy to call for comprehensive treatment." Frankfurter also suggested that all suits brought by a bankruptcy trustee (some of which might be based on federal law) could be regarded as "one litigation" to collect the assets of the bankrupt. If bankruptcy litigation is so regarded, individual suits based on state law could be "analogized to . . . ancillary or pendent jurisdiction cases."

2) Justice Jackson's View

In his plurality opinion in **National Mutual Insurance Co. v. Tidewater Transfer Co.**, *supra,* p. 74, Justice Jackson argued that jurisdiction over bankruptcy cases based on state law was not authorized by Article III. Rather, he argued, Congress in the exercise of its Article I powers could confer additional jurisdiction on an Article III court. (*See* discussion of *Tidewater, supra,* p. 74, but recall that the majority of the Court disagreed with Jackson's conclusion that an Article III court outside the District of Columbia could exercise jurisdiction not authorized by Article III.)

(4) Protective Jurisdiction

It has been argued that Congress has the power to confer federal question jurisdiction on the district courts to hear claims based on state law under a theory of "protective jurisdiction." Justice Frankfurter discussed, and rejected, the concept of protective jurisdiction in his dissent in **Textile Workers' Union v. Lincoln Mills**, *supra,* but the Court as a whole did not rule on the issue. Two versions of protective jurisdiction have been suggested by academic commentators:

(a) Professor Wechsler's Position

Professor Wechsler has suggested that the federal courts should be able to exercise a "protective jurisdiction" over matters of federal concern in "all cases in which Congress has authority to make the rule to govern disposition of the controversy" but has allowed the states' substantive laws to govern the dispute and has conferred jurisdiction in the federal courts to enforce the state laws. [Wechsler, *Federal Jurisdiction and the Revision of the Judicial Code,* 13 Law & Contemp. Probs. 216 (1948)]

(b) Professor Mishkin's Version

In a variant of Professor Wechsler's position, Professor Mishkin has suggested that protective jurisdiction should be available to allow federal courts to decide cases based on state law only when there is "an articulated and active federal policy regulating a field." [Mishkin, *The Federal "Question" in the District Courts,* 53 Colum. L. Rev. 57 (1953)]

(c) Relevance to *Osborn* and to Bankruptcy

A theory of "protective jurisdiction," if adopted, would justify the exercise of jurisdiction challenged in *Osborn,* as well as the federal district court's exercise of jurisdiction over bankruptcy cases based on state law.

(d) Judicial Reluctance to Embrace Protective Jurisdiction

Although the Court has had opportunities to do so, it has refused to embrace protective jurisdiction under Article III.

Example: Federal postal workers removed a state criminal proceeding without asserting any federal defense. The Court held that jurisdiction was unavailable under the statute, unless the officers raised a substantial federal claim or defense. It did so to avoid the constitutional issue that would arise from the assertion of removal jurisdiction over a proceeding that was entirely dependent on state law. The Court rejected the government's argument that such jurisdiction was appropriate to protect federal officers from possible bias in the application of state law. [**Mesa v. California**, 489 U.S. 121 (1989)]

(5) Supplemental Jurisdiction

Supplemental jurisdiction, the statutory embodiment of the former pendent and ancillary jurisdiction, permits federal district courts to adjudicate certain state law claims for which there is no independent jurisdictional basis in Article III. (*See infra,* pp. 146 *et seq.*)

(a) Test

In **United Mine Workers v. Gibbs**, *supra,* p. 76, the Supreme Court permitted the federal district court to adjudicate a state law claim in a nondiversity suit because it was related to a claim over which the court had federal question jurisdiction. The constitutional test applied by the Court was whether, in a case over which there was already federal court jurisdiction, state and federal law claims derived from a "common nucleus of operative fact."

3. Statutory Basis

a. General Original Federal Question Jurisdiction

The general original federal question jurisdictional statute is written in words that parallel the grant of federal question jurisdiction in Article III. The statute provides, "The district courts shall have original jurisdiction of all civil actions arising under the constitution, laws, or treaties of the United States." [28 U.S.C. § 1331]

(1) Narrower than the Constitutional Grant

Despite the parallel wording, the statutory grant of federal question jurisdiction under section 1331 has been construed to grant less than the full extent of the federal question jurisdiction authorized by Article III. [**Verlinden B.V. v. Central Bank of Nigeria**, 461 U.S. 480 (1983)]

(2) Federal Common Law Can Provide Basis for Jurisdiction

The basic federal question jurisdiction statute refers to the "constitution, laws, or treaties of the United States." Federal common law is federal law for purposes of federal question jurisdiction. (See *infra,* pp. 200 *et seq.,* for discussion of federal common law.)

b. Other Grants of Original Jurisdiction

In addition to the general federal question jurisdiction statute quoted above (section 1331), there are a number of other statutes granting jurisdiction over specific kinds of federal question suits, *e.g.:* 28 U.S.C. section 1338(a) (patent and copyright); section 1339 (postal service); section 1340 (internal revenue); and section 1343 (civil rights). In general, the rules of construction governing jurisdiction conferred by these statutes are similar to those governing jurisdiction conferred by the general federal question jurisdiction statute.

c. Concurrent and Exclusive Jurisdiction

Unless specifically stated otherwise, statutes conferring federal question jurisdiction on the federal courts confer a jurisdiction *concurrent with the state courts.* (*See infra,* pp. 214 *et seq.*) If there is concurrent jurisdiction, a plaintiff may choose to file her suit in either federal or state court (subject to a right of removal; *see infra,* pp. 158 *et seq.*).

(1) Examples of Concurrent Jurisdiction

General federal question jurisdiction (section 1331) and civil rights jurisdiction (section 1343) are concurrent with the state courts.

(2) Examples of Exclusive Jurisdiction

Bankruptcy proceedings (section 1334) and patent and copyright cases (section 1338(a)) are within the exclusive jurisdiction of the federal courts because the statute explicitly so provides.

(3) Anomalous Example of Exclusive Jurisdiction

Federal antitrust cases are within the exclusive jurisdiction of the federal courts even though no federal statute explicitly so provides. [**Freeman v. Bee Machine Co.**, 319 U.S. 448 (1943)]

d. Scope of Statutory Original Federal Question Jurisdiction

No satisfactory single test has been formulated to describe the scope of statutory original federal question jurisdiction. Several tests have been proposed.

(1) Cause of Action Test

Justice Holmes suggested that federal question "arising under" jurisdiction should exist when federal law *creates the cause of action.* [**American Well Works Co. v. Layne & Bowler Co.**, 241 U.S. 257 (1916)]

(a) Criticism

The Holmes "cause of action" test has proved too narrow, for it excludes from district court jurisdiction some cases in which the cause of action is created by state law, but whose decision actually depends upon the resolution of a question of federal law.

(b) Present Status

The Supreme Court described the Holmes "cause of action" test as "more useful for describing the vast majority of cases that come within the district courts' original jurisdiction than it is for describing which cases are beyond district court jurisdiction." [**Franchise Tax Board v. Construction Laborers Vacation Trust**, 463 U.S. 1 (1983)] In other words, if a case satisfies the "cause of action" test, it is almost certainly within the district court's jurisdiction; but it may be within the court's jurisdiction even if the "cause of action" test is not satisfied.

(2) "Depends upon the Construction or Application" of Federal Law

Some cases do not arise under federal law in the sense intended by Justice Holmes because state law creates the cause of action relied upon. Yet the decision in such cases may depend substantially, or even entirely, upon the determination of a disputed question of federal law. If it appears from the plaintiff's complaint that the decision in a case "depends upon the construction or application of the Constitution or laws of the United States," then the federal district court has federal question jurisdiction. [**Smith v. Kansas City Title & Trust Co.**, 255 U.S. 180 (1921)] But as the following examples show, this test is easier to state than apply.

Example: A shareholder derivative suit sought to enjoin a corporation from purchasing bonds alleged to be invalid. The right to enjoin a corporation from engaging in such behavior was based on state law. However, the bonds in question were federal bonds that plaintiff contended were invalid under federal law, and the only matter actually in dispute was the validity of the bonds. The Supreme Court held that the district court had federal question jurisdiction. [**Smith v. Kansas City Title & Trust Co.**, *supra*]

Compare: State law tort actions were brought against a drug manufacturer for birth defects allegedly caused by its drug. Plaintiffs contended that the company had violated federal law by failing to include proper warnings on the label. This violation of federal law, if proved, would have constituted a presumption of negligence under state law. The Supreme Court held that even though the violation of federal law might be a critical issue, there was no federal question jurisdiction created. [**Merrell Dow Pharmaceuticals Inc. v. Thompson**, 478 U.S. 804 (1986)]

Example: The plaintiff brought a state court quiet title action, seeking to reclaim property that the IRS had seized and sold to the defendant to satisfy the plaintiff's tax delinquency. The plaintiff argued that the IRS notice was defective, thus invalidating the sale and the defendant's title. The Court found that this federal issue was a "substantial and disputed" issue of federal law warranting federal jurisdiction over the state law quiet title proceeding. [**Grable & Sons Metal Products, Inc. v. Darue Engineering & Manufacturing**, 545 U.S. 308 (2005)]

(a) Relevance of Congressional Intent

The Court in *Grable & Sons* distinguished *Merrell Dow*. In *Merrell Dow*, the Court treated Congress's presumed failure to create a private federal right of action as an argument against federal jurisdiction. *Merrell Dow* also emphasized the relatively modest federal interest and the potential impact on the district court's dockets. By contrast, in *Grable & Sons*, the Court ascribed less significance to Congress's failure to create a private suit, found the federal interest more substantial, and saw little threat to the federal docket. Thus, the Court in *Grable & Sons* recognized the relevance of congressional intent. However, in a departure from the approach that some lower courts had taken after *Merrell Dow*, the Court in *Grable & Sons* refused to treat the absence of a federal right of action as precluding federal jurisdiction over state law claims with federal ingredients. Such an approach would have ended federal jurisdiction over state claims by making a federal right of action essential to sustain jurisdiction.

Example: The plaintiff brought suit, alleging that his attorneys' malpractice in earlier litigation had led to the invalidation of his patent. Under the malpractice law of Texas (and many other states), plaintiff was obliged to show that he had a valid patent in order to demonstrate that the defendant's malpractice, if any, caused him injury. The state law claim thus necessarily presented a question of federal patent law. But the Court concluded that the federal issue was insufficiently substantial to warrant an assertion of federal question jurisdiction (and the finding of exclusive federal jurisdiction that would follow). The state court's assessment of the patent issue, in the hypothetical "case within a case" would not affect the ultimate validity of the patent or influence the corpus of federal patent law. [**Gunn v. Minton**, 568 U.S. 251 (2013)]

(3) Well-Pleaded Complaint

It is a long-standing rule that the federal question must appear in a well-pleaded complaint. Even though the decision in a case "depends upon the construction or application" of federal law, there can be no federal question jurisdiction in the district court unless that question of federal law appears in a properly pleaded complaint.

(a) Cannot Arise as a Defense

When the federal question arises only as a defense to the plaintiff's cause of action, there is no federal question jurisdiction because the question does not appear in the complaint. In other words, the plaintiff cannot confer jurisdiction by anticipating in the complaint a federal defense that the defendant may assert.

(b) Function of Well-Pleaded Complaint Rule

The well-pleaded complaint rule serves as a quick and fairly reliable sorting device for allocating original jurisdiction between the federal and state courts.

(c) Rule Not Infallible

However, there are some cases in which the presence or validity of a federal defense is the critical legal issue. But such cases are excluded from the federal district courts by the well-pleaded complaint rule. The Supreme Court has noted that although the rule "makes sense as a quick rule of thumb," it "may produce awkward results." [**Franchise Tax Board v. Construction Laborers Vacation Trust**, *supra,* p. 118]

(d) Present Status

Despite its conceded awkwardness on occasion, the vitality of the rule has been reaffirmed by the Supreme Court, which called it a "powerful doctrine." [**Franchise Tax Board v. Construction Laborers Vacation Trust**, *supra*]

(e) Rule Applies to Original and Removed Cases

The well-pleaded complaint rule applies both to cases *filed originally* in the district court and to cases *removed* to the district court.

e.g. **Example: original case:** Plaintiffs sued to enforce a contract under which they were entitled to free lifetime passes on a railroad. They contended that a recent federal statute did not forbid the issuance of the passes. The Court held that the defense of the federal statute could not be anticipated in the plaintiffs' complaint and denied jurisdiction in the district court. [**Louisville & Nashville Railroad v. Mottley**, *supra,* p. 60]

Example: original case: Plaintiff filed a state law quantum meruit suit in federal district court. The Court held that the potential availability of a federal law defense did not confer federal question jurisdiction. [**Phillips Petroleum Co. v. Texaco, Inc.**, 415 U.S. 125 (1974)]

Example: removed case: Plaintiff, the state collector of taxes, sued in state court to collect taxes from a national bank, contending that federal law permitted such taxation. Defendant bank removed to federal district court. The Supreme Court held that although federal law might permit taxation by renouncing the defense that the bank was a federal instrumentality, the issue concerning the federal defense did not belong in a well-pleaded complaint. Even in a case removed from state court to federal court, a federal defense could not confer jurisdiction. [**Gully v. First National Bank in Meridian**, *supra*, p. 115]

(f) Special Rule When Complete Federal Preemption Is a Defense

Even though federal preemption of an asserted state law cause of action is a federal defense, it has sometimes been permitted as a basis for removal. If a particular area of law is completely preempted, there is no possibility of a state law claim. In such an area, "any civil complaint . . . is necessarily federal in character" because the only possible claim will be one based on federal law. [**Metropolitan Life Insurance Co. v. Taylor**, 481 U.S. 58 (1987)]

1) Refining the Test for Complete Preemption Removal

Complete preemption removal includes two elements: (i) federal law must completely preempt the state cause of action, and (ii) it must provide an exclusively federal right of action. [**Beneficial National Bank v. Anderson**, 539 U.S. 1 (2003)] Preemption without an exclusive federal right of action does not warrant removal.

2) Three Areas of Complete Federal Preemption—Labor, Pensions, and Usury Claims

So far, the Court has permitted federal preemption removal in three areas of law: labor law under the Labor Management Relations Act [**Avco Corp. v. Aero Lodge No. 735**, 390 U.S. 557 (1968)], pension law under the Employee Retirement Income Security Act ("ERISA") [**Metropolitan Life Insurance Co. v. Taylor**, *supra*], and claims that federal banks violated applicable usury restrictions on interest rates [**Beneficial National Bank**, *supra*].

EXAM TIP   🔲 GILBERT

For your exam, although the "general rule" is that a federal defense will not provide a basis for removal, there is an important exception based on federal preemption: When federal law *completely* preempts state law and provides an *exclusive* federal right of action, the complete preemption doctrine *may* enable a defendant to remove to federal court. Note the important difference between an *exclusive* federal right of action (required) and *exclusive* federal jurisdiction (neither required nor relevant).

(g) Criticism of Rule as Applied to Removed Cases

The function of the well-pleaded complaint rule is to provide a quick and reliable sorting device. The well-pleaded complaint rule makes sense in original cases because jurisdiction can be determined immediately upon the filing of the complaint. Furthermore, since federal question jurisdiction is designed to provide a federal forum to litigants relying on federal law, the rule makes sense because it permits plaintiffs relying on federal law to come into district court. These reasons should apply with equal force to permit defendants relying on a federal defense to *remove* to federal district court. At the time of attempted removal from state court, defendant could be required to file her answer. In that event, there would be no speculation and no time lost waiting to see whether defendant would in fact plead a federal defense. Furthermore, if defendant pleads a federal defense, she should have as much right as plaintiff to have a federal forum determine the federal question.

1) Comment

This criticism has long been familiar to students of federal courts. [*See, e.g.,* Wechsler, *Federal Jurisdiction and the Revision of the Judicial Code,* 13 Law & Contemp. Probs. 216, 233–234 (1948)] But supporters of the well-pleaded complaint rule argue that defendants might too readily plead federal defenses to secure a federal docket, thus burdening federal courts with cases that turn primarily on state law. Furthermore, as the Supreme Court has noted, none of the proposals to change the law has been adopted by Congress. [**Franchise Tax Board v. Construction Laborers Vacation Trust**, *supra,* p. 120]

(h) Declaratory Judgments

The well-pleaded complaint rule applies to suits for declaratory judgments. But rather than looking to see whether the federal question appears in the well-pleaded declaratory judgment complaint that has actually been filed, the district court asks whether the federal question would have appeared in a *hypothetical well-pleaded complaint* if a "coercive" action had been filed concerning the transaction in dispute. (A coercive action is an action for an injunction or for damages.) In other words, the district court must ask what the complaint *would have looked like* if the plaintiff had filed suit for an injunction or for damages. If the federal question would have appeared in a well-pleaded complaint in such a suit, then the rule is satisfied. It is immaterial whether the federal question appeared in the well-pleaded declaratory judgment complaint actually filed in the case.

1) Rationale

The rationale behind this odd application of the well-pleaded complaint rule is that the Declaratory Judgment Act [28 U.S.C. § 2201] was not designed to expand federal court jurisdiction. If a well-pleaded complaint in a declaratory judgment action contains a federal question, when a well-pleaded complaint in an injunction or damage suit arising out of the same transaction would not, the district court's federal question jurisdiction would thus have been expanded by the availability of a declaratory judgment under the Act. To avoid this result, the district court must look only to the sort of complaint (*i.e.,* for an injunction or for damages) that could have been filed before the passage of the Declaratory Judgment Act.

2) Applicable to Federal and State Declaratory Judgments

The rule that a district court must look to complaints in hypothetical damage and injunction actions has been applied to both federal and state declaratory judgment actions.

e.g. **Example: declaratory judgment in federal court:** Plaintiffs sought a declaratory judgment in federal district court that the defendants had no valid federal defense to a state law contract claim. The Court held that if plaintiffs had brought an action for contract damages or for specific performance, the federal question could only have been raised as a defense. Therefore, federal question jurisdiction was denied. [**Skelly Oil Co. v. Phillips Petroleum Co.**, 339 U.S. 667 (1950)]

e.g. **Example: declaratory judgment in state court:** Plaintiff sought a declaratory judgment that a federal defense was not available to the levying of state taxes allegedly due. The action was brought in California state court under California declaratory judgment procedure. Defendant sought to remove to federal district court. The Supreme Court held that the *Skelly Oil* rule applied here, because otherwise litigants would be able to avoid the effect of *Skelly Oil* simply by bringing a state declaratory judgment action and then *removing* to federal district court. If litigants were permitted to confer federal question jurisdiction in this fashion, *Skelly Oil* would become a "dead letter." [**Franchise Tax Board v. Construction Laborers Vacation Trust**, *supra,* p. 122]

e. Requirement of Substantiality

A federal question must be more than frivolous to support federal question jurisdiction. [**Hagans v. Levine**, 415 U.S. 528 (1974)]

(1) Does Not Require Finding of Federal Right

The successful assertion of federal question jurisdiction does *not* require that the litigant prevail on the merits of his federal claim. It is enough that the federal claim be arguable.

e.g. **Example:** Plaintiff brought suit after having been served with a subpoena by the House Un-American Activities Committee. He claimed that the subpoena had been issued in violation of federal law. The Supreme Court held that there was *federal question jurisdiction,* even though it also held that there was no valid claim of right under federal law. [**Wheeldin v. Wheeler**, 373 U.S. 647 (1963)]

e.g. **Example:** Plaintiff sued federal agents in damages for alleged violation of Fourth and Fifth Amendment rights. The claim of federal right was not sustained on the merits, but the Court *sustained federal question jurisdiction.* "[T]he failure to state a proper cause of action calls for a judgment on the merits and not for a dismissal for want of jurisdiction." [**Bell v. Hood**, 327 U.S. 678 (1946)]

(2) Consequences of Dismissal on Merits Rather than for Lack of Federal Question Jurisdiction

A federal court has federal question jurisdiction over a case even if the federal right asserted is eventually denied on the merits. A finding of jurisdiction in such a case has two consequences:

(a) Supplemental Jurisdiction

Since the district court has federal question jurisdiction, it can exercise supplemental (formerly, pendent and ancillary) jurisdiction over related claims or parties.

(b) Waiver

Objections to federal question subject matter jurisdiction cannot be waived. But a litigant who contends that the asserted federal right has no basis in law must move under Federal Rule of Civil Procedure 12(b)(6) to dismiss for failure to state a claim upon which relief can be granted. Such an objection *can be waived* if the motion is not timely made, but the time limits are lenient. [*See* Fed. R. Civ. P. 12(h)(2)]

f. Distinguish—Federal Question Jurisdiction in Supreme Court

The above discussion of original federal question jurisdiction in the district court under 28 U.S.C. section 1331 and related statutes should be distinguished from the Supreme Court's jurisdiction to review federal questions in cases coming up from state courts under 28 U.S.C. section 1257.

(1) Well-Pleaded Complaint Rule Does Not Apply

Unlike in the district courts, the well-pleaded complaint rule does not apply to cases coming to the Supreme Court from the state courts. In such cases, it is only required that the federal question have been raised and decided in the state court.

(a) Rationale

The primary function of the well-pleaded complaint rule in the district court is to screen out cases in which it is unlikely that a federal question will actually be presented. This screening function is performed at the outset of the litigation. When a case reaches the Supreme Court on certiorari from a state court, this screening function is unnecessary, for a federal question is present by definition.

C. Diversity Jurisdiction

1. In General

Diversity jurisdiction is *authorized* by Article III of the Constitution and is specifically *conferred* on the district courts by statute. Congress has conferred diversity jurisdiction on federal trial courts since the beginning of the federal judicial system under the Judiciary Act of 1789. As is also true of federal question jurisdiction, the scope of the constitutionally authorized diversity jurisdiction is broader than that actually conferred by statute. The purposes of diversity jurisdiction will be discussed, and then the constitutional and statutory bases for the jurisdiction will be considered in turn.

2. Purposes of Diversity Jurisdiction

a. Original Purposes of Diversity Jurisdiction

The *primary* original purpose of diversity jurisdiction was probably to provide a neutral federal forum so that *out-of-state citizens could avoid possible prejudice* in state courts. A possible *secondary* purpose was to provide a nationwide system of courts that could decide questions of general common law in a uniform way and thereby encourage the growth of a *uniform common law system* in the states. (*See* discussion of *Swift v. Tyson, infra*, pp. 184 *et seq.*)

b. Modern Functions of Diversity Jurisdiction

(1) Original Purposes Largely Gone

The problem of prejudice against out-of-state citizens in state-law-based litigation is not very severe today. And now that *Swift v. Tyson* has been overruled by *Erie Railroad v. Tompkins (see infra*, pp. 186 *et seq.*), the federal courts no longer decide cases according to the general common law.

(2) Remaining Functions

(a) Out-of-State Prejudice

To some degree, out-of-state prejudice exists today, and diversity jurisdiction protects out-of-state citizens in such cases.

(b) Alternate Forum

Even without the spur of prejudice against out-of-state citizens, litigants often prefer an alternate forum because of perceived sympathies of particular judges, because of more advantageous procedures, or for other reasons.

(c) Familiarizing Federal Judges with State Law

Diversity cases familiarize federal judges with state law. This helps federal judges be generalists who are broadly familiar with the texture of American law.

(d) Development of State Law

It is sometimes argued that federal courts in diversity cases can help in the development of state law by writing influential opinions about what the state law is or should be.

(e) Rural Bias

It has even been argued that diversity jurisdiction helps litigants avoid the bias of rural juries. Litigants in rural areas ordinarily must try their cases in small town courts if they sue in state court. But since federal district courts are located almost exclusively in cities, a diversity case in federal court is tried with an urban rather than rural jury.

(f) Corporate Defendants

As a practical matter, corporations often appear as defendants in diversity proceedings. Diversity may be seen as protecting firms from state court decisions that would transfer wealth from national enterprises to in-state claimants. This rationale for diversity may explain its persistence in the face of efforts to secure its repeal, but has little to do with bias on the basis of state citizenship.

3. Constitutional Basis

a. Article III

The Constitution provides that the "judicial power" shall extend to "controversies . . . between citizens of different states" and between citizens of a state and "foreign States, Citizens or Subjects." [U.S. Const, art. III, § 2, cl. 1]

b. Scope of Constitutional Authorization

The scope of the constitutionally authorized diversity jurisdiction is quite broad.

(1) Complete Diversity Not Required

Complete diversity (*see infra*, p. 126) is not required by Article III. All that is constitutionally required is minimal diversity—one plaintiff's state citizenship must differ from that of one defendant. [**State Farm Fire & Casualty Co. v. Tashire**, *supra*, p. 59]

4. Statutory Basis

a. Basic Statute

The basic diversity jurisdiction statute [28 U.S.C. § 1332] provides for federal district court jurisdiction when there is diversity between:

(1) *Citizens of different states* [§ 1332(a)(*l*)];

(2) *Citizens of a state and citizens or subjects of a foreign state (except those admitted as lawful permanent residents and domiciled in the same state)* [§ 1332(a)(2)];

(3) *Citizens of different states with citizens or subjects of a foreign state as additional parties* [§ 1332(a)(3)];

(4) *A foreign state as plaintiff and state citizens* [§ 1332(a)(4)].

b. Complete Diversity Required Under Basic Statute

The basic diversity statute has been construed to require complete diversity of citizenship. [**Strawbridge v. Curtiss**, *supra*, 59] Complete diversity requires that *each* plaintiff's citizenship be different from that of *each* defendant. Compare this to Article III, which does *not* require complete diversity (*see supra*, p. 126).

e.g. **Example: complete diversity:** Plaintiffs are citizens of states A and B. Defendants are citizens of states C and D. There is complete diversity because all of the plaintiffs are citizens of different states from all of the defendants. The same would be true if the defendants in this example were all citizens of state C, or if the plaintiffs all were citizens of state A.

e.g. **Example: incomplete diversity:** Plaintiffs are citizens of states A and B. Defendants are citizens of states B and C. There is still diversity because the plaintiffs are citizens of states A and B and because one of the defendants is a citizen of state C. But the diversity is incomplete because the other defendant is a citizen of state B, as is one of the plaintiffs.

c. Diversity Under Interpleader Statute

Diversity of citizenship is also the basis for jurisdiction under the federal interpleader statute. [28 U.S.C. § 1335]

(1) Complete Diversity Not Required

Unlike the basic diversity statute, the federal interpleader statute does not require complete diversity of citizenship. [**State Farm Fire & Casualty Co. v. Tashire**, *supra,* p. 126]

Example: An uncontroversial case of incomplete (but statutorily sufficient) diversity is presented when the plaintiff (the interpleading party) is a citizen of state A and the defendants (the interpleaded parties) are citizens of states A, B, and C. [**Treinies v. Sunshine Mining Co.**, 308 U.S. 66 (1939)] Note that in this example there is complete diversity among the interpleaded parties, who are the truly adverse parties.

Example: A more controversial case of incomplete (but statutorily sufficient) diversity is presented when the plaintiff (the interpleading party) is a citizen of state A and the defendants (the interpleaded parties) are citizens of states A, A, and B. The Supreme Court has held that complete diversity is not required among the interpleaded parties. It is sufficient that there is diversity between two of the interpleaded parties. [**State Farm Fire & Casualty Co. v. Tashire**, *supra*]

(2) Distinguish—"Rule Interpleader"

Complete diversity is required when interpleader is sought under Federal Rule of Civil Procedure 22 rather than under the federal interpleader statute. When "rule interpleader" is employed, jurisdiction is founded on the basic diversity statute [28 U.S.C. § 1332], rather than on the interpleader statute. Thus, in "rule interpleader" cases, the complete diversity requirement of the basic diversity statute applies.

(a) But Note

Complete diversity under "rule interpleader" requires only that the plaintiff (the interpleading party) be a citizen of a different state from all of the defendants (the interpleaded parties). It does not matter whether there is diversity of citizenship among the defendants. Thus, plaintiff may be a citizen of state A, and defendants may all be citizens of state B. (*See supra*, p. 126.)

d. Definition of Citizenship

(1) Territories, District of Columbia, and Puerto Rico

United States territories, the District of Columbia, and the Commonwealth of Puerto Rico are considered *states* for purposes of diversity of citizenship. [28 U.S.C. § 1332(d)] Thus, for example, a citizen of the District of Columbia can sue a citizen of Maryland in federal district court in diversity.

(a) Note

The constitutionality of treating the territories, the District of Columbia, and Puerto Rico as if they were states was sustained by the Supreme Court in **National Mutual Insurance Co. v. Tidewater Transfer Co.**, *supra*, p. 116. As discussed, the Court was unable to agree on a rationale for its holding.

(2) Natural Person's Citizenship

A natural person's state citizenship is determined by his *domicile.* Domicile is a person's permanent home, where he resides *with the intention to remain or to which he has the intention of returning.* Children are ordinarily presumed to have the same domicile as their parents. One spouse is ordinarily presumed to have the same domicile as the other spouse and children. However, a person residing in a state is not necessarily domiciled in that state, and thus is not necessarily a citizen of that state; it is the intent to remain or return to another state that controls.

Example: A college student may live in California nine months out of the year, but retain a domicile in (and therefore be a citizen of) Illinois. A member of the armed forces may be stationed in Georgia, but retain a domicile in (and therefore be a citizen of) New York.

EXAM TIP

Although a person's domicile is important in determining both personal jurisdiction and diversity jurisdiction, be sure to keep these concepts separate. Personal jurisdiction gives a court *power over the defendant,* which requires that a defendant have a legal relationship to the forum. On the other hand, diversity jurisdiction, which is a type of subject matter jurisdiction, gives the court the authority to hear the *type of case.* In other words, the law of domicile that governs issues of personal jurisdiction may differ subtly from the domicile rules that govern a person's citizenship for purposes of diversity jurisdiction.

(a) United States Citizens with Foreign Domicile

United States citizens who have their permanent home (domicile) abroad are not citizens of a state for purposes of federal diversity jurisdiction. Therefore, they cannot come within diversity jurisdiction.

(b) Resident Aliens

At one time, an alien admitted for permanent residence in the United States was deemed a citizen of the state in which he or she is domiciled. The purpose of this deeming provision was to curtail jurisdiction, but it caused other problems. Congress repealed this deeming provision in 2012, instead providing that jurisdiction was improper over a dispute between a citizen of a state and a resident alien domiciled in the same state. [28 U.S.C. 1332(a)(2)]

(3) Representative Suits

(a) Class Actions

The citizenship of the *named representatives* of a class in a Federal Rule of Civil Procedure 23 class action suit determines citizenship for purposes of federal diversity jurisdiction. [**Supreme Tribe of Ben-Hur v. Cauble**, 255 U.S. 356 (1921)] The citizenship of unnamed class members is irrelevant to diversity jurisdiction. Thus, as long as there is complete diversity between the named parties, diversity jurisdiction is proper even if unnamed members of the plaintiff class are citizens of the same state as the defendant. The Class Action Fairness Act has further relaxed the diversity requirements for some class actions (*see infra*, p. 140).

Note that because only the citizenship of the **named representatives** is considered in determining diversity in a class action, it is irrelevant that some members of the class are citizens of the defendant's state; diversity still exists. Don't be fooled by a fact pattern where the defendant is a large company, like Firestone, and members of the plaintiff class live in every state. Diversity may be preserved by carefully selecting the class representatives.

(b) Trusts

The citizenship of a **trustee** determines citizenship for purposes of federal diversity jurisdiction when she has the customary powers of a trustee to hold, manage, and dispose of assets for the benefit of others. [**Navarro Savings Association v. Lee**, 446 U.S. 458 (1980)]

(c) Estates and Guardianships

The **legal representative** of an estate is deemed to have the **citizenship of the decedent.** The **legal guardian** of an infant or an incompetent is deemed to have the **citizenship of the infant or incompetent.** [28 U.S.C. § 1332(c)(2)]

(4) Corporations

For purposes of diversity jurisdiction, a corporation is a citizen **both** of the state in which it has its principal place of business **and** of the state of its incorporation. [28 U.S.C. § 1332(c)] A corporation may thus be a citizen of more than one state.

e.g. **Example:** ABC Corp. is incorporated in Delaware and has its principal place of business in Missouri. If citizens of either Delaware or Missouri wish to sue ABC, there is no diversity of citizenship.

(a) "Principal Place of Business"

Some corporations have offices and manufacturing plants in several states, which once made it difficult to determine principal place of business. But the Supreme Court resolved the issue by adopting the "nerve center" test.

1) "Nerve Center"

According to the Court, a corporation's principal place of business is where the corporation's executive and administrative office, or "nerve center," is located. [**Hertz Corp. v. Friend**, 559 U.S. 77 (2010)]

2) Place of Operations Rejected

Although earlier lower court cases suggested that a corporation's principal place of business is where the corporation carries on its primary production or service activities, the Court rejected that approach. [**Hertz Corp. v. Friend**, *supra* p. 129—indicating in a considered dictum that a firm with its visible business operations in NJ and its corporate headquarters in NY would be regarded as a citizen of NY]

(b) Special Problem—Corporation Incorporated in More than One State

A corporation will sometimes take out papers of incorporation in more than one state, potentially making it a citizen of all the states in which it is incorporated. The courts have struggled with the status of such corporations.

1) Forum Doctrine

Prior to 1958, many courts adopted the "forum doctrine," under which a corporation incorporated in more than one state was deemed a citizen only of the forum state.

e.g. **Example:** ABC Corp. is incorporated in New York and Delaware. A New York citizen may not sue ABC in diversity in a federal district court in New York because ABC will be deemed a citizen of the forum state, New York. However, a Delaware citizen may sue ABC in diversity in a federal district court in New York. Even though ABC is incorporated in Delaware, the "forum doctrine" holds that for purposes of diversity jurisdiction the corporation is only a citizen of the state in which the suit is brought (in this case, New York).

2) Effect of 1958 Amendment

In 1958, 28 U.S.C. section 1332(c) was amended to provide that a corporation will be "deemed a citizen of *any* state by which it has been incorporated." Although the Supreme Court has not ruled on the point, this language may mean that the "forum doctrine" is overruled. Thus, under the present statute, a corporation may be deemed a citizen of *all the states* in which it is incorporated, regardless of where the suit is brought.

e.g. **Example:** ABC Corp. is incorporated in New York and Delaware. New York and Delaware citizens cannot sue ABC in federal diversity jurisdiction, regardless of where the suit is brought.

(c) Special Problem—Foreign Country Corporation

Although once a matter of some uncertainty, the diversity statute makes clear that a corporation with foreign ties should be regarded as a citizen of both its country (or state) of incorporation and of the state or foreign state in which it has its principal place of business. Thus, a Swiss corporation with its principal place of business in California is a citizen of Switzerland and of California under 28 U.S.C. section 1332(c).

(d) Special Problem—Direct Action Against an Insurance Company

If a direct action is brought against an insurer, the insurer is deemed to have the citizenship of the insured, in addition to the citizenship of the insurer itself. Thus, if the insurer is a corporation, it will have the citizenship: (i) of the insured; (ii) of the insurer's state of incorporation; and (iii) of the state of the insurer's principal place of business. [28 U.S.C. § 1332(c)(*l*)]

1) But Note

An insurer has the same citizenship as its insured in a direct action suit when it is a defendant, but *not* when it is a plaintiff. [**Northbrook National Insurance Co. v. Brewer**, 493 U.S. 6 (1989)]

(5) Unincorporated Associations

An unincorporated association is considered to be a citizen of *all the states* of which its *members* are citizens. [**Chapman v. Barney**, 129 U.S. 677 (1889)]

Example: If an unincorporated association has members who are citizens of all 50 states, the association will be deemed a citizen of all 50 states for purposes of diversity jurisdiction.

(a) Labor Unions

The **Chapman v. Barney** rule for unincorporated associations applies to labor unions. [**United Steel Workers of America v. R.H. Bouligny, Inc.**, 382 U.S. 145 (1965)]

(b) Partnerships

The **Chapman v. Barney** rule also applies to business partnerships. For limited partnerships, the citizenship of both limited and general partners is considered. [**Great Southern Fire Proof Hotel v. Jones**, 177 U.S. 449 (1900); **Carden v. Arkoma Associates**, 494 U.S. 185 (1990)]

(c) Effect of Rule

The consequence of the **Chapman v. Barney** rule is that unincorporated associations are frequently unable to come into federal court in diversity. The Supreme Court has noted the arguably inconsistent treatment for corporations and unincorporated associations, but has concluded that any change in the rule should come from Congress. [**United Steel Workers of America v. R.H. Bouligny, Inc.**, *supra*]

(d) Unincorporated Business Associations

The Supreme Court held that a real estate trust, organized under Maryland state law as an unincorporated association, was to be viewed as a citizen of every state in which its members were citizens. [**Americold Realty Trust v. ConAgra Foods, Inc.**, 136 S. Ct. 1012 (2016)]

An increasingly common form of business organization, the limited liability company, or LLC, has been treated by federal courts as an unincorporated association for citizenship purposes. [**Johnson v. Smithkline Beecham Corp.**, 724 F.3d 337 (3d Cir. 2013); **Rolling Greens MHP, LP v. Comcast SCH Holdings LLC**, 374 F.3d 1020 (11th Cir. 2004)] The numbers speak for themselves: the IRS received returns from some 300,000 such firms in 1993, but the figure had grown to nearly 2.5 million by 2008. The ABA adopted a resolution in 2015 calling upon Congress to confer entity status on LLCs to facilitate their access to federal diversity dockets. No such legislation has been adopted.

e. No Improper or Collusive Creation of Diversity

A litigant cannot create diversity by improper or collusive assignment of claims to or joinder of parties.

(1) Historical Background

Until 1948, diversity could not be created by the assignment of a promissory note or chose in action to a party of diverse citizenship. This flat prohibition proved awkward because it prevented the exercise of diversity jurisdiction in numerous cases of bona fide assignments. Furthermore, some kinds of assignments to create diversity were not subject to the statute, and thus were subject to abuse. In light of these factors, Congress in 1948 repealed the "assignee clause" and attempted to control improper creation of diversity by a statute speaking directly to improper motivation.

GILBERT

SUMMARY OF CITIZENSHIP RULES FOR DIVERSITY CASES

PARTY	CITIZENSHIP DETERMINED BY
Natural person	*Domicile*—the state in which person resides or to which he intends to return
U.S. citizen living abroad	*No state citizenship* for diversity purposes
Class (in a class action lawsuit under general diversity statute)	Domicile of *class representative*
Corporation	*State(s) of incorporation* and the *one principal place of business*
Insurance company	*State(s) of incorporation* and the *one principal place of business;* for *direct actions against it,* citizenship of *insured* is an *additional* citizenship
Trust	Citizenship of *trustee*
Legal representative of an estate	Former citizenship of *decedent*
Guardian	Citizenship of *infant or incompetent*
Unincorporated association; labor union; partnership; LLCs	State(s) in which its *members* are citizens

(2) Present Statute

The present statute provides that a district court "shall not have jurisdiction of a civil action in which any party, by assignment or otherwise, has been improperly or collusively made or joined to invoke the jurisdiction of such court." [28 U.S.C. § 1359]

(3) Change of State Citizenship

A party may create diversity by a *bona fide change* of domicile between the time of the cause of action's occurring and the filing of the suit. But if the change of domicile is a sham or for the sole purpose of conferring diversity jurisdiction on the federal courts, it will be disregarded. [**Korn v. Korn**, 398 F.2d 689 (3d Cir. 1968)]

---

(4) Assignment of Claim

A *bona fide assignee* of a claim may rely on his own citizenship to determine whether diversity of citizenship exists. But if the sole purpose of the assignment was to create diversity, the citizenship of the assignee will be disregarded and that of the *assignor* will control.

e.g. **Example:** Two foreign corporations were involved in a contract dispute. One of the corporations assigned its claim under the contract to its lawyer, a Texas citizen. The lawyer assigned back to the corporation a 95% interest in any recovery that might be had, retaining a 5% interest "for the use of his name and the trouble in collecting." The attorney then filed suit in his own name in federal district court, relying on the assignment and his Texas citizenship to provide the requisite diversity. The Supreme Court found that this was a "manufacture of federal jurisdiction" forbidden by 28 U.S.C. section 1359. [**Kramer v. Caribbean Mills, Inc.**, 394 U.S. 823 (1969)]

(5) Distinguish—Collusion or Improper Joinder to Defeat Diversity

The statute prohibits only improper *creation* of diversity jurisdiction. [28 U.S.C. § 1359] It says nothing about collusion or other improper methods of *defeating* diversity jurisdiction. Thus, a party is usually permitted to assign claims or to appoint representatives to defeat diversity.

e.g. **Example:** A citizen of Oklahoma three times brought wrongful death actions in state court as administrator of her husband's estate. The actions were all removed to federal district court on the basis of diversity of citizenship. The plaintiff voluntarily dismissed each of the actions. Finally, she resigned as administrator, and a Louisiana citizen was appointed as administrator so that the defendant, a Louisiana corporation, could not remove to federal court. The Supreme Court upheld the objection to diversity jurisdiction. [**Mecom v. Fitzsimmons Drilling Co.**, 284 U.S. 183 (1931)]

(a) But Note

Because of a later amendment to the diversity statute, assignment could not today defeat diversity on the facts of **Mecom v. Fitzsimmons Drilling Co.** Section 1332(c)(2) of the present statute now provides that a representative of a decedent's estate has the same citizenship as the decedent (*see supra*, p. 129).

(b) Possible Erosion of *Mecom* Rule

A few lower federal courts have limited the power of parties to defeat diversity by collusive means. The Supreme Court has not addressed the matter.

f. Dismissal of Nondiverse Party to Preserve Jurisdiction

Federal district courts and courts of appeals have the power to dismiss a dispensable *(see* Civil Procedure Summary) nondiverse party whose presence would defeat complete diversity and thus "spoil" diversity jurisdiction. [**Newman-Green, Inc. v. Alfonzo-Larrain**, 490 U.S. 826 (1989)]

g. Jurisdictional Amount

There must be *more than $75,000* "in controversy" for a federal district court to have jurisdiction over a suit brought under the basic diversity statute. [28 U.S.C. § 1332(a)] (This "amount in controversy" had been $10,000 until a 1989 statutory change raised it to $50,000; in 1997, the amount was again raised to $75,000.)

EXAM TIP

Don't miss easy points on your exam! The amount in controversy requirement in diversity is *more than $75,000*—meaning at least $75,000.01—not $75,000.

---

(1) Purpose of Requirement

The "amount in controversy" requirement ensures that only diversity disputes of some importance are heard by the federal courts.

(a) No Jurisdictional Amount in Federal Question Cases

At one time, there was a $10,000 amount in controversy requirement for suits brought under the basic federal question jurisdiction statute. That provision was removed in 1980, and there is now no amount in controversy requirement for federal question cases. [28 U.S.C. § 1331]

(2) When Computed

The amount in controversy is determined when the *complaint is filed.* A reduction in the amount actually in controversy due to a later change in circumstances does not defeat jurisdiction. [**St. Paul Mercury Indemnity Co. v. Red Cab Co.**, 303 U.S. 283 (1938)]

(3) "Legal Certainty" Test

An allegation made *in good faith* by plaintiff that more than $75,000 is in controversy will suffice to confer jurisdiction unless it appears "to a legal certainty" that the claim is really for less than the jurisdictional amount. [**St. Paul Mercury Indemnity Co. v. Red Cab Co.**, *supra*]

(a) Note

It must be established "to a legal certainty" that plaintiff's claim cannot meet the jurisdictional minimum. Thus, a good faith allegation of a claim in excess of $75,000 and a *possibility* that more than $75,000 can be recovered suffice to confer jurisdiction.

e.g. **Example:** Plaintiff claimed $4,000 in damages in a state court suit arising out of a personal injury, and defendant removed to federal district court. (The jurisdictional amount at the time of the suit was $3,000.) Sometime later, plaintiff filed a bill of particulars in which the actual sums claimed were less than $3,000. The Supreme Court nevertheless sustained jurisdiction on the ground that when the complaint was filed and when the suit was removed to federal court, the claim for damages could have been made in good faith and could not to a legal certainty have been thought to result in an actual recovery of less than the jurisdictional amount. [**St. Paul Mercury Indemnity Co. v. Red Cab Co.**, *supra*]

cf. **Compare:** Plaintiff sued for property damage and personal injuries arising out of an automobile accident. He alleged a little over $7,000 in property damage and about $600 in medical bills. Plaintiff did not claim loss of wages or permanent injury. (The jurisdictional amount at the time of the action was $10,000.) The district court permitted plaintiff to supplement the pretrial record as to further possible damage claims but plaintiff failed to do so. Therefore, the court dismissed the suit. The court of appeals, referring to a "plethora of cases which do not belong in federal courts," affirmed. [**Nelson v. Keffer**, 451 F.2d 289 (3d Cir. 1971)]

(4) Valuing Claims

(a) Plaintiff's Viewpoint

It sometimes happens that the value of the claim to the plaintiff is different from the cost to the defendant of providing the relief sought. Most lower federal courts have adopted the viewpoint of the plaintiff in determining the value of a claim for purposes of jurisdictional amount. Although the Supreme Court has not explicitly adopted this rule, several of its decisions appear to be consistent with it.

e.g. **Example:** Plaintiff sought an injunction forcing defendant, a rival company, to remove its electrical poles and wires. The economic value to plaintiff of defendant's removal of the poles and wires was more than the jurisdictional amount. The cost to defendant of removing them, however, was less than the jurisdictional amount. *Held*: The jurisdictional amount was satisfied. [**Glenwood Light & Water Co. v. Mutual Light, Heat & Power Co.**, 239 U.S. 121 (1915)]

(b) Injunctive and Declaratory Relief

The economic value to the plaintiff of the injunctive or declaratory relief sought is generally the measure for purposes of determining the jurisdictional amount.

e.g. **Example:** Plaintiff sued to enjoin the enforcement of a state statute that would have interfered with the purchase of installment sales contracts. The amount in controversy was the amount the enforcement of the statute would have cost plaintiff. [**McNutt v. General Motors Acceptance Corp.**, 298 U.S. 178 (1935)]

1) Personal and Civil Rights Suits

Injunction suits seeking to protect personal rights, such as civil rights, are inherently difficult to value. Lower federal courts struggled with the amount in controversy issue when there was a $10,000 jurisdictional amount for federal question cases. Now that the $10,000 requirement has been removed for federal question cases, however, the issue rarely arises because diversity cases almost invariably involve some form of economic injury rather than nonpecuniary personal or civil rights violations.

(c) Collateral Consequences

The amount of *money actually sought* in the suit will determine the amount in controversy rather than the value of the collateral consequences of the judgment.

Example: Plaintiff sues for amounts due under an installment contract. There is $2,000 now due. Over the life of the contract $80,000 will become due. The amount in controversy is only $2,000, even though the collateral consequence of a judgment in favor of plaintiff will probably be to obligate the defendant to pay the remaining installments when they come due.

(d) Counterclaims

1) No Aggregation to Confer Jurisdiction

The general rule is that the amount sought in a counterclaim cannot be aggregated with the amount sought in the complaint to make up the amount in controversy.

Example: Plaintiff asks for $60,000 in her complaint. Defendant counterclaims for $25,000. The jurisdictional amount is not met because the amount in the counterclaim cannot be added to the amount in the complaint.

a) Exception

One Supreme Court case does not fit the general rule. A worker sought $14,035 in workers' compensation from a Texas administrative body, and was eventually awarded $1,050. The insurer brought suit in *federal district court* to set aside the award. The worker then sued for $14,035 in *state* court and sought to dismiss the federal district court suit since the insurer only sought to set aside an award of $1,050. In the alternative, the worker sought to file a counterclaim of $14,035 in the federal district court suit. The Supreme Court held in a 5-to-4 decision that the $10,000 jurisdictional amount was satisfied in the federal district court suit. [**Horton v. Liberty Mutual Insurance Co.**, 367 U.S. 348 (1961)]

1/ Note

Professors Wright and Kane criticize this decision [C. Wright & M. Kane, *The Law of Federal Courts* § 37 (6th ed. 2002)], and it is probably best viewed as limited to its special facts rather than as a threat to the general rule.

2) Counterclaim When Plaintiff's Suit Satisfies the Jurisdictional Amount

When plaintiff's suit already satisfies the jurisdictional amount, a counterclaim may or may not have to meet the jurisdictional amount, depending on whether it is *compulsory* or *permissive.*

a) Compulsory Counterclaim

If a counterclaim is compulsory under Federal Rule of Civil Procedure 13(a), it need *not* satisfy the amount in controversy requirement. The district court has supplemental jurisdiction over compulsory counterclaims. (*See infra*, pp. 146 *et seq.*, for discussion of supplemental jurisdiction.)

b) Permissive Counterclaim

If a counterclaim is permissive under Rule 13(b), it *must satisfy* the amount in controversy requirement or be dismissed. There is no supplemental jurisdiction over permissive counterclaims in diversity cases.

(e) Interest and Costs

Interest and court costs are *excluded* from the calculation of the jurisdictional amount. [28 U.S.C. § 1332(a)] Note, however, that "interest" in the statute refers to what is usually called "prejudgment interest." Interest that is *part of the claim* itself *is* counted as part of the jurisdictional amount.

e.g. **Example:** Plaintiff sued upon a note under which $10,000 in principal and 8% interest had been agreed to be paid. Principal and interest were now alleged to be due and owing. Since the interest was due as part of the note agreement, it counted as part of the amount in controversy. [**Brainin v. Milikian**, 396 F.2d 153 (3d Cir. 1968)]

(f) Failure to Obtain a Judgment in Excess of Jurisdictional Amount

If the judgment actually recovered is less than the jurisdictional amount, the district court does *not* lose jurisdiction. But the court does have discretion to deny costs or even to assess costs against plaintiff. [28 U.S.C. § 1332(b)]

(5) Aggregation of Claims

(a) Single Plaintiff Against Single Defendant

A single plaintiff suing a single defendant *may aggregate* all claims against that defendant to satisfy the jurisdictional amount—even if the other claims are *unrelated* to one another.

e.g. **Example:** Plaintiff claims $50,000 in damages for negligent injury by defendant, and further claims damages of $28,000 for an unrelated breach of contract by the same defendant. These amounts may be aggregated to meet the $75,000 requirement.

(b) Multiple Plaintiffs—Undivided Interest

The claims of multiple plaintiffs can be aggregated *if the plaintiffs claim an undivided interest* in the claim.

Example: A, B, and C are tenants in common in a parcel of real estate. They sue defendant for trespass, alleging total damages of $90,000 to the property. Each plaintiff has suffered only $30,000 damage to his own interest, but the three plaintiffs own an undivided interest in the property that has been injured. In this circumstance, they may aggregate their claims to meet the $75,000 requirement.

(c) Multiple Plaintiffs—Separate Claims and Class Actions

The supplemental jurisdiction statute, 28 U.S.C. section 1367(b), includes an intricate set of exceptions under which supplemental jurisdiction does not apply, with the aim apparently being to preserve some features of complete diversity. Importantly, the exceptions do not mention plaintiffs joined under Rules 20 and 23 of the Federal Rules of Civil Procedure, two common provisions for joining plaintiffs.

1) Multiple Plaintiffs—Separate Claims

The separate claims of multiple claimants permissively joined under Rule 20 may be heard only if: (i) each claimant *satisfies the diversity of citizenship* test; (ii) one of the plaintiff's claims *satisfies the $75,000 amount in controversy requirement;* and (iii) the remaining claims *arise from the same common nucleus of operative facts.* In such a case, the court has diversity of citizenship jurisdiction over the claim exceeding $75,000 and supplemental jurisdiction over the claims that do not exceed $75,000. [**Exxon Mobil Corp. v. Allapattah Services, Inc.**, 545 U.S. 546 (2005)]

a) Complete Diversity Required

Each plaintiff joined under Rule 20 must meet the complete diversity requirement. Supplemental jurisdiction does not allow the joinder of additional nondiverse plaintiffs, whether or not their claims meet the statutory 575,000 requirement. [**Exxon Mobil Corp. v. Allapattah Services, Inc.,** *supra*]

Example: Plaintiff, a nine-year-old child, suffered a severe personal injury that resulted in more than $75,000 in damages. Her parents suffered emotional distress, but they could not claim $75,000 in damages. Given that the parents' presence in the suit would not destroy diversity, that the child's claim met the minimum amount in controversy requirement, and that the parental claims arose from the same case or controversy as the claims of their child, the district court's supplemental jurisdiction extended to the claims of the parents. [**Exxon Mobil Corp. v. Allapattah Services, Inc.,** *supra*]

EXAM TIP   **GILBERT**

Don't panic if you encounter a fact pattern on your exam that has multiple plaintiffs and the question asks if the court has jurisdiction over the claims. Just keep in mind the distinction between separate claims and common and undivided claims. For **separate** claims, the **aggregate value does not control**. Rather, a single $75,000.01 claim within the district court's original jurisdiction provides the basis for supplemental jurisdiction over other related claims of lesser value, provided that the additional claims bear a close relationship to a claim that satisfies the threshold. For **common and undivided** claims, supplemental jurisdiction is not needed—the claim is essentially considered to be a single claim, but note that all parties must be of diverse citizenship.

2) Multiple Claimants—Class Actions

Federal jurisdiction over class actions is now governed by two statutes: First, the general diversity statute, 28 U.S.C. section 1332(a), coupled with the supplemental jurisdiction statute, 28 U.S.C. section 1367, now govern traditional diversity class actions. Second, the Class Action Fairness Act of 2005 ("CAFA") establishes a framework for jurisdiction over class actions on the basis of minimal diversity of citizenship and an aggregation of claims to satisfy an amount in controversy requirement currently set at $5 million.

a) No Aggregation in Section 1332 Class Actions

In a class action based on 28 U.S.C. section 1332, plaintiff members of a class may not aggregate their separate claims to satisfy the amount in controversy requirement. [**Snyder v. Harris**, 394 U.S. 332 (1969)—former $10,000 amount in controversy requirement not met]

b) Supplemental Jurisdiction over Class Members

The Supreme Court has held that a federal district court could exercise supplemental jurisdiction over the claims of other class members with claims that do not satisfy the $75,000 threshold, provided that there is at least one member of the plaintiff class with a claim that satisfies both diversity of citizenship and the amount in controversy requirement. [**Exxon Mobil Corp. v. Allapattah Services, Inc.**, *supra—overruling* **Zahn v. International Paper Co**, 414 U.S. 291 (1973)] *Exxon Mobil* does not permit aggregation of claims; instead, there must be at least one claim that meets the jurisdictional requirement and the remaining claims must bear a close enough relationship to that claim to satisfy the same case or controversy test of supplemental jurisdiction.

1/ Note

While not expressly considering the question, the Court in *Exxon Mobil* apparently assumed that the general rule for determining the citizenship of a class action would apply. But the rule announced in **Supreme Tribe of Ben-Hur v. Cauble**, *supra*, p. 128—that the citizenship of the named representative controls whether diversity of citizenship exists—was announced in a Rule 23(b)(1) class action and has not been explicitly extended (by the Supreme Court) to Rule 23(b)(3) class actions.

c) Class Action Fairness Act

CAFA broadened the diversity statute, 28 U.S.C. section 1332(d), and included provisions that regulate class action notices and settlements. Subsection 1332(d) authorizes the exercise of jurisdiction over state law class actions on the basis of *any* diversity of citizenship between a member of the plaintiff class and a defendant. In addition to this minimal diversity provision, section 1332(d) provides for the aggregation of claims to satisfy the amount in controversy requirement of the Act ($5 million). CAFA includes a number of exceptions and restrictions that are apparently designed to preserve state court control of some class actions. Amendments to the removal statute allow defendants to remove any action from state to federal court that satisfies the jurisdictional requirements of CAFA.

EXAM TIP

For your exam, be sure to be able to distinguish between the diversity requirements for a class action brought under *the basic diversity statute* and for a class action brought under *CAFA*. In a class action brought under the basic diversity statute, *the citizenship of the named representative* controls whether diversity exists, whereas under CAFA, one plaintiff, *whether or not she is the named representative*, must be of diverse citizenship from *any* one defendant.

1/ Discretionary Decline of Jurisdiction

Under CAFA, the federal district court may, in its discretion, decline jurisdiction if one-third of the plaintiff class members (or more) and the "primary" defendants are from the same state.

2/ Mandatory Decline of Jurisdiction

The district court must decline jurisdiction if two-thirds of the plaintiff class members and the "primary" defendant(s) are from the same state and other conditions are met. Additionally, federal district courts may not hear class actions under section 1332(d) that seek relief from officials of the state.

3/ Class Must Have at Least 100 Members

District courts lack jurisdiction under 1332(d) of class actions with fewer than 100 members in the plaintiff class.

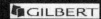
THE FEDERAL DISTRICT COURT HAS JURISDICTION UNDER THE CLASS ACTION FAIRNESS ACT WHEN:

- ☑ The class has *100 members or more;* and

- ☑ The value of the *aggregated* claims of the class is at least $5 million.

- ☑ The court *may* decline jurisdiction *if one-third of the plaintiff class and the "primary" defendant(s) are from the same state.*

- ☑ If other conditions are met, the court *must* decline jurisdiction *if two-thirds (or more) of the plaintiff and the "primary" defendant(s) are from the same state.*

EXAM TIP

While CAFA controls many federal court class actions, it's important to keep in mind that a class action *may still be brought under 28 U.S.C. section 1332(a),* in which case *the restrictions of CAFA do not apply.* Furthermore, pending state court class actions that were previously unremovable may now be removed under CAFA. Finally, when the class action arises under federal law, rather than state law, the jurisdictional provisions of 28 U.S.C. section 1331 apply, instead of CAFA.

h. Domestic Relations and Probate Exceptions

For more than a century, federal courts have refused to decide cases otherwise within their diversity jurisdiction when the cases involve domestic relations disputes or probate matters.

(1) Judge-Made Exceptions

The exceptions for domestic relations and probate cases are largely judge-made. A predecessor statute to the present diversity statute granted jurisdiction over suits "in law and equity," and it is possible that the statute meant to exclude domestic relations cases because they were traditionally tried in ecclesiastical courts rather than in the law courts or equity courts. The present statute, however, speaks of "all civil actions" [28 U.S.C. § 1332(a)], and domestic relations and probate cases are clearly civil actions.

(2) Scope of Exceptions

(a) Domestic Relations

Under the domestic relations exception, federal courts refuse to hear cases involving matrimonial status and cases involving child custody.

1) Supreme Court Interpretation

According to the Supreme Court, "[t]he domestic relations exception . . . divests the federal courts of power to issue divorce, alimony, and child custody decrees," but other issues may fall outside the scope of the exception. [*See* **Ankenbrandt v. Richards**, 504 U.S. 689 (1992)—state-law tort claims brought by mother on behalf of her children against her former husband (children's father) and his companion for physical and sexual abuse of children not within domestic relations exception]

(b) Probate

Under the probate exception, federal courts refuse to admit wills to probate or to administer estates. Other claims, although they bear some relationship to decedents' estates, fall outside the exception and *within the scope of federal judicial power,* assuming that they otherwise meet jurisdictional requirements (diversity or federal question).

1) Supreme Court Interpretation

Under the Court's latest decision, the probate exception simply restates the principle that the federal courts must defer to state court proceedings when the state court has exercised *in rem jurisdiction* over a piece of property or a *res.* Thus, the exception "reserves to the state courts the probate or annulment of a will and the administration of a decedent's estate," but it preserves federal jurisdiction over *in personam* claims. [**Marshall v. Marshall**, 547 U.S. 293 (2006)]

Example: The claim in **Marshall v. Marshall**, *supra*, was brought in a federal bankruptcy court to obtain damages from the beneficiary of a wealthy decedent. The plaintiff (Anna Nicole Smith), who was the decedent's wife, alleged that the decedent's son had tortiously interfered with the decedent's plan to make a gift to her. As an *in personam* claim, it implicated the frayed relations between beneficiaries of a decedent's estate, but did not involve probate, annulment, or administration; thus, the claim fell outside the probate exception.

(c) Lines Unclear

The lines around the domestic relations exception, and particularly around the probate exception, are unclear and in individual cases sometimes difficult to draw. A detailed analysis of the scope of these exceptions is (mercifully) outside the scope of most Federal Courts courses.

D. Admiralty Jurisdiction

1. Introduction

Admiralty jurisdiction is *authorized* by Article III of the Constitution and is specifically *conferred* on the district courts by statute. Congress has conferred admiralty jurisdiction on the district courts since the beginning of the federal judicial system under the Judiciary Act of 1789. In the late 1700s and early 1800s, admiralty jurisdiction was an exceedingly important, perhaps the most important, head of federal trial court jurisdiction. But today, admiralty has been greatly eclipsed in importance by federal question cases.

2. Constitutional Basis

Article III provides that the "judicial power shall extend . . . to all cases of admiralty and maritime jurisdiction." [U.S. Const. art. III, § 2, cl. 1]

3. Statutory Basis

The present statute provides that federal district courts "shall have original jurisdiction, exclusive of the courts of the States, of . . . [a]ny civil case of admiralty or maritime jurisdiction saving to suitors in all cases all other remedies to which they are otherwise entitled." [28 U.S.C. § 1333(1)]

a. Exclusive Jurisdiction

Except as qualified by the "saving to suitors" clause, federal admiralty jurisdiction is *exclusive in the federal courts.*

b. "Saving to Suitors" Clause

The "saving to suitors" clause of section 1333(1) permits the state courts to exercise a *concurrent jurisdiction* with the federal courts over maritime disputes that were traditionally within the jurisdiction of English and American common law courts, and over certain other suits as well. *(Note:* Most maritime transactions are within the scope of the "saving to suitors" clause.)

4. Jurisdiction Based on Maritime Character of Transaction

The existence of admiralty jurisdiction depends on the maritime character of the transaction in dispute. Generally speaking, admiralty jurisdiction requires that the transaction take place on navigable waters (such as a maritime collision) or be intimately connected to transactions taking place on the navigable waters (such as marine insurance).

a. Role of Federal Law

The law applied in admiralty cases is generally federal law, but admiralty jurisdiction does not derive from the general federal question jurisdiction statute [28 U.S.C. § 1331]. The source of jurisdiction in admiralty is section 1333. [**Romero v. International Terminal Operating Co.**, 358 U.S. 354 (1959)]

Chapter Six

Special Problems of District Court Jurisdiction

Key Exam Issues

As discussed in the previous chapter, a federal district court must have subject matter jurisdiction over a case. In addition, the district court must consider:

   (i)   Whether there is *supplemental jurisdiction* over additional claims or parties;

   (ii) Whether *removal from state court* is proper;

   (iii) Whether *venue* is proper; and

   (iv) In rare cases, whether a case should be dismissed on grounds of *forum non conveniens.*

The doctrines are detailed and complex. If your Federal Courts class covers these topics, you must learn the details carefully. However, once you have learned the details, exam questions involving these doctrines can usually be answered in a fairly straightforward, nonspeculative manner. Unlike some other areas of Federal Courts, there are few imponderables, and there are fairly clear answers to most questions. Keep in mind the following:

1. Supplemental Jurisdiction

Supplemental jurisdiction is governed by 28 U.S.C. section 1367. In preparing for your exam, you should learn this statute and the constitutional test of **United Mine Workers v. Gibbs** (*see infra*, p. 148). You should also learn the various situations in which supplemental jurisdiction is, and is not, permitted.

2. Removal Jurisdiction

Removal of cases from state to federal court is governed by statute. In particular, pay attention to the *general removal statute,* 28 U.S.C. section 1441, which largely tracks original jurisdiction. Also note that the scope of removal jurisdiction under other removal statutes is not identical to the scope of original jurisdiction.

3. Venue

Venue is governed almost entirely by explicit statutory provisions. Pay particular attention to the general venue statute, 28 U.S.C. section 1391. Be sure you understand the *definition of "residence,"* and the different treatment given natural persons, corporations, unincorporated associations, and aliens. Finally, learn the difference between change of venue for greater convenience under 28 U.S.C. section 1404(a) and change of venue to cure defects under section 1406(a).

4. Forum Non Conveniens

The doctrine of forum non conveniens is important for state courts but in federal courts retains importance only when the arguably more convenient forum is in a foreign country. The critical case to understand is **Piper Aircraft Co. v. Reyno** (*see infra*, p. 179).

A. Supplemental Jurisdiction

1. Introduction

Federal district court jurisdiction is limited to that authorized by Article III of the Constitution and explicitly conferred by statute. The federal statutes include not only basic subject matter jurisdiction statutes, such as 28 U.S.C. sections 1331 (federal question), 1332 (diversity), and 1333 (admiralty), but also a statute passed in December 1990, conferring *"supplemental jurisdiction."* [28 U.S.C. § 1367] Supplemental jurisdiction allows a district court to entertain additional claims against the existing parties, or claims against additional parties, that cannot be heard under a basic jurisdictional statute standing alone.

a. Basic Purpose

The basic purpose of supplemental jurisdiction is to permit legal disputes to be resolved efficiently. The limited scope of the federal courts' subject matter jurisdiction can result in multi-claim and multi-party litigation being cut into two pieces—some of it coming into federal court and the rest of it going into state court because there is no basis for federal subject matter jurisdiction. The supplemental jurisdiction statute prevents this result, to the extent permitted by the Constitution, in federal question cases, and to some extent in diversity cases.

b. Product of Liberal Joinder Provisions

Supplemental jurisdiction is the natural outgrowth of the provisions of the Federal Rules of Civil Procedure permitting liberal joinder of claims and parties. Without supplemental jurisdiction, the purpose of the liberal joinder rules would often be defeated, because the limited jurisdiction of the federal courts under the basic subject matter jurisdiction statutes alone would prevent or severely limit the joinder contemplated by the rules.

2. Background—Pendent and Ancillary Jurisdiction

Before enactment of the supplemental jurisdiction statute, federal district courts could hear disputes beyond those permitted under the basic jurisdictional statutes under the doctrines of *pendent* and *ancillary jurisdiction.* Because case law before enactment of the supplemental jurisdiction statute speaks in terms of pendent and ancillary jurisdiction, it is useful to know how those words were employed.

a. Practical Definitions

The Supreme Court never provided precise definitions of pendent and ancillary jurisdiction, but general usage suggested the following practical definitions.

(1) Pendent Jurisdiction

Pendent jurisdiction permitted a plaintiff with a jurisdictionally sufficient claim to join a *related claim* against the *same defendant* for which there was no independent basis for jurisdiction. Pendent jurisdiction was usually asserted when a plaintiff had a federal question claim to which she sought to join a related state law claim against the same defendant.

(2) Ancillary Jurisdiction

Ancillary jurisdiction permitted a party, usually a defendant, to assert a *related claim* for which there was no independent basis for jurisdiction against *another defendant, the plaintiff, or a third party.* Ancillary jurisdiction was usually employed when a state law claim was asserted against a nondiverse party or when less than the jurisdictional amount was in controversy.

b. Short Definitions

Pendent claims were usually "asserted *by plaintiffs in their complaints,*" and *ancillary claims* were usually asserted *"by one other than the plaintiff"* after the complaint was filed. [*See* **Corporation Venezonala de Fomento v. Vintero Sales Corp.**, 477 F. Supp. 615 (S.D.N.Y. 1979)]

c. Principal Cases

There are two principal pendent and ancillary jurisdiction cases: **United Mine Workers v. Gibbs**, *supra*, p. 117, and **Owen Equipment & Erection Co. v. Kroger**, *supra*, p. 111. The analysis of these cases continues to be relevant, even under the "supplemental jurisdiction" statute.

d. Relation to Supplemental Jurisdiction

Under the current statute, the term *"supplemental jurisdiction"* includes *both "pendent"* and *"ancillary"* jurisdiction and is designed to replace those terms. Whether "supplemental jurisdiction" will entirely replace the other terms in actual usage remains to be seen.

3. Structure of Supplemental Jurisdiction Statute

28 U.S.C. section 1367 confers very broad "supplemental jurisdiction" on the federal district courts. Section 1367(a) confers supplemental jurisdiction to the extent permitted by the Constitution over claims and parties for which there is no independent basis for jurisdiction, subject to exceptions set out in subsections (b) and (c). Section 1367(b) excepts from supplemental jurisdiction specified claims and parties in suits based solely on diversity of citizenship [28 U.S.C. § 1332]. Section 1367(c) specifies circumstances under which a district court may decline to exercise supplemental jurisdiction.

a. Supplemental Jurisdiction Under Section 1367(a)

A district court has supplemental jurisdiction "over all other claims that are so related to claims in the action within [the court's] original jurisdiction that they form part of the same case or controversy under Article III of the United States Constitution. Such supplemental jurisdiction shall include claims that involve the joinder or intervention of additional parties." [28 U.S.C. § 1367(a)]

(1) "Case or Controversy"

The core meaning of "case or controversy" under section 1367(a) is based on **United Mine Workers v. Gibbs**, *supra*. In *Gibbs*, the Supreme Court held that a district court has constitutional power to hear a pendent claim when two conditions are met:

(i) The state and federal claims derive from a *common nucleus of operative fact;* and

(ii) The plaintiff's claims are such that they would *ordinarily be expected to be tried in one judicial proceeding.*

The "common nucleus of operative fact" language is likely the touchstone for determining the meaning of "case or controversy" under section 1367(a).

(a) Possible Extension Beyond *Gibbs*

Supplemental jurisdiction might extend beyond the *Gibbs* "common nucleus of operative fact." Prior to enactment of the supplemental jurisdiction statute, several lower courts allowed ancillary jurisdiction over permissive counterclaims for setoff not arising out of the facts giving rise to the complaint. [*See, e.g.,* **Ambromovage v. United Mine Workers of America**, 726 F.2d 972 (3d Cir. 1984); **United States v. Heyward-Robinson Co.**, 430 F.2d 1077 (2d Cir. 1970)—Friendly, J., concurring] Such a counterclaim obviously does not derive from a common nucleus of operative fact. However, if it meets the constitutional definition of "case or controversy" (a matter not free from doubt), jurisdiction is available under the supplemental jurisdiction statute. [See **Jones v. Ford Motor Credit Company**, 358 F.3d 205 (2d Cir. 2004) (upholding supplemental jurisdiction over permissive counterclaim) (citing Fletcher, "Common Nucleus of Operative Fact" and Defensive Set-Off: Beyond the Gibbs Test, 74 Ind. L.J. 171 (1998)]

b. Exceptions from Supplemental Jurisdiction Under Section 1367(b)

Under section 1367(b), a district court does not have supplemental jurisdiction for certain additional claims and parties in diversity suits [28 U.S.C. § 1332]. Section 1367(b) is complicated and inartfully drafted. Essentially, it provides that *in diversity suits,* claims recited under section 1367(b) are excluded from supplemental jurisdiction.

(1) Text of Section 1367(b)

Section 1367(b) provides that "district courts shall not have supplemental jurisdiction under subsection (a) over claims by plaintiffs against persons made parties under Rules 14, 19, 20, or 24 of the Federal Rules of Civil Procedure, or over claims by persons proposed to be joined as plaintiffs under Rule 19 of such rules, or seeking to intervene as plaintiffs under Rule 24 of such rules, when exercising supplemental jurisdiction over such claims would be inconsistent with the jurisdictional requirements of section 1332."

(2) Basic Purpose

The basic purpose of section 1367(b) is clear. In federal question cases, supplemental jurisdiction is as broad as the Constitution will permit, because the core business of the federal courts is deciding cases involving federal questions in an effective and efficient way. In diversity cases, by contrast, supplemental jurisdiction is restricted as a way of conserving the resources of the federal courts and of encouraging litigants to take such disputes to the state courts. Section 1367(b), therefore, carves out a number of claims and parties in diversity cases from the broad grant of supplemental jurisdiction contained in section 1367(a).

(3) Specified Exceptions from Supplemental Jurisdiction

The analytic structure of section 1367(a) and (b) is that a broad grant of supplemental jurisdiction is conferred under subsection (a), from which is excepted the specific claims and parties in diversity suits described in subsection (b). If a claim or party satisfies the test in subsection (a) and is not mentioned in subsection (b), the supplemental jurisdiction may be exercised under subsection (a).

EXAM TIP

Many exams will provide student access to the text of the statute. If yours will not, you may best prepare through plain old memorization. You should *memorize the text of section 1367(b)* (while keeping in mind that *complete diversity is required* even if the Rule is not mentioned; *see infra,* p. 153) and the basic provisions of *the Federal Rules mentioned in that section.*

(a) Claims Made by Plaintiffs

In diversity cases, claims made by plaintiffs against persons made parties under Rules 14, 19, 20, and 24 that fail to meet the requirements of diversity jurisdiction *(i.e.,* complete diversity and an amount in controversy of more than $75,000) are excepted from supplemental jurisdiction.

1) Rule 14—Impleader

A claim *by the plaintiff* directly against a third-party defendant impleaded under Rule 14(a) that fails to meet the diversity jurisdiction requirements is also forbidden. This provision codifies the result of **Owen Equipment & Erection Co. v. Kroger** (*see supra*, p. 148), in which the Supreme Court held that a plaintiff in a diversity suit could not claim directly against a third-party defendant unless there was an independent basis for subject matter jurisdiction over that claim.

a) But Note

An impleader claim *by the defendant* against a third-party defendant, and a claim by the *third-party defendant* against the plaintiff, under Rule 14(a) *are* within supplemental jurisdiction (*see infra*).

2) Rule 19—Joinder of Persons Needed for Just Adjudication

A claim by the plaintiff against a defendant joined under Rule 19 that fails to meet the diversity jurisdiction requirements is again forbidden. This is a codification of previously established lower court case law.

3) Rule 20—Permissive Joinder of Parties

A claim against a defendant joined by the plaintiff under Rule 20 that fails to meet the diversity jurisdiction requirements is yet again forbidden. This is a partial explicit codification of the "complete diversity" rule that has existed since **Strawbridge v. Curtiss**, *supra*, p. 126.

4) Rule 24—Intervention

A claim against a defendant who has intervened under Rule 24, either as of right (Rule 24(a)) or permissively (Rule 24(b)), is forbidden if the diversity jurisdiction requirements are not met. This is a slight change from prior law. Previously, there had been ancillary jurisdiction over the claim against an intervenor as of right under Rule 24(a) unless that person would have been "indispensable" if he had been sought to be joined under Rule 19. This odd interrelationship between Rules 24 and 19 had been criticized as an anomaly, and has now been eliminated.

(b) Claims by Persons Who Might Become Plaintiffs

A claim brought by a party proposed to be joined as a plaintiff under Rule 19, or seeking to intervene as a plaintiff under Rule 24, is forbidden in a diversity case if the requirements for diversity jurisdiction are not met.

(c) Alignment of Parties

Diversity depends on the way the parties are aligned. The federal courts have long claimed the power to re-align the parties in accordance with their true interests, even where that re-alignment has an impact on the court's jurisdiction. Thus, a party proposed for joinder as a plaintiff may be re-aligned as a defendant if the court regards the interests of the party as running counter to those of the plaintiff.

SECTION 1367(b) DOES NOT ALLOW SUPPLEMENTAL JURISDICTION OVER:
☑ A claim by a plaintiff against an ***impleaded defendant*** (Rule 14);
☑ A claim by or against ***any party joined as a person needed for just adjudication*** (Rule 19);
☑ A claim by the plaintiff against a ***permissively joined defendant*** (Rule 20); and
☑ A claim by or against ***intervening parties*** (Rule 24).

(4) Two Problem Cases—Now Resolved

Inartful drafting of section 1367 has resulted in two problem cases—joinder of plaintiffs' claims under Rule 20 and claims of unnamed plaintiffs in class actions under Rule 23.

(a) Joinder of Plaintiffs' Claims Under Rule 20

Rule 20 allows permissive joinder of both plaintiffs' and defendants' claims when they arise out of the same transaction or occurrence. Section 1367(b) excepts from supplemental jurisdiction "claims by plaintiffs against persons made parties under Rule . . . 20"—*i.e.,* claims ***against multiple defendants*** joined under Rule 20. However, it does ***not*** except claims ***by multiple plaintiffs*** joined under Rule 20. Thus, if section 1367 is read literally, there is supplemental jurisdiction in multiple-plaintiff cases when one plaintiff is diverse from the defendant but other plaintiffs are not, or when one plaintiff alleges the jurisdictional amount but other plaintiffs do not.

(b) Claims of Unnamed Plaintiffs in Class Actions Under Rule 23

Prior to the enactment of the supplemental jurisdiction statute, the Supreme Court, in **Zahn v. International Paper Co.**, *supra*, p. 139, faced a diversity class action in which the named class representatives asserted claims in excess of the jurisdictional requirement and proposed to include unnamed class members with claims below that amount. The Court held that ancillary jurisdiction did not extend to the plaintiffs with below-threshold claims. However, the supplemental jurisdiction statute, in section 1367(b), does not except from supplemental jurisdiction claims by plaintiffs under Rule 23. Thus, if read literally, section 1367 would overturn *Zahn* and supplemental jurisdiction would extend to the claims of unnamed plaintiffs that fall below the jurisdictional amount, if at least one of the members of the class met the requirements of diverse citizenship and the jurisdictional amount.

(c) Alternative to the Literal Reading of Section 1367

Recognizing that the drafters of the statute may not have intended to alter the rules of diversity jurisdiction, some federal courts adopted an alternative to the literal reading of section 1367. Under this alternative view, supplemental jurisdiction would come into play only after original jurisdiction attaches to the claims in the initial complaint, and pendent party and pendent claim jurisdiction would be available only in federal question proceedings (allowing the plaintiff to join claims arising under state law with related claims arising under federal law). In diversity proceedings, by contrast, pendent party jurisdiction would have no place where it operated to undermine the complete diversity rule. Rules of original jurisdiction would continue to require the plaintiffs to frame an initial complaint that complied with the traditional rules of complete diversity. Only then would supplemental jurisdiction come into play, primarily in the form of what was once known as ancillary jurisdiction. Such an interpretive approach would preserve the complete diversity rule in Rule 20 and Rule 23 proceedings and would maintain the result in *Zahn*.

(d) Problem Cases Resolved

In **Exxon Mobil Corp. v. Allapattah Services, Inc.**, *supra*, p. 139, the Supreme Court resolved these two problem cases. Although the Court reaffirmed the requirement of ***complete diversity***, it concluded that supplemental jurisdiction would extend to related claims that fell below the $75,000 threshold.

e.g. **Example:** Three plaintiffs joined their claims under Rule 20 against the manufacturer of an allegedly defective product. All three satisfied the diversity of citizenship requirement, but the claim of only one of the plaintiffs met the jurisdictional threshold of $75,000. Since original jurisdiction attached to the claims of that one plaintiff, section 1367 conferred supplemental jurisdiction over the related claims of the other plaintiffs. [**Exxon Mobil Corp. v. Allapattah Services, Inc.**, *supra*] The Court indicated in a considered dictum that supplemental jurisdiction would not attach to the related claims of plaintiffs if they lack the requisite diversity of citizenship. (The Court described this as an application of a contamination rule whereby the presence of a non-diverse citizen precludes jurisdiction. Claims below the $75,000 threshold were not viewed as triggering this contamination principle.)

e.g. **Example:** Plaintiffs brought a Rule 23 class action against Exxon Mobil. The named plaintiffs satisfied both the diversity of citizenship requirement and the amount in controversy; the claims of unnamed plaintiff class members fell below the threshold. Nonetheless, the Court ruled that section 1367 conferred supplemental jurisdiction over these below-threshold claims. It thus concluded that the statute had overturned the rule in **Zahn v. International Paper Co.**, *supra*, p. 151.

1) Note

The Court in *Exxon Mobil* assumed (without deciding) that the members of the plaintiff class satisfied the complete diversity rule and were asserting claims that met the same case or controversy test of section 1367(a). Under the rule of *Ben Hur, supra*, p. 128, federal courts have generally determined the citizenship of a plaintiff class by looking to the citizenship of the named class representatives. The Court in *Exxon Mobil* did not discuss the application of the *Ben Hur* rule to Rule 23(b)(3) class actions. But the claims of the named class representative appear to be decisive both for purposes of determining the citizenship of the class and the amount in controversy; supplemental jurisdiction extends to the claims of nondiverse unnamed plaintiff class members with related but below-threshold claims. The Court did not consider whether the acceptance of non-diverse class members violated the complete-diversity-preserving contamination principle.

2) Complete Diversity Preserved

The Court's resolution does not seem fully consistent with the literal interpretation of section 1367, which it seemed to embrace. A strictly literal interpretation would treat the supplemental jurisdiction statute as overriding both the jurisdictional amount requirement and the complete diversity requirement, but the Court went out of its way to preserve the complete diversity rule. Apparently, the Court viewed the complete diversity rule as more significant, perhaps due to the fact that Article III requires diversity of citizenship whereas the amount in controversy rule is a creature of statute.

(5) Nonexcepted Supplemental Jurisdiction in Diversity Cases

Supplemental jurisdiction in the following cases has not been specifically excepted by section 1367(b) and therefore exists in diversity cases.

(a) Rule 13(a)—Compulsory Counterclaim

When a defendant asserts a *compulsory counterclaim* under Rule 13(a), there is supplemental jurisdiction over that claim. Rule 13(a) requires that a compulsory counterclaim arise out of the "transaction or occurrence that is the subject matter of the opposing party's claim." Thus, Rule 13(a), by its terms, ensures that a compulsory counterclaim will be closely related to the claim over which there is an independent basis for jurisdiction.

e.g. **Example:** Plaintiff of nondiverse citizenship sues defendant on a federal claim. Defendant asserts a compulsory counterclaim based on state law under Rule 13(a). There is no independent jurisdictional basis because there is no diversity, but there is supplemental jurisdiction over the compulsory counterclaim.

(b) Rule 13(b)—Permissive Counterclaim

Lower court cases previously held that there was ancillary jurisdiction over a *permissive counterclaim* for a *setoff,* even though the claim giving rise to the setoff was unrelated to the plaintiff's primary claim that formed the basis for original jurisdiction. [**Ambromovage v. United Mine Workers of America**, *supra*, p. 148; **United States v. Heyward-Robinson Co.**, *supra*, p. 148] If such jurisdiction is within the constitutional definition of a "case or controversy" (which is somewhat unclear), there is supplemental jurisdiction under section 1367. [See **Jones v. Ford Motor Credit Co.**, 358 F.3d 205 (2d Cir. 2004) (upholding supplemental jurisdiction over permissive counterclaim) (citing Fletcher, "Common Nucleus of Operative Fact" and Defensive Set-Off: Beyond the Gibbs Test, 74 Ind. L.J. 171 (1998)]

1) Caveat

The *general rule* for permissive counterclaims, however, is that there is *no supplemental jurisdiction* because, by definition, a permissive counterclaim does not arise out of the "transaction or occurrence that is the subject matter of the opposing party's claim." Supplemental jurisdiction over permissive counterclaims for setoff is a narrow exception to that general rule.

(c) Rule 13(g)—Cross-Claim

When a party asserts a *cross-claim* against a co-party (usually a defendant asserting a cross-claim against a co-defendant) under Rule 13(g), there is supplemental jurisdiction over that cross-claim. Rule 13(g) requires that the cross-claim arise out of the "transaction or occurrence that is the subject matter either of the original action or of a counterclaim therein or relating to any property that is the subject of the original action." Thus, like Rule 13(a), Rule 13(g) by its terms insures that a cross-claim will be closely related to a claim over which there is an independent basis for jurisdiction.

(d) Rule 14—Impleader

A *defendant* may *implead* a third-party defendant under Rule 14(a) when that third party "is or may be liable to him for all or part of plaintiff's claim against him." (A plaintiff may also implead a third party under Rule 14(b)—for possible liability under a *counterclaim*—but that situation arises relatively infrequently.) Three different situations can arise under Rule 14 impleader. Supplemental jurisdiction is permitted in two of them.

1) The Impleader Itself

There is supplemental jurisdiction over the impleader claim asserted against the third-party defendant. Since Rule 14 impleader is based on possible liability on the plaintiff's claim, an impleader will necessarily be closely related to the claim over which there is an independent basis for jurisdiction.

e.g. **Example:** Plaintiff sues defendant in diversity for injury caused when defendant served spoiled food to plaintiff. Defendant brings a third-party claim under Rule 14(a) against the company that supplied him with the spoiled food. There is no diversity of citizenship between the defendant and the third-party defendant. There is supplemental jurisdiction over the third-party impleader claim.

2) Claim by Third-Party Defendant Against Plaintiff

A few lower court cases held that there was ancillary jurisdiction over a claim filed by an *impleaded third-party defendant* against the original plaintiff. This jurisdiction is continued, although now called supplemental jurisdiction. Rule 14 requires that such a claim arise out of the "transaction or occurrence" that is the subject matter of the plaintiff's claim against the defendant, thus insuring that the third-party defendant's claim will be closely connected to the claim over which there is an independent basis for jurisdiction.

e.g. **Example:** Plaintiff sues a defendant in diversity on a surety bond. Defendant impleads third-party defendant on the ground that liability on the bond is due to the fault of third-party defendant. Third-party defendant then claims against plaintiff, alleging misconduct by plaintiff in the transaction in question. There is no diversity between third-party defendant and plaintiff. There is supplemental jurisdiction over the claim of third-party defendant against plaintiff. [**Revere Copper & Brass, Inc. v. Aetna Casualty & Surety Co.**, 426 F.2d 709 (5th Cir. 1970)]

3) Distinguish—Claim by Plaintiff Against Third-Party Defendant Under Rule 14(a)

There is *no* supplemental jurisdiction over a claim by the plaintiff against the impleaded third-party defendant. Such a claim is specifically excepted out of supplemental jurisdiction under section 1367(b). (*See supra*, p. 150.)

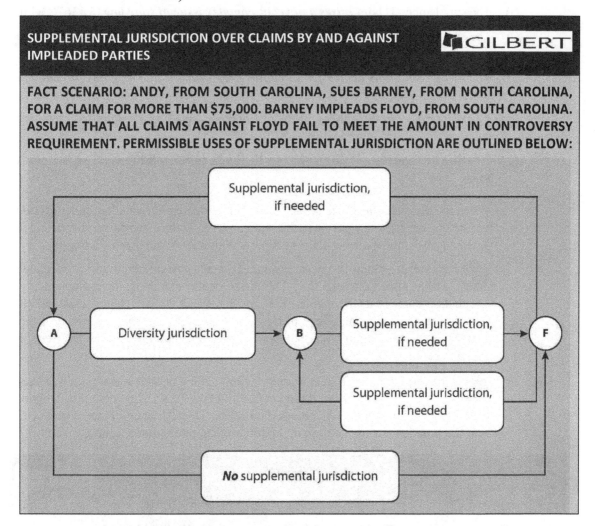

SUPPLEMENTAL JURISDICTION OVER CLAIMS BY AND AGAINST IMPLEADED PARTIES

GILBERT

FACT SCENARIO: ANDY, FROM SOUTH CAROLINA, SUES BARNEY, FROM NORTH CAROLINA, FOR A CLAIM FOR MORE THAN $75,000. BARNEY IMPLEADS FLOYD, FROM SOUTH CAROLINA. ASSUME THAT ALL CLAIMS AGAINST FLOYD FAIL TO MEET THE AMOUNT IN CONTROVERSY REQUIREMENT. PERMISSIBLE USES OF SUPPLEMENTAL JURISDICTION ARE OUTLINED BELOW:

(e) Rule 23—Class Actions

As long as there is diversity of citizenship between the named members of a class and the opposing parties in a diversity-based class action, it does not matter that there is no diversity between unnamed members of the class and opposing parties. There is supplemental jurisdiction over the claims of the unnamed nondiverse parties—at least in a Rule 23(b)(1) class action. [**Supreme Tribe of Ben-Hur v. Cauble**, *supra*, p. 152]

c. District Court May Decline to Exercise Supplemental Jurisdiction Under Section 1367(c)

Even if supplemental jurisdiction is available to a district court, the court is not always compelled to exercise that jurisdiction. Section 1367(c) specifies the circumstances in which a "district court may decline to exercise supplemental jurisdiction of a claim under subsection (a)." [28 U.S.C. § 1367(c)] These circumstances are derived from (but are not identical to) the criteria set forth in **United Mine Workers v. Gibbs**, *supra*, p. 148, for declining to exercise pendent jurisdiction. The circumstances are:

(i) The supplemental claim *raises a novel or complex issue of state law* [§ 1367(c)(1)];

(ii) The supplemental claim *substantially predominates* over the claims over which the district court has original jurisdiction [§ 1367(c)(2)];

(iii) The district court *has dismissed all claims over which it had original jurisdiction* [§ 1367(c)(3)]; or

(iv) In *exceptional circumstances*, there are *other compelling reasons* for declining supplemental jurisdiction [§ 1367(c)(4)].

(1) Decline of Exercise of Jurisdiction Extends to Supplemental Jurisdiction Only

When the district court exercises its discretion to decline jurisdiction under section 1367(c), it declines to hear only the supplemental claims. It has no discretion to decline jurisdiction over the claims properly within its original jurisdiction.

e.g. **Example:** Plaintiff asserts a single federal question claim and four related claims based on state law. The district court concludes that supplemental jurisdiction extends to the whole case, but that the state law claims substantially predominate over the single federal claim. The district court may decline to assert supplemental jurisdiction over the state claims, but may not dismiss the federal question claim.

e.g. **Example:** Same facts as above, except that the district court initially agrees to hear the whole case. After several months of discovery, defendant obtains summary judgment on the federal question claim. The district court may continue to hear the state law claims or may, in its discretion, dismiss those claims.

GROUNDS FOR DISCRETIONARY DECLINE OF SUPPLEMENTAL JURISDICTION	GILBERT
THE FEDERAL DISTRICT COURT MAY DECLINE SUPPLEMENTAL JURISDICTION WHEN:	

☑ The supplemental claim *raises a novel or complex issue of state law;*

☑ The supplemental claim *substantially predominates* over the claims within original jurisdiction;

☑ The district court *has dismissed all claims over which it had original jurisdiction;* or

☑ In *exceptional circumstances*, there are *other compelling reasons* for declining supplemental jurisdiction.

d. Statute of Limitations

District courts may exercise supplemental jurisdiction over state law claims for a time and then dismiss those claims in the exercise of their discretion (or after concluding that they do not come within the scope of the court's supplemental jurisdiction). Sometimes, however, the statute of limitations will have expired before the court declines to exercise supplemental jurisdiction. The question then becomes whether the plaintiff may timely file the dismissed claims in an appropriate state court. Section 1367(d) answers that question by providing that the statute of limitations is tolled during the pendency of the federal proceeding and for at least an additional 30 days following dismissal, unless state law provides a longer period. It thus guarantees at least a 30-day period during which the plaintiff may re-file the state claims.

(1) Constitutional Doubts About Tolling the Limitations Period

Despite the straightforward justification for the rule, state and local governments have questioned Congress's power to apply a federal tolling rule to extend the time for filing state law claims against them in state court. Generally, the tolling rule does not apply to state law claims joined in federal court with a claim that was later dismissed *on Eleventh Amendment* grounds.

Example: supplemental claims against the states: The plaintiff brought suit in federal court against the University of Minnesota, alleging both a federal and state law claim of discrimination in employment. Following dismissal of the federal claim as barred by the Eleventh Amendment, the district court dismissed the related state law claim. Plaintiff re-filed the state law claim in state court, invoking the tolling rule of section 1367(d). The state court invalidated the federal tolling rule, concluding that the state was immune from suit in federal court and could not be subjected to suit in state court on a claim that would have been untimely as a matter of state law but for the provisions of section 1367(d). The Supreme Court avoided the issue through use of the clear statement canon: It found that Congress had not clearly stated its intention to apply the tolling rule to claims brought against the state. As a result, the tolling rule does not apply to state claims against a state joined in federal court with a federal claim that was later dismissed on Eleventh Amendment grounds. [**Raygor v. Board of Regents of the University of Minnesota**, 534 U.S. 533 (2002)]

Compare: supplemental claims against counties: The plaintiff brought a section 1983 claim against a *county* government in connection with her husband's death during his confinement in jail, and she joined related state law claims for wrongful death. Following dismissal of the federal claim, the plaintiff re-filed the state law claims in state court. The county invoked the clear statement rule from *Raygor, supra*, and further argued that the statute exceeded the power of Congress. The Court rejected both of the county's arguments. As for its Eleventh Amendment/clear statement claim, the Court followed established law in finding that counties cannot invoke Eleventh Amendment immunity (and thus have no right to a clear statutory statement). As for the scope of congressional power, the Court found that the tolling rule, even though it applied to state law claims brought in state court, was a necessary and proper response to the problems of timeliness that supplemental jurisdiction had caused in the federal system. Any impact on state practice was incidental. [**Jinks v. Richland County, South Carolina**, 538 U.S. 456 (2003—affirming constitutionality of section 1367(d))]

(2) Applying the Tolling Rule

Granted that Congress has the power to extend the limitations period for local law claims that were litigated as supplemental claims in federal court and then returned to state court, how does the statute actually work? Some courts ruled that the tolling provision in section 1367(d) stops the clock during the pendency of federal litigation; others found that the state clock continues to run but that federal law provides a 30-day grace period after the completion of the federal litigation to refile supplemental claims in state court. The Supreme Court answered that question in **Artis v. District of Columbia**, 138 S. Ct. 594 (2018), adopting the "stop-the-clock" interpretation. Artis sued first in federal court, pursuing a federal employment discrimination claim and three supplemental claims under the law of the District of Columbia. After nearly three years of litigation, the federal court dismissed her federal claim and then exercised discretion to dismiss her local law claims as well. Artis re-filed the local law claims in the District of Columbia courts, too late to meet the 30 day grace period but in plenty of time to satisfy the local three-year timeliness standard if federal litigation of those claims stopped the clock. Relying on plain meaning and rejecting the argument that such a view would impinge on local control of timeliness, the Court adopted the broader stop-the-clock interpretation and upheld the timeliness of Artis's suit.

B. Removal Jurisdiction

1. In General

Generally, the plaintiff chooses the forum by filing her suit in either state or federal court. However, many suits originally filed in state court may be "removed" by the defendant to federal district court before trial. In some respects, removal jurisdiction is almost, but not quite, as broad as the district court's original jurisdiction. In other respects, removal jurisdiction is broader. The most important statute is the basic removal statute [28 U.S.C. § 1441]. Other statutes permit removal of suits against federal officers [28 U.S.C. § 1442] and in certain civil rights cases [28 U.S.C. § 1443].

a. Note

There is no removal *from* federal district court *to* state court. Thus, if the plaintiff files suit in federal court, the defendant cannot remove the case to state court. The defendant can, however, seek dismissal if the federal court lacks jurisdiction or ask the federal court to abstain.

EXAM TIP   ▐ GILBERT

For your exam, remember that there is no such thing as removal *from* a federal district court *to* a state court—the plaintiff's choice of a federal forum will prevail (assuming there is federal subject matter jurisdiction and none of the abstention doctrines apply).

---

2. Basic Removal Statute

The first section of the basic removal statute provides: "Except as otherwise expressly provided by Act of Congress, any civil action brought in a State court of which the district courts of the United States have original jurisdiction, may be removed by the defendant or defendants, to the district court of the United States for the district and division embracing the place where such action is pending." [28 U.S.C. § 1441(a)]

a. District Court Must Have Original Jurisdiction

To be removable, a suit must be within the district court's original jurisdiction. Therefore, all jurisdictional requirements of federal question or diversity jurisdiction must be satisfied. For example, a state court suit must satisfy the well-pleaded complaint rule before it can be removed on the basis of federal question jurisdiction. Once the requirements of original jurisdiction have been met, the district court on removal can assert supplemental jurisdiction over state law claims to the same extent it could in an action filed in federal court.

(1) Criticism of Well-Pleaded Complaint Rule as Applied to Removal

The justification of the well-pleaded complaint rule in original suits is that it permits the district court to determine its jurisdiction at the earliest possible stage merely by looking at the plaintiff's complaint. Furthermore, it permits a plaintiff who relies on federal law to come into federal court for vindication of that right. But these justifications do not support the application of the rule to removal. Removal is sought by the defendant, so the federal court must wait until after the filing of the complaint before determining its jurisdiction. Also, the defendant who asserts a federal defense has an interest in coming into federal court for vindication of his asserted federal right. (For a more detailed discussion of the well-pleaded complaint rule and its application to removed cases, *see supra*, pp. 120 *et seq.*)

b. State Court Need Not Have Jurisdiction

A case may be removed from state to federal court even if the state court from which it is removed did not have subject matter jurisdiction. This means that if a case within the exclusive jurisdiction of the federal courts (*e.g.*, a federal antitrust suit) is filed erroneously in state court, the case generally may be removed to federal court despite the fact that the state court never had jurisdiction over it. [28 U.S.C. § 1441(e)] *Note:* Under an old rule, federal courts regarded their removal jurisdiction as derivative of the jurisdiction that first attached in state court. If the defendant removed an action to federal court of which the state court lacked jurisdiction, then federal court would dismiss (thus requiring the plaintiff to re-file in federal court). Some federal courts have revived this approach when removal occurs under other statutes, particularly that governing federal officer removal.

c. All Defendants Must Seek to Remove

Section 1446(b)(2) prescribes the timing of removal and confirms the long-standing rule that all properly joined defendants must join together in consenting to remove. If any defendant refuses, removal is not permitted.

In general, section 1446(b) provides that removal must occur within 30 days of the receipt by the defendant(s) of a copy of the initial complaint. Although there had been some disagreement among lower federal courts, the statute now clarifies that the time for removal runs from the date on which the *last* defendant was served. The statute also gives a second opportunity to earlier served defendants. Even if they declined to remove within 30 days of their notice date, the statute permits them to join in a removal by a later-served defendant.

d. No Removal by Plaintiff

The right to remove belongs solely to the defendant(s). Thus, if the defendant counterclaims based on federal law, the plaintiff may not remove even though as to the counterclaim she is in a position analogous to a defendant.

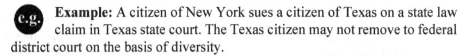 **Example:** Plaintiff sued a citizen of Texas in Texas state court on a state law claim. There was diversity of citizenship, but defendant could not remove because it was a citizen of the forum state. [28 U.S.C. § 1441(b); *see infra*, p. 160] Defendant counterclaimed for an amount in excess of the jurisdictional amount. If the counterclaim had been brought as an original claim, plaintiff (who is not a Texas citizen and who would have been a true defendant in such a case) could have removed. But since it was a counterclaim, no removal was permitted. [**Shamrock Oil & Gas Corp. v. Sheets**, 313 U.S. 100 (1941)]

e. No Removal in a Few Cases

There is no removal in a few cases in which the district court would have had jurisdiction had the suit been filed in its original jurisdiction.

(1) Diversity

Two kinds of diversity cases cannot be removed:

(a) Defendant a Citizen of Forum State

When the defendant in a state court case is a citizen of the forum state, she may not remove even if there is diversity of citizenship. [28 U.S.C. § 1441(b)(2)]

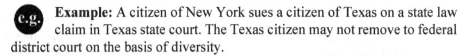 **Example:** A citizen of New York sues a citizen of Texas on a state law claim in Texas state court. The Texas citizen may not remove to federal district court on the basis of diversity.

1) Rationale

If an out-of-state plaintiff chooses to sue an in-state defendant in state court, there is no reason to fear undue prejudice against the in-state defendant. Moreover, by filing in state court, the out-of-state plaintiff has indicated that he trusts the state court to decide his case fairly.

####### a) But Note

This rationale is not carried to its logical extreme. Under this rationale, an in-state plaintiff should not be permitted to sue an out-of-state defendant in diversity in the federal courts of plaintiff's home state. Yet such an original suit even by an in-state plaintiff is permitted (assuming that the court has personal jurisdiction over the defendant and the venue requirements of section 1391(a) can be met). [28 U.S.C. § 1332]

(b) Workers' Compensation Cases

Removal of state law workers' compensation cases is ***prohibited*** even if there is diversity of citizenship and the amount in controversy exceeds $75,000. [28 U.S.C. § 1445(c)]

(2) Federal Question

In certain federal question cases, Congress has provided that a plaintiff shall have an irrevocable choice of forum. Under such statutes, a plaintiff may choose to sue in either federal or state court. If she chooses to sue in state court, the defendant cannot remove. [*See, e.g.,* 28 U.S.C. § 1445(a), *and* 45 U.S.C. §§ 51 *et seq.*—Federal Employers' Liability Act ("FELA"); 28 U.S.C. § 1445(b), *and* 49 U.S.C. § 14706 *et seq.*—Carmack Amendment to the Interstate Commerce Act]

f. Removal of Civil Action That Contains Both Removable Federal Law Claims and Non-Removable Claims

Section 1441(c), as revised in 2012, authorizes the removal of the whole action whenever the complaint includes a claim within the district court's federal question jurisdiction and another claim to which the district court's removal jurisdiction does not extend. Section 1441(c)(1)(B) describes these non-removable claims as follows: "a claim not within the original or supplemental jurisdiction of the district court or a claim that has been made nonremovable by statute." Section 1441(c)(2) further provides that, upon removal, the district court shall sever the non-removable claims and shall remand them to state court.

The purpose of the act is to protect the right of defendants to a federal forum for claims within federal jurisdiction and to avoid the exercise of jurisdiction over matters that do not fall within federal competence on removal. In analyzing the need for a severance and remand, therefore, one must assess claims to determine if they are non-removable. Non-removability may result from the joinder of a totally unrelated state law claim, one so distinct from the federal question claim that confers federal jurisdiction that it does not fall within the district court's supplemental jurisdiction under 28 U.S.C. section 1367(a). Or it may result from federal legislation that makes certain claims non-removable. [See p. 160] In either case, the district court is directed to remand all non-removable matters. [28 U.S.C. § 1441(c)]

(1) Limitation to Federal Question Cases

An old section 1441(c) permitted removal of "separate and independent" claims in both diversity and federal question cases. A later version limited such removal to federal question cases, but posed a set of procedural difficulties. The current section 1441(c) limits such removal to *federal question* cases.

g. Ways in Which Plaintiff Can Prevent Removal

In some circumstances, plaintiff can prevent removal.

(1) Pleading Less than Jurisdictional Amount

A plaintiff in a diversity case can allege that *$75,000 or less* is in controversy, thereby keeping the case out of federal court but also waiving any claim to a greater recovery. [**St. Paul Mercury Indemnity Co. v. Red Cab Co.**, *supra*, p. 134; **Sponholz v. Stanislaus**, 410 F. Supp. 286 (S.D.N.Y. 1976)]

(2) Joining Nondiverse Defendant or Assigning Claim to Nondiverse Plaintiff

To prevent removal, plaintiff can join additional defendants of nondiverse citizenship, thereby destroying complete diversity. [**Illinois Central Railroad v. Sheegog**, 215 U.S. 308 (1909)] Similarly, plaintiff may assign her claim to a party of nondiverse citizenship. [**Mecom v. Fitzsimmons Drilling Co.**, *supra*, p. 133]

(a) Limitation

The plaintiff may not defeat removal by "fraudulent" joinder—*i.e.*, a joinder that has *no legal basis*. [**Dodd v. Fawcett Publications, Inc.**, 329 F.2d 82 (10th Cir. 1964)] A few courts have also held that some assignments to nondiverse plaintiffs do not operate to defeat removal.

> **e.g.** **Example: fraudulent assignment:** Nine potato farmers, citizens of Maine, sued an Oregon corporation in Maine state court. Each plaintiff had assigned 1/100 of his claim to an Oregon citizen (a law school classmate of plaintiffs' lawyer) in order to defeat diversity. The district court permitted removal, disregarding the assignment as a "cynical device" designed to provide the benefit of local prejudice against a foreign corporation. [**Gentle v. Lamb-Weston, Inc.**, *supra*, p. 134]

1) Note

> The decision in **Gentle v. Lamb-Weston**, *supra*, runs contrary to the prevailing wisdom. It is well understood that 28 U.S.C. section 1359 prevents improper or collusive *creation* of diversity, but it is commonly thought that there is no such prohibition against comparable maneuvers to *defeat* diversity. (*See supra*, pp. 131–133.) But the decision in **Gentle v. Lamb-Weston** has been followed by a few lower courts.

(3) Pleading Only a State Law Claim

To prevent removal, the plaintiff may choose to rely only on state law claims, forgoing possible federal claims arising out of the dispute.

> **e.g.** **Example:** Plaintiff sued for wrongful discharge from employment under California state law. Plaintiff alleged no federal claim. Removal was not permitted because plaintiff "is the master of his or her own complaint." [**Garibaldi v. Lucky Food Stores, Inc.**, 726 F.2d 1367 (9th Cir. 1984)]

(a) Limitation

When plaintiff's state law claims are *completely preempted* by federal law, the true federal nature of the dispute will support removal jurisdiction even though the plaintiff attempted to couch the claim in state law terms.

> **e.g.** **Example:** An employer sued in state court to enjoin a strike, relying on a "no strike" clause in its collective bargaining agreement with the union. Removal was permitted because such a claim under collective bargaining agreements is governed by preempting federal law, rather than by state law. [**Avco Corp. v. Aero Lodge No. 735**, *supra*, p. 121]

> **e.g.** **Example:** An employee filed suit against his employer in state court under state law, seeking recovery of benefits under the employer's plan for ill and disabled workers. The employer was permitted to remove to federal court on the ground that the plaintiffs state law claims were completely preempted by the federal Employee Retirement Income Security Act ("ERISA"). [**Metropolitan Life Insurance Co. v. Taylor**, *supra*, p. 121]

> **e.g.** **Example:** A plaintiff filed suit under state law, seeking damages from a federally chartered national bank for usurious loan policies. The Court held that federal law preempted state law and provided an exclusive right of action. When those two factors coincide, the complete preemption doctrine

comes into play and the defendant can remove the state law claim. [**Beneficial National Bank v. Anderson**, 539 U.S. 1 (2003)]

---

1) Note

Some may wonder why a defendant would, as a matter of strategy, remove a completely preempted state law claim. By hypothesis, preemption will defeat the state claim and the state court would be expected to recognize that fact and dismiss the action. Removal transforms the preempted state claim into a viable federal claim and shifts the claim to a court competent to hear the matter. Although the removal strategy may seem counterintuitive, defendants in complete preemption cases typically remove because they have an alternative defense to the (transformed) federal claim and prefer to have a federal court rule on their complete preemption claim.

h. Procedure for Removal

A defendant seeking removal must file a notice of removal in the district court for the district in which the action is pending. The notice must contain a short and plain statement of the grounds for removal and must be accompanied by copies of all process, pleadings, and orders that have been served on the defendant. After filing for removal, defendant must notify adverse parties in writing and must file a copy of the notice in the state court. The state court may then proceed no further unless the case is remanded. [28 U.S.C. § 1446(a)]

(1) Timing

The notice of removal must be filed within 30 days of service of the summons or complaint on defendant, or within 30 days of an amended pleading or other paper making the case removable. A case based on *diversity* may not ordinarily be removed *more than one year* after it was commenced. [28 U.S.C. § 1446(c)] But the one-year limitation may be set aside by the district court on a finding that the plaintiff acted in bad faith to prevent the defendant from removing the action. [28 U.S.C. 1446(c)(2)]

e.g. **Example:** Plaintiff brought suit against a pharmaceutical company, and named the treating physician as an additional party to defeat complete diversity. Shortly after the one-year period for removal ran its course, plaintiff dismissed claims against the non-diverse defendant. The defendant removed anyway, arguing that the one-year limitation period on diversity-based removal was subject to an equitable exception in cases of manipulation. The Fifth Circuit agreed. [**Tedford v. Warner-Lambert Co.**, 327 F.3d 423 (5th Cir. 2003)] At the time, the one-year limit did not include a bad faith exception; it was added to the statute in 2012 essentially to codify the result in **Tedford**.

(2) Ruling by the District Court

Following removal, the plaintiff may file a motion to remand the case to state court. Such remand motions may contend either that the district court lacks removal jurisdiction or that the removal violated some procedural feature of federal law. Under section 1445, procedural defects are waived unless made the subject of a remand motion within 30 days of removal. Jurisdictional defects remain open for further consideration after the 30-day period has passed.

SUMMARY OF REMOVAL ISSUES　　　　　　　　　　　　　　　　**⬛GILBERT**

THE KEY REMOVAL ISSUES ARE:

- ☑ A federal court **must have jurisdiction** over the case; jurisdiction need not have been proper in the state court.

- ☑ Removal is to the federal district court whose **territory encompasses the state court.**

- ☑ **Only defendants** can remove, and **all** defendants must join in the removal.

- ☑ If the case contains a **claim based on a federal question** and **other non-removable claims** defendant may remove the whole case, but the district court must remand the non-removable claims.

- ☑ A case may **not be removed on diversity grounds** if any defendant is a citizen of the forum state.

- ☑ **Notice of removal** must be filed within 30 days of the date defendant receives a copy of the initial pleading unless the case becomes removable later (as by voluntary dismissal of a nondiverse defendant), in which event the case may be removed within 30 days of the date it becomes removable, but a case removable on **diversity** grounds may be removed only **within one year** after it was brought in state court, unless the plaintiff acted in bad faith to prevent removal.

- ☑ **In multiple defendant cases**, the 30 day period runs from the date on which the last defendant was served. Earlier served defendants who failed to act within 30 days of their date of service may nonetheless join in a removal initiated by the later-served defendant.

---

i. Appellate Review of Remand to State Court

Remand of a case to state court after removal under 28 U.S.C. section 1441 is "not reviewable on appeal or otherwise." [28 U.S.C. § 1447(d)] However, this prohibition against appellate review is not as unqualified as it seems. In **Thermtron Products, Inc. v. Hermansdorfer**, 423 U.S. 336 (1976), a federal district judge remanded a diversity case to state court on the openly stated grounds that the federal court's docket was too crowded and that other cases had higher priority. The Supreme Court held that section 1447(d) does not prevent appellate review of a remand when a district court makes it clear that it is remanding on a discretionary (if ultimately improper) ground, rather than on the basis of an absence of jurisdiction or a procedural error in effecting removal.

Example: Plaintiff filed state court action in which federal law claims were joined with supplemental claims under state law. Following removal, the district court dismissed the federal question claim and exercised its discretion to refrain from hearing the state law claims, remanding them to state court. Because the remand was a matter of discretion, rather than jurisdiction, the Court found that appellate jurisdiction was available to review the remand order. [**Carlsbad Technology, Inc. v. HIF Bio, Inc.**, 556 U.S. 635 (2009)]

(1) Note

It may appear that *Thermtron Products* does not significantly inhibit a district judge who desires to remand improperly. If the district judge simply recites, in the statutory language, that the case had been "removed improvidently and without jurisdiction," the court of appeals will probably be unable to inquire into the real reasons for remand.

e.g. **Example:** In **Powerex Corp. v. Reliant Energy Systems, Inc.**, 551 U.S. 224 (2007), the Supreme Court ruled that remand orders based on a "colorable" finding of a lack of subject matter jurisdiction were not subject to appellate review. As a consequence, an appellate court may not review the merits of the subject matter jurisdiction conclusion of the district court, but may only consider if the issue was debatable. The Court's approach apparently leaves open the possibility of review for a wholly groundless jurisdictional remand.

(2) Also Note

There may be statutes elsewhere in federal law that so clearly foreclose a remand that the appellate courts may intervene notwithstanding the terms of section 1447(d).

e.g. **Example:** In **Osborn v. Haley**, 549 U.S. 225 (2007), the Court concluded that the Westfall Act operates as a clear bar to remand, and thereby authorizes appellate review of erroneous remand orders. The Westfall Act supplements the right of federal officers to remove suits from state to federal court (*see infra*, pp. 167 *et seq.*). It provides for substitution of the federal government as the defendant following a certification by the Attorney General of the United States that a federal officer, sued for damages, was acting in the course of employment. The Act treats the certification as conclusive for removal purposes, and thus forecloses a district court from reviewing the certification in the course of determining its removal jurisdiction (although the district court can review the certification in the course of adjudicating the merits). The Court found that the Westfall Act also created an implied exception to section 1447(d)'s prohibition against the review of erroneous remand orders.

3. Civil Rights Removal

A post-Civil War statute provides for removal of civil and criminal suits to federal district courts when civil rights protecting racial equality are in jeopardy. [28 U.S.C. § 1443] This statute has been interpreted narrowly, however, and removal is rarely available under it.

a. Statutory Language

The statute provides for removal of civil and criminal suits in which the defendant "is denied or cannot enforce in [state court] a right under any law providing for the equal civil rights of citizens of the United States . . . ." [28 U.S.C. § 1443(1)]

b. Racial Equality

Although the statute refers to "equal civil rights," it has been construed to permit removal only when rights concerning *racial* equality are at issue. [**Georgia v. Rachel**, 384 U.S. 780 (1966)]

c. Inability to Protect Rights in State Court

A defendant seeking removal must show that he is "denied" his civil rights in state court or "cannot enforce" those rights in state court.

(1) Cases Permitting Removal

Removal under section 1443(1) has been permitted in two kinds of cases. It bears emphasis, however, that neither kind of case occurs frequently.

(a) State Law Denying Racial Equality

If there is a "pervasive and explicit" state law that denies racial equality in state court proceedings, removal will be permitted. [**Greenwood v. Peacock**, 384 U.S. 808 (1966)]

e.g. **Example:** A black man was indicted for murder in West Virginia. West Virginia law specifically provided that only white men could sit on petit and grand juries in the West Virginia court system. The Supreme Court held that the black defendant was entitled to pretrial removal to federal court. [**Strauder v. West Virginia**, 100 U.S. 303 (1880)]

(b) Federal Law Protecting Against State Court Prosecution

If federal law protects against state court prosecutions that would violate rights to racial equality, removal will be permitted.

e.g. **Example:** Twenty defendants were charged with violating Georgia's criminal trespass statute after they conducted "sit-ins" at segregated restaurants. The federal Civil Rights Act of 1964 prohibited state trespass *prosecutions* (not just convictions) arising out of peaceful attempts to receive nondiscriminatory service. Removal to federal court was permitted to protect the right not to be prosecuted. [**Georgia v. Rachel**, *supra*, p. 165]

(2) Cases Denying Removal

(a) State Statute Not Considered by State Courts

Even though a state statute might deny equal rights in such a way as to permit removal, no removal is proper until the state courts have considered the validity of the statute. [Gibson v. Mississippi, 162 U.S. 565 (1896)]

(b) Illegal Acts by State Officials

Removal is not permitted merely because state officials have acted, or are acting, in a way that denies rights to racial equality.

e.g. **Example:** Two black men were indicted for murder in Virginia. They alleged that the practice in Virginia courts was to choose only white men as jurors. The Supreme Court held that such an allegation did not support removal. The Court said that such a practice would violate the Constitution, but was not a state *statutory* denial of right necessary for removal. [**Virginia v. Rives**, 100 U.S. 313 (1880)]

e.g. **Example:** Criminal charges against numerous defendants were brought under Mississippi law. The defendants sought to remove to federal court on the ground that they were being prosecuted because of their civil rights activities, and that they were unable to get a fair trial on the charges in state court. Removal was denied. There was no allegation of a statute denying racial equality that prevented a fair trial. Furthermore, there was no federal statute forbidding the prosecutions in question. [**Greenwood v. Peacock**, *supra*, p. 166]

d. Rationale Behind Narrow Construction of Section 1443(1)

The rationale behind the narrow construction of section 1443(1) is that, except in rare instances, state courts should be trusted to protect federal rights. Only where a state statute clearly mandates discriminatory treatment by the court [*see* **Strauder v. West Virginia**, *supra*, p. 166—all-white jury], or where a federal statute specifically prohibits prosecution [*see* **Georgia v. Rachel**, *supra*], will removal be permitted. Predicting whether a fair trial will take place on "particular federal claims before particular state courts" would involve federal courts in "the unseemly process of prejudging their brethren of the state courts." [**Georgia v. Rachel**, *supra*]

e. Other Ways of Protecting Litigants Against Unequal Treatment by State Courts

The Supreme Court in **Greenwood v. Peacock**, *supra*, suggested three mechanisms other than removal by which a litigant's federal rights to equal treatment could be protected.

(1) Direct Review in Supreme Court

Direct appellate review in the Supreme Court is a statutorily available remedy. [28 U.S.C. § 1257; *see supra*, p. 85] But the large number of cases seeking review and the relatively small number of cases actually heard mean that, as a practical matter, the ability of the Supreme Court to protect rights by direct review in individual cases is extremely limited.

(2) Injunction Against State Court Proceedings

Federal courts have the power, under certain circumstances, to enjoin state court proceedings that threaten to violate federal rights. The exercise of this power is governed by principles of "equitable restraint." The power is employed relatively rarely. (*See infra*, pp. 240–248.)

(3) Federal Habeas Corpus

Federal courts can review asserted denials of federal rights in state court criminal prosecutions. Despite recent decisions and legislation cutting back its availability, habeas corpus is still a useful remedy for violation of federal rights by state courts. (*See infra*, pp. 249 *et seq.*)

f. Appellate Review

Decisions to remove under section 1443, and to remand after removal, are both reviewable on appeal. [28 U.S.C. § 1447(d)] *Note:* Recall that decisions to remand after removal under the basic removal statute, section 1441, are *not* reviewable "on appeal or otherwise," except as provided in **Thermtron Products, Inc. v. Hermansdorfer** and its progeny (*see supra*, p. 164).

4. Removal of Suits Against Federal Officers

A federal officer sued in a civil or criminal proceeding in state court for acts performed *under color of office* may remove the suit to federal court. [28 U.S.C. § 1442(a)(*l*)]

a. Historical Background

The most important predecessor to the modern federal officer statute was the "Force Bill" of 1833, designed to protect officers collecting customs revenue. A successor statute was also applied to collection of federal internal revenue and associated seizures of illegal distilleries. [**Tennessee v. Davis**, 100 U.S. 257 (1880)]

b. Modern Scope

The present removal statute applies to federal officers in general and is not limited to customs and revenue officers. (A related statute specifically provides for removal by members of the armed forces.) [28 U.S.C. § 1442(a)]

c. Connection to Federal Duties

The statute permits removal by a federal officer when the suit arises out of an act performed under color of the federal office; out of an act performed under federal authority; out of the apprehension or punishment of criminals; or out of the collection of federal revenue. [28 U.S.C. § 1442(a)(*l*)] The removal provision is "broad enough to cover all cases where federal officers can raise several defenses arising out of their duty to enforce federal law." [**Willingham v. Morgan**, 395 U.S. 402 (1969)]

e.g. **Example:** An inmate in a federal penitentiary charged in a civil suit in state court that the warden and the chief medical officer had physically abused him in various ways. The warden and medical officer were permitted to remove on a showing that the acts charged "occurred inside the penitentiary, while [defendants] were performing their duties." [**Willingham v. Morgan**, *supra*]

d. Federal Defense Required

A federal officer seeking removal must allege a colorable federal defense or immunity to the state criminal prosecution. It is not enough simply to allege that the act occurred during the performance of the defendant's federal duties. [**Mesa v. California**, 489 U.S. 121 (1989)]

(1) Effect of Westfall Act in Suit for Damages

The *Mesa* case may have less practical significance in suits for damages against federal government officials now that the adoption of the Westfall Act makes the government's certification that the employee was acting within the scope of employment at the time of the alleged tort a sufficient basis for removal of the action. [*See* **Osborn v. Haley**, *supra*, p. 165]

After removal, the suit proceeds against the government (rather than the federal officer) under the Federal Tort Claims Act.

e. Law Applied

The same **criminal** law applies after removal that would have been applied in the absence of removal. [**Arizona v. Manypenny**, 451 U.S. 232 (1981)] Thus, if a state criminal prosecution against a federal officer is removed, the federal district court will conduct a trial of a criminal prosecution based on state law.

cf. **Compare:** As noted above, in **civil** actions against federal officers removed under the Westfall Act, federal law will be substituted for state law following removal of an action against a federal officer acting in the scope of employment. Federal law may incorporate state law as to the standard of care and the measure of liability.

C. Venue

1. In General

Even if the federal district court already has subject matter jurisdiction of a dispute and in personam jurisdiction over the parties, there must also be **proper venue** in that court. Venue is a separate, largely statutory requirement that is designed to fine-tune the decision as to the proper place to bring the action.

EXAM TIP

Don't confuse venue with jurisdiction. Jurisdiction involves the **power** of the court to decide a case (subject matter jurisdiction) and to exercise its power over a particular defendant or piece of property (territorial or personal jurisdiction). Venue involves the **proper place** to bring the action.

---

a. Primarily Designed to Protect Defendant

The primary purpose of venue is to protect the defendant, since one may presume that the plaintiff, who chose the forum, has already taken her own interests into account. "In most instances, the purpose of statutorily specified venue is to protect the **defendant** against the risk that a plaintiff will select an unfair or inconvenient place of trial." [**Leroy v. Great Western United Corp.**, 443 U.S. 173 (1979) (emphasis in original)]

b. Waivable Defect

Unlike a defect in subject matter jurisdiction, a defect in venue *is waivable.* A failure to register a timely objection to improper venue will be deemed a waiver. [Fed. R. Civ. P. 12(b)(3)(h)]

c. Overall Statutory Scheme

The overall statutory scheme is composed of a general venue statute [28 U.S.C. §§ 1390–91] and a large number of special venue statutes for particular kinds of suits [*e.g.*, 28 U.S.C. § 1396—internal revenue; 28 U.S.C. § 1400—patents and copyrights]. In most cases the general and special venue statutes are supplemental; in such cases, venue is proper if it can be found under *either* the general or applicable special venue statute. In other cases, the special venue statute is exclusive; in such cases venue is proper *only if* it can be found under the applicable special venue statute. (*See infra*, p. 174.)

2. General Venue Statute—Section 1390–91

The current version of the general venue statute took effect in 2012 and represents a significant departure from prior law.

a. Definition

28 U.S.C. § 1390 defines venue as a "geographic specification" of the proper court or courts for the litigation of a civil action" and specifically distinguishes venue from subject matter jurisdiction.

b. The General Rule—Three Bases

In civil actions brought in the federal district courts, venue is proper in a judicial district:

(i) "In which *any defendant resides,* if all defendants are residents of the State in which the district is located" [28 U.S.C. § 1391(b)(*l*)]; or

(ii) "In which *a substantial part of the events or omissions giving rise to the claim occurred,* or where a substantial part of the property that is the subject of the action is situated" [28 U.S.C. § 1391(b)(2)]; or

(iii) "*if there is no district in which the action may otherwise be brought as provided in this section,* any judicial district in which any defendant is *subject to the court's personal jurisdiction* with respect to such action" [28 U.S.C. § 1391(b)(3)].

(1) Relationship Among Three Bases for Venue

The first two bases for venue (section 1391(b)(1) and (b)(2)) may be used without restriction. The third basis for venue (section 1391(b)(3)) may be used only if the first two bases for venue fail; *i.e.,* it may be used *only as a fallback.*

(2) Choice of Forums Broad

The second and third bases for venue are particularly generous, giving the plaintiff a wide choice of forums.

(a) "A Substantial Part of Events or Omissions"

The provision allowing venue where "a substantial part of the events or omissions giving rise to the claim occurred" is broader than the former provision, which allowed venue "where the claim arose." Venue is more likely to be available in several districts under the new provision than under the old provision, because "*a substantial part* of the events or omissions" can easily take place in several districts, but it is not likely that a claim will arise in more than one district. [*See* **Leroy v. Great Western United Corp.,** *supra,* p. 169]

EXAM TIP

Remember that in venue questions you must analyze venue under the first two bases for venue—defendant's residence, and location of a substantial part of the events or omissions or of the property—*before* considering the fallback provisions. *Only if neither of the first two bases is available* do you consider the application of the fallback provision.

---

c. No Distinction Between "Diversity" and "Federal Question" Venue

At one time, the venue statute specified different rules for venue depending on whether the claims in question were brought within the diversity or federal question subject matter jurisdiction of the district court. The 2012 enactment eliminated this oft-criticized distinction, establishing a single general venue rule for all civil actions.

d. Meaning of "Resides"

The first basis for venue is the judicial district "where any defendant *resides*" provided that all defendants reside in the state in which the district is located. [28 U.S.C. § 1391(b)(1)] "Resides" has several meanings in the general venue statute, which will be detailed below.

(1) Natural Persons

The statute specifies that a natural person's residence for federal venue purposes is the judicial district in which she has her *domicile*. [28 U.S.C. § 1391(c)(1)] The statutory specification adopts the majority view in the lower courts that the residence of natural persons should be defined by reference to their domicile, not to the place of actual residence.

(a) "Residence" Compared to "Domicile"

In many cases, the terms residence and domicile will mean the same thing. But often, a person may reside in a place different from her permanent home or domicile.

Example: Defendant is a college student residing in Massachusetts. Massachusetts is not her domicile because she does not expect to stay there after she receives her degree. Her *domicile is California,* her last permanent home. (Even if she has no intention of returning to California, it remains her domicile until she establishes a new domicile.) Residence-based venue would be proper in Massachusetts but not in California.

(b) Aliens

Aliens who lack a venue "privilege" may be sued in any judicial district. Current law provides a venue privilege only for aliens admitted as lawful permanent residents of the United States, deeming them to reside in the judicial district in which they have their domicile. [28 U.S.C. § 1391(c)(1)] Undocumented aliens cannot invoke this limitation on venue.

(c) Non-Resident Defendants

Natural persons and other defendants who reside outside the United States may not claim a venue privilege, but may be sued in any judicial district. The rule applies equally to citizens of the United States and aliens. [28 U.S.C. § 1391(c)(3)]

(2) Corporations and Other Entities

Corporations have long been "deemed to reside" in any judicial district in which they are subject to the court's personal jurisdiction. [28 U.S.C. § 1391(c)(2)] The same rule now applies to other entities with the capacity under applicable law to sue and be sued.

Note: Apart from venue on the basis of residence, a corporation would be subject to venue under section 1391(b)(2) in any judicial district that met the substantial event test.

(a) State with Multiple Districts

A corporate defendant subject to personal jurisdiction in a state having more than one judicial district is deemed to reside in any district in the state "within which its contacts would be sufficient to subject it to personal jurisdiction if that district were a separate state," or if there is no such district, "in the district within which it has the most significant contacts." [28 U.S.C. § 1391(d)]

EXAM TIP

Be sure that you do not confuse the issue of the citizenship of a corporation or other entity for purposes of determining diversity with the issue of where such a defendant is deemed to reside for *venue* purposes, *i.e.,* in any judicial district in which it is subject to personal jurisdiction at the time the action is commenced.

(3) Unincorporated Associations

The Supreme Court held in 1967 that if an unincorporated association has the capacity to sue and be sued, it should be treated analogously to corporations. **[Denver & Rio Grande Western Railroad v. Brotherhood of Railroad Trainmen**, 387 U.S. 556 (1967)] The rule was written into law in 2012; the statute extends the corporate venue rule to any "entity with the capacity to sue and be sued in its common name under applicable law." [28 U.S.C. § 1391(c)(2)] As a practical matter, then, most unincorporated associations and partnerships with the capacity to be sued as entities will be deemed to reside for venue purposes in any judicial district in which they are subject to personal jurisdiction.

(a) Determining Capacity in Federal Court

The Federal Rules of Civil Procedure specify the rules of capacity to sue and be sued in federal court. Rule 17(b)(3) indicates that the capacity of all parties (excluding corporations and natural persons) shall be determined "by the law of the state where the court is located." To the extent such law gives such an association the capacity to sue and be sued in its common name, the association will be treated as an entity for residence purposes.

(b) State Law Denial of Capacity

If the unincorporated association or partnership lacks capacity to sue and be sued in its common name as a matter of applicable state law, the residence calculus for venue purposes becomes more complex.

1) Federal Law Claims and Defenses

Rule 17 provides that, for purposes of enforcing rights under federal law, a partnership or unincorporated association may sue in its common name. Under this provision, it would appear that defendants responding to claims or setting up defenses under federal law would be regarded as residing for venue purposes wherever they are subject to personal jurisdiction.

2) State Law Claims and Defenses

As for claims based on state law in a district court located in a state where the association lacks capacity, it would appear that the deeming provision would not come into play and the determination of the association's "residence" would turn on some other mode of analysis. Some district courts may return to prior law governing the residence of an association, perhaps focusing on where they are *"doing business"* or are *"licensed to do business."* The absence of a specific rule creates potential uncertainty.

(c) Distinguish—Diversity Jurisdiction

For purposes of diversity of citizenship, an unincorporated association is *not* treated like a corporation. Rather, an unincorporated association is a citizen of the states of *all of its members* [**United Steelworkers of America v. R.H. Bouligny, Inc.**, *supra*, p. 131], while a corporation is a citizen of the state of its incorporation and of its principal place of business [28 U.S.C. § 1332(c); *see* *supra*, p. 129; *and see supra*, p. 130, for discussion of foreign country corporations]

(d) Labor Unions and Business Partnerships

The venue rule for unincorporated associations applies at least to labor unions [**Denver & Rio Grande Western Railroad v. Brotherhood of Railroad Trainmen**, *supra*] and to business partnerships [**Penrod Drilling Co. v. Johnson**, 414 F.2d 1217 (5th Cir. 1969)].

e. Local Actions

For much of the nation's history, federal venue statutes were interpreted to permit venue in disputes over real property (known as a "local action") only in the judicial district in which the real estate involved in the dispute was located. The venue law of 2012 abolished this local action requirement. But note that a party bringing suit that implicates title to real property must still satisfy one of the other venue rules (and those will typically allow, but not require, venue in the place of the property's situs).

 Example: local actions: Examples of local actions include mortgage foreclosures, trespass actions, suits to abate a nuisance, and actions trying title to land.

 Historical Example: The most famous local action venue case is **Livingston v. Jefferson**, 15 F. Cas. 660 (C.C.D. Va. 1811) (Marshall, J.). Livingston claimed title to land near New Orleans. President Jefferson, claiming that the land belonged to the United States, caused United States marshals to eject Livingston from the land. After Jefferson returned to private life, Livingston brought a trespass suit in Virginia, where Jefferson lived. The federal court refused to hear the case because it was a "local action" that could be tried only in the judicial district where the land was located. Since Jefferson was not susceptible to process in Louisiana, the effect of the holding was that no suit could be brought against him.

Abolition of local action rule: The venue statute declares that proper venue shall be determined "without regard to whether the action is local or transitory in nature." [28 U.S.C. § 1391(a)(2)]

f. Removed Cases

The federal venue statutes need *not* be satisfied if the suit is removed from state to federal court. The removal statute [28 U.S.C. § 1441] requires only that the action be "pending" in state court and that the district court would have had "original jurisdiction of the suit." [**Polizzi v. Cowles Magazine Inc.**, 345 U.S. 663 (1953)] Venue under the removal statute is proper in the district court for the district in which the state court action was pending. [See also 28 U.S.C. § 1390(c)—confirming that removal law determines the venue of removed cases]

g. Supplemental Jurisdiction

If venue is proper for the original claim by the plaintiff, it will also be proper for counterclaims, cross-claims, and impleader claims. The general rule is that venue requirements need not be independently satisfied for any claim that is "supplemental" to the original claim.

3. Special Venue Statutes

There are a number of special venue statutes. Most special venue statutes *supplement* the general statute. For cases coming under these supplemental statutes, venue is proper if the requirements of *either* the general or the special venue statutes are satisfied. Some special venue statutes, however, are *exclusive.* For cases coming under exclusive statutes, venue is proper *only if* the requirements of the special statutes are satisfied.

a. Supplemental Statutes

After the 1990 expansion of venue under the general venue statute (*see supra*, pp. 169 *et seq.*), the practical importance of supplemental venue statutes has diminished substantially. Examples of special venue statutes that supplement the general venue statute include:

(1) *Antitrust suits.* [15 U.S.C. §§ 15, 22] These venue provisions are largely redundant of the general venue statute.

(2) *Suits for the collection of internal revenue.* [28 U.S.C. § 1396]

b. Exclusive Statute

An example of a special venue statute that is exclusive of the general venue statute is the venue rule for *patent and copyright suits.* [28 U.S.C. § 1400; *and see* **Fourco Glass Co. v. Transmirra Products Corp.**, 353 U.S. 222 (1957)]

The Supreme Court confirmed the exclusive character of patent venue, which authorizes suit either in the district where the defendant committed acts of infringement or where the defendant resides. As noted above, the 2012 amendment declared, for "all venue purposes," that corporations reside for venue purposes in any district in which they were subject to personal jurisdiction. But the Court refused to apply this definition of residence to defendants sued for patent infringement. [**TC Heartland LLC v. Kraft Foods Group Brands LLC**, 137 S.Ct. 1514 (2017)] Reaffirming **Fourco**, the Court held that corporations were subject to patent venue as residents only in the district in which they were incorporated. The Court apparently failed to recognize that LLCs were not necessarily corporations for purposes of the relevant definitions.

4. Change of Venue

There are special statutory provisions that permit a change of venue for the *convenience of parties and witnesses* [28 U.S.C. § 1404(a)], or when *venue is improper* in the original forum [28 U.S.C. § 1406(a)]. These provisions will be considered in turn.

a. Change of Venue for Convenience

A change of venue may be granted on grounds of convenience. [28 U.S.C. § 1404(a)]

(1) Historical Background

Prior to 1948, suits brought in a federal district court with proper venue could not be transferred to other district courts merely because the original forum was inconvenient for parties and witnesses. The only available alternative was to dismiss on grounds of forum non conveniens and file a new suit in the more convenient forum. [**Gulf Oil Corp. v. Gilbert**, 330 U.S. 501 (1947)—sustaining a forum non conveniens dismissal] In 1948, Congress passed section 1404(a), which permitted a district court to *transfer* a case to the more convenient forum.

(2) Statutory Terms

The statute provides that "[f]or the convenience of parties and witnesses, in the interest of justice, a district court may transfer any civil action to any other district or division where it might have been brought **or to any district or division to which all parties have consented.**" [28 U.S.C. § 1404(a)] This section is designed to fine-tune the forum selection process beyond the fine-tuning already provided by the venue statutes governing the original choice of forum. The provision for transfer by consent (highlighted in bold) was added to the statute in 2012.

(3) Transfer Standard More Lenient than Forum Non Conveniens Dismissal Standard

It is easier to obtain a transfer under section 1404(a) than to obtain a dismissal on grounds of forum non conveniens. [**Norwood v. Kirkpatrick**, 349 U.S. 29 (1955)]

(4) Either Party May Seek Transfer

Ordinarily a motion to transfer under section 1404(a) is made by the defendant, but a plaintiff may also move for transfer if after filing suit he "discovers that there are good reasons for transfer." [**Philip Carey Manufacturing Co. v. Taylor**, 286 F.2d 782 (6th Cir. 1961)]

(5) Forum Selection Clause Will Be Given Weight

A valid forum selection clause in an agreement between the parties will be given substantial, though not necessarily controlling, weight in determining whether a case will be transferred under section 1404(a). [**Stewart Organization, Inc. v. Ricoh Corp.**, 487 U.S. 22 (1988)] See also **Atlantic Marine Const. Co., Inc. v. U.S. Dist. Court for Western Dist. of Texas**, 571 U.S. 49 (2013).

(6) Venue Must Be Proper in Transferee Court or All Must Consent

Section 1404(a) permits a transfer to a judicial district *"where it might have been brought."* This has been construed to mean that venue must be proper in the transferee forum. The Supreme Court ruled that a defendant seeking a change of venue cannot waive an objection to venue in the transferee forum. [**Hoffman v. Blaski**, *supra*, p. 169]

(a) Criticism

The rule of **Hoffman v. Blaski**, *supra*, has been criticized as unnecessarily limiting the utility of section 1404(a). Since the defendant typically enjoys the venue privilege, the defendant's willingness to waive a venue objection to secure a transfer of the action would seem to address any fairness concerns.

(b) Analogous Result When in Personam Jurisdiction Lacking

The language of section 1404(a), permitting transfers only to districts where the suit "might have been brought," has also been interpreted to require that there be in personam jurisdiction over the defendant in the transferee forum. If that court does not have in personam jurisdiction over the defendant, the suit cannot be transferred to that court. The defendant cannot waive his objection to in personam jurisdiction to obtain a transfer. [**Foster-Milbum Co. v. Knight**, 181 F.2d 949 (2d Cir. 1950)]

(c) Transfer by Consent of All Parties

In 2012, Congress partially overrode these strict interpretations of the "where it might have been brought" language of the statute. While section 1404(a) retained the "might have been brought" requirement as a general rule, Congress added a provision authorizing transfer to a district or division "to which all parties have consented."

Note: By requiring consent of **all** parties, the statute gives the plaintiff and other parties a right to block a change of venue to a more convenient forum if venue or personal jurisdiction would be improper there. As a result, a defendant still cannot unilaterally waive venue and personal jurisdiction defects that would prevent transfer of the action.

(7) Law Applied After Transfer

After transfer to a new forum on motion by the defendant, the law of the *original forum* will ordinarily be applied in a diversity case. A change of venue under section 1404(a) "generally should be, with respect to state law, but a change of courtrooms." [**Van Dusen v. Barrack**, 376 U.S. 612 (1964)] The same law will be applied regardless of whether the defendant or plaintiff moves for transfer. [**Ferens v. John Deere Co.**, 494 U.S. 516 (1990)]

Example: defendant moves to transfer: Plaintiffs brought 40 wrongful death actions in federal district court in the Eastern District of Pennsylvania. The deaths occurred when an airplane bound for Philadelphia crashed into Boston Harbor shortly after takeoff. Defendants successfully moved to transfer to federal district court in Massachusetts under section 1404(a). State law governing damages in wrongful death actions was more favorable in Pennsylvania than in Massachusetts. The Supreme Court held that Pennsylvania law would be applied, even after transfer to Massachusetts. [**Van Dusen v. Barrack**, *supra*]

Example: plaintiff moves to transfer: Plaintiff lost a hand in a farming accident in Pennsylvania. After the statute of limitations had expired in Pennsylvania, plaintiff filed suit in federal court in Mississippi, where, under Mississippi law (applicable under *Erie*), the statute of limitations had not run. Plaintiff then successfully moved to transfer the case to federal district court in Pennsylvania under section 1404(a). The Supreme Court held that the Mississippi statute of limitations applied. [**Ferens v. John Deere Co.**, *supra*]

(a) Unresolved Issues After *Van Dusen* and *Ferens*

1) Suit Where Forum Non Conveniens Motion Would Have Been Successful

Van Dusen specifically refused to decide whether its rule applied to a case in which the initial forum choice was so inconvenient that the forum state would have dismissed on the ground of forum non conveniens if the suit had been filed in state court.

a) Different Considerations

If the *Van Dusen* rule were applied to suits that would have been dismissed from state court on forum non conveniens grounds, the result could be seen to conflict with **Erie Railroad v. Tompkins** (*see infra,* pp. 186 *et seq.*). That is, if a suit were filed in state court and dismissed on grounds of forum non conveniens, plaintiff would have to refile the suit in another forum, and the law of the new forum would be applied in the new suit. *Erie* probably requires that the same result be obtained when the suit is filed in federal court. Thus, if the suit transferred by the federal district court under section 1404(a) would have been dismissed for forum non conveniens by a state court in that state, the law in the transferee federal district court should be the law that would be applied in the state of the transferee court.

2) Suit Transferred from One Federal Circuit to Another, and There Is a Conflict Between the Circuits

Neither *Van Dusen* nor *Ferens* mentioned the question of whether the *Van Dusen* rule should apply to questions of federal law when the transfer is from a district court in one circuit to a district court in another circuit, and when there is a conflict between the circuits on the appropriate interpretation of the federal law at issue. However, an influential decision, by then Circuit Judge Ruth Bader Ginsburg, holds that the federal court to which federal question claims have been transferred for convenience under section 1404 may apply the law of its own circuit, rather than looking to the law of the circuit in which the action was initiated. [*See In re* **Korean Air Lines Disaster of September 1, 1983**, 829 F.2d 1171 (D.C. Cir. 1987)]

b. Change of Venue to Cure Defects

A change of venue may be granted under section 1406(a) when venue is improper in the original forum.

(1) Statutory Terms

The statute provides that a district court with a case "laying venue in the wrong division or district shall dismiss or, if it be in the interest of justice, transfer such case to any district or division in which it could have been brought." [28 U.S.C. § 1406(a)] This section is designed to permit a district court to transfer rather than to dismiss a case when it would be just to do so. The most important practical consequence of a transfer, rather than a dismissal, is to protect a plaintiff when the statute of limitations has run by the time the motion is made.

(2) In Personam Jurisdiction Defect May Also Be Cured

Section 1406(a) refers only to defects in venue, but it has been employed to permit transfer of a case in which there was no in personam jurisdiction over the defendant, as well as improper venue, in the transferor forum. [**Goldlawr v. Heiman**, 369 U.S. 463 (1962)]

(a) In Personam Defect Only

Goldlawr permitted transfer under section 1406(a) where there was *both* improper venue *and* lack of in personam jurisdiction in the transferor forum. The *Goldlawr* principle has been extended by some lower courts to permit transfer when venue is *proper* but there is no in personam jurisdiction, provided that the defendant consents. [**Dubin v. United States**, 380 F.2d 813 (5th Cir. 1967)]

(3) Venue and in Personam Jurisdiction Must Be Proper in Transferee Court

Venue and in personam jurisdiction must be proper in the transferee court after a transfer under section 1406(a). [**Sharp Electronic Corp. v. Hayman Cash Register Co.**, 655 F.2d 1228 (D.C. Cir. 1981)—venue; **Ellis v. Great Southwestern Corp.**, 646 F.2d 1099 (5th Cir. 1981)—in personam jurisdiction]

Note: 28 U.S.C. section 1406(a) does not include a provision authorizing transfer by consent of all parties.

(4) Law Applied After Transfer

The *Van Dusen* rule for transfers under section 1404(a) (law of the original forum is applied after transfer) does ***not*** apply to transfers under section 1406(a). The law of the ***transferee*** court is applied after a section 1406(a) transfer. [**Nelson v. International Paint Co.**, 716 F.2d 640 (9th Cir. 1983)]

(a) Contrasting Rationale

The *Van Dusen* rule for a section 1404(a) transfer is premised on plaintiff's having filed suit in a forum where both venue and in personam jurisdiction exist. When defendant (or even plaintiff) moves to change venue for reasons of his own convenience, plaintiff is permitted to keep the substantive law of the first forum because the original forum choice was proper. By contrast, the premise for a transfer under section 1406(a) is that plaintiff's original forum choice is ***improper.*** Either venue or in personam jurisdiction, or both, are lacking. Thus, it makes no sense for plaintiff to keep the law that would have been applied by the first forum, because that forum could not have entertained the suit.

(5) Law Applied After Transfer to Enforce Forum-Selection Contract

The Supreme Court views forum-selection clauses in contracts as presumptively enforceable and has taken steps to facilitate the transfer of litigation to ensure their effectiveness. [See **Stewart Organization v. Ricoh Corp.**, *supra* p. 175] Parties to such a contract may ignore its provision, by filing suit in a venue or district that's proper under the venue statute but different from the forum the parties selected in their contract. Following *Stewart Organization*, the Court views the matter as presumptively subject to transfer under the federal change of venue statute. [28 U.S.C. section 1404] But the Court has held that the applicable law differs from that which usually accompanies a transfer under section 1404. Instead of treating the forum's state choice of law rules of the transferor court as presumptively applicable under the rule of *Van Dusen v. Barrack*, the Court held that the forum state choice of law rules of the transferee district would apply, post-transfer. [**Atlantic Marine Const. Co., Inc. v. U.S. Dist. Court for Western Dist. of Texas**, 571 U.S. 49 (2013)]

D. Forum Non Conveniens

1. General Background

Forum non conveniens is a traditional doctrine under which a case is dismissed when venue and jurisdiction are proper but the forum is nevertheless seriously inconvenient. Forum non conveniens has not had much practical importance in federal courts since 1948, when section 1404(a) (*supra*, p. 174) was added to the judicial code. Section 1404(a) permits transfer to another federal court, rather than dismissal, when the first forum is inconvenient.

2. Present Use of Forum Non Conveniens

Forum non conveniens remains an important doctrine in *state courts,* since they do not have the power to transfer to more convenient forums in other states. Also, forum non conveniens remains the relevant doctrine in federal court when the convenient forum is in a *foreign country.* [**Piper Aircraft Co. v. Reyno,** 454 U.S. 235 (1981)—forum non conveniens dismissal when convenient forum is in Scotland]

EXAM TIP   **GILBERT**

An easy way to remember the transfer rules for cases is to compare it to trying to use a hairdryer made for the United States in France. A federal district court generally can transfer a case to another federal district court because they are *both part of the same system* (*i.e.,* they use the same type of electricity). However, a federal district court can't transfer a case to a foreign country (and a state court can't transfer a case to another state) because they aren't part of the same system (they use a different type of electricity). Like the hairdryer in France, it just doesn't work. *Dismissal is the only option.*

---

3. Relevant Factors

Many factors are relevant to consideration of forum non conveniens motions: access to proof, availability of witnesses, viewing of property, vexation of litigants, enforceability of judgments, and imposition of forum on a community having little to do with the dispute. [**Gulf Oil Corp. v. Gilbert**, *supra*, p. 174]

a. Change in Substantive Law

The fact that the more convenient forum has a substantive law less favorable to plaintiffs "should not ordinarily be given conclusive or even substantial weight." [**Piper Aircraft Co. v. Reyno,** *supra*]

4. Alternative Forum Must Be Available

A forum non conveniens dismissal is not appropriate unless a more convenient forum is available. As a precondition to a forum non conveniens dismissal, a court will usually insist that a defendant waive any venue or personal jurisdiction objections to suit in the more convenient forum. A court may also insist on waiver of any statute of limitations bar that would apply in the more convenient forum.

5. Limited Appellate Review

The trial judge's decision on a forum non conveniens motion will not be reversed on appeal unless there has been an abuse of discretion.

Chapter Seven

Law Applied in the Federal Courts

CONTENTS

Key Exam Issues

Exam questions about the law applied in federal courts usually concern what are loosely called "*Erie* problems." **Erie Railroad v. Tompkins** and its progeny have produced a complex body of case law that cannot easily be reduced to a tidy and quickly stated set of rules. Your best approach to *Erie* is to begin by understanding **Swift v. Tyson,** for the history that led to *Erie* makes the case much easier to understand. In analyzing the law after *Erie*, keep in mind the following structure:

1. **General Rule**

    In state law matters (generally diversity cases), the federal courts apply *state substantive law* and *federal procedural law.* The problem then arises what is "substantive" or "procedural."

2. **Arguably Procedural Law Governed by Federal Rules of Civil Procedure**

    If an arguably procedural question is governed by a valid Federal Rule of Civil Procedure, the Federal Rule controls. [*See* **Hanna v. Plumer**, *infra*]

3. **Arguably Procedural Law Not Governed by Federal Rule of Civil Procedure**

    If no Federal Rule governs, and the matter is arguably procedural, the decision whether to apply state law is primarily determined under:

    (i)   The *"outcome determinative" test* of **Guaranty Trust Co. v. New York**; and

    (ii) The *balancing test* of **Byrd v. Blue Ridge.**

4. **Federal Common Law**

    In some nonprocedural areas, the strength and nature of the federal interest are such that *federal substantive common law* has grown up. It is supreme federal law under the Supremacy Clause, meaning that it must be followed by the state courts and will confer appellate jurisdiction of the Supreme Court. (Do not confuse federal common law with the federal *general* common law that existed under *Swift*. Federal general common law was not supreme law.)

As a matter of general approach in this area, remember the important fact that federal law is usually "interstitial" in nature; it exists against a background of existing state law. Also, you should be familiar enough with the key cases in this area to be able to discuss them in a fairly detailed and nuanced fashion. The outline has been written in such a way as to enable you to do so.

A. Introduction

1. Principles Underlying Choice of Law Decisions

The fundamental principle governing the law applied in federal and state courts is that the *substantive law should be the same* in both court systems. A related principle is that there should be *no forum shopping* between federal and other courts based on a difference in the substantive law that is applied. The two principles are embodied in **Erie Railroad v. Tompkins**, *supra*, p. 4, and its progeny. Although the principles are relatively clear, their application in particular cases can be complicated. The principles embodied in *Erie*, and the associated complications, are worked out in the following sections.

B. Historical Background

1. Rules of Decision Act

The Rules of Decision Act was enacted as section 34 of the first judicial statute, the Judiciary Act of 1789.

a. Text

Section 34 provided: "[T]he laws of the several states, except when the constitution, treaties or statutes of the United States shall otherwise require or provide, shall be regarded as rules of decision in trials at common law in the courts of the United States in cases where they apply." [*See* 28 U.S.C. § 1652—-modern version of the Rules of Decision Act, only slightly changed from the 1789 statute]

b. Original Meaning

Scholars of legal history have disagreed about the original meaning of section 34. [*Compare* Warren, *New Light on the History of the Federal Judiciary Act of 1789*, 37 Harv. L. Rev. 49 (1923), *with* W. Crosskey, *Politics and the Constitution in the History of the United States* 867 (1953)] More recent historical scholarship has suggested that the adopters of section 34 had the following scheme in mind [Fletcher, *The General Common Law and Section 34 of the Judiciary Act of 1789*, 97 Harv. L. Rev. 1513 (1984)]:

(1) Federal Positive Law

When federal constitutional, treaty, or statutory law applied to a case, it governed.

(2) State Law

When state law was not displaced by positive federal law, it governed in cases where it applied. However, state law within the meaning of section 34 did not have the same meaning as state law today. In 1789, state law was understood to mean *"local"* law. Such local law included judge-made law concerning local subjects such as mortgages, land titles, and family relationships, and clear statutory law that deviated from the rules of the general common law.

(3) General Common Law and Other Law

When neither federal positive law nor local state law governed a case, some other law governed. Such other law could be international law, maritime law, or general common law. These kinds of law were not specifically mentioned in section 34, but it was assumed that they would be relied upon in cases where they applied.

(a) Role of General Common Law Under Section 34

When the general common law was capable of supplying the rule of decision, the federal courts relied upon it in deciding a case. The state courts also relied on the general common law.

(b) General Common Law Was Not Federal Law

The general common law was not federal law in the sense of the Supremacy Clause. That is, state courts and federal courts could, and sometimes did, differ as to what the general common law required. Additionally, general common law did not supply a federal question for purposes of conferring jurisdiction on the federal courts.

2. *Swift v. Tyson*

In 1842, the Supreme Court held that in a case not concerned with a local subject and not covered by a state statute, a federal court sitting in New York was not required by the Rules of Decision Act to follow the general common law decisions of the New York state courts. (The substantive question involved the law of negotiable instruments.) Rather, the federal court could follow the rule it thought faithful to the general common law. [**Swift v. Tyson**, *supra*, p. 4]

a. Historical Significance of *Swift*

At the time it was decided, *Swift* does not appear to have been regarded as a terribly important case. Rather, it appears to have been viewed as applying the Rules of Decision Act in a relatively uncontroversial and well-established way. However, in retrospect, *Swift* has been regarded as a watershed case. It was the first case in which the Supreme Court clearly held that a federal court could follow its own rules of general common law, even when the state courts of the state in which it sat followed a different rule on the same point.

b. Practical Significance of *Swift*

The principle that the federal courts could follow their own view of the common law had great practical significance in the 19th century. It was regarded as desirable by many (including Justice Story, who wrote *Swift*) that the states have largely uniform commercial laws. But the states were without any ready means to coordinate their general common law decisions in commercial cases. *Swift* provided a mechanism to facilitate such coordination, and to encourage a uniform general common law with a national perspective.

(1) Supreme Court as a Coordinating Mechanism

The United States Supreme Court's general common law decisions provided a coordinating mechanism for several reasons:

(a) Relatively Large Number of Common Law Cases

In the 19th century, unlike today, the Supreme Court's docket was very largely made up of general common law decisions in commercial cases decided under the federal courts' diversity jurisdiction.

(b) Visibility of Supreme Court Decisions

The decisions of the Supreme Court were fairly accurately and promptly reported. State supreme courts had relatively ready access to these reports after about 1810.

(c) Uniformity of Law Within Federal Court System

On points of general common law on which the Supreme Court had ruled, all inferior federal courts were required to follow the Supreme Court's decision. Thus, the federal courts' general common law was uniform throughout the country. The state courts, not wanting to have a different rule applied in the federal and state courts within their own states, were pressured to conform their views of the general common law to that of the federal courts.

(2) Favorable Reception by State Courts

Until the Civil War, the state courts usually followed the lead of the United States Supreme Court on matters of general common law. (Note that since this was general common law rather than federal law, the state courts were not *required* to follow the lead of the Supreme Court.) Thus, during this period, *Swift* provided a useful (and usually welcome) mechanism by which the state and federal courts were able to fashion and apply a general common law. Perfect uniformity was never achieved, but *Swift* helped provide more uniformity than would otherwise have been possible.

c. Decline of *Swift*

(1) Post-Civil War

After the Civil War, the federal courts under *Swift* relied on the general common law to impose liability on many local communities for defaulted municipal bonds when state courts would not do so. [*See, e.g.,* **Gelpke v. City of Dubuque**, 68 U.S. (1 Wall.) 175 (1864)] These cases aroused great resentment against the federal courts' use of the general common law and, hence, against *Swift*.

(2) Early 20th Century

By the early 20th century, a number of things had changed. The cumulative result of these changes was to deprive *Swift* of its former usefulness. These changes included:

(a) Fewer Diversity Cases in Supreme Court

By the early 20th century, the Supreme Court's docket had changed significantly. The Court increasingly decided cases involving federal law rather than general common law. By the 1930s, the Court used its discretion under the writ of certiorari to deny review in most diversity cases. (*See supra,* pp. 100–101, for the beginnings of the certiorari jurisdiction.) Thus, the Supreme Court no longer acted as an important central coordinator of the general common law.

(b) Rise of Other Coordinating Mechanisms

New mechanisms had arisen that encouraged uniformity and permitted fairly effective coordination of state law. These included the widespread availability of state case reports, uniform model statutes, learned treatises on private law subjects, and American Law Institute Restatements of the law. [*See* Gilmore, *Legal Realism: Its Cause and Cure*, 70 Yale L.J. 1037 (1961)]

(3) Increasing Awkwardness of *Swift*

Since the Supreme Court no longer provided any significant coordinating role for commercial law, and since other effective means of achieving this goal became available, the awkwardness created by *Swift* became increasingly intolerable. The primary problems of *Swift* were:

(a) Forum Shopping

Litigants were encouraged to forum shop between federal and state courts, since different general common law rules were sometimes available in the two court systems.

(b) Unfairness to Some Litigants

Litigants who satisfied the diversity of citizenship jurisdictional requirements of the federal courts could engage in forum shopping. But litigants who could not meet the federal courts' diversity requirements were deprived of this opportunity.

(c) Rulemaking Beyond Powers of Federal Courts

Some felt that under *Swift* the federal courts were moving beyond the limited powers delegated to the federal government. It was argued that in formulating general common law rules in certain areas of contract or tort law, the federal courts were invading the domain of substantive law constitutionally reserved to the states.

(4) Rise of Positivism and Decline of Natural Law

By the early 20th century, *Swift* was perceived as resting on an outmoded theory of natural law. To modern positivist legal thinkers like Justice Holmes, law could not be understood except as it was tied to a particular lawmaking government. Under positivist theories, there could be state law and federal law because there were state and federal governments. But there could not be a "general common law" because it was not tied to any particular government. In Justice Holmes's famous phrase, "the common law is not a brooding omnipresence in the sky, but the articulate voice of some sovereign or quasi-sovereign that can be identified." [**Southern Pacific Co. v. Jensen**, 244 U.S. 205 (1917)—Holmes, J., dissenting]

C. Modern Obligation to Follow State Law—*Erie* Doctrine

1. In General

In 1938, the Supreme Court ***overruled*** Swift v. Tyson in **Erie Railroad v. Tompkins**, *supra*, p. 182. The *Erie* decision profoundly shapes the law applied in federal courts today.

2. Decision in *Erie*

Tompkins was injured by a passing freight train while walking beside railroad tracks in Pennsylvania. He sued in diversity in federal district court in New York. The lower federal courts found for Tompkins based on the general common law rules of liability applied in federal courts. Defendant Erie Railroad sought certiorari on the ground that the "local" law of Pennsylvania should govern because the dispute involved a matter of local rather than "general" law. Although neither party contended that *Swift* should be overruled, the Court, in an opinion by Justice Brandeis, overruled *Swift*, holding that "[t]here is no federal general common law." In cases not governed by genuine federal law, ***state law*** must govern.

(c) Possible Constitutional Analog

To find a modern constitutional analog to Brandeis's objection to *Swift*, some have argued that Congress's power to regulate commerce on a uniform basis and to adopt rules binding on both state and federal courts undercuts any argument that Congress may also empower the federal courts to formulate rules of decision to govern disputes brought to federal court on the basis of diversity. [*See* Friendly, *supra*, p. 187] The resulting rules, if applicable only in diversity, would suffer from the same spurious quality that eventually led the Court to overturn *Swift*.

3. Structure of Modern Law Under *Erie*

Under *Erie's* reading of the Rules of Decision Act, federal courts are required to follow state laws "in cases where they apply." [28 U.S.C. § 1652] In general, this means that the federal courts will follow *state substantive law* and *federal procedural law.*

a. *Erie* Applicable in Diversity and Federal Question Cases

The Rules of Decision Act does not distinguish among cases depending on the source of federal jurisdiction. It merely refers to the rules of decision "in the courts of the United States." [28 U.S.C. § 1652] As a practical matter, state laws will be applied most frequently in diversity cases, but the Rules of Decision Act also requires that state laws be applied in cases coming into the federal courts on other jurisdictional bases—*e.g.,* federal question cases under 28 U.S.C. section 1331 [**Maternally Yours, Inc. v. Your Maternity Shop, Inc.**, 234 F.2d 538 (2d Cir. 1956)], or supplemental jurisdiction cases under section 1367.

b. Valid and Controlling Federal Law Must Be Followed

The Rules of Decision Act provides that state law shall be followed "except where the Constitution or treaties or Acts of Congress otherwise require or provide." [28 U.S.C. § 1652] This means that where a valid federal law controls, it prevails over an inconsistent state law because of the Supremacy Clause.

c. Determining Where State Laws Apply

The Rules of Decision Act is singularly unhelpful in providing guidance about precisely where state laws should be followed. It says simply that they should be followed "in cases where they apply." [28 U.S.C. § 1652] Subsequent to the *Erie* decision, the Supreme Court developed a framework for deciding when state laws apply. Under this framework it is crucial to know:

(1) *If an arguably procedural matter is at issue, is it covered by the Federal Rules of Civil Procedure?* If an arguably procedural matter is controlled by a Federal Rule of Civil Procedure, one kind of analysis is applied. (*See infra*, pp. 190–194.) But if such a matter is *not* controlled by a Federal Rule, another kind of analysis is applied. (*See infra*, pp. 194–198.)

(2) *Should an issue be governed by federal common law?* If a matter is clearly governed by federal constitutional or statutory law, it is clear that federal law applies and, under the Supremacy Clause, supersedes any inconsistent state law. But if no federal constitutional or statutory law governs the matter at issue, a court must decide whether federal common law should govern. If federal common law governs, it is supreme and it *supersedes inconsistent state law.* (Compare this kind of federal common law to the "federal general common law" renounced in *Erie*; the "federal

general common law" under *Swift* was not supreme federal law, *see supra*, pp. 184 *et seq.*)

D. Arguably Procedural Matters and the Federal Rules of Civil Procedure

1. Substance-Procedure Distinction

The basic principle of *Erie* is that valid state substantive law and federal procedural law should apply in federal court. This is fairly straightforward when the state law at issue is clearly substantive. But matters become complicated when the law at issue is rationally capable of classification as either substantive or procedural, or in other words, when the law is "arguably procedural."

2. Arguably Procedural Matter Controlled by a Federal Rule of Civil Procedure

When an arguably procedural matter is controlled by a valid Federal Rule of Civil Procedure, the ***Federal Rule governs.*** This results from the Supreme Court's decision in the important case of **Hanna v. Plumer**, 380 U.S. 460 (1965).

a. *Hanna v. Plumer*

A personal injury suit in diversity was brought in federal district court in Massachusetts. Service of process was made upon defendant's wife in accordance with what was then Federal Rule of Civil Procedure 4(d)(1). Service in this manner did not comply with the Massachusetts rule that would have applied had the suit been brought in state court. Defendant sought to dismiss on the ground that *Erie* and the "outcome determinative" test of **Guaranty Trust Co. v. York** required that service of process be made in accordance with the Massachusetts rule. (*See infra*, p. 194.) The Court held that the *federal* rather than the state rule should be followed. In so doing, it upheld the "power of Congress to prescribe housekeeping rules for federal courts even though some of those rules will inevitably differ from comparable state rules."

(1) Reformulation of "Outcome Determinative" Test

The Court said that the "outcome determinative" test "was never intended to serve as a talisman." Rather, it must be understood in light of the "twin aims of *Erie*": the discouragement of forum shopping, and the avoidance of inequitable administration of the laws.

(2) *Hanna* Test

Under *Hanna*, the ***Federal Rules of Civil Procedure validly control any matter that is arguably procedural:*** "[T]he constitutional provision for a federal court system ... carries with it congressional power to make rules governing the practice and pleading in those courts, which in turn includes a ***power to regulate matters which, though falling within the uncertain area between substance and procedure are rationally capable of classification as either.***" [**Hanna v. Plumer**, *supra*— emphasis added]

b. Structure of the Law After *Hanna*

After *Hanna*, a matter purportedly governed by Federal Rules of Civil Procedure must be analyzed in three steps. [*See* Ely, *The Irrepressible Myth of Erie*, 87 Harv. L. Rev. 693 (1974)—analysis of three steps]

(1) Applicability of a Federal Rule of Civil Procedure

First, a Federal Rule must actually control the matter at issue.

(2) Validity of Rule Under Rules Enabling Act

Second, the Federal Rule must be valid under the Rules Enabling Act. [28 U.S.C. § 2072]

(a) Limitation on Scope of Rules Passed Under Rules Enabling Act

The Rules Enabling Act provides that the Supreme Court shall prescribe rules for federal judicial proceedings. However, procedural rules passed under the Act "shall not abridge, enlarge or modify any substantive right." [28 U.S.C. § 2072]

1) Purpose and Scope of Limitation

It has traditionally been assumed that the limitation on the scope of rules passed under the Rules Enabling Act was designed to protect substantive state law from interference or erosion by federal procedural rules. Such an assumption derives from the principle behind *Erie* that substantive state law should be applied the same way in federal and state court.

a) But Note

Professor Burbank has demonstrated that the traditional assumption is wrong. The Rules Enabling Act was passed in 1934, four years before *Erie* was decided. Thus, the protection of state law could not have been the intention of the limitation. According to Professor Burbank, the limitation was designed to ensure that the power to formulate Rules, delegated to the Supreme Court under the Act, would not interfere with the power of Congress to make substantive law. [*See* 130 U. Pa. L. Rev. 1015 (1982)]

b) Comment

It is possible to synthesize the traditional assumption and Professor Burbank's argument. The protection of substantive federal law from modification by Court-initiated Rules also serves to protect substantive state law from incursions by federal rulemaking. Thus, what began as a limitation based on a separation of powers justification has a further, and continuing, justification based on federalism.

(b) Application of Limitation to Federal Rules

Hanna makes it clear that a Federal Rule of Civil Procedure is valid under the Rules Enabling Act as long as it regulates a matter that is ***arguably procedural.*** The power delegated by the Act is a power to regulate matters "falling within the uncertain area between substance and procedure" and "rationally capable of classification as either."

(3) Rule Must Not Exceed Constitutional Powers of Federal Government

Under the third step for analyzing a matter purportedly governed by the Federal Rules, a Rule must not exceed the powers given to the federal government by the Constitution, as it would then invade the domain reserved to the states.

(a) Comment

This final step is necessary in a theoretical sense but superfluous in a practical sense, given the limitation on the scope of the Rules contained in the Rules Enabling Act. (*See supra,* p. 191.) Rules that meet the "arguably procedural" test will represent rules that are necessary and proper to the creation of lower federal courts under Articles I and III of the Constitution.

c. Relation of Rules of Decision Act to Federal Rules of Civil Procedure

Erie held that the Rules of Decision Act (*see supra,* p. 183) requires that federal courts follow state laws "in cases where they apply" except where positive federal law otherwise requires. The Federal Rules of Civil Procedure, as long as they are validly passed under the Rules Enabling Act, are positive federal law. Thus, *Erie's* reading of the Rules of Decision Act permits federal district courts to follow valid Federal Rules of Civil Procedure.

d. Application of *Hanna*-Type Analysis

(1) Pre-*Hanna*

In **Sibbach v. Wilson & Co.**, 312 U.S. 1 (1941), shortly after the Federal Rules of Civil Procedure were first adopted in 1938, the Supreme Court reached a result consistent with its later analysis in *Hanna.* In a personal injury suit, plaintiff contended that she should not be required to submit to a physical examination, even though such examination was expressly required under Federal Rules of Civil Procedure 35 and 37. Plaintiff contended that she would not have had to submit to such an examination if the suit had been brought in state court, and that the right to avoid an examination was "important" and "substantial." The Court upheld the application of Rules 35 and 37: "If we were to adopt the suggested criterion of the importance of the alleged right we should invite endless litigation and confusion more confounded. The test must be whether a *rule really regulates procedure.*" [Emphasis added]

(2) Post-*Hanna*

In **Walker v. Armco Steel Corp.**, 446 U.S. 740 (1980), plaintiffs argued that Federal Rule of Civil Procedure 3 allowed the Oklahoma statute of limitations to be tolled when the complaint was filed, even though the rule in Oklahoma courts was that only *service* of the complaint tolled the statute. The Court followed the Oklahoma rule requiring service of process. However, the Court's analysis was consistent with *Hanna*, for it held that Rule 3 *did not apply* to the statute of limitations issue. Thus, the case fell into the category of cases in which an arguably procedural matter is at stake but in which there is no applicable Federal Rule.

(a) Note

The result in *Walker* is the same as that in **Ragan v. Merchants' Transfer & Warehouse Co.**, 337 U.S. 530 (1949). *Ragan* was decided under the pre-*Hanna* regime when the Court followed a state procedural rule if it was "outcome determinative." (*See infra*, pp. 194 *et seq.*)

(3) *Gasperini v. Center for Humanities Inc.*

In **Gasperini v. Center for Humanities, Inc.**, 518 U.S. 415 (1996), the Court held that a federal court should follow New York law requiring federal judges to determine whether a jury damage award "deviates materially from what would be reasonable compensation." Plaintiff, a professional photographer, had obtained a jury verdict of $450,000 as compensatory damages for misplaced photographic transparencies. Affirming a remittitur to $100,000 under the New York standard, the Court found the New York law outcome determinative because "*Erie* precludes a recovery in federal court significantly larger than the recovery that would have been tolerated in state court." The Court also found that the federal interest in maintaining the judge/jury division of responsibility was not impaired by a rule directing federal judges to review jury verdicts for compliance with New York's standard. Justices Scalia and Thomas, in dissent, contended that Federal Rule of Civil Procedure 59 directly controlled the issue, but the Court found that Rule 59 did not apply. By thus narrowing the scope of the federal rule, the Court preserved the application of state law.

(4) *Shady Grove Orthopedic Assocs. v. Allstate Insurance Co.*

Shady Grove brought suit in the form of a diversity class action under Fed. R. Civ. P. 23, seeking to recover statutory interest due on behalf of a class. New York state law had been interpreted to bar class actions to recover statutory interest claims. The lower federal courts dismissed the action, ruling that Rule 23 did not apply and deferring to the state policy. The Supreme Court reversed, holding that Rule 23 conflicted with the state law and controlled under **Hanna**. A fifth vote for the result came from a Justice who offered a more nuanced assessment of Rule 23's applicability under the Rules Enabling Act; a vigorous four-Justice dissent argued that the conflict should have been avoided through a narrow interpretation of Rule 23. The disagreement among the Justices produced a narrow and contested holding with uncertain implications for the future. [**Shady Grove Orthopedic Assocs. v. Allstate Insurance Co.**, 559 U.S. 393 (2010)]

e. Distinguish—Federal Rules of Evidence

In late 1972, the Supreme Court transmitted to Congress a comprehensive set of proposed Federal Rules of Evidence under the procedures of the Rules Enabling Act. But rather than following the procedure for making the Rules law, Congress debated the proposed rules for a little over two years, and finally, in early 1975, passed them as a *separate statutory enactment* independent of the Rules Enabling Act.

(1) Effect—Rules Enabling Act Irrelevant

Since the Federal Rules of Evidence were passed as a separate statutory enactment, they are *not* subject to the limitation of the Rules Enabling Act that rules enacted thereunder "not abridge, enlarge or modify any substantive right." [28 U.S.C. § 2072, para. 2]

(2) Relevance of *Erie* to Federal Rules of Evidence

The fact that the Federal Rules of Evidence have been enacted as a separate statutory enactment does not mean that all *Erie* issues have disappeared. As to any particular evidentiary rule, one must still inquire whether that rule is within the enumerated constitutional powers of the federal government. (*See supra,* p. 192.) However, it is very unlikely that any of the present Federal Rules of Evidence are beyond the power of the federal government to enact.

3. Matters Not Covered by Federal Rules of Civil Procedure

The Federal Rules of Civil Procedure govern most procedural or arguably procedural matters that arise during the trial of a case in federal court. However, the Federal Rules do not cover all such matters. In cases where the Federal Rules do not provide a rule governing the issue, the Supreme Court has struggled to provide a framework of analysis.

a. "Outcome Determinative" Test

In **Guaranty Trust Co. v. York**, 326 U.S. 99 (1945), the Supreme Court formulated the "outcome determinative" test: A state law rule that substantially determines the outcome of the litigation must be applied.

e.g. **Example:** A state statute of limitations had run on an equitable action. Plaintiff argued that a federal court could apply a federal equitable limitations period, which would permit the suit to be brought even though the state statute of limitations would have barred the suit if it had been brought in state court. The Court, in an opinion by Justice Frankfurter, said that the basic policy of *Erie* was that the outcome of litigation in federal court should be *substantially the same,* so far as legal rules determine the outcome of the litigation, as it would be *if tried in a state court.*

(1) Application of Outcome Determinative Test

The outcome determinative test, if applied in a rigorous fashion, would go very far in requiring the federal courts to follow state procedural rules. Almost any legal rule can have an impact on the outcome of the case. Whenever there are different federal and state rules, the application of the state rule to the behavior of someone who has followed the federal rule may result in a sanction against that person and often even the loss of the lawsuit. Despite these problems, the Court applied the test rather rigorously in a number of succeeding cases.

e.g. **Example: service of process and tolling state statute of limitations:** In **Ragan v. Merchants' Transfer & Warehouse Co.**, *supra*, p. 193, the plaintiff filed a personal injury suit in federal court in Kansas. Federal Rule of Civil Procedure 3 provides that "[a]n action is commenced by filing a complaint with the court." Kansas law provided that the action was commenced when the defendant was *served with process.* When the suit was filed, the state statute of limitations had not run, but process was not served until after the statute had run. Thus, if the action had "commenced" when filed, the statute had not run, but it had run if service of process was required. The Court held that the Kansas rule requiring service of process was "an integral part of the state's statute of limitations" and thus applied the state rule determining when the statute was tolled. *Note:* The Court in *Ragan* did not hold that Federal Rule 3 violated *Erie.* The Court's opinion left room for the conclusion that Rule 3 simply did not address the question of when a statute of limitations was tolled. [*See* **Walker v. Armco Steel Corp.**, *supra*, p. 192—Court held that Rule 3 was not intended to affect state statutes of limitation]

Example: posting bond in shareholder derivative suits: In **Cohen v. Beneficial Industrial Loan Corp.**, 337 U.S. 541 (1949), the plaintiff filed a shareholder derivative suit in federal court in New Jersey. New Jersey law required that plaintiffs in shareholder derivative suits post bonds to cover possible attorneys' fees awards against them. Federal Rule of Civil Procedure 23 prescribed certain procedures in shareholder derivative suits, but was silent on the issue of bonds. The Court held that New Jersey law requiring a bond should be applied in federal court because it had important practical consequences and was more than "a mere procedural device."

Example: qualification to sue in state court: In **Woods v. Interstate Realty Co.**, 337 U.S. 535 (1949), a Tennessee corporation had not complied with a Mississippi statute requiring corporations doing business in the state to designate an agent for receiving service of process. A corporation not complying with the statute was not permitted to file suit in state court. The Tennessee corporation filed suit in federal rather than state court in Mississippi. The Supreme Court held that the Tennessee corporation was barred from suing in federal court, just as it was barred from suing in state court.

(2) *Hanna's* Gloss on the Outcome-Determinative Test

In **Hanna v. Plumer**, *supra*, p. 190, the Court ultimately concluded that the conflict between state and federal law in that case was to be resolved under the Rules Enabling Act test for Federal Rules of Procedure, rather than through use of the outcome determinative test. Yet, the Court nonetheless provided a gloss on the outcome determinative test of **Guaranty Trust Co. v. York**, *supra*, p. 194. In assessing the possible impact on the outcome of the dispute (and the possible incentives to engage in forum shopping that such differences in outcome may engender), the Court admonished that the proper vantage point was from the time of the suit's commencement, rather than from the time a state rule was made the subject of a motion to dismiss a federal claim. This prospective vantage point for assessing the impact on outcome can often provide some insight into the incentives of the plaintiff.

Example: In **Hanna v. Plumer,** the plaintiff filed suit in federal court and relied on the Federal Rules of Procedure to effect service on the defendant by leaving court papers with the defendant's spouse at his home. Presumably, the plaintiff could have just as easily complied with state rules that required in-hand service on the defendant if the plaintiff had known them to be applicable. It seems doubtful that the plaintiff chose the federal forum to take advantage of the (slightly) more liberal rules for service of process. Viewed from the time of forum choice, therefore, the difference in the state and federal rule does not appear outcome determinative. But the difference in service rules took on greater significance at the time of the defendant's motion to dismiss for improper service. At that time, the statute of limitations had run and the plaintiff could no longer timely satisfy the state rule of in-hand service, if applicable. Application of the state rule would have thus been outcome determinative only in the sense that it would have required dismissal of pending litigation, even though the rule had not apparently influenced forum choice at the outset.

Example: In **Cohen v. Beneficial Industrial Loan Corp.**, *supra*, the bond requirement might be viewed as outcome determinative in the sense in which *Hanna* used that term. Plaintiffs might prefer to avoid the state law bond requirement by filing in federal court, thereby reducing the cost to them of initiating litigation and the risk of loss should the court conclude that the action so lacked merit as to warrant an award of attorneys' fees.

e.g. **Example:** In **Guaranty Trust Co. v. York**, *supra*, the difference in the rules of timeliness would also be outcome determinative in the *Hanna* sense. If federal courts were free to apply an equitable rule of laches to govern the timeliness of suit, rather than the more rigid state statute of limitations, plaintiffs with claims barred under state law would have an obvious incentive to prefer the federal forum.

b. "Interest Balancing" Approach

In **Byrd v. Blue Ridge Rural Electric Cooperative, Inc.**, 356 U.S. 525 (1958), the Supreme Court did not employ the outcome determinative test, but rather balanced state and federal interests.

(1) The *Byrd* Case

Plaintiff Byrd had been injured while working as an employee of a contractor with Blue Ridge Electric Cooperative. Byrd sued for negligence in federal court in South Carolina. Defendant Blue Ridge claimed that Byrd was its "statutory employee" under South Carolina law, and thus could recover, if at all, only under the state's workers' compensation law (which permitted a much lower recovery than a tort suit would have). If the suit had been brought in South Carolina state court, Byrd's status as a "statutory employee" would have been determined by a judge rather than a jury. Thus, Blue Ridge claimed that under *Erie*, and under the outcome determinative test, the federal court was required to use a judge to determine Byrd's status. The Court held that Byrd was entitled to a *jury* determination of his status in federal court, even though he would not have had a jury on that issue in state court. The Court conceded that the outcome could be "substantially affected" by the different fact finder, and stated that "were 'outcome' the only consideration, a strong case might appear for saying that the federal court should follow the state practice." But the Court balanced the state interest in having its procedures followed against the federal interest in administering justice as an "independent system." Given the strength of the policy in favor of jury trials in the federal courts, the Court refused to follow the state practice.

(2) *Byrd* as an Anomaly

Byrd is an anomalous case. It can be convincingly justified, if at all, only by the strength of the Seventh Amendment policy in favor of jury trials in federal court. Two cases show the anomalous nature of *Byrd*.

(a) Arbitration in Federal Court

In **Bernhardt v. Polygraphic Co. of America**, 350 U.S. 198 (1956), plaintiff brought suit in federal court on a contract. The contract provided for mandatory arbitration of disputes arising out of the contract, but the parties conceded that the state court would not have enforced the arbitration provision. The Supreme Court held that the arbitration provision could not be honored in federal court any more than it would have been honored in state court: "The change from a court of law to an arbitration panel may make a radical difference in ultimate result."

1) Comparison to *Byrd*

The choice of decisionmaker (arbitrator or judge) was thus controlled by state practice in *Bernhardt.* In *Byrd*, by contrast, the choice of decisionmaker (jury or judge) was controlled by federal practice.

(b) Jury Trial in State Court

In **Dice v. Akron, Canton & Youngstown Railroad**, 342 U.S. 359 (1952), suit was brought in Ohio state court under the Federal Employers' Liability Act ("FELA"). The Ohio Supreme Court held that under state practice an issue involving a fraudulent inducement to sign a release was to be decided by a judge. The United States Supreme Court held that the right to jury trial on that issue was "part and parcel" of the federal remedy under the FELA. Thus, the state court had to provide a jury trial in accordance with federal practice.

1) Comparison to *Byrd*

In *Dice*, the choice of judge or jury in state court was controlled by federal practice in a suit brought under federal law. The analogous treatment in *Byrd* would have been for the choice of judge or jury in federal court to have been controlled by state practice in a suit brought under state law. But the court decided the issue by a jury in *Byrd*, even though the state court would have decided the issue by a judge.

(3) Significance of *Byrd*

Even though *Byrd*, on its facts, appears to be an anomalous case, it stands for the proposition that in cases not governed by the Federal Rules of Civil Procedure, the Court no longer looks merely to "outcome." It also *balances the strength of the state interest and the interest in uniformity* of outcome, on the one hand, *against* the *interest of the federal courts in following their own procedures,* on the other.

c. Combination of Outcome Determinative and Interest Balancing Approaches

The Supreme Court has sometimes used both approaches to reach its decision. In **Gasperini v. Center for Humanities, Inc.**, 518 U.S. 415 (1996), the Court held that a federal court should follow New York law requiring federal judges to determine whether a jury damage award "deviates materially from what would be reasonable compensation." Affirming use of the New York standard, the Court found the New York law outcome determinative because "*Erie* precludes a recovery in federal court significantly larger than the recovery that would have been tolerated in state court." The Court also found that Rule 59, governing review of jury verdicts, did not apply.

d. Other Matters Outside the Scope of the Federal Rules

Several other arguably procedural matters are not covered by the Federal Rules of Civil Procedure. They include:

(1) Choice of Law

A federal court follows the choice of law rules of the state in which it sits. [**Klaxon Co. v. Stentor Electric Manufacturing Co.**, 313 U.S. 487 (1941)] Two cases demonstrate the reach and current vitality of *Klaxon.*

(a) Reach of *Klaxon*

A federal interpleader suit under the predecessors to 28 U.S.C. sections 1335 and 2361 was brought in federal district court in Texas. Nationwide service of process was permitted under the federal interpleader statute; such service would not have been available if the suit had been brought in state court. Even though certain parties were brought before the federal court that could not have been brought before a Texas court, the Supreme Court held that *Klaxon* required the federal court to follow Texas law, as the Texas court would have done. [**Griffin v. McCoach**, 313 U.S. 498 (1941)]

(b) Current Vitality of *Klaxon*

Plaintiffs sued in federal court in Texas to recover for death and personal injuries suffered when a howitzer shell prematurely exploded in Cambodia. The lower federal courts found that Texas state courts would follow Cambodian law on critical issues; nevertheless, the federal courts followed Texas substantive law on those issues. The Supreme Court summarily reversed, saying, "A federal court in a diversity case is not free to engraft onto . . . state rules exceptions or modifications which may commend themselves to the federal court, but which have not commended themselves to the State in which the federal court sits." [**Day & Zimmermann, Inc. v. Challoner**, 423 U.S. 3 (1975)]

(2) In Personam Jurisdiction

In the absence of a federal long arm statute or procedural rule to the contrary, a federal court can exercise in personam jurisdiction only to the extent that a state court in that state would exercise in personam jurisdiction. This restriction on the power of the federal courts' in personam jurisdiction applies in both federal question and diversity cases. [**Omni Capital International v. Rudolf Wolff Co.**, 484 U.S. 97 (1987)—federal question; **Arrowsmith v. United Press International**, 320 F.2d 219 (2d Cir. 1963)—(Friendly, J.) diversity]

(3) Forum Non Conveniens

The Supreme Court has so far left open the question of whether a federal court must apply the forum non conveniens doctrine of the state in which it sits, or whether there is a federal standard for forum non conveniens dismissals. [**Piper Aircraft Co. v. Reyno**, *supra,* p. 179] Most lower federal courts assume a federal standard applies.

(4) Claim and Issue Preclusion

The Supreme Court has suggested that the entire subject of claim and issue preclusion lies outside the Federal Rules of Civil Procedure. In **Semtek International, Inc. v. Lockheed Martin Corp.**, 531 U.S. 491 (2001), the Court faced the question of what preclusive effect a federal court diversity judgment was to have in subsequent state court litigation. It concluded that the preclusive effect was to be defined by federal common law and was not controlled by Rule 41 (which specifies when certain kinds of dismissals operate with and without prejudice). The Court also found that the federal common law preclusion rule in diversity proceedings should (at least in this instance) incorporate the preclusion rules of the state court, so as to avoid any forum-shopping incentives that a variation in preclusion rules might create.

4. Determining State Law

Once it has been determined that a federal court is required by *Erie* to follow state law, the next step is to determine what that state law is.

a. Problem—Structural Difference Between State and Federal Courts

State courts are often required to follow federal law, just as federal courts, under *Erie*, are often required to follow state law. Subject to certain limitations, state courts are subject to both direct (*see supra,* p. 84 *et seq.*) and collateral (*see infra,* pp. 233 *et seq.*) review by federal courts of their decisions on questions of federal law. By contrast, federal court decisions on questions of state law are not subject to review by state courts. Thus, if a federal court makes a mistake in the application of state law to a case before it, a litigant harmed by that decision has no recourse except by appeal to a higher federal court.

b. Federal Court Must Give "Proper Regard" to Relevant Rulings

A federal court need not follow blindly the precedents of state trial courts, intermediate appellate courts, or even an old precedent of a state supreme court if it is of questionable validity. In holding that a federal court is not necessarily bound by intermediate state appellate court rulings, the Supreme Court has said that only "proper regard" need be given such rulings. [**Commissioner of Internal Revenue v. Estate of Bosch**, 387 U.S. 456 (1967)]

(1) Note

In the first years after *Erie* was decided, the Supreme Court required that a federal court follow the precedents of a state trial court even if the federal court thought the state supreme court would eventually decide the issue differently. [**Fidelity Union Trust Co. v. Field**, 311 U.S. 169 (1940)] Such a rigid approach to state law determination reduced a federal court to the role of a "ventriloquist's dummy." The present, more flexible approach is that of *Estate of Bosch, supra.*

c. Intervening Changes in State Law

If the state law changes between the time of the district court's decision and that of the court of appeals, the court of appeals must follow the now-current law even though it means reversing a district court decision that was correct when made. [**Vanderbark v. Owens-Illinois Glass Co.**, 311 U.S. 538 (1941)]

d. No Deference to District Court on Question of State Law

A federal court of appeals must review *de novo* a decision by a district court on a question of state law, just as it would review a district court's decision on a question of federal law. [**Salve Regina College v. Russell**, 499 U.S. 225 (1991)] Prior to the Supreme Court's decision in *Salve Regina College*, the practice in several circuits had been to leave undisturbed a district court's decision on a question of state law unless the decision was clearly erroneous.

EXAM TIP

On your exam, don't fall into the trap of mixing up similar or related material. For instance, although a federal appellate court will give the lower court's findings of fact deference (because the lower court heard the evidence firsthand), it will **not** give the lower court's **interpretation** *of state law similar deference* (because it can determine state law as effectively as a lower federal court).

e. Special Techniques for Ascertaining State Law

Two special techniques are sometimes used to determine state law:

(1) Certification

If state law is unsettled and state statutes permit the procedure, a federal court may "certify" a question of law to the state supreme court. In this way, a federal court obtains an answer to the state law question from the state supreme court, rather than answering the question itself. Such a course of action is often desirable, but rests with the "sound discretion of the federal court." [**Lehman Brothers v. Schein**, 416 U.S. 386 (1974)] When federal courts choose to certify such questions, they must follow the procedural rules and limits specified by state law. Some states, for example, do not permit federal trial courts to ask certified questions.

(2) Abstention

A federal court may also "abstain" from decision on a state law question in order to permit the parties to bring an appropriate proceeding in *state court* to obtain a ruling on the question. [**Railroad Commission of Texas v. Pullman Co.**, 312 U.S. 496 (1941); **Burford v. Sun Oil Co.**, 319 U.S. 315 (1943); *and see* discussion, *infra*, pp. 225–232]

E. Federal Common Law

1. In General

In some circumstances, federal courts have developed and applied judge-made rules of "federal common law." Such common law has three essential characteristics:

a. Supreme Federal Law

Federal common law is federal law in the sense that it is supreme federal law. Thus, state courts as well as federal courts must follow federal common law in cases where it applies.

(1) Distinguish—Federal General Common Law

The federal *general* common law developed by the federal courts under **Swift v. Tyson** was not federal law in the sense of the Constitution's Supremacy Clause. State courts were never required to follow the federal court's version of the general common law under **Swift v. Tyson.** (*See supra*, p. 185.)

EXAM TIP GILBERT

You have probably heard that there is no such thing as federal general common law. That is true, but be sure you understand the context of the statement and the distinction between "federal *general* common law" and "federal common law." *"Federal general common law"* means the body of judge-made law that, way back when, sometimes developed when neither federal law nor state law governed a case. (Recall the basic decision of *Swift v. Tyson*—that a federal court was not required to follow the general common law of a state court. Also recall that the Supreme Court, at the time, used as a coordinating mechanism to provide a uniform

---

body of law, which acted as a catalyst for interstate commerce; *see supra*, pp. 184–185.) This is the "federal general common law" that was effectively done away with in *Erie Railroad v. Tompkins.* On the other hand, federal judges obviously still decide cases that have current precedential value, and this body of law, if not closely tied to the interpretation of a controlling provision of the Federal Constitution or laws, may be referred to as ***"federal common law."*** And it indeed exists.

b. Can Be Overruled by Federal Statute

Almost all federal common law can be overruled by federal statute. Federal common law is judge-made law, developed in the absence of clear legislative command, and is generally nonconstitutional in nature.

(1) Exception—Common Law Inferred from Constitution

Federal common law that is inferred from constitutional provisions generally cannot be overruled by federal statute. [*See, e.g.*, **Bivens v. Six Unknown Named Federal Narcotics Agents**, 403 U.S. 388 (1971); *and see infra*, p. 208]

c. Jurisdiction-Conferring

Most federal common law is jurisdiction-conferring. That is, it is generally federal law within the meaning of federal question jurisdiction under 28 U.S.C. section 1331. [**Illinois v. City of Milwaukee**, *supra*, p. 106]

(1) Exception—Admiralty Suits

Admiralty suits are heard under 28 U.S.C. section 1333, which confers admiralty jurisdiction on federal district courts. Admiralty suits are not heard under section 1331, even though admiralty law is federal law. Thus, the federal law in admiralty suits is not jurisdiction-conferring law under section 1331. [**Romero v. International Terminal Operating Co.**, *supra*, p. 143]

2. Federal Common Law and Rules of Decision Act

The Rules of Decision Act provides that state laws shall govern in cases where they apply "except where the Constitution or treaties of the United States or Acts of Congress otherwise require or provide." [28 U.S.C. § 1652; *and see supra*, pp. 183 *et seq.*] The language of the Act does not mention federal common law. The question thus arises whether the development of federal common law is permitted by the Rules of Decision Act.

a. History

(1) Rules of Decision Act

In the 19th century, the Rules of Decision Act was thought to permit the development of a federal general common law by the federal courts. [**Swift v. Tyson**, *supra*, p. 184] The Act was not thought to speak to the question of whether there was a *federal* common law.

(2) Federal Common Law

After a long initial period of uncertainty, the Supreme Court finally held in 1834 that there was no federal common law, when it refused to create a common law of federal copyright in the absence of an applicable federal copyright statute. [**Wheaton v. Peters**, 33 U.S. (8 Pet.) 498 (1834)]

b. Modern Practice

The practice since the 20th century has been to develop federal common law without regard to the Rules of Decision Act. The early refusal of the Court to find that there was no federal common law has been read narrowly (or ignored).

3. Different Types of Federal Common Law

Federal common law can be divided into two subcategories: (i) common law inferred from the strength of federal policy; and (ii) common law inferred from federal statutory or constitutional provisions. These subcategories will be considered in turn:

a. Federal Common Law Inferred from Strength of Federal Policy

When there is a strong federal policy, but no federal statute or constitutional provision governs the issue, federal common law has sometimes been developed to provide a uniform federal rule. Such federal common law has been developed in several areas:

(1) When United States Is a Party

Federal common law has been developed in some cases when the United States is a party and where federal proprietary or other interests are at stake.

Example: A government check made out to a private individual was accepted by a retail store after a forged endorsement was written on the check. Clearfield Trust Co. collected the amount of the check from the Federal Reserve Bank and paid that money to the store. After the money had been paid out, the United States notified Clearfield Trust of the forgery. In this case, federal common law, rather than state law, governed the issue of whether the United States had unreasonably delayed in notifying Clearfield Trust of the forgery. [**Clearfield Trust Co. v. United States**, 318 U.S. 363 (1943)]

Compare: The federal Small Business Administration made a loan to Mr. and Mrs. Yazell after a natural disaster in Texas. The Yazells defaulted on the loan, and the United States sued them. Mrs. Yazell argued that under Texas law of coverture she was protected from enforcement of the loan agreement against her. *Held:* State law rather than federal common law governed the availability of the coverture defense. [**United States v. Yazell**, 382 U.S. 341 (1966)]

(a) Analysis

A comparison of *Clearfield Trust Co.* and *Yazell* shows that the fact that the United States is a party and has a financial stake in the outcome is *not* enough, by itself, to dictate that a federal common law rule be developed. The Court must, in addition, look to the nature of the interests involved. In *Clearfield Trust*, where commercial banking practices were at issue, the Court stated that the "desirability of a uniform rule is plain." In *Yazell*, where "family and family-property arrangements" were at issue, there was no federal interest that justified invading the "peculiarly local jurisdiction" of the states.

(2) Foreign Relations

Federal common law can govern questions of foreign relations when there is no applicable federal statute. The need for a single federal rule is particularly great when the foreign relations of the United States are at stake.

Example: An assignee of contract rights held by the Cuban government sued on the contract in the United States. The Supreme Court held that the contours of the "act of state" doctrine, which governed the case, were to be determined according to federal common law. [**Banco Nacional de Cuba v. Sabbatino**, 376 U.S. 398 (1964)]

(3) Interstate Disputes

Disputes between the states are peculiarly a subject of national concern because of the need for a neutral, non-state arbiter. Moreover, suits in which the states themselves are the actual parties are within the exclusive jurisdiction of the Supreme Court. [*See* 28 U.S.C. § 1251(a)] Because of the exclusive Supreme Court jurisdiction, some of the questions arising in such cases have never been addressed by the state courts. Thus, it sometimes turns out that the *Erie* problem does not even arise in the ordinary sense, since in some cases there are no directly applicable state rules. *Examples:*

(a) Allocation of Water

The Supreme Court relies on principles of federal common law to allocate water of an interstate stream. [**Hinderlider v. La Plata River Cherry Creek Ditch Co.**, 304 U.S. 92 (1938)]

1) Note

The *Hinderlider* opinion was handed down on the same day as *Erie*, making it clear that the Court did not intend that *Erie* eliminate federal common law. [*See also* **Arizona v. California**, 373 U.S. 546(1963)]

(b) Interstate Pollution

Federal common law can govern interstate pollution caused by the states or their agencies. [**Illinois v. City of Milwaukee**, *supra*, p. 201]

1) But Note

Congress has supplanted much of the federal common law previously governing interstate pollution by the passage of the federal Water Pollution Control Act Amendments of 1972. [**Milwaukee v. Illinois**, 451 U.S. 304 (1981)]

2) Standard for Displacement

The Supreme Court continues to recognize that Congress can supplant federal common law in the environmental context. [**American Elec. Power Co. v. Connecticut**, 564 U.S. 410 (2011)—indicating that the standard for displacement is lower than that for the preemption of state law]

(4) Admiralty

From the beginning, admiralty suits were seen as involving uniquely national interests because of their effect on international trade and foreign relations. Admiralty jurisdiction is exclusive in the federal courts, subject to the significant qualification of the "saving to suitors" clause. [28 U.S.C. § 1333; *see supra*, p. 143] Much of the maritime law applied in admiralty suits is federal common law in the sense that it is judge-made. Federal maritime law is supreme federal law under the Supremacy Clause. [**Southern Pacific Co. v. Jensen**, *supra*, p. 186] (But federal common law developed in admiralty suits is not federal law in the jurisdiction-conferring sense of federal question jurisdiction under 28 U.S.C. section 1331; *see supra*, p. 202.)

Example: Federal maritime law employs a comparative negligence rather than a contributory negligence standard in personal injury suits. The admiralty comparative negligence standard must be followed whether the suit is filed in a federal admiralty court or in a state or federal common law court, as long as the nature of the injury is maritime. [**Pope Talbot, Inc. v. Hawn**, 346 U.S. 406 (1953)]

Example: An oral contract entered into between a sailor and a ship-owner respecting the manner in which medical care would be provided was unenforceable if the New York Statute of Frauds governed. But if the usual admiralty rule applied, the contract was enforceable. The Supreme Court held that the federal, judge-made admiralty rule should govern because the subject of the contract was maritime and not "local" in nature. [**Kossick v. United Fruit Co.**, 365 U.S. 731 (1961)]

(5) Other Federal Interests

Other federal interests have sometimes provided the basis for the development of federal common law, but the Supreme Court has been quite cautious in developing such law.

Example: Plaintiff had been the owner of bearer bonds issued by the Federal Home Owners' Loan Corporation. The bonds mysteriously disappeared in 1944 and were presented for payment by someone other than plaintiff in 1948. Two defendant banks argued that they had paid off the bonds in good faith, and that the bonds were not overdue when paid. The Supreme Court held that the burden of persuasion on the defendants' good faith was governed by a state rather than a federal common law standard since the litigation over the propriety of payment was "purely between private parties." However, since the bonds were federal government bonds, the question of their "overdueness" was a matter of federal law. [**Bank of America National Trust & Savings Association v. Parnell**, 352 U.S. 29 (1956)]

b. Federal Common Law Inferred from Federal Statutory or Constitutional Provisions

Federal common law is sometimes inferred from federal statutes or from the federal Constitution. To call this law "common law" is something of a misnomer, for it derives from a statutory or constitutional base. But the label "common law" is employed because it is judge-made law, consisting of significant clarifications or additions to statutory or constitutional provisions.

(1) Federal Common Law Inferred from Statutes

Federal common law has been used on a number of occasions to fill out an existing statutory structure.

(a) Inferred from Jurisdictional Grant

In one instance, the Court inferred the authority to fashion federal common law from a statute that some had interpreted as merely a jurisdictional grant. Section 301 (a) of the federal Labor Management Relations Act (LMRA) conferred jurisdiction on the federal courts to hear suits arising out of breaches of collective bargaining agreements regardless of the citizenship of the parties. If the section had been construed merely to grant jurisdiction to hear disputes arising under *state law* of contract, a serious constitutional question would have arisen as to the permissible scope of an Article III court's jurisdiction. [*See* **National Mutual Insurance Co. v. Tidewater Transfer Co.**, *supra*, pp. 74–75] But the Court found that the section authorized the federal courts to develop a substantive federal common law governing collective bargaining agreements. The Court concluded that the substantive law to apply in suits under section 301(a) is "federal law which the courts must fashion from the policy of our national labor laws." [**Textile Workers Union v. Lincoln Mills**, *supra*, p. 116]

1) Note

It is sometimes suggested that the federal common law developed in *Lincoln Mills* is comparable to the common law developed in interstate disputes and in admiralty. (*See supra*, p. 203.) In all three instances, the authority to develop a federal common law is inferred from a jurisdictional grant rather than from a substantive statutory or constitutional rule.

But one can read section 301(a) of the LMRA as establishing a federal duty to comply with labor contracts and to authorize suits for their "violation," in which case the statute would go beyond a mere jurisdictional grant.

(b) Inferred from Substantive Statute

In a number of instances, the Court has inferred federal common law from incomplete or unclear substantive statutes.

1) Private Causes of Action

Sometimes a federal statute will prescribe a standard of conduct without specifying who is entitled to recover in the event the statute is violated. The Supreme Court has occasionally inferred private causes of action from such statutory commands. (**Note on terminology:** Federal courts will sometimes refer to the causes of action that they have recognized through a process of inference as "implied" rights of action. This usage treats the statute as implying the existence of a right to sue and downplays the creative role of courts in the process.)

The law in this area remains in a state of flux. For some time, an emerging majority of the Court has insisted that Congress take the lead in the creation of private rights of action and has been less willing to recognize implied rights of action than was true at an earlier day. This renewed emphasis on the text as the best measure of congressional intent has familiar analogs in other areas of federal law. As a result, students should view older precedents, which rely on various non-textual clues to legislative intent, with caution.

a) Old Test for Private Cause of Action

Plaintiff shareholder sought damages from directors of a corporation for alleged violation of a federal criminal statute prohibiting certain corporate political contributions. The Supreme Court formulated a four-part test to determine whether a private cause of action should be inferred: (i) is the plaintiff part of a class "for whose *especial benefit* the statute was enacted"; (ii) is there any indication of *legislative intent* to create or deny the remedy; (iii) is the proposed remedy *consistent* with the underlying legislative scheme; and (iv) is the proposed cause of action *traditionally relegated to state law*? Applying this test, the Court refused to infer a private cause of action for damages. [**Cort v. Ash**, 422 U.S. 66 (1975)]

e.g. **Example:** Plaintiff alleged that she had been denied admission to medical school because of her sex. Educational institutions receiving federal funds are prohibited by Title IX of the Educational Amendments of 1972 from discriminating on the basis of sex. The Supreme Court applied the four-part **Cort v. Ash** test (*supra*) and inferred a private cause of action from Title IX. [**Cannon v. University of Chicago**, 441 U.S. 677 (1979)]

Important dissent: Justice Powell dissented in **Cannon**, arguing that Congress should take the lead in fashioning rights of action and courts should generally refrain from doing so. Powell's dissent ranged widely, arguing in part that the recognition of rights of action had a jurisdiction-conferring element (given the availability of federal question jurisdiction over any right of action the courts chose to recognize). Powell also argued on separation-of-powers grounds that the responsibility for both jurisdiction and rights of action was legislative.

b) **Modern Tendency**

In recent years, the Supreme Court has been particularly cautious in inferring private causes of action from bare statutory commands. As the Court stated in **Touche Ross & Co. v. Redington**, 442 U.S. 560 (1979): "[I]n a series of cases since *Borak* we have adhered to a stricter standard for the implication of private causes of action . . . . The ultimate question is one of congressional intent, not one of whether this Court thinks it can improve on the statutory scheme that Congress enacted into law."

e.g. **Example:** The federal Parental Kidnapping Prevention Act imposes on the state courts the obligation to give full faith and credit to child custody decrees entered by courts of other states. Plaintiff was awarded custody of his child under a California court decree. He sought a declaratory judgment and an injunction from federal court that would have required the sister state to observe the California decree. The Supreme Court held that the federal Act was not intended to create a private cause of action in federal court, but rather was intended only to create an obligation enforceable directly in the courts of the sister state. [**Thompson v. Thompson**, 484 U.S. 174 (1988)]

e.g. **Example:** Plaintiffs brought suit, alleging that an English-only requirement in the administration of drivers' license exams had an adverse impact in violation of Title VI of the Civil Rights Act (prohibiting discrimination on the basis of race in various programs supported by federal financial aid). The Court, reaffirming its emphasis on congressional primacy and legislative intent, refused to recognize a disparate impact right of action. [**Alexander v. Sandoval**, 532 U.S. 275 (2001)]

> **Example:** Plaintiffs brought suit, alleging that the defendant aided and abetted a violation of the federal securities laws and that the violation was actionable under 10b–5. Although the Court had previously recognized a 10b–5 action, it expressed a reluctance to broaden the action to embrace a new collection of potential defendants, particularly given Congress's failure to adopt that course. [**Stonewall Investment Partners, LLC v. Scientific-Atlanta**, 552 U.S. 148 (2008)—"it is settled that there is an implied cause of action only if the underlying statute can be interpreted to disclose the intent to create one."]

c) Assessing Proposed Implied Rights of Action

With growing skepticism toward implied rights of action, the Court has declined to invoke the **Cort v. Ash** test in conducting its inquiry into congressional intent. The **Cort** analysis may still be relevant for statutory rights enacted during the 1970s and 1980s, before the turn to textualism cast doubt on its approach. [See **Alexander v. Sandoval**, *supra* p. 206—acknowledging the possible relevance of **Cort's** framework to older statutes, which were enacted during its interpretive heyday, but denying that such reliance was compelled.]

2) Federal Defenses

Sometimes a federal defense has been inferred from a statutory policy.

> **Example:** Three plaintiffs were all injured while on active military duty—one during a barracks fire and two due to negligent medical care by military doctors. The Court held that persons injured while on active duty in military service may not sue the United States for recovery for their injuries. This defense, called the *Feres* doctrine, is a judge-made exception to the Federal Tort Claims Act. [**Feres v. United States**, 340 U.S. 135 (1950)]

> **Example:** Defense contractors that have supplied equipment to the United States may assert a "government contractors" defense to product liability suits brought by those injured by their equipment. The defense is available when (i) the United States *approved reasonably precise specifications* for the equipment; (ii) the equipment *conformed to those specifications*; and (iii) the contractor *warned* the United States of dangers inherent in the use of the equipment known to the contractor but unknown to the United States. The government contractors' defense was *inferred in part from the policies of the Federal Tort Claims Act.* [**Boyle v. United Technologies Corp.**, 487 U.S. 500 (1988)]

3) Statutes of Limitations

Federal statutes often explicitly create causes of action but are silent on the issue of what statute of limitations period should be employed.

a) Fallback Statute of Limitations

A statute provides that all civil actions arising under Acts of Congress enacted after December 1, 1990, have a fallback statute of limitations of *four years*. [28 U.S.C. § 1658] Thus, if an Act of Congress is silent regarding a statute of limitations, the fallback period of four years applies. For cases brought prior to the statute's enactment, the Court would either "borrow" an analogous state statute [*see, e.g.*, **Board of Regents v. Tomania**, 446 U.S. 478 (1980)] or rely on federal law [**Del Costello v. International Brotherhood of Teamsters**, 462 U.S. 151 (1983)—Court "borrowed" NLRB provision in suit against a union; **Holmberg v. Ambrecht**, 327 U.S. 392 (1946)—Court applied federal equitable principles of laches to determine the limitations period.]

(2) Federal Common Law Inferred from Constitution

Federal common law has been employed on a few occasions to infer private causes of action from constitutional provisions. Such actions are frequently referred to as "*Bivens* actions," after the first case to infer a private cause of action directly from the Constitution.

Example: Plaintiff alleged that he had been arrested and his apartment searched by federal narcotics agents without probable cause, in violation of the Fourth Amendment. He sued the agents for damages. Had the search been conducted by *state* officers, a statutory cause of action for damages would have been available under 42 U.S.C. section 1983, which provides remedies for violations of constitutional rights under color of state law. However, there is no comparable statute for constitutional violations by federal officers. The Supreme Court inferred a private cause of action for damages directly from the prohibition of the Fourth Amendment. [**Bivens v. Six Unknown Named Federal Narcotics Agents**, *supra*, p. 201]

Example: Plaintiff, a female staff employee of a member of Congress, was fired because the Congressman had decided "that it was essential that the understudy to my Administrative Assistant be a man." The Supreme Court inferred a private cause of action for damages due to sex-based discrimination directly from the Due Process Clause of the Fifth Amendment. [**Davis v. Passman**, 442 U.S. 228 (1979)]

Example: The mother of a deceased prisoner sued federal prison officials for damages, alleging that they had not provided adequate medical care. The Supreme Court inferred a private cause of action for damages directly from the Eighth Amendment. The Court noted that the Federal Tort Claims Act potentially provided a statutory cause of action against the prison officials, but characterized the statutory remedy as "parallel" and "complementary." A constitutional cause of action could be defeated only "when Congress has provided an alternative remedy which is explicitly declared to be a *substitute* for recovery directly under the Constitution and viewed as equally effective." [**Carlson v. Green**, 446 U.S. 14 (1980)]

Compare: Plaintiff was demoted after he made critical public remarks about the federal agency where he worked. After a series of administrative proceedings, he was reinstated to his former position with back pay. Plaintiff sought a further damage recovery based upon an asserted violation of his First Amendment rights. The Supreme Court assumed both that there had been a constitutional violation and that the statutory administrative remedy was less "complete" than a full damage remedy would be. The Court nevertheless refused to infer a private cause of action directly from the First Amendment. The test was stated in softer terms than in **Carlson v. Green**, *supra:* "When Congress provides an alternative remedy, it may, of course, indicate its intent, by statutory language, by clear legislative history, or perhaps even by the statutory remedy itself, that the Court's [common law] power should not be exercised." [**Bush v. Lucas**, 462 U.S. 367 (1983)]

(a) Reluctance to Infer Additional *Bivens* Actions

Since **Bush v. Lucas**, *supra*, the Court has been notably reluctant to infer additional rights of action from the Constitution. These cases suggest that the Court may no longer insist on an adequate alternative remedy under federal law or on evidence that Congress meant to substitute such a remedy for the constitutional common law remedy.

Example: Claimants denied disability benefits by the Social-Security Administration ("SSA") filed an action for damages for violation of their due process rights. The Court rejected the claim in deference to its perception that Congress had fashioned limited but effective administrative remedies within SSA. In particular, administrative remedies would restore benefits, but would not redress losses for delays and emotional distress. [**Schweiker v. Chilicky**, 487 U.S. 412 (1988)]

Example: A former member of the military brought suit for damages resulting from the administration of the drug LSD to him without his knowledge or consent. The Court refused to permit a *Bivens* action, citing the special relationship between superiors and subordinates in the military and the system of veteran's benefits to which the claimant was entitled. [**United States v. Stanley**, 483 U.S. 669 (1983)]

Example: The Bureau of Prisons contracted with a private firm to run a prison facility. An inmate suffered a heart attack, allegedly due to the firm's disregard of his condition, and sued for resulting personal injuries. A narrow 5–4 majority of the Court rejected the claim, citing the fact that the inmate had sued a corporate entity rather than an individual and the fact that adequate remedies were available under state tort law. Reliance on state law remedies to displace a federal common law remedy marked a new departure and suggests a deep skepticism about the wisdom of *Bivens* itself. Indeed, two concurring Justices frankly questioned the doctrine and proposed to confine it narrowly within its established bounds. [**Correctional Services Corp. v. Malesko**, 534 U.S. 61(2001)]

Example: An owner of a dude ranch out West took title free and clear of an unrecorded federal government easement. Government officials bargained for the restoration of the easement, and then launched a pattern of retaliation against the owner when he refused. The owner sued, alleging that he was the victim of retaliation for exercising his Fifth Amendment right to just compensation for any transfer of his property rights. The Court held that there was no implied right of action for retaliation under the Fifth Amendment. [**Willkie v. Robbins**, 551 U.S. 537 (2007).

Example: Plaintiff, an inmate in a privately-run federal prison, brought a **Bivens** action against various officers, alleging that his medical care was so substandard as to constitute cruel and unusual punishment. The Court refused to recognize a federal right of action. [**Minecci v. Pollard**, 565 U.S. 118 (2012)—emphasizing the availability of private tort remedies for the misconduct of private prison firms]

(b) Limiting the *Bivens* Action to Its Three Established Contexts

In **Ziglar v. Abbasi**, 137 S.Ct. 1843 (2017), the Supreme Court apparently confined *Bivens* to its three established contexts: suits by victims of a Fourth Amendment violation (as in *Bivens* itself); suits by prisoners under the Eighth Amendment (as upheld in *Carlson v. Green*); and suits by victims of gender discrimination under the Fifth Amendment (as in *Davis v. Passman*). The case arose from religious and ethnic discrimination claims brought against high government officials said to have been responsible for the round up and detention under harsh conditions of Muslim men in the greater New York City area after 9/11. The Court refused to allow the suits to proceed, and announced a new more restrictive framework for the recognition of rights to sue. First, lower courts must treat every claim that does not fall squarely within the three existing contexts as presenting a new *Bivens* question. Second, the lower courts must ordinary defer to the primacy of Congress in fashioning rights to sue and approach the judicial creation of a new right to sue with caution, giving appropriate weight to a host of factors that might counsel hesitation. The Court treated the absence of alternative remedies as a possible factor in the analysis but gave little weight to that consideration. Third, the Court indicated that it did not view the *Bivens* action as an appropriate vehicle for testing broad questions of federal policy, preferring to rely on suits for habeas and injunctive relief for that purpose.

F. Federal Law Against a State Law Background

1. In General

It is important to keep in mind that federal law is not comprehensive. It is generally "interstitial in nature. It rarely occupies a legal field completely, totally excluding all participation by the legal systems of the states .... It builds upon legal relationships established by the states, altering or supplanting them only so far as necessary for the special purpose. Congress acts, in short, against the background of the total corpus juris of the states in much the way that a state legislature acts against the background of the common law, assumed to govern unless changed by legislation." [*Hart & Wechsler's The Federal Courts and the Federal System* 521 (4th ed. 1996)]

2. Federal Common Law Cause of Action Not Created

In a number of cases, the Supreme Court has declined to create a federal cause of action under federal common law because existing state law rules already governed the matter satisfactorily.

Example: An American soldier was injured by defendant's truck. The United States sued to recover for the soldier's hospitalization costs and his pay during his period of disability. The Supreme Court left the matter to existing state law (which gave no cause of action) rather than create a federal common law cause of action. [**United States v. Standard Oil of California**, 332 U.S. 301 (1947)]

Example: Plaintiffs were survivors of persons killed in an airplane crash. Plaintiffs claimed that the cause of the crash was birds swarming from a nearby dump. Plaintiffs sought to recover from the operator of the airport on the ground that the operator had violated a contract with the Federal Aviation Administration to restrict land near the airport to uses compatible with safe operation of aircraft. The Supreme Court declined to create a federal common law cause of action, leaving the matter to state law (which provided governmental immunity to the defendant). [**Miree v. DeKalb County**, 433 U.S. 25 (1977)]

Example: Petitioner, a corporate defendant in a federal antitrust suit, sought to file a third-party complaint against those who might be found to have conspired with it. The Supreme Court held that federal law governed, but declined to create a federal common law right of contribution under the antitrust laws. [**Texas Industries, Inc. v. Radcliff Materials, Inc.**, 451 U.S. 630 (1981)]

3. Incorporation of State Law into Federal Law

Federal statutes ordinarily do not incorporate state standards that would make the application of federal law vary from state to state, depending on the content of state law. [**Mississippi Band of Choctaw Indians v. Holyfield**, 490 U.S. 30 (1989)] Sometimes, however, federal courts explicitly or implicitly incorporate state standards as part of the federal law.

Example: The federal Copyright Act gives to the "children" of the author the right to renew a copyright. The Act gives the renewal right to an illegitimate child if, under state law, that child would be an heir to the author. [**De Sylva v. Ballentine**, 351 U.S. 570 (1956)]

Example: Agencies of the federal government lent money secured by liens on property. Since the rights of the federal government under nationwide programs were involved, federal law governed. But the Supreme Court held that federal law incorporated state law in determining priority among competing liens on the property. [**United States v. Kimball Foods**, 440 U.S. 715 (1979)]

Example: Federal statutes enacted prior to December 1990 are usually deemed to incorporate state statutes of limitation. [**Board of Regents v. Tomania**, *supra*, p. 208]

4. Special Problems with the Enforcement of Treaties

The Supremacy Clause of the Constitution expressly includes treaties as part of supreme federal law and requires state courts to give them effect notwithstanding anything to the contrary in state law. By giving treaties binding force in the domestic legal order, the (monist) Constitution departed from the (dualist) treaty-enforcement model in Great Britain, where treaties were negotiated and signed by the Crown but took effect only after the adoption of implementing legislation by Parliament. Early decisions, such as **Ware v. Hylton**, 3 U.S. 199 (1796), viewed the Supremacy Clause as effectuating the US treaty of peace with Great Britain (1783) without any need for implementing legislation by Congress.

Not all treaties enjoy this self-executing quality. In a useful summary, Professor Vazquez has identified the following four situations in which treaties require further action:

1) The parties intended that legislation would be adopted to effectuate treaty

2) The treaty norm was addressed to the legislature

3) The Constitution requires a statute (or constitutional amendment) to effectuate the treaty

4) The plaintiff has a right under the treaty but lacks a private right of action.

Vazquez, The Four Doctrines of Self-Executing Treaties, 89 Am. J. Int'l L. 695 (1995).

Today, the federal courts have been slow to recognize implied rights of action to enforce federal treaty obligations. In **Medellin v. Texas**, 552 U.S. 491 (2008), the Supreme Court refused to treat a treaty-based decision by the International Court of Justice in a Texas state court death penalty matter as binding in the domestic order, and on that basis declined to require the state court to effectuate the ICJ decision. Such decisions will have the practical effect of requiring Congress to implement many treaty-based obligations.

Chapter Eight

Federal Law in the State Courts

Key Exam Issues

State courts hear many cases based on federal questions or in which federal questions are involved. Learning about state courts is important because the state courts form an important backdrop to the federal courts' jurisdiction. Recall that under the "Madisonian Compromise," it is the state courts that decide federal question cases whenever the cases do not, or cannot, go into federal court.

In analyzing an exam question in this area, use the following basic approach:

1. ***Distinguish between concurrent and exclusive jurisdiction.*** The general rule (with the exception of antitrust suits) is that where a federal statute is silent, the state courts have ***concurrent*** jurisdiction. If the federal statute explicitly so provides, the federal courts have ***exclusive*** jurisdiction.

2. ***If jurisdiction is concurrent*** (and thus the state court can hear the case), consider whether under the principle of *Testa v. Katt*, the state court ***must hear*** the case. Unless the court's jurisdiction is inadequate for that type of case, it cannot refuse to hear a case merely because it is based on federal law. State courts must follow federal law just as, under *Erie*, federal courts must follow state law.

3. ***Consider whether the state court must apply federal procedural rules.*** Although generally the state court applies its own procedural rules, in a few cases state courts are required to go further than federal courts are required to go under *Erie*.

One final note: In studying this material, learn the basic doctrinal rules; in this area, they are not terribly difficult. When answering examination questions, keep in mind as well that these rules help the state courts fit into an overall ***system*** of federal and state courts.

A. Introduction

1. In General

State courts have jurisdiction to decide questions of federal law, and in deciding those questions the state courts must faithfully follow federal law. These two characteristics of the state court correspond to characteristics of the federal courts.

2. Jurisdiction to Hear Cases Involving Law of Other Sovereign

State courts have a ***concurrent jurisdiction*** with federal courts over most cases involving questions of federal law, just as federal courts have a concurrent jurisdiction with state courts over many cases involving questions of state law. (State courts' jurisdiction over cases involving questions of federal law will be considered below, pp. 215 *et seq.*)

3. Obligation to Follow Substantive Law of Other Sovereign

State courts have an obligation to faithfully follow federal law in cases within their jurisdiction, just as federal courts have an obligation to faithfully follow state law in cases within their jurisdiction. (The state courts' obligation to follow federal law will be considered below, pp. 215 *et seq.*)

B. State Courts' Jurisdiction over Cases Involving Questions of Federal Law

1. State Courts May Hear Many Federal Law Cases

State courts are permitted to decide a wide range of cases brought under federal law.

a. Concurrent Jurisdiction Ordinarily Assumed

The normal rule of construction is that *if a federal statute is silent*, state and federal courts have *concurrent jurisdiction* over cases brought under that statute. [**Claflin v. Houseman**, 93 U.S. 130 (1876); **Charles Dowd Box Co. v. Courtney**, 368 U.S. 502 (1962)]

Example: State courts have concurrent jurisdiction with the federal courts over federal civil rights suits brought under 42 U.S.C. section 1983. [**Maine v. Thiboutot**, 448 U.S. 1 (1980)]

Example: State courts have concurrent jurisdiction with the federal courts over federal civil Racketeer Influenced and Corrupt Organizations Act ("RICO") suits. [**Tafflin v. Levitt**, 493 U.S. 455 (1990)]

Example: State courts have concurrent jurisdiction with the federal courts over suits under Title VII of the Civil Rights Act of 1964. [**Yellow Freight Systems v. Donnelly**, 494 U.S. 820 (1990)]

Compare: antitrust cases: Federal courts have *exclusive* jurisdiction over federal antitrust actions, even though the relevant statutes do not explicitly provide for exclusive federal jurisdiction.

b. Exclusive Federal Jurisdiction When Explicitly Stated

Federal courts have exclusive jurisdiction over federal statutory claims when the statute explicitly provides for exclusive jurisdiction.

Example: As provided in the federal statute, federal courts have exclusive jurisdiction over patent and copyright cases. [28 U.S.C. § 1338]

2. State Courts *Must* Hear Federal Law Cases When Congress So Requires

Congress has the power not merely to authorize, but to *require*, state courts to hear cases based on federal causes of action.

Example: The federal Emergency Price Control Act passed during World War II provided that state and federal courts should have concurrent jurisdiction over suits brought to recover treble damages for violation of federal price controls. Rhode Island state courts refused to hear a treble damage suit brought under the statute on the ground that a state need not enforce the "penal" laws of a government that is "foreign in the international sense." The Supreme Court held that the United States government stands on a different footing vis-a-vis the states from foreign governments, and that the state courts had a constitutional obligation to hear even "penal" treble damage suits based on federal law. [**Testa v. Katt**, 330 U.S. 386 (1947)]

Example: The plaintiff brought a section 1983 action against the local school board. Under federal law, such an entity could be held liable under section 1983, but enjoyed sovereign immunity under state law. The Court held that a state court must entertain a federal civil rights action under 42 U.S.C. section 1983. The state court cannot allow a state sovereign immunity defense to a federal claim if that defense would not be available in federal court. [**Howlett v. Rose**, 496 U.S. 356 (1990)]

a. But Note

Although state courts must entertain most federal actions, state courts *need not provide a forum for federal claims when a federal court would not entertain the claim; e.g.*, suits that implicate the state's *federal* sovereign immunity from suit. [**Alden v. Maine**, 527 U.S. 706 (1999)]

Example: A group of employees sued the state of Maine in state court, seeking back pay to remedy violations of federal fair labor standards. Such an action for retrospective monetary relief could not proceed in federal court, under the prevailing view of the Eleventh Amendment. (*See infra*, pp. 287 *et seq.*) The Court held that state courts were also permitted to close their doors to the suit. [**Alden v. Maine**, *supra*]

3. When State Courts Can Refuse to Hear Federal Law Case

When a state court does not have subject matter jurisdiction over, or would dismiss, a certain kind of case, the state court *may* refuse to hear federal cases of that kind. But a refusal to hear a federal case *may not he based on a hostility to federal law.*

a. Language in *Testa v. Katt*

In **Testa v. Katt**, *supra*, the Supreme Court noted that Rhode Island courts had jurisdiction to hear similar claims if brought under Rhode Island law and that Rhode Island courts had previously heard claims for double damages under federal labor laws. The Court stated, "Thus the Rhode Island courts have jurisdiction adequate and appropriate under established local law to adjudicate this action." This statement suggests that if the Rhode Island courts were without jurisdiction over this type of claim, the federal government could not require a Rhode Island court to hear it. So read, *Testa* is only an antidiscrimination case, requiring a state court not to discriminate against cases brought under federal law.

b. Clear Statement of the Antidiscrimination Principle

The Supreme Court has stated the antidiscrimination principle as follows: "While Congress has not attempted to compel states to provide courts for the enforcement of the Federal Employers' Liability Act . . ., the Federal Constitution prohibits state courts of general jurisdiction from refusing to do so solely because the suit is brought under a federal law . . . . *A state may not discriminate against rights arising under federal laws.*" [**McKnett v. St. Louis & San Francisco Railway**, 292 U.S. 230 (1934) (emphasis added)]

c. Successful Refusals to Hear Federal Cases

In a few instances, state courts have successfully refused to hear federal cases. It is important to note that their refusal was based on grounds equally applicable to state and federal cases. Examples include:

(1) State Court of Limited Jurisdiction

A municipal court of limited jurisdiction can decline jurisdiction over a claim under the Federal Employers' Liability Act when under state law it is without jurisdiction over this kind of suit. [**Herb v. Pitcairn**, 324 U.S. 117 (1945)]

(2) Forum Non Conveniens

A state court may dismiss a suit brought under the Federal Employers' Liability Act because of the doctrine of forum non conveniens, provided the doctrine is applied as a "general local practice" to "all causes of action begun in its courts." [**Missouri ex rel. Southern Railway v. Mayfield**, 340 U.S. 1 (1950)]

d. Jurisdictional Limits on State Authority

Plaintiffs brought suit in state court of general jurisdiction, seeking to impose liability on state prison guards under 42 U.S.C. section 1983 for violation of their civil rights. States generally enjoy concurrent jurisdiction over such actions. New York had adopted a law, however, forbidding any suit against state prison guards in state courts of general jurisdiction. Instead, claimants were expected to sue the state itself in the court of claims. The state courts ruled that this jurisdictional restriction, which applied to both state and federal law claims against prison guards, was a non-discriminatory restriction on state power that did not violate the federal Supremacy Clause.

The Supreme Court reversed. For starters, it pointed to the fact that the state courts had ample jurisdiction to entertain claims against state officials, including section 1983 claims. While it acknowledged that the jurisdictional limit was non-discriminatory, that alone did not save the statute. Having opened its courts of general jurisdiction to such claims, New York could not selectively refuse to entertain claims against prison guards, even by way of jurisdictional limits. [**Haywood v. Drown**, 556 U.S. 729 (2009)]

Importance: Haywood is important both for extending the **Testa** rule to even-handed jurisdictional restrictions and for suggesting that state courts have limited power to restrict access to state courts for those who wish to enforce federal rights.

C. State Court Obligation to Follow Federal Law

1. In General

A fundamental principle of the federal system is that state courts must faithfully follow and apply federal law.

a. Rationale

The rationale for this fundamental principle is essentially the same as the rationale underlying **Erie Railroad v. Tompkins.** It should not matter, in terms of the substantive law applied, whether a suit is brought in state or federal court.

b. Origin of State Court Duty

The state court obligation stems from the Constitution itself, which proclaims that federal law is supreme and binding on state judges, anything to the contrary in state law notwithstanding.

c. Task of Ascertaining the Content of Federal Law

Although state courts clearly have an obligation to follow the precedents of the Supreme Court, they do not owe a similar loyalty to the decisions of the lower federal courts (including those of the federal circuit court that embraces the state). As with the role of federal courts in finding state law under the *Erie* doctrine, state courts may treat precedents of the lower federal courts as persuasive, but not binding.

2. Distinguish—Holding in *Martin v. Hunter's Lessee*

The famous case of **Martin v. Hunter's Lessee**, *supra*, p. 85, is often cited for the proposition that state courts must follow federal law. The obligation of the state courts to follow federal law was indeed assumed in that case. But the question at issue, and the Supreme Court's holding, was that the Supreme Court had *appellate jurisdiction* over state courts *to ensure* that they were fulfilling that obligation.

3. Scope of Obligation to Follow Federal Law

a. General Rule

The principle that state courts must faithfully follow federal law in cases in which federal law applies is symmetrical with the *Erie* principle that federal courts must faithfully follow state law in cases in which state law applies. Generally speaking, state courts may follow their *own procedural rules* in enforcing substantive federal law, just as federal courts may follow their own procedural rules in enforcing substantive state law. [*See* **Hanna v. Plumer**, *supra*, pp. 190–192]

EXAM TIP

This is an important point to remember for your exam: In a case to enforce a federal right, a *state* court may apply its own *procedural rules*, but it *must* apply *federal substantive law*—this mirrors the *Erie* requirement that a *federal* court may apply its own procedural rules in enforcing state substantive law.

---

b. Cases Going Beyond General Rule

Occasionally, the Supreme Court has required state courts to follow *federal* procedures in enforcing substantive federal law. In such cases, the rationale of the Court is that the federal procedures are "part and parcel" of the federal remedy. [**Dice v. Akron, Canton & Youngstown Railroad**, *supra*, p. 197]

e.g. **Example:** State courts trying Federal Employers' Liability Act cases must divide decisionmaking authority between the judge and jury in the same manner as federal courts do, even if uniform state practice is otherwise. The right to have certain issues tried by a jury is "part and parcel" of the remedy under the federal act. [**Dice v. Akron, Canton & Youngstown Railroad**, *supra*]

e.g. **Example:** State courts trying Federal Employers' Liability Act cases cannot use "strict local rules of pleading" that "impose unnecessary burdens" on plaintiffs, even if the local pleading rules are uniformly applied in the state courts. [**Brown v. Western Railway of Alabama**, 338 U.S. 294 (1949)]

(1) Inconsistency with *Hanna v. Plumer*

The *Dice* and *Brown* cases are inconsistent with the approach to procedural issues in federal courts. Under **Hanna v. Plumer** (*see supra*, pp. 190–192), federal district courts follow the Federal Rules of Civil Procedure, without sensitive inquiry into the effect of the federal procedure on the enforcement of state law.

(2) Special Character of Federal Employers' Liability Act

Both *Dice* and *Brown* were Federal Employers' Liability Act cases. From the late 1940s to the early 1960s, the Supreme Court was very concerned that plaintiffs under that Act be treated fairly, or, depending on one's point of view, unduly generously. Justice Black was particularly anxious to protect such plaintiffs. Justice Frankfurter was particularly opposed to the Court's singling out Federal Employers' Liability Act plaintiffs for such attention. Given the special character of Federal Employers' Liability Act cases, it may be wise to regard *Dice* and *Brown* as idiosyncratic and aberrational, rather than representative of a broadly applicable general principle.

4. Power of State Courts to Enter Orders Against Federal Officers

Even though state courts are obliged to follow federal law, they have *limited* power to enter orders directly against federal officers.

a. No Habeas Corpus

State courts do not have power to grant writs of habeas corpus against federal officers alleged to be holding prisoners in violation of federal law. [**Tarble's Case**, 80 U.S. (13 Wall.) 397 (1872)]

(1) Historical Explanation

A state court ordered a man's release from the United States military on habeas corpus, on the ground that under federal law he was underage when he enlisted. The Supreme Court was very reluctant to allow state courts to grant habeas corpus to persons held by the federal government because many state courts during the Civil War had granted habeas in situations where it was clearly not warranted in attempts to protect state citizens and hinder the operation of the federal government. There was no federal statute authorizing state courts to grant habeas. Without such a federal statute, the Court refused to permit a state court to grant habeas to persons in federal custody. [**Tarble's Case**, *supra*]

(2) Current Status of *Tarble's Case*

Despite the radical change in political climate since the 1860s and '70s, *Tarble's Case* remains good law. State courts, even today, are not permitted to grant habeas against federal officers.

(3) Exception to Presumption of Concurrent State Power

As noted earlier (*see supra*, p. 214), state courts presumptively enjoy concurrent jurisdiction over federal rights of action. Like the federal antitrust statute (*see supra*, p. 215), the federal statute conferring habeas power on the federal courts does not contain any language making that authority exclusive of state court jurisdiction. *Tarble's Case* thus represents another judge-made exception to the usual presumption of state court concurrent jurisdiction.

b. No State Injunction Against Federal Judicial Proceedings

State courts have no power to enjoin federal judicial proceedings, even to prevent relitigation of matters already fully decided by the state court. [**Donovan v. City of Dallas**, 377 U.S. 408 (1964)]

(1) Exception—In Rem or Quasi in Rem Jurisdiction

When the state court's jurisdiction is based on possession of a res, the state court may enjoin a federal court from exercising jurisdiction over the res. Additionally, in what amounts to the same thing as a practical matter, the state court may enjoin the parties from proceeding in federal court. [**Princess Lida of Thurn & Taxis v. Thompson**, 305 U.S. 456 (1939)]

(2) Distinguish—Federal Injunctions Against State Procedures

Federal courts are limited by the Anti-Injunction Act from enjoining state judicial proceedings, but exceptions to the Act permit injunctions in certain circumstances. [28 U.S.C. § 2283] Generally, federal courts may enjoin state courts in many more circumstances than state courts may enjoin federal courts. A federal court may enjoin relitigation to "protect or effectuate its judgments." It may also enjoin a state court's interference with a res where "necessary in aid of its jurisdiction." (*See* discussion of the Anti-Injunction Act, *infra*, pp. 233–238.)

c. Other Actions Against Federal Officers

(1) No Mandamus

State courts cannot grant mandamus against federal officers. [**McClung v. Silliman**, 19 U.S. (6 Wheat.) 598 (1821)]

(2) Injunctions

Lower courts are in conflict on the question of whether state courts may enjoin federal officers. The Supreme Court has never addressed the question, except in the context of state court power to enjoin federal *judicial proceedings*, where injunctions are not permitted (*see supra*, p. 220).

(3) Damage Awards

State courts are permitted to grant damage awards against federal officials. [**Buck v. Colbath**, 70 U.S. (3 Wall.) 334 (1866)] Note, however, that such awards are limited, in both state and federal courts, by doctrines of sovereign and official immunity.

d. Removal to Federal Court

To a significant extent, the protection of federal officers provided by *Tarble's Case* and related cases is unnecessary, or at least redundant. Under 28 U.S.C. section 1442, suits brought against federal officers in state court are removable to federal court. [*See* **Tennessee v. Davis**, *supra*, p. 168]

e. Power of Federal Courts over State Officers

The federal courts are not as limited in their power to enter orders against state officials as the state courts are in relation to federal officers. For example, federal courts can grant writs of habeas corpus against state officers for violations of the Constitution. [28 U.S.C. § 2254; *and see infra*, pp. 252 *et seq.*] Federal courts can also grant injunctions against state officers, subject to the limitations imposed by the various statutes and the Eleventh Amendment. (*See infra*, pp. 290–293.)

Chapter Nine

Collateral Relations Between Federal and State Courts— Abstention and Equitable Restraint

CONTENTS

Key Exam Issues

The collateral relations between federal and state courts are governed by three important doctrines. The first two—abstention and equitable restraint—are covered in this chapter. The third—federal habeas corpus for state prisoners—is covered in the next chapter. These doctrines are often fruitful sources of exam questions. Keep in mind the following points:

1. Abstention

Federal courts sometimes "abstain" from deciding state law questions in cases within their jurisdiction. In general, they abstain because they do not wish to decide state law incorrectly or to interfere with the ordinary administration of state-law-based schemes. In this area, you should learn the four subcategories of federal abstention: (i) *Pullman abstention*; (ii) *Burford abstention*; (iii) *Thibodaux abstention*; and (iv) *abstention to avoid duplicative litigation.* Remember that these doctrines are untidy and flexible. In most cases where abstention may be appropriate, the federal court has considerable discretion in deciding whether to abstain. Thus, for most exam questions, your task will be to argue why abstention *may be* appropriate rather than to give definitive reasons why the court *must* abstain.

2. Federal Injunctions Against State Court Proceedings—Statutory Prohibitions and "Equitable Restraint"

If a question presents a situation where a federal court is asked to enjoin a state court proceeding to protect federal rights, recall that there are two hurdles to surmount:

(i) *There must be no statutory prohibition against the injunction.* Here you should particularly focus on the Anti-Injunction Act. Many questions involve federal injunctions to protect federal civil rights under 42 U.S.C. section 1983. Remember that the Anti-Injunction Act does not prohibit such injunctions.

(ii) *Even if there is no statutory prohibition*, the principles of *"equitable restraint"* must be satisfied. The case of *Younger v. Harris* is your starting point in analyzing equitable restraint. Look to see whether any exceptions to *Younger* apply; whether the state action is *"pending"* (using the special definition of "pending" used in this area); whether a *preliminary injunction* is sought (it can be obtained more quickly than a permanent injunction); whether *declaratory* rather than injunctive relief is sought; and whether *"civil Younger"* is at issue.

A practical tip: Exam questions often involve federal civil rights actions under 42 U.S.C. section 1983. Since section 1983 suits constitute one of the statutory exceptions to the Anti-Injunction Act (but not the Tax Injunction Act), you ordinarily need to consider in detail only the requirements of "equitable restraint" in answering such a question.

A. In General

1. Governing Doctrines

Doctrines governing collateral relations between federal and state courts must reconcile the competing needs and capacities of the two court systems. There are three important sets of doctrines:

a. *Abstention*—see infra, pp. 225 et seq.;

b. *Federal injunctions against state proceedings—statutory prohibitions and "equitable restraint"*—see infra, pp. 233 et seq.; and

c. *Habeas corpus for state prisoners*—see infra, pp. 250 et seq.

2. Two Fundamental Facts

Doctrines governing the relations of federal and state courts largely stem from two fundamental facts about the federal system.

a. Concurrent and Overlapping Jurisdiction

Federal and state courts have concurrent jurisdiction over many cases, with the consequence that federal courts decide questions of state law, and state courts decide questions of federal law. Even when the jurisdictions are not concurrent in the sense that both the federal and state systems have subject matter jurisdiction over a case, the jurisdictions are frequently overlapping. Thus, for example, a federal court may have to decide a question of state law even in the course of deciding a case within its exclusive jurisdiction.

b. Federal and State Supreme Courts as Authoritative Expositors

The United States Supreme Court is the authoritative expositor of federal law, and state supreme courts are the authoritative expositors of state law.

3. Combined Effect of Two Facts

The combined effect of these two facts is that a case in the federal court may depend for its resolution on a question of state law, or vice versa. In such a case, a federal or state court may be required to decide a question of law as to which it can never be the authoritative expositor. A particularly acute problem is posed when a state law question arises in a federal court, for there is no appellate review by state courts of federal court decisions. But a significant problem is also posed when a federal law question arises in a state court, for as a practical matter, the United States Supreme Court has a very limited ability to provide appellate review of state court decisions.

4. Doctrines Mitigate Unavoidable Problems

The problems posed by two systems of courts are, to a significant extent, unavoidable. But doctrines of abstention, of federal injunctions against state court proceedings under statutory standards and "equitable abstention," and of habeas corpus have been developed to mitigate those problems.

B. Abstention

1. In General

Abstention doctrines are employed when a federal court has been asked to decide a question of state law in a case *properly within its jurisdiction*, but when it is *inappropriate* for the federal court to decide the question. Abstention is used (i) when a state court decision on a state law question may avoid a constitutional question raised in federal court; (ii) when a federal decision on a state law question would disrupt an important state administrative policy; (iii) when state law is unsettled and involves an area of particular local concern; and (iv) occasionally, when federal litigation would duplicate litigation pending in state court.

a. Judge-Made Law

Federal abstention doctrines are judge-made rules under which the federal courts refuse to decide cases or questions within their statutory jurisdiction.

(1) Arguable Inconsistency with *Cohens v. Virginia*

When a federal court abstains from deciding a case within its statutorily authorized jurisdiction, its refusal to decide may be inconsistent with Chief Justice Marshall's famous dictum in **Cohens v. Virginia**, *supra*, p. 53: "It is most true that this court will not take jurisdiction if it should not; but it is equally true, that it must take jurisdiction, if it should . . . . We have no more right to decline the exercise of jurisdiction which is given, than to usurp that which is not given."

(2) Postponement Rather than Renunciation of Jurisdiction

One may argue that Marshall's dictum in *Cohens* is not violated by abstention, at least insofar as abstention does not "involve the abdication of federal jurisdiction, but only the postponement of its exercise." [**Harrison v. NAACP**, 360 U.S. 167 (1959)] Note, however, that the "postponement" rationale does not justify all abstention, for the entire case is sometimes decided by the state court after the federal court abstains.

b. Four Categories of Abstention

It has become common to divide abstention into four categories, each of which is discussed below.

SUMMARY OF WHEN ABSTENTION IS USED	🔲GILBERT
***ABSTENTION* IS USED WHEN**	

☑ A state court ***decision on a state law question*** may ***avoid a constitutional question*** raised in federal court (*"Pullman abstention"*);

☑ A ***federal*** decision on a ***state*** law question would disrupt ***an important state administrative policy*** ("Burford abstention");

☑ State law is ***unsettled and involves an area of particular local concern*** (*"Thibodaux abstention"*); and

☑ Federal litigation would ***duplicate*** litigation pending in state court (used occasionally).

2. *Pullman* Abstention

Pullman abstention takes its name from **Railroad Commission of Texas v. Pullman Co.**, *supra*, p. 200. It is used when state action is challenged in federal court as violating the federal Constitution, and a decision on a question of state law may permit the constitutional question to be avoided.

a. The *Pullman* Case

The Texas Railroad Commission required that sleeping cars on trains always be in the charge of a conductor rather than a porter. On trains with only one sleeping car, the Pullman company desired to put a porter in charge of the car. (Conductors, who were white, had higher rank and salary than porters, who were black.) Pullman, the railroads, and intervening porters contended that the order was beyond the statutory power of the Commission, and that it violated the United States Constitution. A three-judge federal district court held that the Commission lacked the power under state law to issue the order and did not reach the constitutional questions. On appeal, the Supreme Court reversed, *requiring the district court to abstain* from decision so that a proceeding could be brought "with reasonable promptness" *in state court* to obtain a "definitive ruling" on the state law question. [**Railroad Commission of Texas v. Pullman Co.**, *supra*]

b. Application of *Pullman*

(1) Avoidance of Federal Constitutional Question

Pullman abstention is used to allow a state court to decide a question of state law that may allow the federal court to avoid deciding a federal constitutional question. Abstention is appropriate when the state statute is "fairly subject to an interpretation which will render unnecessary or substantially modify the federal constitutional question." [**Babbitt v. United Farmworkers National Union**, 442 U.S. 289 (1979)]

(a) But Note

Pullman abstention is not used simply to avoid deciding federal constitutional questions. Rather, it is used to allow a *state* (rather than a federal) court to determine whether the federal constitutional question may be avoided, when the avoidance would be achieved by reliance on state law. If the purpose were simply to avoid constitutional questions, a federal court could perform that function as well as, or better than, a state court. For example, in the *Pullman* case itself, the federal district court had already avoided the constitutional question by deciding that the Railroad Commission was without power under state law to issue the order. In *Pullman*, the only different result that could be achieved by abstention would be to obtain the opposite decision under state law, which would require a decision of the constitutional question the district court had sought to avoid. Thus, it is wrong to say simply that *Pullman* permits the avoidance of a federal constitutional question. It is more accurate to say that *Pullman* gives *to the state court* the power to decide whether state law will be construed so as to avoid the constitutional question.

Be careful how you phrase your answers on your exam! For example, it may be fairly easy to write that *Pullman* abstention is used to avoid a constitutional question. However, a better answer would explain that *Pullman* abstention is used to allow a *state* court to decide a *state* law issue that may allow a *federal* court to avoid deciding a federal constitutional question.

(2) Unsettled Law

Pullman abstention is available *only* when there is an "*unsettled* question of state law." [**Harris County Commissioners Court v. Moore**, 420 U.S. 77 (1975)] It would be pointless to abstain to obtain a state court decision when state law is already clear.

(3) Availability of State Forum

Pullman abstention is proper only if a decision can be obtained from the state court. The Court in *Pullman* indicated that it would not order abstention if "methods for securing a definitive ruling in the state courts cannot be pursued."

(4) Relevance of *Erie*

Note that *Pullman* came down shortly after the decision in **Erie Railroad v. Tompkins**, *supra,* p. 217. Under *Erie*, the federal courts cannot provide a definitive interpretation of state law that would avoid, once and for all, any further litigation of the federal question. *Pullman* operates in part to empower the state courts to perform that interpretive function, thus highlighting the importance of an *unsettled* question of state law.

c. Retention of Federal Jurisdiction

A federal court abstaining under *Pullman* ordinarily retains jurisdiction over the case while a decision on the state law question, is sought from the state court.

(1) Obligation to Present Constitutional Question to State Court

When a federal court has abstained under *Pullman*, the plaintiff will ordinarily bring suit in state court on the state law portion of the case. The plaintiff must also "expose" the federal constitutional issue to the state court so that it may "interpret the [state] statute in light of the constitutional objections presented." [**Government & Civic Employees Organizing Committee v. Windsor**, 353 U.S. 364 (1957)]

(2) Retention of Jurisdiction to Decide Constitutional Question

A plaintiff's submission of the federal constitutional question to the state court in compliance with **Government & Civic Employees Organizing Committee v. Windsor** does not constitute a waiver of the right to have that federal question ultimately decided by the federal court. The federal court will retain jurisdiction of the case after abstaining, and a party may *return to the federal court* for decision of the federal question *after* the state court has decided the state issue. A party will be found to have submitted a federal claim to the state court for ultimate disposition only if it "clearly appears that he voluntarily did more than *Windsor* required and fully litigated his federal claims in the state courts." [**England v. Louisiana State Board of Medical Examiners**, 375 U.S. 411 (1964)]

(3) Overlap of State and Federal Questions

The *England* reservation procedure may not preserve the federal question for federal judicial determination if the state law issue is "functionally identical" to the federal question. [**San Remo Hotel, L.P. v. City of San Francisco**, 545 U.S. 323 (2005)] In that case, the hotel challenged a city ordinance requiring payment of a fee to convert residential rooms to tourist rooms. The federal court abstained on the federal taking claim, sending the parties to state court. There, the hotel presented a variety of facial and as-applied challenges to the ordinance under state law. The Court found that these issues were functionally identical to the hotel's federal takings claims, thereby triggering the application of claim preclusion.

(a) Note

In most cases involving *Pullman* abstention, the state law and federal constitutional issues do not overlap. Thus, in *Pullman* itself, the state law issue involved the power of the agency under Texas law, and the federal claims were based on Due Process and Equal Protection Clauses of the Fourteenth Amendment.

(4) Refusal of State Courts to Decide

A few state courts refuse to decide state law questions presented to them while a federal district court retains jurisdiction. These state courts consider a decision in such circumstances to be an advisory opinion. [*See, e.g.,* **United Services Life Insurance Co. v. Delaney**, 396 S.W.2d 855 (Tex. 1965)]

d. Benefit of *Pullman*

Pullman abstention serves the values of federalism. In particular, the doctrine allows the state courts to decide the meaning of state law when constitutional challenges are made to that law. As the Court said in **Harrison v. NAACP**, *supra*, p. 226, "the federal courts should not adjudicate the constitutionality of state enactments fairly open to interpretation until the state courts have been afforded a reasonable opportunity to pass on them."

e. Cost of *Pullman*

The great cost of *Pullman* abstention is delay. The Court has sometimes refused to abstain, recognizing that "abstention operates to require piecemeal adjudication in many courts, . . . thereby delaying ultimate adjudication on the merits for an undue length of time." [**Baggett v. Bullitt**, 377 U.S. 360 (1964)—deciding First Amendment challenge to state loyalty oath for teachers]

3. *Burford* Abstention

Burford abstention takes its name from **Burford v. Sun Oil Co.**, *supra,* p. 200. It requires a federal court to abstain when its decision on a question of state law would disrupt state efforts to establish coherent policy on a matter of substantial importance to the state.

a. Note

The Supreme Court has not been able to define the contours of *Burford* abstention with precision. The Court has described *Burford* abstention as proper when "the exercise of jurisdiction by the federal court would disrupt a state administrative process" [**County of Allegheny v. Frank Mashuda Co.**, 360 U.S. 185 (1959)], and when "federal review . . . would be disruptive of state efforts to establish a coherent policy with respect to a matter of substantial public concern" [**Colorado River Water Conservation District v. United States**, 424 U.S. 800 (1976)].

b. The *Burford* Case

In *Burford*, Sun Oil challenged an order of the Texas Railroad Commission granting Burford a permit to drill four oil wells. The Commission had the authority to regulate oil drilling under a complex state-law-based regulatory scheme. State court review of Commission orders was funneled into a single court to ensure expertise in the reviewing court. Federal court suits attacking Commission orders constituted less than 10% of the cases in which orders were reviewed, and federal court orders were obviously not subject to review by the single state court that had developed expertise in the area. Previous federal decisions in this area had produced great confusion and had substantially interfered with the Commission's regulatory practices. Under these circumstances, the Supreme Court ordered that the federal suit be dismissed.

c. **Application of *Burford* Abstention**

In **Alabama Public Service Commission v. Southern Railway**, 341 U.S. 341 (1951), the railroad challenged an order of the Alabama Public Service Commission requiring the railroad to continue operating two intrastate passenger trains. The railroad contended that since the trains operated at a loss, the order requiring continued operation violated the Fourteenth Amendment. The Supreme Court noted that an effective appeal from the administrative order was available in the state courts and ordered the federal court to abstain.

d. **Illustration of When *Burford* Abstention Does Not Apply**

Where a state utility rate-setting proceeding was challenged in federal court as preempted by federal law, ***Burford*** abstention was not appropriate. The state law aspects of the rate-setting process were potentially complex, but the federal preemption question could be decided without getting "entangled in a skein of state law." [**New Orleans Public Service, Inc. v. Council of City of New Orleans**, 491 U.S. 350 (1989)]

e. **Dismissal of Federal Suit**

When a federal court abstains under *Burford*, it ***dismisses*** the suit.

(1) **Distinguish—*Pullman* Abstention**

By contrast, a federal court abstaining under ***Pullman*** retains jurisdiction pending decision by the state court of the unsettled state law issue.

4. *Thibodaux* Abstention

Thibodaux abstention takes its name from **Louisiana Power & Light Co. v. City of Thibodaux**, 360 U.S. 25 (1959). But the case name is not so firmly affixed to this type of abstention as the case names in ***Pullman*** and ***Burford*** abstentions. ***Thibodaux*** abstention permits a federal court to abstain when there is an unsettled question of state law in an area of particular local concern.

a. **The *Thibodaux* Case**

In ***Thibodaux***, the city of Thibodaux sued to condemn private property belonging to the Louisiana Power and Light Company. The federal district court, to which the condemnation suit had been removed, abstained pending resolution of state law questions concerning the city's authority to condemn. The Supreme Court sustained the district court's abstention, pointing to the involvement of the state's "sovereign prerogative" in eminent domain proceedings, as well as to the fact that state law was unsettled and subject to many local variations.

(1) **But Note—Uncertain Reach of *Thibodaux***

The reach of ***Thibodaux*** is uncertain, particularly in light of a similar case decided on the same day, in which the Supreme Court did ***not*** require abstention. In **County of Allegheny v. Frank Mashuda Co.**, *supra,* p. 229, private property owners challenged in federal district court a condemnation undertaken by the county. The district court abstained. The Supreme Court ordered the district court to hear the case, saying that "a state's power of eminent domain no more justifies abstention than the fact that it involves any other issue related to sovereignty." The Court did not find that state law was unsettled.

(2) Reconciling the Two Cases

The decision was 5-to-4 in *Thibodaux*, and 6-to-3 in *Allegheny County*, suggesting that the Court itself had difficulty distinguishing the two cases. Although there is room for disagreement, the best way to reconcile the results is probably to conclude that eminent domain is not enough by itself to require abstention; but when eminent domain is involved **and** state law is unclear, then abstention is appropriate.

b. Unsettled State Law Ordinarily Not Enough by Itself

Standing alone, the fact that state law is unclear does not justify abstention under the *Thibodaux* rationale. [**Meredith v. City of Winter Haven**, 320 U.S. 228 (1943)] Eminent domain (or perhaps some other intensely local matter) must also be involved.

c. Availability of Certification

In a number of states, a federal court may certify a question of unsettled state law to a state court for decision. Such a procedure is much less cumbersome than staying federal court proceedings while plaintiff files a separate suit in state court. The Supreme Court has indicated that when a certification procedure is available, abstention may not be required. [**Lehman Brothers v. Schein**, *supra,* p. 200] (While awaiting a resolution of the certified question, federal courts will often stay the case. Stays contemplate the eventual revival of federal proceedings in a way that some abstention doctrines do not.) In many cases, the federal court may either abstain or certify the question to state court in the exercise of discretion. (An exception may be *Pullman* abstention, where the Court has suggested that the district court should ordinarily invoke an available certification procedure, rather than ordering abstention. *See infra*, p. 232.)

5. Abstention to Avoid Duplicative Litigation

In rare cases, a federal court will stay or dismiss a suit to avoid duplicative litigation already going forward on the same subject in state court. [**Colorado River Water Conservation District v. United States**, *supra*, p. 229] The Court in *Colorado River* declined to attach the label "abstention" to its decision to dismiss the federal court suit, but academic commentators have commonly referred to it as a form of abstention.

a. Special Facts Necessary to Support Abstention

The reluctance of the Supreme Court to abstain solely to avoid duplicative proceedings may be illustrated by the following cases.

(1) Abstention Proper

In *Colorado River*, the United States sued in federal district court for a declaration of its rights to water in certain Colorado rivers. Shortly after the federal suit was filed, the United States was joined as a defendant in an ongoing state proceeding in which all the government's claims, both state and federal, could be decided. Joinder of the United States in the state proceedings was specifically authorized by the federal McCarran Act. The Supreme Court sustained the federal district court's dismissal because of the **adequacy of the state proceeding to resolve the federal claims**; the **lack of sustained proceedings in federal court** at the time of dismissal; and, particularly, the **McCarran Act's policy** of "avoidance of piecemeal adjudication of water rights in a river system." [**Colorado River Water Conservation District v. United States**, *supra*]

(2) Abstention Improper

In **Moses H. Cone Hospital v. Mercury Construction Corp.**, 460 U.S. 1 (1983), Mercury Construction sued a hospital in federal district court to compel arbitration on a contract under the Federal Arbitration Act. Nineteen days earlier, the hospital had sued Mercury in state court for a declaratory judgment that it owed nothing under the contract and that Mercury had waived its right to arbitration. The Supreme Court ordered the district court to go forward because the basic issue was governed by the Federal Arbitration Act, and because of the "probable inadequacy of the state-court proceeding to protect Mercury's rights."

b. Strong Presumption Against Abstention

A federal court will stay or dismiss an order to avoid duplicative proceedings only in exceptional circumstances. The Supreme Court has emphasized the federal courts' "heavy obligation to exercise jurisdiction." [**Colorado River Water Conservation District v. United States**, *supra,* p. 231]

6. Certification

As noted above, federal courts may certify a question of state law to the state supreme court when state statutes permit such a result. Certification of state law questions often fit into one or more of the abstention categories above, but they need not do so.

a. Certification More Easily Available than Abstention

Certification has advantages over abstention: "reducing the delay, cutting the cost, and increasing the assurance of gaining an authoritative response." Certification is therefore available in circumstances where abstention might not be warranted. Certification requires only that there be "novel, unsettled questions of state law." [**Arizonans for Official English v. Arizona**, *supra,* p. 21]

b. Application—Certification in a Diversity Case

The Supreme Court was confronted with an uncertain issue of state securities law in a diversity case, and remanded to the court of appeals to allow it to consider whether it should certify the question to the Florida Supreme Court. The case did not fit any of the four conventional categories of abstention cases. [**Lehman Brothers v. Schein**, *supra,* p. 231]

c. Application—Certification by Supreme Court

The United States Supreme Court can certify questions directly to state supreme courts provided that state statutes permit the procedure. The Court need not first remand to a district court or court of appeals. [**Virginia v. American Booksellers Association**, 484 U.S. 383 (1988)—certifying two questions of Virginia law to the Virginia Supreme Court in an obscenity case]

7. Postponement vs. Dismissal—Suit for Damages

In a suit seeking damages, a federal court may abstain only *by postponing its decision.* It may not abstain by *dismissing the suit.* By contrast, a federal court may abstain by dismissing a suit seeking injunctive or declaratory relief. [**Quackenbush v. Allstate Insurance Co.**, 517 U.S. 706 (1996)]

C. Federal Injunctions Against State Court Proceedings— Statutory Prohibitions and "Equitable Restraint"

1. Introduction

Federal courts are sometimes asked to enjoin state court proceedings in order to protect federal rights. Generally speaking, federal courts are reluctant to grant such injunctions. Before a federal court may enjoin a state court proceeding, it must engage in a three-part analysis:

a. No Statutory Prohibitions

There are important statutory prohibitions against federal injunctions of state court proceedings. The court must determine that no statutory prohibition applies.

b. Injunction Permitted Under "Equitable Restraint"

If there is no statutory prohibition, the court must decide whether injunctive relief is proper under the doctrine of "equitable restraint." The doctrine is concerned with the conditions under which a court of *equity* should *abstain* from granting injunctive relief.

c. Apply Test for Injunctive Relief

Assuming no barrier to injunctive relief, the court must evaluate such factors as likely success on the merits and the prospect of irreparable harm in determining whether to issue injunctive relief.

2. Statutory Prohibitions

There are several statutes limiting the power of federal courts to enjoin state court proceedings:

a. Anti-Injunction Act

The most important statutory prohibition is the Anti-Injunction Act.

(1) Background

The Anti-Injunction Act was first passed in 1793, providing that a writ of injunction shall not be "granted to stay proceedings in any court of a state." In 1874, the Act was modified to *permit* injunctions to prevent state court proceedings from interfering with federal bankruptcy proceedings. Other exceptions to the prohibition also grew up, such as decrees to protect federal interpleader or federal in rem suits against state court interference. However, in 1941, the Supreme Court refused to find an additional exception to prevent relitigation in a state court of a suit already decided in federal court. [**Toucey v. New York Life Insurance Co.**, 314 U.S. 118 (1941)]

(2) Present Act

The Act was passed in its present form-in 1948. The revision was designed to overrule the Court's decision in **Toucey v. New York Life Insurance Co.**, *supra,* and to incorporate the other exceptions that had grown up. The Act provides: "A court of the United States may not grant an injunction to stay proceedings in a State court except as expressly authorized by Act of Congress, or where necessary in aid of its jurisdiction, or to protect or effectuate its judgments." [28 U.S.C. § 2283]

(3) Purpose of Act

The purpose of the Anti-Injunction Act is to protect the functioning of state courts and to avoid needless friction between the federal and state court systems. An underlying premise of the Act is that in the majority of cases, state courts can be trusted to protect federal rights. Stated in a more cautious way, the premise is that state courts can be sufficiently trusted that the radical remedy of an injunction against their proceedings is not necessary. In keeping with this premise, exceptions to the Act are limited to situations where the need for protection from state court process is particularly strong.

(4) Exceptions to Act

The Act has three explicit exceptions to its prohibition. The Supreme Court has indicated that they are exclusive and "should not be enlarged by loose statutory construction." [**Atlantic Coast Line Railroad v. Brotherhood of Locomotive Engineers**, 398 U.S. 281 (1970)] The exceptions are:

(a) "Expressly Authorized by Statute"

The first exception allows an injunction when it is "expressly authorized by statute." [28 U.S.C. § 2283] A significant number of federal statutes have been found to come within this exception. The language of section 2283 is poorly chosen to convey the scope of the exception, for express words are not in fact necessary to a finding that a federal statute is an exception to the Anti-Injunction Act.

1) Statutory Exceptions in 1948

In 1948, when the Act was passed in its present form, the exception was understood to encompass several federal statutes. These statutes include:

a) Injunctions Authorized Under Federal Bankruptcy Laws

11 U.S.C. §§ 1(a)(15), 29(a)—bankruptcy injunctions had been the one explicit exception to the Anti-Injunction Act between 1874 and 1948.

b) Removal

28 U.S.C. § 1446(d)—a federal court may enjoin a state court from proceeding further with a suit that has been removed to federal court.

c) Admiralty Limitation of Liability

46 U.S.C. § 185—a federal admiralty court may entertain an action under which a shipowner transfers ownership in a vessel to a trustee for the benefit of claimants, thereby limiting the liability of the shipowner to the value of the vessel. The federal court may enjoin state proceedings interfering with this limitation of liability action.

d) Federal Interpleader

28 U.S.C. § 2361—a federal court in a statutory interpleader action may enjoin state court proceedings that would interfere with the interpleader action.

e) Habeas Corpus

28 U.S.C. § 2251—a federal court entertaining a habeas corpus petition from someone detained by state process may enjoin state court proceedings.

2) Later Statutory Exceptions

a) Civil Rights

42 U.S.C. § 1983—after a long period of uncertainty, the Supreme Court held in 1972 that civil rights suits under section 1983 constitute a statutory exception to the Anti-Injunction Act. [**Mitchum v. Foster**, 407 U.S. 225 (1972)]

1/ Rationale

The test enunciated in **Mitchum v. Foster** was "whether an Act of Congress . . . could be given its intended scope only by the stay of a state court proceeding." Section 1983 satisfied the test because its very purpose was to "interpose the federal courts between the states and the people, as guardians of the people's federal rights—to protect the people from unconstitutional action under color of state law, 'whether that action be executive, legislative, or judicial.' "

2/ Importance

Mitchum v. Foster is an important case because federal injunctions to protect federal civil rights jeopardized by pending state court proceedings are possible only because the Court found that section 1983 was an exception to the Anti-Injunction Act. But note that injunctions against state court proceedings are still not readily available in section 1983 suits. Before an injunction will issue, a litigant must also satisfy the requirements of equity and comity inherent in the doctrines of equitable restraint. (*See infra*, p. 240.)

3/ But Note

Unlike the Anti-Injunction Act, the Tax Injunction Act applies to civil rights suits. (*See infra*, p. 239.)

b) Antitrust

15 U.S.C. § 26, "Clayton Act"—section 16 of the Clayton Act authorizes injunctive relief against threatened conduct that would violate the federal antitrust laws. A five-person majority of the Supreme Court held that section 16 is ***not always*** an exception to the Anti-Injunction Act. A different majority of the Court in the same case said, however, that where the ***state suit was itself part of an***

anticompetitive scheme, section 16 would permit an injunction against the state proceeding. Four dissenting justices would have held that section 16 was, in all circumstances, an exception to the Anti-Injunction Act. [**Vendo Co. v. Lektro-Vend Corp.,** 433 U.S. 623 (1977)]

(b) "Necessary in Aid of Its Jurisdiction"

The second exception allows an injunction when "necessary in aid of [the federal court's] jurisdiction." [28 U.S.C. § 2283] This exception has been applied in two kinds of cases.

1) In Rem Jurisdiction

When the federal court's jurisdiction is founded on its possession of a res, the court may enjoin state courts from entertaining suits involving the same res. [**Kline v. Burke Construction Co.**, 260 U.S. 226 (1922)] The in rem exception under the "necessary in aid of its jurisdiction" clause is a continuation of the exception that existed even before the adoption of the 1948 version of the Act.

2) Structural Injunctions

When a federal court has given structural injunctive relief, as in a school desegregation case or a legislative reapportionment case, it may enjoin state suits involving the same matter as long as it continues to exercise jurisdiction over the matter. [**Swann v. Charlotte-Mecklenburg Board of Education**, 501 F.2d 383 (4th Cir. 1974)—school desegregation; **Moss v. Burkhart**, 220 F. Supp. 149 (W.D. Okla. 1963), *aff'd without opinion*, 378 U.S. 558 (1964)—legislative reapportionment; § 2283 not specifically mentioned]

(c) "Protect or Effectuate Its Judgments"

The third exception allows an injunction to "protect or effectuate" a federal court's judgments. [28 U.S.C. § 2283] This exception was added to the Act in 1948 to overrule the Court's decision in **Toucey v. New York Life Insurance Co.**, *supra*, p. 233. It is commonly referred to as the "relitigation exception."

1) Scope of Exception

The relitigation exception permits a federal court to enjoin a state court suit on the ground that a federal court has *already decided* the matter. The exception applies to both *res judicata* (claim preclusion) and *collateral estoppel* (issue preclusion).

2) Limitation—Parallel Proceedings Permitted

The relitigation exception does *not* permit a federal court to enjoin parallel state court litigation *prior to* the granting of a federal court judgment.

3) Limitation—Federal Injunction Must Be Sought Before Final State Judgment

If a final federal judgment is reached and a final state court judgment is obtained later, the relitigation exception does not apply. An injunction against the state court action must be obtained before a final judgment is reached in the state court action. [**Parsons Steel, Inc. v. First Alabama Bank**, 474 U.S. 518 (1986)]

4) Injunction No Broader than the Scope of Preclusion

Assuming a prior decision of the federal court triggers the relitigation exception, the injunction can extend no more broadly than the scope of the issues actually concluded by the prior decision.

Example: Texas federal district court granted motion to dismiss for forum non conveniens, ruling that the action should proceed before a foreign tribunal. Plaintiff re-filed in state court in Texas. Federal defendant obtained injunction against state proceeding on the basis that it conflicted with federal court's forum non ruling. Supreme Court held that state of Texas was free to apply a different body of forum non conveniens law and was therefore not obliged to give effect to the district court's federal forum non decision. [**Chick Kam Choo v. Exxon Corp.**, 486 U.S. 140 (1988)]

Example: Minnesota federal district court denied class certification under Rule 23 and then enjoined the prosecution of a similar class action in West Virginia state court. Supreme Court held that the denial of class certification was not an order entitled to preclusive effect, both because West Virginia was free to follow a different set of certification standards and because the absence of certification meant the non-party class members were not precluded by the Minnesota judgment. [**Smith v. Bayer Corp.**, 564 U.S. 299 (2011)—vacating the injunction as inconsistent with the Anti-Injunction Act]

EXCEPTIONS TO ANTI-INJUNCTION ACT	GILBERT
A FEDERAL COURT MAY ENJOIN A STATE COURT ACTION WHEN	

- ☑ The issuance of an injunction is *expressly authorized by statute*;
- ☑ The issuance of an injunction is *necessary in aid of the federal court's jurisdiction*; and
- ☑ The issuance of an injunction is needed *to protect or effectuate the federal court's judgment.*

(5) Distinguish—Federal Injunctions Against Other Federal Courts

Federal courts have power in some circumstances to enjoin parallel proceedings in other federal courts. [**Kerotest Manufacturing Co. v. C-O-Two Co.**, 342 U.S. 180 (1952)—dictum] There is, however, no statute that directly addresses the question, and the Supreme Court has decided too few cases to give a clear sense of the circumstances in which an injunction against proceedings in another federal court is proper.

(6) Actions Outside the Scope of Act

Generally speaking, the Anti-Injunction Act applies to federal court injunctions against state judicial proceedings. But in certain instances, the Act does not apply and a federal injunction of the state proceeding is permitted.

(a) United States as Party

When the United States is a party to the suit in federal court, the Anti-Injunction Act does *not* apply. [**Leiter Minerals, Inc. v. United States**, 352 U.S. 220 (1957)]

1) Note

The *Leiter* principle has been extended to mean that the Act does not apply to federal injunctions sought by an administrative agency of the United States. [**NLRB v. Nash-Finch Co.**, 404 U.S. 138 (1971)]

(b) Prior to Beginning Proceedings

The Act does *not* apply to injunctions forbidding persons from instituting state court proceedings. It applies only to proceedings already begun. [*Ex parte* **Young**, 209 U.S. 123 (1908)]

(c) Nonjudicial Proceedings

The Act does *not* apply to injunctions against nonjudicial proceedings in state courts. For example, if a state court affirming an order of a state railroad rate-setting commission is engaging in legislative rather than judicial proceedings, it may be enjoined. [**Prentis v. Atlantic Coast Line Co.**, 211 U.S. 210 (1908)]

(d) Declaratory Judgments

The Act itself says nothing about declaratory judgments. It has been construed *not* to prohibit a declaratory judgment covering a question at issue in parallel state proceedings. [**Thiokol Chemical Corp. v. Burlington Industries, Inc.**, 448 F.2d 1328 (3d Cir. 1971)] *But note:* Unlike the Anti-Injunction Act, the Tax Injunction Act does apply to declaratory judgments. [*See infra*, p. 238.)

Comment: The exception allowing injunctions in section 1983 actions makes the Act's application to declaratory judgment proceedings less pressing.

b. Tax Injunction Act of 1937

The Tax Injunction Act of 1937 provides: "The district courts shall not enjoin, suspend or restrain the assessment, levy or collection of any tax under State law where a plain, speedy, and efficient remedy may be had in the courts of such State." [28 U.S.C. § 1341]

(1) Purpose of Act

The purpose of the Act is to protect state taxing authorities from federal court interference. Only when there is no "plain, speedy, and efficient remedy" in state court for allegedly unlawful collection of state taxes may a federal court interfere.

(2) Scope of Act

The Act is more complete in its prohibition than the Anti-Injunction Act. The three exceptions to the Anti-Injunction Act have been neither written nor read into the Tax Injunction Act.

(a) Declaratory Judgments

The Act *prohibits* declaratory judgments just as it prohibits injunctions. [**California v. Grace Brethren Church**, 457 U.S. 393 (1982)] But recall that declaratory judgments are **not** prohibited by the Anti-Injunction Act. (*See supra*, p. 238.)

(b) Damages

The Court has refused, on grounds of comity, to entertain suits for damages against state and local tax officials. It has refused to "decide whether the [Tax Injunction] Act, standing alone, would require such a result." [**Fair Assessment in Real Estate Association Inc. v. McNary**, 454 U.S. 100 (1981)]

(c) Civil Rights

The Tax Injunction Act *appears to apply* to civil rights suits brought under 42 U.S.C. section 1983. In **Rosewell v. LaSalle National Bank**, 450 U.S. 503 (1981), the Court refused to allow an injunction in a section 1983 suit, on the ground that the state court remedy was "plain, speedy, and efficient." The Court did not discuss the issue, but its implicit holding was necessarily that section 1983 suits were covered by the Act. Again, recall that suits for injunctive relief under section 1983 are not prohibited by the Anti-Injunction Art. [**Mitchum v. Foster**, *supra*, p. 235]

(d) Distinguish—United States as Party

The Act does **not** apply to actions brought by the United States to restrain state tax collection against itself or its instrumentalities. [**Department of Employment v. United States**, 385 U.S. 355 (1966)]

1) Indian Tribes

Where the United States could have sued on their behalf, Indian tribes may also sue in federal court to restrain state tax collection. [**Moe v. Confederated Salish and Kootenai Tribes**, 425 U.S. 463 (1976)]

(e) Distinguish—Suits to Enjoin Tax Credits

The Act does **not** bar suits to enjoin the state's provision of a tax credit to religious groups as a claimed violation of the Establishment Clause. The Act was adopted to prevent taxpayers from mounting pre-enforcement challenges to the assessment or collection of their own tax liability; it requires taxpayers to pay their taxes first and litigate later, so long as state court remedies are adequate. A suit to enjoin state tax credits was different because the injunction would not prevent the state from assessing or collecting any taxes. [**Hibbs v. Winn**, 542 U.S. 88 (2004)]

(3) Meaning of "Plain, Speedy, and Efficient"

The requirement of the Act is only that a state-court remedy meet "certain minimal *procedural* criteria." [**Rosewell v. LaSalle National Bank**, *supra*, p. 239 (emphasis in original)]

(a) Refund Enough

A state need not provide prior injunctive relief against the collection of taxes. A state procedure permitting *post hoc suits* for refunds meets the statutory criteria. [**California v. Grace Brethren Church**, *supra*, p. 238]

(b) Two-Year Delay and No Payment of Interest

A state procedure that results in refunds after two years, and under which the state pays no interest on funds wrongfully withheld, meets the statutory criteria. [**Rosewell v. LaSalle National Bank**, *supra*]

c. Johnson Act of 1934 (State Utility Rate-Setting)

The Johnson Act of 1934 provides that a federal district court shall not enjoin orders of state utility rate-setting bodies where a "plain, speedy, and efficient" remedy may be had in state courts. [28 U.S.C. § 1342] The statute contains other requirements, but they usually have little practical importance and will not be described here.

(1) Purpose of Act

The Johnson Act was designed to protect state utility rate-setting from federal court interference. In a sense, the statute was at least a quarter of a century late, for federal courts had interfered most substantially with state rate-setting bodies shortly before and after the turn of the century. [*See, e.g.,* ***Ex parte* Young**, *supra*, p. 238—injunction preventing Minnesota attorney general from enforcing railroad rates set by state]

(2) Scope of Act

Like the Tax Injunction Act, the Johnson Act applies to declaratory judgments and to civil rights suits under section 1983.

(3) Construction of Act

The language of the Johnson Act is construed similarly to that of the Tax Injunction Act.

3. Equitable Abstention or Restraint

Even if no statute prohibits a federal injunction against state judicial proceedings, *requirements of equity and comity* must still be satisfied before an injunction may issue.

a. In General

(1) "Our Federalism"

The doctrine of equitable abstention or restraint is often referred to as "Our Federalism." The phrase comes from Justice Black's opinion for the Court in **Younger v. Harris**, 401 U.S. 37 (1971): "Our Federalism" "is a system in which there is sensitivity to the legitimate interests of both state and National Governments, and in which the National Government, anxious though it may be to vindicate and protect federal rights and federal interest, always endeavors to do so in ways that will not unduly interfere with the legitimate activities of the States."

(2) Two Underlying Policies

Justice Black's opinion in **Younger v. Harris**, *supra*, relied on three grounds supporting the doctrine of equitable abstention. They are:

(a) Traditional Equitable Principles

The party seeking an injunction must show, under traditional equitable principles, that she has *no adequate remedy at law*, and that she will suffer *irreparable injury.*

(b) Comity

A federal court should not enjoin the functioning of a state court if the injunction would violate the principle of "comity"—a doctrine that requires "a proper respect for state functions" and that rests on the "belief" that the federal system will "fare best if the States and their institutions are left free to perform their separate functions in their separate ways."

(c) The Anti-Injunction Act

Although the Court did not view the Anti-Injunction Act as controlling, preferring to base its decision on judge-made law, it did rely on the Act as support for the traditional reluctance of the federal courts to intervene in pending state proceedings. An enduring puzzle for students of the decision is why the Court chose to fashion a federal common law doctrine of equitable restraint, rather than relying upon an existing statutory restriction on federal judicial power.

(3) Application of Doctrine

(a) Criminal Proceedings

The heart of equitable abstention deals with injunctions against state criminal proceedings. The general rule is that a federal court may not enjoin a pending state criminal prosecution except in narrowly defined and unusual circumstances.

(b) Civil Proceedings

Equitable abstention has been extended to certain state civil proceedings. (*See infra*, pp. 246–247.)

(c) Civil Rights Cases

Equitable abstention issues arise most frequently in federal civil rights cases brought under 42 U.S.C. section 1983. (This is true for suits to enjoin both state criminal and civil proceedings.) Injunctions in section 1983 suits are an exception to the prohibition of the Anti-Injunction Act [28 U.S.C. § 2283]. [**Mitchum v. Foster**, *supra*, p. 239] But a person seeking a federal injunction against a state judicial proceeding that allegedly violates her civil rights must still satisfy the requirements of the equitable restraint doctrine. (*See infra*, pp. 242 *et seq.*)

b. Historical Background

Federal court injunctions have traditionally been issued against state criminal proceedings only in exceptional circumstances. [*See, e.g.*, **Douglas v. City of Jeanette**, 319 U.S. 157 (1943)—"It is a familiar rule that courts of equity do not ordinarily restrain criminal prosecutions"]

(1) *Dombrowski v. Pfister* and "Chilling Effect"

In **Dombrowski v. Pfister**, 380 U.S. 479 (1965), the Court appeared to permit injunctions more readily than under the old **Douglas v. City of Jeanette** standard. Civil rights activists in Louisiana sought an injunction against threatened state court prosecutions, contending that the prosecutions were not in good faith and that their First Amendment rights were being infringed. The Court permitted the injunction, pointing both to bad faith harassment and to the "chilling effect" upon the exercise of First Amendment rights deriving from "the fact of the prosecution." *Dombrowski* and its "chilling effect" language were seen by many as an endorsement of injunctive relief whenever state proceedings were alleged to have a "chilling effect" on First Amendment rights.

(2) But Note—*Younger v. Harris* Cuts Back *Dombrowski*

In **Younger v. Harris**, *supra*, p. 240, decided six years after *Dombrowski*, the Court made it clear that allegations of "chilling effect" standing alone were not sufficient to obtain an injunction against state court proceedings.

c. Current Equitable Restraint Doctrine Under *Younger v. Harris*

The Court in **Younger v. Harris** held that federal equitable relief was *generally unavailable* against *pending* state criminal prosecutions.

(1) Rationale

The primary justification of the equitable abstention rule is that the federal right asserted in the federal injunctive suit can be used as a defense in the state criminal proceeding. State courts are presumed under *Younger* to be as competent as federal courts in deciding federal claims or defenses, and there is little reason to grant the federal injunction if the state proceeding is actually pending, since the federal defense can be presented to the state court with reasonable promptness. Thus, the litigant will be assured of having his federal defense decided in a timely fashion by some competent forum.

(2) Exceptions to *Younger*

There are three exceptions to *Younger:*

(a) Bad Faith Harassment

If the state prosecution is brought in bad faith or for purposes of harassment, *Younger* does not forbid a federal injunction. The *Younger* Court suggested that a "series of repeated prosecutions" might, in some circumstances, constitute harassment.

(b) Flagrant and Patent Unconstitutionality of State Statute

The *Younger* Court indicated that state prosecution under a *patently* unconstitutional statute might be enjoinable. It alluded to a statute that "might be flagrantly and patently violative of express unconstitutional prohibitions in every clause, sentence, and paragraph, and in whatever manner and against whomever an effort might be made to apply it." [**Younger v. Harris**, *supra— quoting from* **Watson v. Buck**, 313 U.S. 387 (1941)]

1) Note

The language of the test suggests that a state statute will rarely, if ever, be so patently unconstitutional as to qualify as an exception to *Younger*. The Court has treated the exception as exceedingly narrow. [*See* **Trainor v. Hernandez**, 431 U.S. 434 (1977)—(Brennan, J., dissenting) *Younger* held to apply even though Illinois attachment statute clearly unconstitutional]

2) Comment

One may argue that an exception for a patently unconstitutional state statute is unnecessary. In a case where the state statute is obviously unconstitutional, the state court can probably be trusted to see its unconstitutionality and to protect the defendant against its application. If this is true, federal court intervention may be **least,** rather than most, justified where the state statute is patently unconstitutional. On the other hand, injunctive relief has more commonly issued to protect parties from an obvious or patent violation of their rights.

(c) "Other Unusual Circumstances"

Without specifying what they might be, the *Younger* Court indicated that in "other unusual circumstances" federal injunctions might be proper. Such circumstances have been found where:

1) Federal Claim or Defense Cannot Be Raised in State Prosecution

In **Gerstein v. Pugh**, 420 U.S. 103 (1975), plaintiffs were held in Florida state prison on state criminal charges. They sought a federal injunction requiring Florida to hold pretrial hearings on whether there was probable cause for their detention. The Court held that **Younger** did not prohibit the injunction because the legality of pretrial detention "could not be raised in defense of the criminal prosecution."

2) Bias of State Tribunal

Where the state tribunal before which the federal claim or defense would be asserted is biased, **Younger** does not apply. [**Gibson v. Berryhill**, 411 U.S. 564 (1973)—state administrative tribunal]

(3) Pending State Proceedings

The general prohibition against injunctive relief applies to **pending,** not threatened, state criminal proceedings. The obvious meaning of "pending" includes state proceedings that are **actually in progress** at the time the federal injunction suit is filed. But the definition also includes:

(a) Later-Filed State Proceedings

A federal injunction is also barred, under the "pending" state proceedings rationale, if a state court prosecution is filed "after the federal complaint is filed but **before any proceedings of substance on the merits** have taken place in federal court." [**Hicks v. Miranda**, *supra*, p. 102 (emphasis added)]

1) Criticism

Four justices dissented in **Hicks v. Miranda.** Justice Stewart, writing for the four, pointed out that if a federal injunctive suit is filed, the state can avoid defending on the merits in federal court simply by filing a prosecution promptly in state court. The *Hicks* rule does not eliminate the "race to the courthouse"; "it merely permits the State to leave the mark later, run a shorter course, and arrive first at the finish line."

2) But Note—Justification for Rule

The rule in *Hicks* can be justified, however, on the same ground as the rule in *Younger* itself. (*See supra*, p. 242.) The aim is to get the federal issue adjudicated in a timely fashion, and the state forum is presumed to be as competent as the federal forum to decide the issue fairly. A filing in state court insures that the federal defense can be presented in a reasonably prompt fashion in the state proceeding. If the state prosecution is not filed, the federal injunction suit may go forward, because in that event, the federal court is the only forum where the federal claim can be decided with reasonable promptness.

a) Ability to Force Decision on Federal Issue

The *Hicks* rule gives to the federal plaintiff the practical ability to force a decision on his federal claim. If he files a federal injunctive suit, he will get a decision on the merits in federal court if he can demonstrate irreparable injury; or he will get a decision in state court if the state invokes the *Hicks* rule by timely filing a state court prosecution.

b) Practical Limitation on *Hicks v. Miranda*

An astute counsel can usually avoid the consequence of **Hicks v. Miranda** by seeking a *preliminary injunction* against the prosecutor's filing a state court prosecution. [**Doran v. Salem Inn, Inc.**, 422 U.S. 922 (1975)] This is an effective tactic because a preliminary injunction can be obtained quickly, leaving little time for a state proceeding to be filed. A preliminary injunction is a "proceeding of substance on the merits." [**Hawaii Housing Authority v. Midkiff**, 467 U.S. 229 (1984)] Thus, as soon as a federal court issues a preliminary injunction, a state court proceeding filed thereafter cannot be a "pending" state proceeding under **Hicks v. Miranda.** It seems unlikely that a temporary restraining order is similarly a "proceeding of substance on the merits" under the *Hicks* principle. However, if the federal court grants the temporary restraining order, it will prevent the state prosecutor from initiating a prosecution so long as the order remains in effect.

(b) Pending Appeals in State Proceedings

"Pending" state proceedings include appeals pending in state proceedings. "Virtually all of the evils at which *Younger* is directed would inhere in federal intervention prior to completion of state appellate proceedings, just as surely as they would if such intervention occurred at or before trial." [**Huffman v. Pursue, Ltd.**, 420 U.S. 592 (1975) (dictum)]

1) Distinguish—No Appeal Taken

The Court in *Huffman, supra*, held that where an appeal is not pending because it was never taken, a federal injunction may not be granted against the operation of the state court judgment. The practical effect of the Court's holding was that a litigant in state court must have exhausted his state appellate remedies before seeking a federal injunction.

a) Res Judicata

Note that res judicata may also be a valid defense to a federal injunction suit when a state judgment has become final by a litigant's failure to appeal. (The res judicata issue was not present in *Huffman* because the state had not asserted it as a defense in the federal court suit.)

(4) Distinguish—Threatened Rather than Pending State Proceedings

Younger does *not* apply to state proceedings that are merely threatened. In such a case, a federal injunction against a state prosecutor's bringing suit *may be proper.*

(a) Rationale

Since no state prosecution is actually pending, a federal injunction does not interfere with or show undue disrespect for a state court. Furthermore, since the person seeking to raise the federal issue has not been brought before a state forum, the federal court is the only forum currently able to address the issue. Federal courts have been permitted to decide federal claims in the following cases:

1) Declaratory Judgment

Plaintiff sought a declaratory judgment that his leafletting was protected by the First Amendment. No state prosecution was pending. [**Steffel v. Thompson**, *supra*, p. 69]

2) Preliminary Injunction

Plaintiffs sought both a declaratory judgment that an ordinance was unconstitutional and a preliminary injunction against its enforcement in state court while the federal court decided the case. No state prosecution was pending when the federal suit was filed. [**Doran v. Salem Inn, Inc.**, *supra*, p. 244]

3) Permanent Injunction

Plaintiff sought a permanent injunction against future state court prosecutions for covering the motto "Live Free or Die" on his license plate. He had previously been convicted three times for covering the motto. No state prosecution was pending when the federal suit was filed. [**Wooley v. Maynard**, 430 U.S. 705 (1977)]

(b) Ripeness Problem

Note that litigants seeking declaratory or injunctive relief against threatened state court prosecutions must show that their dispute is "ripe" for adjudication. Such a showing is not always easy to make. [*See* **United Public Workers v.**

Mitchell, *supra*, p. 48—federal employees not permitted to seek a declaratory judgment that the federal Hatch Act was unconstitutional when they merely alleged that they wished to engage in conduct prohibited by the Act; *and see* discussion of ripeness, *supra*, pp. 22–24]

(5) Declaratory Judgments

As a general rule, equitable restraint forbids both federal injunctive and declaratory relief against pending state prosecutions. [**Samuels v. Mackell**, 401 U.S. 66 (1971)]

(a) But Note—Declaratory Judgment Sometimes More Readily Available

In **Steffel v. Thompson**, *supra*, p. 245, the Court permitted a declaratory judgment that a threatened state prosecution would be unconstitutional. Justice Brennan's opinion for the Court stated that declaratory judgments should be more readily available than injunctions. The opinion justifies the distinction between declaratory and injunctive relief on two grounds:

1) A declaratory judgment is *less intrusive* than an injunction.

2) The *equitable requirements are less strict.* Traditionally, declaratory judgments have required a lesser showing of immediacy and irreparability of harm than injunctions.

(6) Possible Application of *Younger v. Harris* to Damage Actions

If damages are sought under 42 U.S.C. section 1983 for violation of civil rights in connection with a state criminal prosecution, *Younger* **may** require abstention. The Court has refused to reach the question of whether *Younger* requires federal court abstention in a damage action. It has held that under principles of comity, a district court should stay proceedings in the damage case until the state criminal proceeding is completed. [**Deakins v. Monaghan**, 484 U.S. 193 (1988)] More recently, it has held that in a suit seeking damages a federal court may abstain by *postponing its decision,* but *not* by *dismissing the suit.* [**Quackenbush v. Allstate Insurance Co.**, *supra*, p. 232]

(7) *Younger* Applied to State Civil Proceedings

Beginning in 1975, the Court applied the principles of *Younger* to prohibit federal injunctions against certain state *civil* proceedings. [**Huffman v. Pursue, Ltd.**, *supra*, p. 244] This extended *Younger* beyond the original context of unwillingness to interfere with criminal prosecutions. This extension is sometimes referred to as "civil *Younger.*"

(a) In General

The general principle of "civil *Younger*" is that federal courts may not enjoin pending state civil proceedings that are alleged to violate civil rights. The rationale of "civil *Younger*" is the same as of *Younger* itself: State courts should decide claims of federal rights in cases pending before them.

(b) Illustrations

1) Quasi-Criminal Proceeding

The state brought a nuisance suit against an adult movie theater in state court. A final judgment was obtained, ordering the theater closed for a year. The operator-owner of the theater sought a federal court injunction that would permit the showing of films during that year if the films had not already been adjudged obscene. The principle of *Younger* prohibits a federal injunction here, where the state "proceeding is both in aid of and closely related to criminal statutes." [**Huffman v. Pursue, Ltd.**, *supra*]

2) Enforcing Orders and Judgments of State Courts

A federal court may not issue an injunction that will interfere with the ability of state courts to enforce their orders and judgments.

Example: A federal court was not permitted to enjoin a state court from holding litigants in contempt in state civil cases. [**Juidice v. Vail**, 430 U.S. 327 (1977)]

Example: A federal court was not permitted to enjoin a litigant from enforcing a state court judgment exceeding $10 billion. Plaintiff's primary federal contention was that the requirement under state law that posting a bond of over $13 billion was necessary to avoid attachment of its property pending appeal violated federal due process guarantees. Citing the "importance to the states of enforcing the orders and judgments of their courts," the Supreme Court held that the federal constitutional arguments should be addressed to the state court and that equitable abstention was required. [**Pennzoil Co. v. Texaco, Inc.**, 481 U.S. 1 (1987)]

3) State Recovery of Welfare Payments

The state sought, in a civil proceeding, to recover welfare payments from defendants who had allegedly fraudulently concealed assets to qualify for benefits. The Court refused to permit an injunction against such an "ongoing civil enforcement action . . . brought by the State in its sovereign capacity." [**Trainor v. Hernandez**, *supra*, p. 243]

4) State Protection of Children

State officials brought a civil suit in state court to take custody of children to protect them from physical abuse by their father. The Court refused to permit a federal injunction against the proceedings. [**Moore v. Sims**, 442 U.S. 415 (1979)]

(8) *Younger* Invoked in Nonjudicial Settings

The Court has invoked the underlying principles of "Our Federalism" in nonjudicial settings. In such cases, the invocation has helped justify federal court refusals to interfere in state affairs.

(a) State Administrative Proceedings

The state brought civil administrative proceedings of a judicial nature under state civil rights law against an employer who had discharged a pregnant employee. The Court refused to permit a federal court to interfere with the administrative proceedings, noting that they vindicated an "important state interest." [**Ohio Civil Rights Commission v. Dayton Christian Schools**, 477 U.S. 619 (1986)]

(b) State Bar Disciplinary Proceedings

An attorney was charged by a local ethics committee appointed by the state supreme court with violating disciplinary rules after he criticized a state trial judge at a press conference. Rather than respond to the charges, the attorney sought a federal injunction against the disciplinary proceedings. Relying on *Younger*, the Court refused to enjoin the disciplinary proceedings which it characterized as "judicial in nature." [**Middlesex County Ethics Committee v. Garden State Bar Association**, 457 U.S. 423(1982)]

(c) Municipal Police Department

In a federal civil rights suit, plaintiffs sought an injunction that would have substantially reorganized the Philadelphia police department. The Court refused the injunction on other grounds, but invoked *Younger* as additional support for its result: "We think [*Younger*] principles likewise have applicability where injunctive relief is sought, not against the judicial branch of the state government, but against those in charge of an executive branch of state or local government." [**Rizzo v. Goode**, 423 U.S. 362 (1976)] This statement is usually interpreted only as a general indication that federal courts should be reluctant to interfere with ongoing operations of state governments.

(9) *Younger* Inappropriate for State or Local Legislative Action

Younger abstention was held inappropriate when a federal court was asked to enjoin a city council's final utility rate-setting order on the ground that it was preempted by federal law. The city council's rate-setting proceeding was essentially legislative in character. Moreover, the proceeding was completed, so a federal court injunction would not interfere with an ongoing legislative process. [**New Orleans Public Service, Inc. v. Council of City of New Orleans**, *supra*, p. 230]

(a) Parallel to the Anti-Injunction Act

Recall that the Anti-Injunction Act does not apply to injunctions against state legislative action. (*See supra*, p. 238.)

(10) *Younger* Confined

In **Sprint Communications v. Jacobs**, 571 U.S. 69 (2013), the Supreme Court refused to direct *Younger*-based abstention in an action seeking injunctive relief against an allegedly preempted state regulatory ruling. The federal plaintiff had also sought review of the disputed ruling in state court, raising the question whether the suit in federal court was subject to equitable restraint. Rejecting that view, the decision confines *Younger* to suits for injunctive relief against three types of state proceedings:

1) Pending criminal proceedings; [e.g., *Younger* itself]

2) Certain civil enforcement proceedings; [e.g., *Huffman v. Pursue*]

3) Civil proceedings uniquely in furtherance of the state courts' ability to perform their judicial function [e.g., *Juidice v. Vail*].

The Court explained that it had not applied *Younger* outside these three "exceptional" categories, and held "that they define *Younger*'s scope." *Sprint v. Jacobs*, 571 U.S. at 78.

4. The *Rooker-Feldman* Doctrine

The *Rooker-Feldman* doctrine takes its name from two decisions in which the Supreme Court held that the federal district courts could not exercise jurisdiction over claims attacking the validity of state court judgments. [**Rooker v. Fidelity Trust Co.**, 263 U.S. 413 (1923); **District of Columbia Court of Appeals v. Feldman**, 460 U.S. 462 (1983)] Federal law permits only the Supreme Court to review state court judgments on appeal. [28 U.S.C. § 1257] Federal district courts thus lack jurisdiction to entertain proceedings seeking the functional equivalent of appellate review of state court judgments. After a period during which the doctrine expanded in the lower federal courts—but was severely criticized in the law reviews—the Court has signaled a reluctance to tolerate such expansion. [**Exxon Mobil Corp. v. Saudi Basic Industries Corp.**, 544 U.S. 280 (2005)]

a. Origins of the Doctrine

(1) The *Rooker* Decision

In *Rooker, supra*, the plaintiff brought an action in federal court to nullify a state court judgment on the ground that it violated various provisions of the Constitution. The Supreme Court affirmed the dismissal of the action on jurisdictional grounds. It found that the state court had jurisdiction of the original cause and the parties, and that the party now seeking to attack the state court judgment could only do so through an appeal to the Supreme Court itself.

(2) The *Feldman* Decision

In *Feldman, supra*, two law school graduates sought admission to the District of Columbia bar. The local court of the District of Columbia (which operates somewhat like a state court within the District) denied the applications, refusing to exempt the applicants from the rule requiring graduation from an accredited law school. The applicants then filed suit in federal district court. On review, the Supreme Court applied *Rooker* and concluded that the applicants could not challenge the local court's adjudicative denial of their waiver application. The Court did allow the applicants to challenge the constitutionality of the bar admission rule; the local court had issued that rule in a "legislative" capacity, not a judicial capacity, and such rules were subject to suit in federal court. (For more on the distinction between "legislative" and "judicial" rulings by state courts, *see supra*, p. 248.)

b. Criticism

Scholars have criticized the *Rooker-Feldman* doctrine as a confusing addition to the doctrine of claim preclusion, which ordinarily forbids a federal court from entertaining a suit seeking to relitigate matters previously resolved in state court. Resting as it does on jurisdictional grounds, moreover, the *Rooker-Feldman* doctrine apparently permits litigants and appellate courts to raise the issue for the first time on appeal. Defenses based on claim preclusion are usually waived if not asserted in the trial court.

c. Lower Court Expansion

Despite these criticisms, lower courts have applied the *Rooker-Feldman* doctrine in new situations. For example, one court applied the doctrine to a litigant that had not been a party to the prior state court proceeding. [**Lemonds v. St. Louis County**, 531 U.S. 1183 (2001)] Another applied the doctrine to bar absent class members from challenging a state court class-wide settlement, even though the absentees argued that the state court lacked jurisdiction over them. [**Kamilewicz v. Bank of Boston Corp.**, 92 F.3d 506 (7th Cir. 1996)]

d. Restriction on *Rooker-Feldman* Doctrine

The Court appears to have signaled a desire to cut back on the reach of the doctrine. In *Exxon Mobil, supra*, the parties filed concurrent litigation in state and federal court. The state court proceeding went to judgment first, and the federal appeals court later ruled that the *Rooker-Feldman* doctrine required dismissal of the overlapping federal proceeding. The Supreme Court reversed, holding that the doctrine permitted dismissal only when a party that lost in state court later files a suit in federal court to undo that result. Here, the federal court had jurisdiction of the concurrent action at the outset, and was not ousted of jurisdiction when the state court proceeding went to judgment. The tone of this unanimous opinion, if not the holding, casts doubt on lower court expansions of the doctrine.

Chapter Ten

Collateral Relations Between Federal and State Courts— Federal Habeas Corpus for State Prisoners

Key Exam Issues

In recent years, the collateral relations between federal and state court have been the most problematic—and unstable—in cases of federal habeas corpus for state prisoners. Prior to 1996, the basic statutory structure of habeas corpus had remained largely unchanged for over a century, although the Supreme Court had substantially changed the law through judicial decisions. In the 1960s, the Warren Court made habeas corpus more available to state prisoners. Then, from the mid-1970s to the mid-1990s, the Burger and Rehnquist Courts reversed direction and made habeas less available. During both periods of change, the Court was motivated in part by considerations of federalism, but also in part by changing political attitudes toward crime and criminal procedure.

In April 1996, Congress adopted the Antiterrorism and Effective Death Penalty Act ("AEDPA"), amending the statute and substantially changing habeas for state prisoners. The amendments are themselves somewhat complex. Moreover, they must be integrated into the already complex decisional law that is only partly displaced by the amendments.

A student learning federal habeas for state prisoners must perform two tasks:

1. **Learn the Law Based on the Earlier Statute**

   The AEDPA was enacted against a background of an existing statute and case law loosely derived from that statute. Much of the earlier statute, and earlier case law, survives and must be integrated with the amended statute.

2. **Learn the Amendments**

   The amended provisions are found in:

   a. **28 U.S.C. section 2244—finality of determination**

   This section sets forth res judicata and statute of limitation provisions. The amended parts of the statute are subsections 2244(b) and (d).

   b. **28 U.S.C. section 2253—appeal**

   This section limits appeals from district court decisions. The amended part of the statute is subsection 2253(c).

   c. **28 U.S.C. section 2254—state custody; remedies in state courts**

   This section sets forth the general rules for state habeas. The amended parts of the statute are subsections 2254(b)(2)–(3), (d)–(e), and (h)–(i).

   d. **28 U.S.C. sections 2261–2266—capital cases**

   These sections provide time limits and preclusive effect for state court convictions in capital cases if a state provides competent counsel in state post-conviction proceedings. These sections are entirely new, but have had little practical significance to date.

A. Introduction

1. Sequence of Events in Habeas Cases

Federal habeas corpus permits prisoners convicted in state courts to raise federal challenges to their imprisonment. To understand federal habeas for state prisoners, keep in mind the following sequence of events:

   a. A criminal defendant is *convicted* in state court.

b.   He ***appeals his conviction*** to the highest state court to which an appeal may be brought.

c.   He may, but need not, ***seek direct review in the United States Supreme Court*** on his federal defenses to the prosecution.

d.   He ***may*** seek habeas corpus ***in the state court system***. He ***must*** do so if he wishes to ***raise new issues*** not previously presented on direct review.

e.   Finally, he ***seeks habeas corpus from a federal court*** based on his federal defenses to the state court prosecution and any new issues developed in state court collateral proceedings. The application for habeas is almost always to a ***federal district court***, although the governing statute also permits an application directly to the Supreme Court, to an individual Justice of the Court, or to a circuit judge.

2. Constitutional and Statutory Basis

a. Constitutional Basis

Article I, Section 9, of the Constitution provides: "The privilege of the writ of habeas corpus shall not be suspended, unless when in cases of rebellion or invasion the public safety may require it."

b. Statutory Basis

(1) General Power

"Writs of habeas corpus may be granted by the Supreme Court, any justice thereof, the district courts and any circuit judge within their respective jurisdictions." [28 U.S.C. § 2241(a)]

(2) Grounds

For a state prisoner, the writ may issue "only on the ground that he is in custody in violation of the Constitution or laws or treaties of the United States." [28 U.S.C. § 2254(a)]

c. Collateral Rather than Direct Review

Habeas corpus is a collateral attack on a state court conviction. It comes after, and is distinct from, direct appellate review.

d. Irritation of State Court Judges

Federal habeas corpus has sometimes been a significant irritant to state court judges. It gives to a single federal district judge (subject to appellate review) the power to order the release of a prisoner from state custody. This power is typically exercised after a number of state court judges, including the justices of the state supreme court, have concluded that the prisoner has been properly convicted.

B. "In Custody"

1. Defendant Must Be in Custody

Habeas corpus is available only if the person seeking the writ is "in custody." [28 U.S.C. § 2254(a)] Custody has been construed liberally to permit habeas as long as there is some ***actual or potential physical restraint***.

a. Parole

A person on parole is in custody. [**Jones v. Cunningham**, 371 U.S. 236 (1963)]

b. Own Recognizance

A person released on his own recognizance, but subject to court order and arrest for disobeying an order to appear, is in custody. [**Hensley v. Municipal Court**, 411 U.S. 345 (1973)]

c. Consecutive Sentences

(1) Present Sentence

A prisoner may challenge the conviction for which he is now serving time even when a consecutive sentence will keep him in custody if his petition is successful. [**Walker v. Wainwright**, 390 U.S. 335 (1968)]

(2) Subsequent Sentence

A prisoner may challenge one conviction, the sentence for which he has not yet begun to serve, while he is in custody on another conviction. [**Peyton v. Rowe**, 391 U.S. 54 (1968)]

(3) Prior Sentence

A prisoner may challenge a conviction for a sentence already served if it is one of a series of consecutive sentences and if a grant of habeas will serve to shorten the overall time served. [**Garlotte v. Fordice**, 515 U.S. 39 (1995)]

"IN CUSTODY" REQUIREMENT	GILBERT
"IN CUSTODY" FOR HABEAS CORPUS PURPOSES INCLUDES BEING	

- ☑ On *parole*;
- ☑ Released *"on recognizance"*;
- ☑ In confinement under a punishment of *consecutive sentences,* even if:
  - ○ The petitioner *would still be in confinement* because of consecutive sentencing if the habeas corpus petition is successful;
  - ○ The petitioner *has not yet begun serving the sentence* for the conviction he is challenging; and
  - ○ The petitioner *had served the sentence for the conviction,* if a successful habeas corpus petition would serve to shorten the overall time served.

d. Mootness

If a person is in custody when a habeas petition challenging his conviction is filed, the petition does not become moot when he is released from custody. [**Carafas v. LaVallee**, 391 U.S. 234 (1968)—discharge from parole does not moot habeas petition]

(1) But Note

The mootness rule of **Carafas v. LaVallee** is limited. If a person attacks only the validity of his sentence, rather than the underlying conviction on which the sentence is based, his petition is moot when he is released from custody. [**Lane v. Williams**, 455 U.S. 624 (1982)]

EXAM TIP

On your exam, be careful not to mix up mootness as it relates to civil actions and mootness as it relates to habeas corpus petitions. Although a civil action may become "moot" with the passage of time, a habeas corpus petition, filed when the person is in custody, *does not become moot because the person has been released from custody*, provided that the petition is attacking his conviction rather than his sentence.

C. Claims Cognizable on Habeas

1. Statute

A state prisoner may seek federal habeas on the ground that he is in custody in violation of "the Constitution or laws or treaties of the United States." [28 U.S.C. § 2254(a); *and see supra*, p. 253]

2. Constitutional Claims

In practice, federal habeas for state prisoners is generally used to raise constitutional due process claims under the Fourteenth Amendment. (Fourth Amendment exclusionary rule claims are excluded from habeas under **Stone v. Powell,** *see infra*, p. 255.) A nonexhaustive list of cognizable claims includes:

a. *Proof of guilt beyond a reasonable doubt.* [**Jackson v. Virginia**, *supra*, 94]

b. *Racial composition of the grand jury.* [**Rose v. Mitchell**, 443 U.S. 545 (1979)]

c. *Ineffective assistance of counsel at trial.* [**Kimmelman v. Morrison**, 477 U.S. 365 (1986)]

d. *Admissibility of a confession in violation of* **Miranda v. Arizona**, 384 U.S. 436 (1966). [**Withrow v. Williams**, 507 U.S. 680 (1993)]

D. Claims Excluded from Habeas

1. Claims Based on Fourth Amendment—*Stone v. Powell*

Fourth Amendment claims under the exclusionary rule may *not* be presented on federal habeas if there was "an opportunity for full and fair litigation" of the Fourth Amendment claim in state court. [**Stone v. Powell**, 428 U.S. 465 (1976)] State courts routinely provide such an opportunity, so as a practical matter Fourth Amendment search and seizure claims cannot be heard on federal habeas.

a. Rationale

The Court's rationale in **Stone v. Powell** is that Fourth Amendment claims are not "guilt-related." That is, a prisoner arguing that evidence was improperly admitted is not arguing that he is innocent. Rather, he is arguing only that the admission of the evidence led to a conviction that would not otherwise have been obtained. Thus, the Court in **Stone v. Powell** refused to hear the Fourth Amendment claim on habeas because the allegedly erroneous admission did not risk the conviction of an innocent person.

(1) Note

Justice Brennan, in his dissent in **Stone v. Powell,** suggested that the "guilt-relatedness" rationale might lead to denial of habeas in other cases in which constitutional rights protect values other than accurate fact-finding at trial, such as "double jeopardy, entrapment, self-incrimination, *Miranda* violations, and use of invalid identification procedures." However, **Stone v. Powell** has not been extended beyond the Fourth Amendment exclusionary rule. For example, the Court has specifically held that the racial composition of a grand jury may be raised on habeas [**Rose v. Mitchell**, *supra,* p. 255], and that a *Miranda* violation may be raised on habeas [**Withrow v. Williams**, *supra,* p. 255].

2. Claims Based on New Rule—*Teague v. Lane*

A *new rule* of criminal procedure cannot be *applied or announced* on habeas unless it falls within two very narrow exceptions (*see infra,* pp. 258 *et seq.*). [**Teague v. Lane**, 489 U.S. 288 (1989)]

a. What Is a New Rule?

The Court has characterized a "new rule" under **Teague v. Lane** in various ways. A rule is new if:

(i) It "*breaks new ground* or *imposes a new obligation* on the States or the Federal Government" [**Teague v. Lane**, *supra*];

(ii) "The result was not *dictated* by a precedent existing at the time the defendant's conviction became final" [**Teague v. Lane**, *supra* (emphasis in original)];

(iii) The "outcome" of the case announcing the rule "*was susceptible to debate among reasonable minds*" [**Butler v. McKellar**, 494 U.S. 407 (1990)]; or

(iv) The rule is the "most reasonable interpretation of prior law." The rule is old only if "*no other* interpretation was reasonable." [**Lambrix v. Singletary**, 520 U.S. 518 (1997)]

e.g. **Example: new rule: In Butler v. McKellar,** *supra,* while defendant was in custody on an assault charge and after he had retained counsel, he was questioned about an unrelated murder. He was informed that he was a suspect in the murder case and given *Miranda* warnings. He then signed "waiver of rights" forms and made incriminating statements about the murder. After his conviction and sentence of death for the murder, he argued on habeas that the police should not have questioned him about the unrelated charge. On the day his conviction became final on direct review, the Supreme Court held in **Arizona v. Roberson**, 486 U.S. 675 (1988), that police questioning in circumstances similar to those of defendant's case was not permitted. The Court held that *Roberson* had announced a "new rule" because lower courts had previously differed on the question and the "outcome" of *Roberson* "was susceptible to debate among reasonable minds."

cf. **Compare: not new rule:** A jury in a "weighing state" (*i.e.,* jury must weigh aggravating and mitigating factors before imposing death penalty) sentenced defendant to death based on three "aggravating factors," one of which was unconstitutionally vague. After the judgment in defendant's case was final, the Supreme Court held in **Clemons v. Mississippi**, 494 U.S. 738 (1990), that an appellate court could affirm a capital sentence in a weighing state only if it "reweighed" the aggravating and mitigating factors without considering the impermissible factor and found capital punishment proper after the reweighing. The Court held that *demons* did not announce a new rule, but rather applied an established principle in a "novel setting, thereby extending the precedent." The Court noted that the Court of Appeals for the Fifth Circuit prior to *Clemons* had not required reweighing by the appellate court; it found the court of appeals' contrary decisions "relevant . . . but not dispositive" on the question of whether *Clemons* announced a new rule. [**Stringer v. Black**, 503 U.S. 222 (1992)]

(1) Comment

As reflected in a comparison of **Butler v. McKellar** and **Stringer v. Black**, *supra,* the difference between an old and a new rule will not always be readily apparent.

b. Cannot Be Applied or Announced

(1) Applied

If the Supreme Court announces a new rule of criminal procedure in another case after the prisoner's conviction has become final on direct review, that rule cannot be *applied* on habeas.

(a) Rationale

The trial court cannot be expected to comply with a rule of criminal procedure that does not exist at the time of trial.

(b) Meaning of "Has Become Final on Direct Review"

To determine when a conviction becomes final on direct review, one looks to the date on which state court appellate proceedings ended, or, in the case of a timely petition for direct review in the Supreme Court, the date on which certiorari was denied.

1) Note

Rules of law that the Court announces (even in other cases) during the course of a defendant's pursuit of direct appellate review bind the state court even though they may be announced after the state trial has been completed. In effect, then, in determining whether to grant relief, the federal habeas court must apply the body of clearly established law that was in place on the date the petitioner's conviction became final on direct review.

(2) Announced

A new rule of criminal procedure cannot be *announced* on habeas.

(a) Comment

The inability to announce a new rule on habeas limits the Supreme Court's ability to formulate and announce new rules of criminal procedure. After

Teague v. Lane, the Court can announce new rules only in cases on direct review. The Court cannot announce a new rule in a habeas case unless the rule fits within one of the two exceptions to the prohibition (*see infra*).

c. Two Exceptions

There are two exceptions to **Teague v. Lane's** prohibition against the use of a new rule on habeas. A federal habeas court can apply or announce a new rule if (i) it applies to private individual conduct that cannot be criminally proscribed; or (ii) it requires procedures that are "implicit in the concept of ordered liberty." [**Teague v. Lane**, *supra*] The wording of these two exceptions is taken from Justice Harlan's separate opinion in **Mackey v. United States**, 401 U.S. 667 (1971). However, applications of the exceptions after **Teague v. Lane** have modified Justice Harlan's ideas.

(1) Private Individual Conduct That Cannot Be Criminally Proscribed

The exception for private individual conduct is broader than Justice Harlan's words suggest. A new rule can be applied under this exception in two circumstances:

(a) Private Conduct

If the new rule states that certain private individual conduct cannot be criminally proscribed by the state, it does not matter that the conduct is newly protected under the rule.

e.g. **Example:** The rule of **Roe v. Wade**, *supra*, p. 27—forbidding states from criminally punishing performance of abortions—could have been applied on habeas to earlier criminal convictions for performing abortions and could have been announced in a case coming to the Supreme Court on habeas.

(b) Certain Categories of Punishment

The Court has expanded the exception for private individual conduct to include certain categories of punishment "for a class of defendants because of their status or offense." [**Penry v. Lynaugh**, 492 U.S. 302 (1989)] Thus, in **Penry v. Lynaugh,** the Court considered whether it was permissible to execute mentally retarded people. The Court concluded on the merits that capital punishment of retarded people is not prohibited by the Eighth Amendment. However, if the Court had held such punishment impermissible, the rule would have been applied on habeas under the first exception to **Teague v. Lane**. (*Note:* The Court, in **Atkins v. Virginia**, 536 U.S. 304 (2002), reversed itself on the merits and ruled that a mentally retarded person cannot be executed.)

(2) Rule "Implicit in the Concept of Ordered Liberty"

The exception for a rule "implicit in the concept of ordered liberty" is narrower than Justice Harlan's words suggest. A new rule does not come within this second exception to **Teague v. Lane** unless it is a "watershed rule of criminal procedure implicating the fundamental fairness and accuracy of the criminal proceedings." [**Saffle v. Parks**, 494 U.S. 484 (1990)—erroneous contention of petitioner that jury can base sentence on feelings of sympathy for defendant not an exception]

e.g. **Example: new rule not within exception:** Petitioner was sentenced to death after the prosecutor argued his future dangerousness to the sentencing jury but petitioner was not permitted to inform the jury that he would be ineligible for parole if sentenced to life in prison. In a later case, **Simmons v. South Carolina**, 512 U.S. 154 (1996), the Supreme Court held that a capital defendant who would be ineligible for parole has a right to inform the jury of that fact if the prosecutor argues future dangerousness. On habeas in petitioner's case, the Supreme Court held that *Simmons* announced a new rule and, further, that the rule did not fall within the exception because it "has hardly 'alter[ed] our understanding of the **bedrock procedural elements'** essential to the fairness of a proceeding." [**O'Dell v. Netherland**, 521 U.S. 151 (1997)—emphasis added]

d. Applies to Capital and Noncapital Cases

Teague v. Lane applies to both capital and noncapital cases. [**Penry v. Lynaugh**, *supra*]

e. Effect of 28 U.S.C. Section 2254(d)(1) on *Teague v. Lane*

Section 2254(d)(1) of the Antiterrorism and Effective Death Penalty Act ("AEDPA"), enacted in 1996, provides that habeas is not available for any claim "adjudicated on the merits in State court proceedings unless the adjudication of the claim . . . resulted in a decision that was contrary to, or involved an unreasonable application of, clearly established Federal law, as determined by the Supreme Court . . . ." The AEDPA replaces the **Teague v. Lane** standard for habeas petitions filed after the effective date of the Act (April 1996), but the new standard draws its inspiration from *Teague*. In one important respect, the statute narrows *Teague* by requiring reference to the clearly established decisional rules of the Supreme Court. State courts need not necessarily comply with lower federal court decisions, except to the extent these decisions reflect the law as established by the Supreme Court. [*See* **Carey v. Musladin**, 549 U.S. 70 (2007)]

f. Applying Teague's Retroactivity Rules Under AEDPA

The interplay of **Teague** and AEDPA gave rise to questions about how a habeas petitioner might gain access to a new rule of constitutional law. As noted above, **Teague** indicates that habeas petitioners may gain such access in two instances, where the new rule amounts to a "watershed" change in criminal procedure and where the Court has interpreted the Constitution to deprive the states of the power to criminalize certain primary conduct. But AEDPA makes it awkward to secure habeas relief on behalf of habeas petitioners who have previously sought habeas review and now seek to claim the benefit of a new rule that, they contend, satisfies the **Teague** standard as one foreclosing punishment of certain primacy conduct. AEDPA permits habeas review only where the Supreme Court has *already* declared the rule retroactively applicable.

The Court attempted to resolve that tension in **Montgomery v. Lousiana**, 136 S. Ct. 718 (2016). At issue was how the petitioner, convicted and sentenced as a juvenile in the 1960s, might claim the benefit of a new rule of constitutional law that forbids the imposition of life imprisonment without the possibility of parole on defendants who were juveniles at the time they committed their offense. Montgomery could not file a second or successive habeas petition; the Supreme Court had yet to rule that its life-without-parole rule for juvenile offenders was meant to apply retroactively. So Montgomery filed a state collateral review petition instead. On review of a state court decision denying relief, the Court held that the state was obliged to apply its **Teague** formula in evaluating such petitions and then ruled that Montgomery was indeed entitled to retroactive application of the juvenile offender rule.

E. Presentation of Federal Defenses to State Court

1. Introduction

A state prisoner seeking federal habeas must have presented his federal defenses to the state court for resolution. This requirement has two aspects: (i) procedural default in state court, and (ii) exhaustion of state judicial remedies.

a. Distinguish—Equitable Restraint

Equitable restraint under **Younger v. Harris**, *supra,* shares with federal habeas the premise that state criminal defendants should present their federal defenses to the state court. Under *Younger* and related cases, once a state criminal proceeding is "pending," a defendant may not (except in very restricted circumstances) seek federal court protection through a suit for declaratory or injunctive relief. (*See supra*, pp. 242 *et seq.*)

2. Procedural Default in State Court

a. In General

Generally speaking, if a state criminal defendant *fails to present a federal defense* to the state court because of a procedural default in that court, he will be *precluded* from asserting that defense on federal habeas. Examples of procedural defaults include failure to bring a timely challenge to the racial composition of a grand jury, failure to make a contemporaneous objection to the introduction of evidence, and failure to take a timely appeal of a state court conviction.

b. Application of *Michigan v. Long* to Habeas

In **Michigan v. Long**, *supra*, p. 87, the Court held that an independent and adequate state ground barring Supreme Court direct review of a state court judgment must be clearly indicated by the state court. The same rule applies to federal habeas review of state court convictions: A state procedural bar does not prevent a federal habeas court from considering the merits of a prisoner's federal claim unless the last state court rendering judgment in the case " 'clearly and expressly' states that its judgment rests on a state procedural bar." [**Harris v. Reed**, 489 U.S. 255 (1989)]

(1) Limitation

If a state court's decision fairly appears to rest primarily on federal law, or is interwoven with federal law, the "clearly and expressly" test of **Harris v. Reed** applies. But if there is no indication that a federal ground was relevant to the state court decision, no explicit statement by the state court is required. [**Coleman v. Thompson**, 501 U.S. 722 (1991)]

c. Distinction Between Direct Appellate Review and Collateral Habeas Relief

One may argue that different standards and different sanctions should apply to state procedural default, depending on whether the prisoner is seeking direct appellate review or collateral habeas review.

(1) Strict Standard for Direct Review

The standard for relief from state procedural default is very strict on direct review. The Supreme Court will not address a federal defense when a procedural default prevented the defendant from raising the issue in state court, unless the state procedural rule is so harsh as to deprive the defendant of a "reasonable opportunity to have the issue . . . determined by the state court." [**Michel v. Louisiana**, *supra*, p. 88]

d. Different and Changing Standards on Habeas for Procedural Default

The Supreme Court has applied different standards on habeas for state procedural default than it has applied on direct review. Furthermore, the Court has changed the standards for habeas over the past several decades. In **Fay v. Noia**, 372 U.S. 391 (1963), the Court adopted a very forgiving "deliberate bypass" standard (*i.e.,* the federal habeas court could address the merits unless the defendant had "deliberately bypassed" the opportunity to raise the objection in state court) for state procedural default. In **Wainwright v. Sykes**, 433 U.S. 72 (1977), the Court overruled **Fay v. Noia** and imposed a much stricter standard. Though it is formulated differently, the **Wainwright v. Sykes** standard on habeas is, as a practical matter, virtually as strict as the standard on direct review.

e. "Cause and Prejudice" Standard—*Wainwright v. Sykes*

In **Wainwright v. Sykes**, *supra*, the Supreme Court made federal habeas relief much more difficult to obtain after a procedural default during the state proceeding. The standard under **Wainwright v. Sykes** is "cause and prejudice." If a claim is barred by a state procedural default, a federal habeas court cannot address the merits of the claim unless there is both "cause" for the default and "prejudice" resulting from the inability to address the claim.

(1) The Case

In **Wainwright v. Sykes**, Sykes was tried for murder in state court. His confession was introduced at trial. Sykes's attorney failed to object to the use of the confession at the time of its admission even though the state court had a contemporaneous objection rule. Sykes later sought federal habeas on the ground that his confession was inadmissible because of a failure to give an effective *Miranda* warning. On the facts of the case, Sykes's failure to object might have been a "deliberate bypass" under **Fay v. Noia**, but the Court declined to rely on that ground. Instead, it imposed the new, more stringent "cause and prejudice" standard.

f. Application

The "cause and prejudice" rule applies to a procedural default during trial. [**Wainwright v. Sykes**, *supra*] It also applies to a failure to appeal within the state court system. [**Coleman v. Thompson**, *supra*]

g. "Cause" Under *Wainwright v. Sykes*

(1) External Impediment

Cause exists if "some objective factor external to the defense impeded counsel's efforts to comply with the State's procedural rule." [**Murray v. Carrier**, 477 U.S. 478 (1986)—but *no* cause where counsel failed to raise error at trial when prosecution refused to allow counsel to examine witness statements prior to trial]

Example: Defendant made no attempt to challenge the racial composition of the jury venire before or during trial. While his case was on appeal, evidence was revealed in a separate civil case that the state district attorney had directed the jury commissioner to draw up jury lists that would underrepresent blacks and women. Defendant tried to raise this issue on appeal, but the state appellate court ruled the argument untimely. The Supreme Court held that the deliberate withholding of evidence of the unconstitutional discrimination constituted "cause" for failure to raise the issue earlier. [**Amadeo v. Zant**, 486 U.S. 214 (1988)]

Example: Habeas petitioner argued that the state had failed to disclose exculpatory material, after adopting an "open files" policy that led counsel to assume that all material available to the government had been disclosed. Although the Court found "cause" in the government's failure to disclose, and thereby forgave petitioner's default in failing to raise the due process claim earlier, it ruled against petitioner on the merits of the due process claim. [**Strickler v. Greene**, 527 U.S. 263 (1999)]

(2) Ineffective Assistance of Counsel

Ineffective assistance of counsel (as opposed to counsel error as in *Murray*, *supra*) constitutes "cause" for failure to raise the issue at trial. It is unrealistic to expect an ineffective counsel to raise the issue of his own ineffectiveness while he is representing the defendant. [**Murray v. Carrier**, *supra*; **Strickland v. Washington**, 466 U.S. 668 (1984)]

(a) Note

Recall that a federal claim of ineffective assistance of counsel must, like all federal claims, be presented to the state court as a prerequisite to seeking federal habeas. The first opportunity to present such a claim is frequently on state habeas, when a new lawyer represents the prisoner. In such a case, the prisoner must exhaust his state remedies by seeking state habeas relief. (*See infra*, pp. 266 *et seq.*)

(b) And Note

The Court has resisted the attempt of some courts to treat ineffective assistance of counsel as a matter to be raised on direct appellate review of the conviction. [**Massaro v. United States**, 538 U.S. 500 (2003)] The Court held that collateral review was the proper mode of presenting such claims after noting (albeit in the context of claims brought by a federal prisoner) that ineffective assistance claims depend on facts outside the record of the trial and may require more investigative time than is usually available in the briefing schedule for direct review.

(c) Ineffective Assistance in First State Habeas Proceeding as Cause

The Supreme Court has held that while the constitutional right to effective assistance of counsel applies at trial and on direct review, it does not apply during post-conviction review. [See **Coleman v. Thompson**, 501 U.S. 722 (1991)] As a consequence, petitioners cannot ordinarily challenge the effectiveness of their post-conviction attorney and cannot set up such ineffective assistance as cause to excuse a procedural default that occurred during the course of post-conviction proceedings. Thus, the attorney's failure to meet a filing deadline on appeal in a state post-conviction proceeding resulted in the default of the petitioner's challenges to his conviction. [**Coleman v. Thompson**, *supra*.]

Nonetheless, the Court has recognized a narrow exception to the rule, enabling habeas petitioners who received ineffective assistance of counsel during their first state habeas proceeding (also known as an "initial-review collateral proceeding") to cite such ineffective assistance as cause to excuse counsel's procedural defaults and open a gateway to federal habeas review. [See **Martinez v. Ryan**, 566 U.S. 1 (2012)] The decision **does not** establish a constitutional right to effective assistance of counsel in state post-conviction proceedings. Rather, the decision opens the way to habeas review in federal court (and thus disables the state from relying on procedural defaults as a bar to federal consideration.) In **Martinez**, the habeas petitioner was convicted at trial, but counsel in the post-conviction proceeding failed to raise any issues, including possible ineffective assistance at trial. The proceeding thus raised the specter of a conviction being affirmed without petitioner's having received effective assistance at any stage of the process. To address that concern, the Court agreed to treat a claim of ineffective assistance in an initial-stage collateral review proceeding as "cause," thereby opening the way to further federal habeas review.

Extension: Although the **Martinez** Court emphasized that Arizona state law required the adjudication of ineffective assistance claims in post-conviction proceedings (rather than on direct review, where the right to counsel obtains), the Court later made clear that the **Martinez** rule applied to situations in which state law as a practical matter compels such a procedure. [See **Trevino v. Thaler**, 569 U.S. 413 (2013)—extending the **Martinez** rule to proceeding in Texas where the procedural system formally allows petitioners to litigate ineffective assistance on direct review but makes it "virtually impossible" as a practical matter]

Extension: In a further erosion of the **Coleman** rule, the Court held that attorney error resulting from the abandonment of post-conviction representation in Alabama provided cause for relief from procedural default. [**Maples v. Thomas**, 565 U.S. 266 (2012)] The procedural default occurred when two young lawyers left their law firm in New York and did not withdraw or transfer representation to the firm. As a result, they did not receive notice of the denial of client's petition for state post-conviction relief and did not take appropriate steps to protect their client's right to appeal. The Court ruled that this abandonment provided cause to excuse the default.

(d) "Cause" Not Necessary—Innocence of Defendant

"[I]n an extraordinary case, where an asserted constitutional violation has resulted in the conviction of one who is actually innocent, a federal habeas court may grant the writ even in the absence of a showing of cause for the procedural default." [**Murray v. Carrier**, *supra*]

1) Actual Innocence

If a prisoner claims to be "actually innocent" in the sense that he did not do the underlying crime, habeas will be granted if he can show that, absent the constitutional violation, "it is *more likely than not* that no reasonable juror would have convicted" him. [**Schlup v. Delo**, 513 U.S. 298 (1992)—emphasis added]

a) But Note

Schlup has been partly overruled by the 1996 statute. When the evaluation of an asserted constitutional violation requires an evidentiary hearing in the federal habeas court (which it frequently does), the availability of that hearing will be governed by the standard of section 2254(e)(2). Among other things, that section incorporates the stricter standard of **Sawyer v. Whitley** (*see* below) for the required showing of innocence.

2) Innocence Standard Satisfied

Despite the demands of the actual innocence standard, at least one habeas petitioner has made the requisite showing. The petitioner was convicted of murder, based largely on circumstantial evidence. On habeas, the petitioner sought to litigate defaulted claims of ineffective assistance of counsel and due process violations arising from the prosecution's failure to disclose exculpatory evidence. The Court agreed that petitioner had made a showing of actual innocence under **Schlup v. Delo**, *supra.* The physical evidence did not match the petitioner's DNA and another possible perpetrator had confessed to the crime on two separate occasions. [**House v. Bell**, 547 U.S. 518 (2006)]

a) Note

The innocence showing in **House v. Bell** serves to open the door to further litigation of otherwise defaulted claims and is therefore known as a "gateway" actual innocence claim. The more demanding "actual innocence" standard of **Herrara v. Collins**, *supra*, if satisfied, would entitle the petitioner to release from custody.

3) Innocence and Equitable Tolling

The Court treated a sufficiently compelling showing of actual innocence as a gateway through the one-year AEDPA statute of limitations. [See **McQuiggin v. Perkins**, 569 U.S. 383 (2013)] Eleven years after his conviction on murder charges, a prisoner sought habeas review. His showing of actual innocence included affidavits tending to establish the guilt of the primary witness against him at the trial. The state argued that he had failed to meet the one-year limitation period, but the Court analogized that limitation to other procedural barriers to habeas review that claims of actual innocence can surmount, citing **Schlup v. Delo** and **House v. Bell.**

4) Innocence of Capital Crime

A prisoner may claim to be "innocent of a capital crime" rather than "actually innocent." In such a case, he is claiming that there is insufficient evidence of culpability to justify the imposition of the death penalty, not that he is innocent of the underlying crime. If a prisoner claims to be "innocent of a capital crime" in this sense, habeas will be granted under a stricter standard than if he claims "actual innocence." Under the stricter standard, he must show "by *clear and convincing evidence* that but for constitutional error, no reasonable juror would find him eligible for the death penalty." [**Sawyer v. Whitley**, 505 U.S. 333 (1992)—emphasis added]

(e) No "Cause"—Failure to Anticipate Change in Law

In **Reed v. Ross**, 486 U.S. 1 (1984), the Supreme Court held that a failure to anticipate a change in the law, and a resulting failure to raise a federal claim based on the new law, was "cause." But five years later, in 1989, the Court held that a "new rule" cannot be applied on habeas. [**Teague v. Lane**, *supra,* pp. 256 *et seq.*] Thus, *Reed* is now a dead letter because any change in the law constituting "cause" under *Reed* almost certainly constitutes a forbidden "new rule" under **Teague v. Lane**.

h. "Prejudice" Under Wainwright v. Sykes

The Supreme Court has provided several formulations of the "prejudice" standard.

(1) "Actual and Substantial Disadvantage" and "Substantial Likelihood" of Different Result

In a sustained discussion of "prejudice" under an analogous statute governing habeas for federal prisoners [28 U.S.C. § 2255], the Court said that a prisoner must show that the violation of federal right "worked to his actual and substantial disadvantage, infecting his entire trial with error of constitutional dimension." The Court held that giving the jury erroneous malice instructions does not constitute "actual prejudice" if there was "no substantial likelihood" that the jury would have convicted of a lesser offense if it had been properly instructed. [**United States v. Frady**, 456 U.S. 152 (1982)]

(2) "Might Not Have Been Convicted"

Where defendant had been forced to bear the burden of proof of lack of malice, this constituted "actual prejudice" because if he had not had to bear the burden "he might not have been convicted of first degree murder." [**Reed v. Ross**, *supra*]

(3) "Reasonable Probability" of Different Result

Where the prisoner contended that he had received inadequate assistance of counsel, he was required to show that there was "a reasonable probability that, but for counsel's unprofessional errors, the result of the proceeding would have been different." [**Strickland v. Washington**, *supra,* p. 262]

(4) Denial of Assistance of Counsel—Presumption of Prejudice

Where there has been an actual or constructive denial of counsel, or an interference by the state with counsel's assistance, *prejudice is presumed.* Where counsel is alleged to have been ineffective because of conflict of interest, there is a limited presumption of prejudice. [**Strickland v. Washington**, *supra* (dictum)]

(5) Cause and Prejudice Under the AEDPA

The AEDPA leaves in place the established framework of **Wainwright v. Sykes** as it applies to review of federal claims that were procedurally defaulted in state court proceedings.

3. Exhaustion of State Judicial Remedies

A state criminal defendant must not only present his federal defenses to the state court at trial. He must also "exhaust" his post-trial state judicial remedies before seeking federal habeas corpus.

a. Statute

A state prisoner must have exhausted his state judicial remedies before seeking federal habeas. [28 U.S.C. § 2254(b), (c)]

(1) *Section 2254(b)(1)* provides that habeas "shall not be granted unless it appears that . . . (A) the applicant has exhausted the remedies available in the courts of the State; or (B)(i) there is either an absence of available State corrective process; or (ii) circumstances exist that render such process ineffective to protect the rights of the applicant."

(2) *Section 2254(b)(2)*, a 1996 amendment, provides that an application for habeas may be denied on the merits even though state remedies have not been exhausted.

   (a) In part, this provision responds to the common circumstance in which an obviously unmeritorious application containing unexhausted claims is presented to a federal district court. Under prior law, the court dismissed without prejudice in order to allow exhaustion. The amended provision *allows the district court to dismiss on the merits despite the failure to exhaust.* The consequence is to save the district court's time, for it can now dispose of obviously unmeritorious applications without having to look at them twice— once before exhaustion and once afterwards.

EXAM TIP   **■**GILBERT

On your exam, be careful not to automatically apply the "exhaustion of remedies" rule without carefully reading the facts of the question. Remember that a habeas petition may be *denied* without requiring exhaustion, but it *may not be granted* without requiring exhaustion.

---

(3) *Section 2254(b)(3)*, a 1996 amendment, provides that a state will not be held to have waived the exhaustion requirement unless it has done so expressly.

(4) *Section 2254(c)* provides that an applicant shall not be deemed to have exhausted his state remedies "if he has the right under the law of the State to raise, by any available procedure, the question presented."

b. Presentation of Federal Claim to State Courts

A federal claim must be presented to the state courts for decision. The Court emphasized "that the federal claim must be fairly presented to the state courts . . . . Only if the state courts have had the opportunity to hear the claim does it make sense to speak of the exhaustion of state remedies." [**Picard v. Connor**, 404 U.S. 270 (1971)]

(1) Claim in State Court Must Be Designated as Federal Claim

A defendant must alert the state court to the *federal* nature of his claim. [**Duncan v. Henry**, 513 U.S. 364 (1995)]

c. Federal Claim Must Be Presented to Appellate as Well as Trial Court

A state prisoner must present his federal claim to the highest available state court on direct (appellate) review. [**Brown v. Allen**, 344 U.S. 443 (1953)]

(1) Petitioner Must Exhaust All State Appeals

A prisoner must take all appeals available as of right within the state system. Additionally, the prisoner whose conviction was affirmed by an intermediate court of appeals is required to seek discretionary review from the state supreme court. [**O'Sullivan v. Boerckel**, 526 U.S. 838 (1999)]

(2) Consequence of Failure to Present Federal Claim to State Courts

If a state criminal defendant fails to present a federal claim to the state courts, including to the state appellate courts, he is precluded from bringing the claim on federal habeas. [**Coleman v. Thompson**, *supra*, p. 41]

d. Unnecessary to Seek Certiorari to United States Supreme Court

A state criminal defendant need *not* seek certiorari of the state court decision to the United States Supreme Court. [**Ulster County Court v. Allen**, 442 U.S. 1 (1979); **Fay v. Noia**, *supra*, p. 261]

e. Must Present Same Federal Claim

It is not enough that the prisoner presented some federal claim to the state courts. He must have presented the *same* federal claim to the state courts. [**Picard v. Connor**, *supra*]

f. Mixed Petitions Containing Exhausted and Unexhausted Claims

State remedies must have been exhausted for *all* the federal claims in the habeas petition. If a petition contains several federal claims, some of which have been previously presented to the state courts and some of which have not, the federal court must dismiss the entire petition for failure to exhaust. [**Rose v. Lundy**, 455 U.S. 509 (1982)]

(1) Stay and Abeyance Process

The management of mixed petitions grew more complicated with the adoption in the AEDPA of a one-year limitation period applicable to all habeas claims. To deal with this problem, the Supreme Court approved a stay and abeyance process. [**Rhines v. Weber**, 544 U.S. 269 (2005)]

g. Elements of the Stay and Abeyance Process

When a district court faces the prospect that dismissal of a habeas petition to allow exhaustion of unexhausted claims could present a limitation issue, it has power to stay the federal habeas proceeding rather than dismissing it altogether. That way, the petitioner may simply revive the petition upon exhausting claims in state court and thereby retain the earlier (timely) filing date for the federal habeas petition. To protect against delay, the Court further held that stay and abeyance should be available only when the petitioner shows good cause for the failure to exhaust previously and when the claims in question are not plainly meritless. [**Rhines v. Weber**, *supra*]

h. Usually Unnecessary to Exhaust State Habeas

Although a prisoner must exhaust state court remedies on direct (appellate) review, he is ordinarily *not* required to exhaust state court habeas. [**Cobb v. Wainwright**, 666 F.2d 966 (5th Cir. 1982)] However, in those instances where a federal claim could *only* be raised on habeas in the state system, a prisoner is required to seek state habeas. An example is a claim of ineffective assistance of counsel. It is unrealistic to expect a trial counsel to raise at trial the issue of his own ineffectiveness, or, if he remains counsel after trial, to raise the issue on appeal. Frequently, the first real opportunity to raise the issue will be on state habeas when the prisoner is represented by new counsel. In such a case, the prisoner will be required to exhaust his state remedies by seeking habeas from the state court before coming to federal court. [**Murray v. Carrier**, *supra,* p. 263]

(1) Note

The Supreme Court has never ruled that a state must make habeas available in the state court system. The question was presented in **Case v. Nebraska**, 381 U.S. 422 (1965), but Nebraska passed a new statute before the Court had a chance to rule.

i. Exhaustion Not Required for Civil Rights Claims

Federal civil rights claims may be brought without first exhausting state administrative or judicial remedies. [**Monroe v. Pape**, 367 U.S. 167 (1961)] One must distinguish carefully between a habeas corpus petition under 28 U.S.C. section 2254 (for which exhaustion is required) and a civil rights complaint under 42 U.S.C. section 1983 (for which exhaustion is not required). The distinction is subtle when state prisoners seek to preserve or recover "good time" credits.

(1) Restoration of Good Time Credits—Habeas Petition

When a prisoner who has been deprived of good time credits seeks to have them *restored*, the appropriate remedy is habeas corpus. This is true whether the writ sought will result in immediate release or merely in shortening the time remaining to be served. [**Preiser v. Rodriguez**, 411 U.S. 475 (1973)]

j. Damages for Deprivation of Good Time Credits—Civil Rights Complaint

When a prisoner who has been deprived of good time credits seeks *damages*, the appropriate remedy is a civil rights complaint. A declaratory judgment concerning past deprivations or injunctive relief seeking to prevent future deprivation of good time credits may be sought as "ancillary relief" to the civil rights damage complaint. [**Wolff v. McDonnell**, 418 U.S. 539 (1974)]

(1) Distinguish—Civil Rights Complaints Concerning Prison Conditions

Under the Prison Litigation Reform Act of 1995, a prisoner bringing a civil rights claim under 42 U.S.C. section 1983 challenging prison conditions must exhaust state *administrative* remedies (though not state *judicial* remedies). [28 U.S.C. § 1997(e)]

k. Damages for Wrongful Conviction

A different exhaustion problem arises when the state criminal defendant seeks damages under section 1983 for wrongful conviction. Federal courts struggled to coordinate such claims with those for habeas relief, which require state court exhaustion of remedies. In **Heck v. Humphrey**, 512 U.S. 477 (1994), the Court resolved this coordination problem. Section 1983 claims that seek damages for an allegedly unconstitutional conviction or for other harms caused by actions whose unlawfulness would render a conviction or sentence invalid cannot proceed unless the section 1983 plaintiff can establish that the conviction or sentence "has been reversed on direct appeal, expunged by executive order, declared invalid by a state tribunal, or called into question by a federal court's issuance of a writ of habeas corpus."

(1) Note

Heck does not foreclose the section 1983 claim but simply defers its assertion until the plaintiff has succeeded in invalidating the conviction through some combination of direct or habeas review. It thus ensures the primacy of habeas remedies for the determination of constitutional challenges to a state conviction.

(2) Accrual of Limitation Period

The *Heck* rule poses a puzzle for the accrual of section 1983 claims that seek damages for unconstitutional police conduct, such as false arrests or imprisonments. (Accrual refers to the date on which the claim ripens and the statute of limitations begins to run.) False arrests may lead to custodial interrogation, trial, and conviction of a criminal offense. A suit brought for damages due to a false arrest may imply the invalidity of both the arrest and any evidence obtained in its wake and thus pose a *Heck* coordination problem. Lower courts divided on the accrual question. Some held that the action accrued upon the reversal or invalidation of any conviction; others found that the action accrued when the arrest occurred. The Court adopted the latter view; a section 1983 claim for false imprisonment accrues at the time of the false arrest (specifically, when the defendant was brought before a magistrate). [**Wallace v. Kato**, 549 U.S. 384 (2007)]

(a) Note

The Court recognized that certain section 1983 claimants may be forced by the early accrual rule to file actions while their state criminal proceedings remain pending at trial or on appeal. The Court suggested that the proper mode of coordination in such cases was to stay the section 1983 claim pending resolution of the criminal action.

(b) Criticism

The dissent criticized this approach as requiring individuals to file claims unnecessarily to protect their right to sue.

l. Actions to Challenge Method of Execution

When individuals on death row wish to challenge the method of their execution, questions arise as to whether the action should proceed as a habeas petition or under section 1983. If the action were to succeed, and were to invalidate the only mode of execution that the state has authorized, it could affect the duration of the prisoner's sentence (and thereby trigger habeas exclusivity). Recognizing this possibility, the Court has nonetheless permitted such actions to proceed as section 1983 claims, thus allowing the claimant to sidestep the bar to filing a second or successive habeas petition. [**Hill v. McDonough**, 547 U.S. 573 (2006)—state had approved alternative to the mode of execution challenged]

m. Actions to Challenge Parole Procedures

When prisoners seek to challenge not the grant or denial of parole, but the procedures by which the application for parole has been evaluated, the *Preiser* principle (*see supra,* p.

268) does not require the action to be treated as a habeas proceeding. [**Wilkinson v. Dotson**, 544 U.S. 74 (2005)] Success on the claim would not have altered the length or level of present custody, but would have simply invalidated as improperly retroactive the new and more restrictive parole guidelines that were applied in denying parole. Any decision on release from custody would await a new parole hearing.

n. Actions Seeking DNA Testing

Prisoner applied for DNA testing under a Texas statute that took effect after his conviction became final. State denied request. Prisoner sought relief under section 1983, arguing that the rejection of proposed test violated rights to procedural due process. Supreme Court held that the suit was brought properly under section 1983, rejecting the state's claim that it was cognizable only in habeas. [**Skinner v. Switzer**, 562 U.S. 521 (2011)—emphasizing the fact that DNA testing would not necessarily imply the invalidity of the conviction; results might be incriminating.]

F. Preclusive Effect of State Court Judgments

1. Effect of the AEDPA

The AEDPA's amendments to federal habeas require the federal district court to give greater preclusive effect to state court criminal judgments than under prior case law.

2. State Court Rulings on Matters of Law

The AEDPA provides that federal habeas shall not be granted with respect to any claim adjudicated on the merits in state court "unless the adjudication of the claim resulted in a decision that was contrary to, or involved an unreasonable application of, clearly established Federal law, as determined by the Supreme Court of the United States." [28 U.S.C. § 2254(d)(*l*)]

a. No New Rule Applied on Federal Habeas

As discussed above, the amended statute fairly clearly codifies **Teague v. Lane**, prohibiting a federal habeas court from applying a new rule. (*See supra,* p. 259.)

b. Deference to State Court Interpretations of Federal Law

In addition to forbidding reliance on a new rule of federal law, the amended statute requires deference to some state court determinations of federal law.

(1) Decision Contrary to Clearly Established Federal Law

The amended statute forbids habeas unless the state court decision was "contrary to . . . *clearly established* Federal law." [28 U.S.C. § 2254(d)(*l*)—emphasis added] The effect is to reject the previous practice permitting de novo review of state court decisions on questions of federal law.

c. Decision Involving Unreasonable Application of Clearly Established Federal Law

The amended statute forbids habeas unless the state court decision "involved an *unreasonable application* of clearly established federal law." This provision precludes federal habeas in cases of reasonable but incorrect state court applications of clearly established federal law.

d. "As Determined by the Supreme Court"

The new statute further provides that the federal law in question must be clearly established "as determined by the Supreme Court."

e. Application of the AEDPA's Standard of Review

Cases interpreting the AEDPA's standard of review answer some questions and raise others.

(1) Objective Standard

The Court requires an objective determination of the reasonableness of the state's application of clearly established law. [**Williams v. Taylor**, 529 U.S. 362 (2000)] Thus, the Court rejected the view that federal habeas corpus courts were required to defer to state court applications of federal law so long as a "reasonable jurist" might plausibly regard the state court application as proper.

f. Standard Applied

A few examples illustrate the approach used to determining if the objective standard of unreasonable application has been met:

e.g. **Example: ineffective assistance of counsel:** The Virginia Supreme Court rejected the claim of a state habeas petitioner that his counsel in the penalty phase of a death penalty case was constitutionally ineffective for having failed to adduce mitigation evidence of petitioner's mental retardation and abusive childhood. The state court identified the correct precedent, **Washington v. Strickland**, but found that that decision had been qualified by later authority and further found that any ineffectiveness did not outweigh the prosecution's evidence of future dangerousness. In reversing the state and lower federal courts (and concluding that habeas relief was warranted), the Court found that the state court had acted both contrary to controlling precedent and had adopted an unreasonable application of such precedent. [**Williams v. Taylor**, *supra*]

e.g. **Example: ineffective assistance of counsel:** The Court granted habeas relief in an ineffective assistance case that challenged the performance of counsel at the penalty phase of a death penalty case. Although trial counsel had made efforts to develop mitigating evidence (unlike the lawyer in **Williams v. Taylor**, *supra*), he had not reviewed the case file in a related case that the prosecutor planned to use. The Court found, over a sharp dissent, that the state court's rejection of the claim was objectively unreasonable. [**Rompilla v. Beard**, 545 U.S. 374 (2005)]

e.g. **Example: cruel and unusual punishment:** The California Supreme Court rejected a challenge to the state's "three strikes" law, concluding that two 25-year prison terms for thefts of some videotapes did not constitute cruel and unusual punishment. The Supreme Court upheld the state court's application of federal law, rejecting a lower court decision to the contrary, after canvassing its own precedent and concluding that the federal law clearly established a "gross disproportionality" principle available only in an extreme case. The particular case was not as egregious as one involving life without the possibility of parole in which the Court had granted relief. [**Lockyer v. Andrade**, 538 U.S. 63 (2003)] *Note:* The Court's approach seemingly calls for deference to state court decisions whenever the constitutional rule requires the application of a general standard with a variety of factors to a specific situation. [**Yarborough v. Alvarado**, 541 U.S. 652 (2004)]

g. Defining Clearly Established Law

The statute makes clear that relief may issue only to address unreasonable applications of clearly established law, as determined by the Supreme Court. The Court has clarified that only the holdings of its prior cases, defined at a fairly narrow range of particularity, constitute "clearly established law" within the statute's meaning. [**Carey v. Musladin**, *supra*, p. 268]

e.g. **Example:** Members of the family of a murder victim attended the trial of the defendant, wearing buttons with the victim's picture on them. The defendant argued that the buttons could prejudice the jury, but the state trial court refused to order the family members to remove the buttons. On appeal, the state court upheld the defendant's conviction and rejected the claim that the buttons created a prejudicial trial atmosphere. Prior decisions of the Supreme Court had found the requisite inherent prejudice when the state required that the defendant appear at trial in a prison jumpsuit [**Estelle v. Williams**, 425 U.S. 501 (1976)], but not when the state positioned state troopers to sit immediately behind the defense table in the courtroom [**Holbrook v. Flynn**, 475 U.S. 560 (1986)]. Because both cases involved government conduct, the Court concluded that there was no clearly established Supreme Court precedent on point for private conduct (and no justification for concluding that the state court had adopted an unreasonable application of clearly established law in rejecting a challenge to the buttons). The dicta in earlier cases, though phrased to prohibit inherently prejudicial conduct more generally, did not establish a rule of law applicable to private conduct. [**Carey v. Musladin**, *supra*] *Note:* The lower courts had divided in considering how far to extend the precedent of **Estelle v. Williams,** a division the Court pointed to in support of its conclusion that the law was not clearly established. But the Court refused itself to define the breadth of *Estelle*, no doubt viewing the question (as in **Teague v. Lane**) as one it could not answer in a habeas proceeding.

(1) Note

The Ninth Circuit followed its own prior decisions about the prejudicial behavior of courtroom spectators in *Musladin*, regarding its own decisions as cementing an established interpretation of the Court's decisions in *Williams* and *Flynn.* The Supreme Court regarded the Ninth Circuit's earlier decision as irrelevant to the task of divining the content of clearly established law as determined by the Supreme Court.

h. Criticism

Although the concurring Justices agreed with the disposition, denying habeas relief, they criticized the Court for taking too narrow a view of established law. In the view of the concurring Justices, considered dicta in prior cases could establish a general rule applicable to other situations of courtroom prejudice not encompassed within the narrow prison jumpsuit holding of **Estelle v. Williams.**

3. State Court Rulings on Matters of Fact

Two provisions of the AEDPA require deference to a state court's findings of fact:

(i) *Habeas shall not be granted* as to a claim adjudicated on the merits in state court *unless the decision "was based on an unreasonable determination of the facts in light of the evidence presented in the State court proceeding."* [28 U.S.C. § 2254(d)(2)]

(ii) ***Furthermore, a determination of a factual issue*** made by a state court shall be ***presumed to be correct.*** "The applicant shall have the burden of rebutting the presumption of correctness by clear and convincing evidence." [28 U.S.C. § 2254(e)(1)]

a. Effect of Statute

The two provisions above are redundant and possibly inconsistent. Whatever their precise meaning, the effect of the provisions is to require substantial deference to state court fact finding, just as section 2254(d)(1) calls for federal deference to reasonable state court applications of established law.

e.g. **Example:** In a case involving the prosecutor's use of peremptory challenges to exclude jurors on the basis of race, the Court carefully reviewed the facts and concluded that the prosecutor's race-neutral justification for striking black jurors was not credible. It thus found a violation of **Batson v. Kentucky**, 476 U.S. 79 (1986), which precludes the racially exclusionary use of peremptory challenges. Some of the evidence on which the Court relied, including juror questionnaires and information cards, had not been in the record of the state court proceeding, but was made a part of the federal habeas proceeding without the state's objection. [**Miller-El v. Dretke**, 545 U.S. 231 (2005)] *Note:* The Court may appear to have relied on evidence from outside the record of the state court proceeding in a manner inconsistent with section 2254(d)(2). But the trial judge clearly had access to the questionnaires and juror information cards at the time of its ruling on the government's proffered race-neutral explanation.

e.g. **Example:** In a case similar in some respects to *Miller-El, supra,* the Court took a much stricter view of the deference required to state court fact-finding. As in *Miller-El,* the state trial court rejected a *Batson* challenge, accepting the proffered race-neutral account of the prosecutor. The federal appeals court found it unreasonable to accept that account. The Court reversed, emphasizing that in habeas proceedings governed by section 2254(d)(2), when reasonable minds can disagree as to the prosecutor's credibility, the trial court's factual conclusion should control. [**Rice v. Collins**, 546 U.S. 333 (2006)] The Court did not address the relevance of the possibly inconsistent provisions of section 2254(e)(1).

(1) Explanation

Although *Miller-El* and *Rice* appear to be in some tension, one might harmonize the two cases by noting that the Court's own review in *Miller-El* persuaded it that the race-neutral account had no reasonable factual basis, whereas the race-neutral account in *Rice* presented a closer question, turning on issues of credibility that the state court had reasonably resolved.

b. Failure to Develop Factual Record in State Court

Under prior law, federal courts rarely exercised their power, sitting in habeas, to conduct a full-blown evidentiary hearing on a disputed issue of fact. When the habeas petitioner failed to seek an evidentiary hearing in state court, moreover, the petitioner was deemed to have defaulted the factual issue, subject to possible revival under the "cause and prejudice" standard of **Wainwright v. Sykes**, *supra.* [**Keeney v. Tamayo-Reyes**, 504 U.S. 1 (1992)] The AEDPA specifies a more restrictive regime.

(1) The AEDPA Governs Evidentiary Hearings

The AEDPA provides that if a prisoner failed to develop a factual record in state court in support of his federal claim, the federal habeas court may not hold a factual hearing on that claim unless:

(A) the claim relies on—

    (i) a new rule of constitutional law, made retroactive to cases on collateral review by the Supreme Court, that was previously unavailable; or

    (ii) a factual predicate that could not have been previously discovered through the exercise of due diligence; and

(B) the facts underlying the claim would be sufficient to establish by clear and convincing evidence that but for constitutional error, no reasonable fact finder would have found the applicant guilty of the underlying offense.

[28 U.S.C. § 2254(e)(2)]

Note: The Supreme Court has ruled that a habeas court cannot consider evidence adduced in an evidentiary hearing if the petition does not otherwise qualify for relief under the "clearly established" law standard in section 2254(d)(1). The imposition of this restriction may further limit access to evidentiary hearings in federal habeas proceedings. [**Cullen v. Pinholster**, 563 U.S. 170 (2011)]

c. Meaning of "Failed to Develop"

The Court has ruled that a habeas petitioner fails to develop the factual basis for a claim in state court only where "there is lack of diligence, or some greater fault" attributable to the prisoner or his attorney. [**Williams v. Taylor**, 529 U.S. 420 (2000)] The Court accordingly rejected the state's contention that any failure to develop the issue in state court, however inadvertent or well intentioned, would operate to bar a subsequent federal hearing. If the prisoner and his attorney had no reason to suspect a juror of lying about her relationship to a witness, there was no lack of diligence in failing to explore the issue in the state proceeding.

d. Limit on Reach of the AEDPA

At least one court has concluded that pre-AEDPA rules governing evidentiary hearings continue to control when the petitioner did not "fail" to present the factual issue to the state court. [**Bryan v. Mullin**, 335 F.3d 1207 (10th Cir. 2003)]

e. Innocence of Prisoner—Due Process Concerns

(1) Evidence Presented at Trial Sufficient to Prove Guilt

Due process prohibits conviction unless sufficient evidence is ***introduced at trial*** to prove guilt beyond a reasonable doubt. [***In re* Winship**, 397 U.S. 358 (1970)— evaluation of evidence introduced into record at trial; **Jackson v. Virginia**, *supra,* p. 255] A claim that the evidence presented at trial does not support a verdict of guilt beyond a reasonable doubt is cognizable on habeas. The standard is "whether there was sufficient evidence to ***convince a rational trier of the facts*** to find guilt beyond a reasonable doubt." [**Jackson v. Virginia**, *supra*—emphasis added]

f. Claim of Actual Innocence Based in Part on Evidence Not Presented at Trial

Due process ***may*** also prohibit the conviction of an innocent person, whether or not the evidence at trial satisfies ***In re* Winship**, *supra.* [*See* **Herrera v. Collins**, 506 U.S. 390 (1993)—although perhaps it is the execution of the defendant that is prohibited; the opinion is not clear] *Herrera* involved a free-standing claim of innocence, not limited to an evaluation of the evidence presented at trial. A claim of ***actual innocence***, based in part on evidence not introduced at trial, ***may*** warrant habeas relief. However, the Court has expressed serious reservations: "We may assume, for the sake of argument . . . that in a capital case a truly persuasive demonstration of 'actual innocence' made after trial would render the execution of a defendant unconstitutional, and warrant federal habeas relief if there were no state avenue open to process such a claim. But . . . the threshold showing for such an assumed right would necessarily be extraordinarily high." [**Herrera v. Collins**, *supra*]

(1) Note

Herrera v. Collins does not specify a standard for deciding a case of claimed actual innocence in a capital case. It says only that if the Constitution forbids the execution of an innocent person, the required showing of innocence would be "extraordinarily high."

(2) Effect of the AEDPA on *Herrera v. Collins*

The AEDPA statutory provision governing the introduction of new evidence does not differentiate between a claim of actual innocence and other constitutional claims. (*See supra,* p. 263.) An applicant claiming actual innocence thus must satisfy the criteria of section 2254(e)(2) in order to introduce new evidence (*see supra,* p. 273); only after section 2254(e)(2) is satisfied may a habeas court consider that evidence under **Herrera v. Collins**, *supra.*

(3) Distinguish—Claim of Innocence as Basis for Excusing State Court Procedural Default

The **Herrera v. Collins** analysis applies to a claim of actual innocence, unaccompanied by any other federal claim. A different analysis is used when a "gatekeeping" claim of innocence is used as a basis for excusing procedural default in state court as a prerequisite for presenting some federal claim other than actual innocence (*e.g.*, a *Miranda* violation). (*See supra,* pp. 260 *et seq.*)

4. Harmless Error

If a federal court decides that a habeas petitioner's federal constitutional right was violated because of a cognizable error by the state court, it must decide whether the error was "harmless."

a. Review of Error on Habeas

An erroneous ruling by the state judge at trial is ordinarily *harmless* when reviewed on habeas unless it had *"substantial and injurious effect or influence"* on the jury's verdict. [**Brecht v. Abrahamson**, 507 U.S. 619 (1993)]

(1) "Deliberate and Especially Egregious" Trial Error

However, it is possible that a "deliberate and especially egregious error of the trial type" may "so infect the integrity of the proceeding" that habeas should be granted without a showing of substantial influence on the jury's verdict. [**Brecht v. Abrahamson**, *supra*]

b. "Structural Defect" in Trial Mechanism

Some severe constitutional errors are "structural defects in the constitution of the trial mechanism, which defy analysis by harmless error standards." Such errors require *automatic reversal* without harmless error inquiry. [**Brecht v. Abrahamson**, *supra*]

Example: Deprivation of right to counsel requires automatic reversal. [**Brecht v. Abrahamson**, *supra*]

c. Distinguish—Direct Review of Error

The standard on direct review is much more favorable to the defendant than the standard on habeas. A federal constitutional error at trial is harmless on direct review only if it is "harmless beyond a reasonable doubt." [**Chapman v. California**, 386 U.S. 18 (1967)]

5. Statute of Limitations

Prior to 1996, there was no statute of limitations for filing a habeas application. Under the AEDPA, a prisoner must file an application for federal habeas within one year from one of four specified dates. The date from which the one-year period will most often run is "the date on which the judgment became final by the conclusion of direct review or the expiration of the time for seeking such review." [28 U.S.C. § 2244(d)(*l*)(A); *and see* § 2244(d)(1)(B)–(D)]

a. Statute Tolled During Pendency of State Application for Collateral Relief

The one-year period does not run during periods when "a properly filed application for state post-conviction or other collateral review . . . is pending." [28 U.S.C. § 2244(d)(2)]

(1) But Note

The statute is tolled only while applications for post-conviction relief in state court are actually ***pending.*** It is not tolled for the periods before and after, or between, the filing of state court applications.

b. Also Note

Equitable tolling may apply to extend the limitation period. See **McQuiggin v. Perkins**, *supra* p. 264 and **Holland v. Florida**, *infra* p. 277]

c. Limited Relation Back of Amendments to Habeas Claims

If more than a year has passed since the conviction became final, questions may arise as to the timeliness of a motion to add new claims to a federal habeas petition or to amend claims that had been previously asserted. (Sometimes, counsel appointed to help a *pro se* petitioner may suggest the proposed amendments.) Under Federal Rule of Civil Procedure 15, amended complaints "relate back" to the earlier, timely filing date so long as the claims to be asserted arose from the same "conduct, transaction, or occurrence" that was set forth in the initial complaint. However, the Court ***rejected*** the Rule 15 test of relation back, ruling instead that the specific legal claim was to provide the relevant transaction for relation back purposes. Thus, a confrontation claim based on introduction of videotaped testimony by another witness was said to differ from a self-incrimination claim based upon the admission of the prisoner's own confession. [**Mayle v. Felix**, 545 U.S. 644 (2005)—defining a transaction for relation back purposes in habeas proceedings as the cluster of facts that underlie specific legal claims]

(1) Criticism

Limitations periods normally serve to place the defendant on notice of the pendency of claims so that their ability to defend will not be prejudiced through the passage of time. Rules of relation back reflect this notice function, and treat broadly related claims as encompassed within a timely initial filing on the same basic claims. In **Mayle v. Felix**, the state was on notice that the petitioner wished to challenge his conviction. As applied, the restrictive relation back rule operates more as a forfeiture device than a rule requiring effective notice within the time specified.

d. Stay and Abeyance to Permit Exhaustion

Mixed habeas petitions contain both exhausted and unexhausted claims. In the past, district courts would dismiss such mixed petitions to allow the petitioner to exhaust the claims through state court proceedings. Re-filing of the claims would come later. Today, simple dismissal may bar the re-filing of a fully exhausted petition if more than one year has passed since the conviction became final on direct review. The limitation period excludes time spent litigating in state, but not federal habeas, court. To deal with this problem, the Supreme Court approved a stay and abeyance procedure. [**Rhines v. Weber**, *supra,* p. 267)] The elements of the stay abeyance process are discussed at p. 267, *supra.*

e. Equitable Tolling

Applying its doctrine governing the jurisdictionality of time limits, see pp. 112–113, the Court concluded that the statute of limitations in section 2244(d) was subject to equitable tolling. The Court based its decision on the absence of any emphatic textual restriction on jurisdiction and on the traditional reliance on equitable principles in connection with habeas review. [**Holland v. Florida**, 560 U.S. 631 (2010)]

G. Preclusive Effect of Earlier Habeas Application

1. Introduction

The AEDPA significantly expanded the preclusive effect of a prior federal habeas application.

2. Same Claim

The same claim may be presented only once in a federal habeas application: "A claim presented in a second or successive habeas corpus application under section 2254 that was presented in a prior application shall be dismissed." [28 U.S.C. § 2244(b)(1)]

3. Different Claim

A different claim—one not presented in an earlier habeas application—may be presented in a later application only in very limited circumstances:

(A) The applicant shows that the claim relies on a *new rule of constitutional law*, made *retroactive* to cases on collateral review by the Supreme Court, that was *previously unavailable*; or

(B) (i) The factual predicate for the claim *could not have been discovered previously* through the exercise of due diligence; and

 (ii) The facts underlying the claim, if proven and viewed in light of the evidence as a whole, would be sufficient to establish by clear and convincing evidence that, but for the constitutional error, *no reasonable fact finder would have found the applicant guilty* of the underlying offense.

[28 U.S.C. § 2244(b)(2)—emphasis added]

4. Applying Teague's "New Law" Framework in Light of AEDPA's Successive Petition Limits

a. In General

As noted above, **Teague v. Lane** forecloses habeas review of new rules of constitutional law. AEDPA follows suit, foreclosing relief except where the law has been clearly established by the Supreme Court. **Teague** qualifies its rule of non-retroactivity, allowing habeas petitioners to claim the benefit of decisions that establish fundamental procedural rules (under the "ordered liberty" test) and make important changes in substantive law that place certain forms of punishment beyond the power of the state. AEDPA does not include these same exceptions; it prohibits habeas relief unless the state court violated the statute's "clearly established federal law" standard.

b. The Tension Between Teague and AEDPA Illustrated

What happens when the Court makes an important change in substantive criminal law that apparently satisfies the **Teague** standard, like the invalidation of certain forms of punishment? Such new rules do not satisfy the AEDPA standard for relief, but they should under the logic of **Teague** apply across the board to all individuals under that (now-prohibited) sentence, even to those who unsuccessfully sought habeas review before on different issues. But AEDPA poses a serious obstacle, by barring consideration on habeas of a claim that the petitioner had previously submitted and by barring any second or successive petition unless the petition "relies on a new rule of constitutional law, made retroactive to cases on collateral review by the Supreme Court, that was previously unavailable."

Under AEDPA, the successive habeas petitioner may gain relief only if the rule in question was one that the Supreme Court made retroactively applicable. The Court has interpreted this retroactivity provision to require a specific Supreme Court decision on point. AEDPA thus makes it awkward at best for any class of second or successive habeas petitioners to secure relief; they will necessarily be seeking the retroactive application of a new rule that the Court has yet, by definition, to make retroactively available to them.

E.G. In Miller v. Alabama, (2012), the Court held that the Eighth Amendment prohibited sentences of life without the possibility of parole for individuals who were minors at the time of their offense. The Court did not, however, declare its decision retroactively applicable. An inmate in Louisiana, one Montgomery, who had been sentenced as a minor for a crime committed in the 1960s to life without parole sought to claim the benefit of the **Miller** rule. AEDPA would, on its face, seemingly bar federal habeas relief.

c. The Supreme Court Addresses the Problem

The Court addressed the tension between **Teague** and AEDPA in **Montgomery v. Louisiana,** 136 S. Ct. 718 (2016), in the context of direct review of the prisoner's state court application for post-conviction relief. Louisiana made such relief available as a matter of state law and applied the **Teague** framework in rejecting Montgomery's argument that, as a minor convicted long ago, he should have the benefit of the Miller rule. On review, the Court held that the state court was constitutionally obliged to apply the **Teague** framework. That meant the issue of retroactive application was not a question of state law but a controlling federal question that would sustain its appellate jurisdiction. On the merits, the Court ruled that the Louisiana court had erred in denying Montgomery retroactive access to the **Miller** rule.

b. Possible Elimination of Appeal by State

The statute may also have the consequence—though almost certainly not the intent—of eliminating appeals by the state. The statute requires a certificate of appealability in all cases in which a state prisoner seeks habeas [28 U.S.C. § 2253(c)(1)(A)], and provides that the only ground for issuance of a certificate is a substantial showing by the applicant of a denial of a constitutional right [28 U.S.C. § 2253(c)(2)]. The statute provides no ground for the issuance of a certificate that would apply to an appeal by the state.

(1) Drafting Mistake

The apparent unavailability to the state of a certificate of appeal is almost certainly the result of a drafting mistake. It is unclear what the federal courts will do if the statute is not amended.

I.   Capital Cases

1. Introduction

The AEDPA includes special provisions for federal habeas in capital cases. [28 U.S.C. §§ 2261–2266] The statute greatly reduces the time between conviction and execution, provided that competent counsel is assured for indigent prisoners during *state* post-conviction proceedings. For the first 10 years of the Act, these provisions were of primarily academic interest. No state succeeded in persuading the federal courts that its system for assuring competent counsel in state post-conviction proceedings met the standards of the statute. In 2006, Congress transferred the task of assessing state compliance from the federal courts to the Attorney General of the United States (subject to judicial review in the D.C. Circuit). If states are deemed to qualify under this new structure, the expedited review provisions of this part of the Act may take effect. As of 2013, the Attorney General had yet to promulgate regulations governing competence of counsel and only one state, Arizona, had petitioned to secure right to expedited review.

2. Competent Counsel Requirement

The provisions shortening the time for habeas in capital cases apply *only if* the state has made arrangements for "the appointment, compensation, and payment of reasonable litigation expenses of competent counsel in State postconviction proceedings brought by indigent prisoners . . . ." [28 U.S.C. § 2261(b)] If the state does not make such arrangements, the normal time limits for federal habeas apply.

a. Note

This provision only requires the appointment of competent counsel during *state* habeas proceedings. A separate federal statute provides counsel in capital cases during federal habeas proceedings. [21 U.S.C. § 848(q)(4)(B)]

b. Comment

As a practical matter, the most critical stage in a capital case is the actual trial rather than post-trial collateral proceedings. Section 2261 neither provides nor encourages the states to provide competent counsel during trial.

3. Time Limits

If the state has made sufficient arrangements for competent counsel during state postconviction proceedings, the following time limits apply:

a. Filing in District Court

A habeas application must be filed in the district court no later than 180 days "after the final State court affirmance of the conviction and sentence on direct review or the expiration of the time for seeking such review." [28 U.S.C. § 2263(a)] That time period is tolled during pendency of a certiorari petition in the Supreme Court or a habeas petition in state court. [28 U.S.C. § 2263(b)]

b. Decision by District Court

The district court must decide a habeas application no later than 180 days after the date it is filed. [28 U.S.C. § 2266(b)(*l*)(A)]

(1) Possible Extension of Time

For good cause (as defined in the statute), the district court may extend the 180-day period by no more than 30 days. [28 U.S.C. § 2266(b)(*l*)(C)]

c. Decision by Court of Appeals

The court of appeals must decide a habeas appeal from the district court no later than 120 days from the date the reply brief is filed, or, if there is no reply brief, from the date of the answering brief. [28 U.S.C. § 2266(c)(*l*)(A)]

d. Note—No Enforcement Mechanism

The statute provides no enforcement mechanism to ensure that the district court and the court of appeals comply with the time limit. It is unclear what should happen if the district court exceeds the time limit for decision.

4. Scope of Review

If the state has made sufficient arrangements for competent counsel in state postconviction proceedings, the scope of federal habeas review is ***somewhat more restricted*** than in regular habeas. [28 U.S.C. § 2264]

a. Consequence of Failure to Raise Claim in State Court

A federal habeas court in a capital case under this section may ***not hear a claim*** that has not been raised and decided in the state court ***unless*** the failure to raise the claim properly is:

(i) The result of state action in violation of the Constitution or laws of the United States;

(ii) The result of the Supreme Court's recognition of a new federal right that is made retroactively applicable; or

(iii) Based on a factual predicate that could not have been discovered through the exercise of due diligence in time to present the claim for state or federal postconviction review.

[28 U.S.C. § 2264(a)(1)–(3)]

b. More Restricted Review than in Noncapital Cases

The above bases for excusing a failure to raise a claim in state court are more restrictive than the "cause" and "prejudice" standards developed under **Wainwright v. Sykes.** (*See supra*, pp. 261 *et seq.*)

(1) Irrelevance of Innocence

For example, innocence—either "actual innocence" or "innocence of a capital crime"—is a basis for excusing state court procedural default under **Schlup v. Delo** and **Sawyer v. Whitley.** (*See supra*, pp. 263–264.) But innocence is *not* a basis for excusing a failure to present a claim to a state court in a capital case that qualifies for treatment under this section.

c. Comment

More restrictive bases for excusing procedural default in capital cases are hard to justify:

(1) Greater Seriousness of Capital Cases

It is not apparent why the consequences of procedural default should be more severe in a case where death rather than imprisonment is the punishment.

EXAM TIP

Sometimes you just can't use logic to arrive at a correct conclusion on an exam. For example, one would logically believe that the consequences of a procedural default would be less severe in a capital case, given the severity of the punishment, ***but that is not true***—in a capital case, unlike in a "regular" habeas proceeding, the failure to raise a claim at trial ***may bar review*** in a habeas proceeding (at least in a state that qualifies for expedited review by providing competent counsel in state habeas proceedings).

---

(2) Irrelevance of the Qualifying Criterion

The qualifying criterion for more severe treatment of capital cases on habeas is that the state makes arrangements for competent counsel *during state habeas.* But a procedural default results from a failure by counsel *during trial.* Thus, the qualifying criterion has no bearing on what caused the procedural default and on whether the default should be excused.

Chapter Eleven

The Eleventh Amendment and State Sovereign Immunity

Key Exam Issues

The Eleventh Amendment is usually baffling to nonexperts. The best way to study the Amendment is probably in two steps:

1. **Review the Historical Background of the Amendment**

   Note that the true historical meaning of the Amendment has not been followed by the Court for about 100 years. In 1985, Justice Brennan, joined by three other Justices, proposed that the Court return to something close to its original meaning, but a majority of the Court has never agreed to do so. (*See infra,* p. 288.)

2. **Learn the Modern Doctrinal Structure**

   The current state of the law treats the Amendment as a ***jurisdictional bar*** to unconsented suits by private citizens against a state. But there are a number of exceptions and qualifications to the bar. Learn both the scope of the bar and all the exceptions and qualifications.

A. Introduction

1. In General

The Eleventh Amendment has traditionally been read as a constitutional text directly protecting the sovereign immunity of the states. But as will be seen below, this reading of the Amendment is highly suspect as a historical matter, and it has produced a complicated modern doctrinal structure.

2. Two Competing Ideas

Eleventh Amendment jurisprudence tries to reconcile the demands of two competing ideas: state sovereign immunity and federal power.

a. State Sovereign Immunity

In Anglo-American law, it is assumed that the "sovereign" is immune from suit by private persons unless the sovereign consents to be sued. The origin, nature, and scope of this immunity are a matter of some historical debate, the details of which are beyond the scope of this Summary. Before the adoption of the Constitution, the states, as "sovereigns," were ***presumed to be immune*** from unconsented suits.

b. Federal Power

The adoption of the Constitution necessarily diminished the "sovereign" status of the states, which were reduced to ***subsidiary sovereigns.*** But it was unclear how much the state's sovereign immunity was reduced by the creation of the new, overarching national sovereign.

3. Working Out Accommodations of Competing Powers

The history of the Eleventh Amendment shows a series of accommodations between the competing powers of the state and federal governments. Eleventh Amendment doctrine has not been stable because it has had to respond to changes in the relative powers of the two governments.

B. Historical Background

1. "State-Citizen Diversity Clause" of Article III

Article III of the Constitution contains a number of bases of jurisdiction, including federal question, diversity, and admiralty. One such basis confers jurisdiction over controversies "between, a State and citizens of another State . . . [or] foreign . . . citizens or Subjects." This basis of jurisdiction depends on the *status of the parties* rather than the nature of the question being litigated. One may call it the "State-Citizen Diversity Clause" to distinguish it from the more familiar Citizen-Citizen Diversity Clause.

2. Chisholm v. Georgia

In **Chisholm v. Georgia**, 2 U.S. (2 Dall.) 419 (1793), the Supreme Court decided a suit brought under the jurisdiction conferred by the State-Citizen Diversity Clause. In that case, a South Carolina citizen had sued the state of Georgia on a contract. The suit was not based on federal law. The Court held that the State-Citizen Diversity Clause conferred jurisdiction, and that state sovereign immunity was abrogated in suits brought under the clause.

3. Passage of Amendment

The political reaction to **Chisholm v. Georgia** was very hostile. Many states had accrued significant contract-based debts during the Revolutionary War and were deeply concerned that *Chisholm* would permit those debts to be enforced against them in federal court without their consent. The Eleventh Amendment was adopted in 1798 to overturn the result in *Chisholm*.

C. Text and Original Meaning of Amendment

1. Introduction

The text of the Eleventh Amendment has been difficult for modern courts to understand, but the meaning at the time of its adoption is fairly clear.

2. Text

The full text of the Amendment provides: "The judicial power of the United States shall not be construed to extend to any suit in law or equity, commenced or prosecuted against one of the United States by Citizens of another State, or by Citizens or Subjects of any Foreign State."

3. Analysis

The Amendment says that the judicial power shall not "be construed" to extend to a certain kind of suit. This suggests that the Amendment is correcting an erroneous construction by the Court. It also suggests that the Amendment applied to the several claims that were pending on the Supreme Court's original docket at the time the Amendment took effect. The suits to which the Amendment speaks are only those suits brought against a state by *out-of-state or foreign citizens.* The Amendment says nothing about suits brought against a state by its own citizens.

4. Original Meaning of Text

The use of the word "construed," as well as the narrow focus on out-of-state and foreign citizens, suggest that the Amendment was intended to address only the Court's erroneous construction of the State-Citizen Diversity Clause. The Court in *Chisholm* had construed the clause to permit suits against the states without their permission. The Amendment said that the clause should not be construed to authorize that jurisdiction.

a. Significance of Original Meaning

So understood, the Amendment did not originally *bar* suits by private citizens against the states. If it had been intended as a bar, it probably would have been drafted to prohibit suits against the states by all citizens, not just by out-of-state and foreign citizens. Instead, the Amendment merely provided that the State-Citizen Diversity Clause *did not confer* jurisdiction over suits against the state.

b. Note—Other Jurisdictional Bases Available

So understood, the Amendment does not bar private citizens' suits against states. If other bases of jurisdiction (such as federal question and admiralty) confer jurisdiction, then a suit may be brought under one of these bases.

5. State Sovereign Immunity after Passage of Amendment

If the Eleventh Amendment is understood in this way, it does not provide a textual basis for state sovereign immunity from federal causes of action under the Constitution. State sovereign immunity may still have some constitutional protection, but it would not depend on the Eleventh Amendment; it would depend, instead, on the scope of the federal government's *enumerated powers* and on inferences from the *structure of the federal system.*

6. Justice Brennan's Position

Justice Brennan, joined by three other Justices, adopted the historical analysis outlined here. But he contended that there was *no* constitutional protection for state sovereign immunity after the adoption of the Eleventh Amendment. [**Atascadero State Hospital v. Scanlon**, 473 U.S. 234 (1985)—Brennan, J., dissenting; *and see* **Welch v. State Department of Highways & Public Transportation**, 483 U.S. 468 (1987)—Brennan, J., dissenting]

a. Position Rejected

A five-justice majority of the Court has explicitly rejected Justice Brennan's historical analysis [**Pennsylvania v. Union Gas Co.,** 491 U.S. 1 (1989)], and there is no majority supporting his analysis today.

7. Academic Literature

The historical analysis presented here and relied in part upon by Justice Brennan in **Atascadero State Hospital v. Scanlon**, *supra,* comes from several law review articles. [*See, e.g.,* Fletcher, *A Historical Interpretation of the Eleventh Amendment,* 35 Stan. L. Rev. 1033 (1983); Gibbons, *The Eleventh Amendment and State Sovereign Immunity: A Reinterpretation,* 83 Colum. L. Rev. 1889 (1983); *and see* Pfander, *History and State Suability: An "Explanatory" Account of the Eleventh Amendment,* 83 Cornell L. Rev. 1269 (1998)]

D. Current Doctrine

1. In General

Current Eleventh Amendment doctrine is quite unlike what the above historical discussion would suggest. Today, the Amendment is a *bar* to federal court jurisdiction whenever a private citizen attempts to sue a state. But this bar is qualified by a complicated patchwork of exceptions.

2. Eleventh Amendment as Jurisdictional Bar

a. Historical Background

Almost a century after the adoption of the Amendment, the Supreme Court held that *in-state* as well as out-of-state citizens were barred from suing a state by the Amendment and the principle for which it stands. [**Hans v. Louisiana**, 134 U.S. 1 (1890)]

b. Extent of Jurisdictional Bar

(1) Suit by Any Private Citizen

Although the Amendment mentions only out-of-state citizens, a suit against a state by any private citizen—whether in-state, out-of-state, or foreign—is barred.

c. Suit by Foreign Country

Although the Amendment says nothing about foreign countries, a suit by a foreign country is barred. [**Principality of Monaco v. Mississippi**, 292 U.S. 313 (1934)— "Behind the words of the constitutional provisions are postulates which limit and control"]

d. Suit by Recognized Indian Tribe

Although the Amendment says nothing about Indian tribes, a suit by a recognized Indian tribe is barred. [**Blatchford v. Native Village of Noatak and Circle Village**, 501 U.S. 775 (1991)]

e. Suit in Admiralty

Although the Amendment mentions only suits "in law or equity," a suit in admiralty by a private citizen is also barred. [*Ex parte* **New York**, 256 U.S. 490 (1921)]

f. Jurisdictional Nature of Bar

The Amendment's bar is "jurisdictional." In practical effect this means:

(1) Defense May Be Raised for First Time on Appeal

By analogy to the "*Mansfield* rule" for a defect in subject matter jurisdiction (*see supra*, p. 111), an Eleventh Amendment defense may be raised on appeal even if the state failed to raise the defense and lost on the merits at trial. [**Edelman v. Jordan**, 415 U.S. 651 (1974)]

(a) Criticism

It seems unfair to allow the state to raise an Eleventh Amendment defense on appeal after a defense on the merits failed in the trial court. This effectively gives the state two bites at the apple: If the state wins on the merits, it wins; if the state loses on the merits, it can get a dismissal by invoking the Eleventh Amendment on appeal.

g. But Note—Defense May Be Waived

Unlike a defect in subject matter jurisdiction, the Amendment's jurisdictional bar may be waived by the state if it consents to suit (*see infra*, p. 293). [**Clark v. Barnard**, 108 U.S. 436 (1883)]

h. Possible Synthesis of *Edelman v. Jordan* and *Clark v. Barnard*

Probably the best reading of *Edelman* is that consent to suit requires more than a mere failure to raise an Eleventh Amendment defense at trial. It probably requires, in addition, that the state's attorney have the power under state law to consent to suit, either by explicitly waiving immunity or by defending on the merits. [*See* **Clark v. Barnard**, *supra*] In support of its holding that the state could raise the Eleventh Amendment for the first time on appeal, the Court in *Edelman* cited **Ford Motor Co. v. Department of Treasury**, 323 U.S. 459 (1945). In *Ford Motor Co.,* the Court held that the state attorney general had not consented to suit because he was not authorized under the law of his state to consent to suit. The Court made it clear that if the attorney general had had the power under state law to consent to suit, he would have done so by his defense on the merits.

EXAM TIP GILBERT

It's important not to mix up similar concepts on your exam. Although a defense of sovereign immunity and a defense of lack of subject matter jurisdiction share a common trait, in that the defenses are jurisdictional and may be raised for the first time on appeal, the application of each is slightly different. For sovereign immunity, if the person representing the state has **the statutory power to waive the defense**, a failure to raise the defense at trial may **waive that defense**, whereas the lack of subject matter jurisdiction may **never** be waived.

---

i. Waiver Through Forum Selection

As noted below, the Eleventh Amendment ordinarily bars federal courts from hearing suits for injunctive relief against state officials to compel compliance with state law. A state that removes such a state law claim from state to federal court will be deemed to have waived its Eleventh Amendment immunity. Otherwise, the state could defeat enforcement of its state law obligation through the selection, by removal, of a federal forum. [**Lapides v. Board of Regents**, 535 U.S. 613 (2002)]

3. Exceptions to Bar

There are a number of exceptions to the Amendment's jurisdictional bar.

a. Suits Against State Officers—The Fiction of *Ex Parte Young*

Ex parte **Young** has come to stand for the principle that a federal court may enjoin a state official from violating federal law. [*Ex parte* **Young**, 209 U.S. 123 (1908)—federal court could enjoin state attorney general from enforcing in state court an unconstitutional state rate-setting order for railroads] The legal fiction behind the principle is that a suit against a state officer is *not a suit against the state* when the remedy sought is an injunction against an illegal action, for an officer is not acting on behalf of the state when he acts illegally.

(1) Distinguish—State Action Under Fourteenth Amendment

The legal fiction of *Ex parte* **Young** is arguably inconsistent with the prohibition against certain kinds of state action under the Fourteenth Amendment. Injunctions are permitted against state officers who act under color of state law to violate the Fourteenth Amendment. Thus, what *is not* the act of the state for purposes of the Eleventh Amendment *is* the act of the state for purposes of the Fourteenth Amendment. [**Home Telephone & Telegraph Co. v. City of Los Angeles**, 227 U.S. 278 (1913)]

b. Modern Application of *Ex Parte Young*

An important modern case distinguishes line between permitted and prohibited forms of relief under the *Ex parte* **Young** principle. **Edelman v. Jordan**, *supra,* p. 289. In that case, plaintiffs sued state officials, alleging that defendants were processing applications for a federal-state aid program more slowly than the applicable federal statute required. Plaintiffs sought an injunction requiring the officials to process the applications in a timely fashion in the future, and they sought to recover money that had not been paid in the past because of the slow processing of applications. The Court permitted the injunctive relief but refused to permit the recovery of money that had been wrongfully withheld. The distinction, according to the Court, was between permitted *prospective* relief and prohibited *retroactive* relief "which requires payment of funds from the state treasury."

(1) Possible Narrowing of *Ex Parte Young* by *Seminole Tribe of Florida v. Florida*

In **Seminole Tribe of Florida v. Florida**, 517 U.S. 44 (1996), the Supreme Court declined to issue an injunction ordering state officers to obey the commands of the federal Indian Gaming and Regulatory Act. The Act created a detailed (and fairly mild) remedial scheme running directly against the state. The Court found the Act unenforceable against the state and held that it would not order the state officers to perform the obligations required by the Act. Instead of the mild sanctions provided against the *state* under the Act, "an action brought against a *state official* under *Ex parte* **Young** would expose that official to the full remedial powers of a federal court, including, presumably, contempt sanctions . . . [We are not] free to rewrite the statutory scheme in order to approximate what we think Congress might have wanted had it known that [the Act] was beyond its authority. If that effort is to be made, it should be made by Congress, and not by the federal courts." The implications of *Seminole Tribe* are not entirely obvious, but it at least is clear that the Court was unwilling to read the Act sympathetically in order to grant injunctive relief against state officers.

(2) Further Narrowing of *Ex Parte Young* by *Coeur d'Alene Tribe*—Degree of Intrusion on State Sovereignty

In **Idaho v. Coeur d'Alene Tribe of Idaho**, 521 U.S. 261 (1997), the Coeur d'Alene Tribe sued Idaho state officials for declaratory and injunctive relief that would have prevented the state from interfering with the tribe's use and enjoyment of banks and beds of a lake and surrounding rivers as to which both the tribe and the state claimed ownership. Although its precise rationale was unclear, the Supreme Court held that the relief was, in substance, no different from a quiet title action against the state, which would have been forbidden by the Eleventh Amendment. Furthermore, the issue in the case was ownership—"sovereign control"—of land located within and claimed by the state. "The dignity and status of its statehood allows Idaho to rely on its Eleventh Amendment immunity and to insist upon responding to these claims in its own courts, which are open to hear and determine the case."

(3) Restoration of *Ex Parte Young*?

In **Verizon v. Public Service Commission**, 535 U.S. 635 (2002), the Court seemingly answered questions about the continued viability of the *Ex parte* **Young** action to enforce federal statutory rights. There, the Court allowed the district court to hear an action against state officials for injunctive and declaratory relief setting aside a state agency ruling alleged to have violated the federal Telecommunications Act of 1996. The Court distinguished *Edelman* as a case in which plaintiffs sought a monetary remedy and *Seminole Tribe* as a case involving a detailed remedial scheme.

(a) Significance

Verizon apparently treats the *Ex parte* **Young** remedy as routinely available, so long as the action seeks relief that satisfies the prospectivity requirement of *Edelman.* But *Verizon* does not overrule or cast doubt on earlier decisions that took a narrower view of the availability of such relief.

(b) Further Restoration

The Supreme Court further restored the presumptive availability of **Ex parte Young**, suggesting that the remedy does not depend on "the identity of the plaintiff." [**Virginia Office of Protection & Advocacy v. Stewart**, 563 U.S. 247 (2011)]. There, the Court concluded that one agency of the state of Virginia could sue another state agency in federal court, seeking to ensure its compliance with federal law.

(c) Qualified Restriction of *Ex Parte Young* in Statutory Cases

In **Armstrong v. Exceptional Living Center**, 135 S.Ct. 1378 (2015), the Supreme Court narrowed access to the *Ex parte Young* remedy in suits brought to enforce rights conferred by federal statute. The claims in question sought to compel the state of Idaho to reimburse Medicaid health care providers at the higher rates the plaintiffs viewed as required by federal law. The Court refused to allow the suit to proceed, after concluding in reliance on *Seminole Tribe*, supra, that the *Ex parte Young/Edelman* remedy had been displaced by the Medicaid statute's remedial scheme. In addition to oversight, the Medicaid agency was empowered to cut federal funds from a non-compliant state. This, coupled with the agency's expertise over rate-making, was said impliedly to have displaced the *Ex parte Young* action.

Caveat: The decision does not by its terms apply to *Ex parte Young* actions brought to enforce rights conferred by the Constitution. Nor does it automatically displace the *Ex parte Young* action in all federal spending programs.

Caveat: The decision does not cast doubt on the viability of the so-called *Ex parte Young* fiction, allowing suits to proceed against the officer when the plaintiff has a right to sue under federal equity.

c. Ancillary Relief

Relief ancillary to injunctive relief is permitted. Such ancillary relief includes an award of attorneys' fees against the state [**Hutto v. Finney**, 437 U.S. 678 (1978)] and an order to send notice to class members informing them that the state had acted illegally and that state administrative remedies might be available [**Quern v. Jordan**, 440 U.S. 332

(1979)]. But note that an order to provide notice of the state's past illegal actions is not permitted when there is no injunctive relief to which that order is ancillary. [**Green v. Mansour**, 474 U.S. 64 (1985)]

d. Principle of *Ex Parte Young* Restricted to Federal Question Cases

Prospective relief is available under *Ex parte* **Young** against state officers who violate federal law, but not against state officers who violate state law. Thus, the so-called authority stripping fiction of *Ex parte* **Young**—"stripping" an officer of the protection of the state when he acts illegally—operates only when *federal law* has been violated. [**Pennhurst State School & Hospital v. Halderman**, 465 U.S. 89 (1984)]

e. Consent to Suit

A state may waive the protection of the Amendment by consenting to suit. Consent may take several forms:

(1) Waiver by Voluntary Appearance

A state may waive the protection of the Amendment by voluntary appearance and defense on the merits in federal court. [**Clark v. Barnard**, *supra*, p. 290]

(a) But Note

For a defense on the merits to constitute a waiver of the Eleventh Amendment, the state's attorney must have the power under state law to consent to suit. [*See* **Ford Motor Co. v. Department of Treasury**, *supra*, p. 290] Also, a state that has defended and lost on the merits in the trial court may still raise an Eleventh Amendment defense on appeal. [**Edelman v. Jordan**, *supra*, p. 291]

f. Waiver by Statute

A state may pass a statute consenting to be sued.

(1) Narrow Construction of Statutes

A statute consenting to suit will be narrowly construed. Consent to suit in state court does not constitute consent to suit in federal court. [**Kennecott Copper Corp. v. State Tax Commission**, 327 U.S. 573 (1946)]

g. Waiver by Administering a Federal-State Program

In theory, a state can consent to be sued by agreeing to administer a federal-state program that imposes certain federal standards upon the state. But the Supreme Court has required that there be such a "clear statement" of the state's agreement that so far consent to suit has never been found. [*See, e.g.,* **Atascadero State Hospital v. Scanlon**, *supra*, p. 288— no consent found]

h. Waiver by Continuing to Act After Federal Statutory Standard Established—Not Sufficient

A state continued to operate a state-owned railroad after the passage of the Federal Employers' Liability Act. This was held to constitute consent to suit under the Act. [**Parden v. Terminal Railway**, 377 U.S. 184 (1964)] However, *Parden* has been overruled. [**College Savings Bank v. Florida Prepaid Postsecondary Education Expense Board**, 527 U.S. 666 (1999)—rejecting the concept that a state constructively consents to suit by entering a field of commerce with knowledge that federal law allows private suit]

i. Congressional Abrogation of State Sovereign Immunity

Congress has the power, under certain provisions of the Constitution, to abrogate the sovereign immunity of the states through statute.

(1) Sources of Congressional Power

(a) Fourteenth Amendment

Congress may abrogate state sovereign immunity under the Fourteenth Amendment. [**Fitzpatrick v. Bitzer**, 427 U.S. 445 (1976)]

(b) Possible Extension to Fifteenth Amendment

The Court has suggested that Congress may also abrogate state sovereign immunity under the Fifteenth Amendment. [**City of Rome v. United States**, 446 U.S. 156 (1980)—dictum]

j. Congress's Indian and Interstate Commerce Powers Insufficient—*Seminole Tribe*

In **Seminole Tribe of Florida v. Florida**, *supra,* p. 291, the Supreme Court held that Congress lacks power to abrogate a state's Eleventh Amendment immunity under either the Indian Commerce Clause or the Interstate Commerce Clause.

(1) Decision Overrules *Pennsylvania v. Union Gas*

The Court's decision in **Seminole Tribe of Florida v. Florida**, overrules **Pennsylvania v. Union Gas Co.**, *supra*, p. 288, in which the Court had held that Congress may abrogate the Eleventh Amendment under the Interstate Commerce Clause.

(2) Implications of *Seminole Tribe* for Other Congressional Heads of Power

The Court in *Seminole Tribe* wrote, "The Eleventh Amendment restricts the judicial power under Article III, and Article I cannot be used to circumvent the constitutional limitations placed on federal jurisdiction." Read literally, this statement means that Congress cannot abrogate the Eleventh Amendment under any Article I head of power. In keeping with that view, the Court has taken a very restrictive view of the sources of congressional power that will support abrogation. While abrogation statutes adopted pursuant to Congress's powers under the Fourteenth Amendment have been upheld, those adopted under its Article I powers have generally been invalidated.

> **e.g.** **Example:** Congress cannot abrogate state sovereign immunity in the exercise of its powers to regulate patents. [**Florida Prepaid Postsecondary Education Expense Board v. College Savings Bank**, 527 U.S. 627 (1999)—stating flatly that Congress cannot abrogate immunity pursuant to its Article I powers]

> **e.g.** **Example:** Congress has adopted a variety of statutes that impose an anti-discrimination obligation on both public and private sector employers. Abrogations of immunity to effectuate these anti-discrimination norms have been consistently rejected, except where they can be seen as adopted to effectuate prohibitions against sex- and race-based discrimination in the Fourteenth Amendment's Equal Protection Clause. [**Kimel v. Florida Board of Regents**, 528 U.S. 62 (2000)—invalidating abrogation under Age Discrimination in Employment

Act; **Board of Trustees of the University of Alabama v. Garrett**, 531 U.S. 356 (2001)—invalidating abrogation under the Americans with Disabilities Act]

(3) Abrogation and the Spending Power

The Supreme Court has held that Congress can condition grants of federal financial assistance to the states on their agreement to waive their sovereign immunity from suit. [**Sossamon v. Texas**, 563 U.S. 277 (2011)] But the Court has insisted on extremely clear language in the statute so conditioning federal funds. A statute that authorized suits "for all appropriate relief against a government" was said not to address the availability of money damages with the requisite clarity.

k. Clear Statement of Congressional Intent Required

Congress must state clearly that it intends a statute to abrogate state sovereign immunity. The mere fact that a statute was passed under the Fourteenth Amendment is not enough to show that Congress intended to nullify state sovereign immunity. [**Atascadero State Hospital v. Scanlon**, *supra*, p. 293]

(1) No Clear Statement

The Court has found no clear statement of intent to abrogate under the basic Civil Rights Act, 42 U.S.C. section 1983 [**Quern v. Jordan**, *supra*, p. 292]; the Rehabilitation Act of 1973 [**Atascadero State Hospital v. Scanlon**, *supra*]; the Education to the Handicapped Act [**Dellmuth v. Muth**, 491 U.S. 223 (1989)]; and the Bankruptcy Code [**Hoffman v. Connecticut Department of Income Maintenance**, 492 U.S. 96 (1989)].

(2) Clear Statement

The Court has found a clear statement of intent to abrogate under Title VII of the Civil Rights Act of 1964 [**Fitzpatrick v. Bitzer**, *supra*, p. 294] and under the Superfund Amendments and Reauthorization Act of 1986 [**Pennsylvania v. Union Gas Co.**, *supra*, p. 294].

l. Section 1983 Does Not Abrogate State Sovereign Immunity

In passing the basic civil rights statute [42 U.S.C. § 1983], Congress did not intend to abrogate state sovereign immunity. [**Quern v. Jordan**, *supra*]

(1) State Officers May Be Sued

Under the *Ex parte* **Young** fiction, state officers may be sued for prospective relief under section 1983. Under the fiction, such suits are not deemed to be against the state within the meaning of the Eleventh Amendment. (*See supra*, pp. 293 *et seq.*)

(2) And Note

Section 1983 suits *can* be brought against counties and municipalities. [**Monell v. Department of Social Services**, 436 U.S. 658 (1978)] Counties and municipalities are not considered part of the state for purposes of the Eleventh Amendment. (*See infra*, p. 298.)

m. Restrictive View of Abrogation Under the Fourteenth Amendment

In an effort to protect the no-abrogation rule announced in *Seminole Tribe*, the Court has taken a very narrow view of the scope of permissible abrogation under the Fourteenth Amendment.

(1) No Abrogation to Enforce Procedural Due Process

Congress created a form of property with the adoption of the patent laws, and state invasions of such property rights could be said to violate the Fourteenth Amendment. But Congress may not use its Fourteenth Amendment powers to abrogate state sovereign immunity from suits to enforce the patent laws. [**Florida Prepaid Postsecondary Education Expense Board v. College Savings Bank**, *supra*] Congress did not make a record of widespread, unremedied state invasions of patent rights that would bring into play its enforcement powers under Section 5 of the Fourteenth Amendment.

(2) No Abrogation to Remedy Age or Disability Discrimination

Discrimination on the basis of age and disability does not violate the Fourteenth Amendment's Equal Protection Clause. Only such discrimination so lacking in justification as to be irrational would give rise to an Equal Protection violation. Accordingly, Congress lacked power under the Fourteenth Amendment to abrogate the state's immunity from suits to enforce federal statutes prohibiting public employers from discriminating on the basis of age and disability. Congress lacked record evidence or findings that widespread forms of irrational state discrimination on these bases had been occurring. [**Kimel v. Florida Board of Regents**, *supra*; **Board of Trustees v. Garrett**, *supra*]

(3) Abrogation Upheld for Claims of Sex Discrimination

Discrimination on the basis of sex violates the Fourteenth Amendment. Therefore, Congress could abrogate the state's immunity to permit suit to enforce the Family Medical Leave Act ("FMLA") which requires public and private employers to provide unpaid leave for employees with newborn children. [**Nevada Department of Human Resources v. Hibbs**, 538 U.S. 721 (2003)]

(a) Note

Hibbs did not involve direct discrimination on the basis of sex, but was based on findings that sex-based stereotypes had long informed official notions of a woman's role in caring for children. The actual violation at issue in *Hibbs* was the state's failure to provide family leave in accordance with the terms of the FMLA, which went well beyond what the Constitution itself would require.

(b) *Hibbs* Restricted?

A second provision of the FMLA requires employers to provide up to 12 weeks of unpaid leave to allow employees to care for their own health needs. The Court held that Congress did not justify subjecting state employers to suit to enforce this right. [**Coleman v. Court of Appeals of Maryland**, 566 U.S. 30 (2012)] According to the Court, Congress did not adequately link this provision to a pattern of constitutional violations; public employers do not owe a constitutional obligation to provide health care, but only to refrain from discrimination in the provision of health care. A spirited dissent argued that the provision was framed in neutral, non-gender terms but was really an attempt to address sex discrimination (just as was the FMLA more generally).

(c) Abrogation Upheld for Claim of Access to Courthouse

Individuals have a right of access to court rooted in the Fourteenth Amendment. Accordingly, Congress could compel the states to make their courthouses accessible to disabled persons and could abrogate state immunity from suits brought to enforce such accessibility rules. [**Tennessee v. Lane**, 541 U.S. 509 (2004)]

1) Note

The provisions at issue appeared in Title II of the Americans with Disabilities Act, which imposes accessibility obligations on a wide variety of public and private buildings, not just state courthouses. To the extent accessibility obligations were adopted pursuant to the commerce power, they would not support abrogation. State-owned courthouses may differ, for abrogation purposes, from state-owned entertainment centers or sports facilities to which constitutional rights of access may not attach.

(d) Prison Disability Abrogation Upheld in Part

Prisoners have a right to freedom from cruel and unusual punishment, made effective through the Fourteenth Amendment. Title II of the ADA subjects the states to suit for violations of the accommodation provisions of the Act. Prisoners may sue under the ADA, seeking damages against the state, for conduct that violates the ADA and actually violates the Fourteenth Amendment. [**United States v. Georgia**, 546 U.S. 151 (2006)—allegations that state prison officials made little effort to accommodate needs of a paraplegic inmate, thus denying him access to shower and toilet facilities] Note that the state's liability will extend only to conduct that violates both the ADA and the Fourteenth Amendment.

n. Anomalous Extension to Bankruptcy Clause

Congress may adopt laws allowing the trustee in bankruptcy to subject states to suit to recover a preference item. [**Central Virginia Community College v. Katz**, 546 U.S. 356 (2006)] The Court did not, strictly speaking, treat the Bankruptcy Clause as a source of power that enabled Congress to abrogate state immunity, but held that the nature of the bankruptcy power was such that the states could not claim immunity from suit on claims within its ambit.

(1) Criticism

The dissent questioned the majority's effort to distinguish the Bankruptcy Clause from other provisions in Article I (such as the commerce, patent and copyright powers) that will not support an abrogation of state immunity. The decision may reflect disagreement with the no-abrogation rule of *Seminole Tribe*, rather than a principled application of the *Seminole Tribe* framework.

o. Requiring State to Entertain Suits Against Itself in Its Own Courts

Plaintiffs turned to state court to enforce their rights under federal statutes that the *Seminole Tribe* Court had barred from federal court. But the Court ruled that the state courts had no federal duty to hear such claims. [**Alden v. Maine**, 527 U.S. 706 (1999)]

(1) Criticism

Alden recognizes immunity on the basis of structural considerations that render the Eleventh Amendment redundant. The Eleventh Amendment refers to the judicial power of the United States, and says nothing about suits brought in state court. [**Nevada v. Hall**, 440 U.S. 410 (1979)—no Eleventh Amendment barrier to suit brought against Nevada in California state court] Prior decisions of the Supreme Court had suggested that states may owe a duty to entertain federal rights of action [**Hilton v. South Carolina Public Railways Commission**, 502 U.S. 197 (1991)], or at least were not free to discriminate against federal rights of action [**Testa v. Katt**, *supra*]. The Court distinguished all these prior cases en route to ruling that a federal statutory right to damages, excluded from federal court, was also barred from state court.

p. Note

States may still be compelled to comply with the terms of a federal statute through actions for declaratory and injunctive relief brought pursuant to ***Ex parte Young***, *supra*. But the combination of *Seminole Tribe* and *Alden* precludes individual suits for damages against the state, absent a viable abrogation.

q. And Note

Individuals can still recover damages in appropriate cases by suing the responsible state government official in his or her personal capacity. But such individual liability applies primarily in the tort context, and the doctrine of qualified immunity may reduce the remedy's effectiveness.

r. Counties and Municipalities Not Protected by Amendment

Subdivisions of the state, such as counties, municipalities, and school boards, are *not* protected by the Amendment. [*See, e.g.,* **Lincoln County v. Luning**, 133 U.S. 529 (1890)]

(1) Civil Rights Suits Permitted Against Counties and Municipalities

Suits may be brought against *counties* and *municipalities* under section 1983. [**Monell v. Department of Social Services**, *supra*, p. 295] However, suits are *not* permitted against the state under section 1983. [**Quern v. Jordan**, *supra*, p. 295]

s. Standard of Care for Municipal Liability

While cities, counties and school boards do not enjoy any qualified immunity from liability under section 1983, the plaintiff must establish that the government body had a policy, practice, or custom that violates the Constitution. Showing that an official violated the Constitution does not suffice; the official must have acted pursuant to a city or municipal policy. [**Monell v. Department of Social Services**, *supra*] When the official violation results from a departmental failure to train, the government body's failures must rise to the level of "deliberate indifference" to warrant imposition of liability. **E.g., Connick v. Thompson**, 563 U.S. 51 (2011).

t. Supreme Court Review of State Court Decisions

The Amendment's jurisdictional bar does *not* extend to the United States Supreme Court's review of cases coming up from the state courts. [**Cohens v. Virginia**, *supra*, p. 226]

Table of Cases